Modernity and Tradition:
The New Latin American and Caribbean
Literature, 1956–1994

SALALM Secretariat
Benson Latin American Collection
The General Libraries
The University of Texas at Austin

Modernity and Tradition: The New Latin American and Caribbean Literature, 1956–1994

Papers of the Thirty-Ninth Annual Meeting of the
SEMINAR ON THE ACQUISITION OF
LATIN AMERICAN LIBRARY MATERIALS

David M. Kennedy Center for International Studies
Brigham Young University, Provo, Utah
Family History Library, Salt Lake City, Utah

Salt Lake City, Utah
May 28-June 2, 1994

Nelly S. González
Editor

SALALM SECRETARIAT
Benson Latin American Collection
The General Libraries
The University of Texas at Austin

ISBN: 0-917617-50-9

Contents

Latin America

IV. Evaluation of Latin American Literary Collections

PART THREE. NEW TRENDS AND CHALLENGES IN ACQUISITION, CATALOGING, MICROFILMING, AND PUBLISHING OF LATIN AMERICAN LIBRARY MATERIALS

I. Issues in Acquisition, Cataloging, and Microfilming of Latin American Library Materials

II. The State of the Art in the Publishing Industry

Preface

The period from 1956 to 1994 witnessed a dramatic explosion in both volume and variety of literature generated in the Americas. Several distinct, creative styles developed and flourished in the nourishing environment before, during, and after the "boom." As evidence of this literary activity, the Nobel Prize for Literature was awarded to Miguel Angel Asturias (Guatemala, 1967), Pablo Neruda (Chile, 1971), Gabriel García Márquez (Colombia, 1982), Octavio Paz (Mexico, 1990), and Derek Walcott (West Indies, 1992). These and other writers expanded the breadth and vision of Latin American literature in this period.

Adopting the theme "Modernity and Tradition: Development of the New Latin American and Caribbean Literature between 1956 and 1994," the Thirty-Ninth Seminar on the Acquisition of Latin American Library Materials afforded us a more intent look into this era. We had the opportunity to examine and appreciate the work of creative men and women who set a new direction in Latin American literature.

Search for Conjunctions in Latin American Literature

Among the highlights of SALALM XXXIX were the General Sessions, where recognized scholars in their respective fields discussed literary trends during this period. Each contributed in the search for common themes amidst wide diversity in Latin American fiction published in the second half of this century. Five different versions of the Spanish American novel from 1970 to 1994 were presented by Raymond Leslie Williams: the novels of the boom, the chronological story (encompassing complex and hermetic novels, fiction with the dictator as theme, and accessible and entertaining writings), the Latin American version of postmodernism, the representation of diversity and marginalization, and the narrative of women writers. Focusing on the boom, David William Foster elaborated on its impact on Latin American literary research, addressing issues in the academic understanding of the boom. He highlighted the use of bibliographic sources in the scholarly study of this subject. Ted Lyon concentrated on the boom's effect on journal publication. He addressed the increase in the number of journals as well as the upgrading of the quality of literary criticism, which were both spawned by the boom. On specific literary genres, Merlin Forster discussed the increasing experimentation and recognition of poetry and drama as literary genres in the twentieth century.

The emergence of Latin American writers of African ancestry is another significant development in Latin American literature. This was set forth in a stirring discourse by Carlos Guillermo Wilson. In his introduction of Wilson, William D. Ilgen pointed out his key contribution to Afro-Hispanic literature and explained the origins of the speaker's pen name, "Cubena."

Eighteen panels offered a variety of intellectually stimulating themes. Provided here is an overview of these presentations, within a thematic organization.

Emergent Trends in Latin American Literature

Trends in contemporary Latin American literature and cinema was the subject of several presentations. A number of speakers focused on Mexican literature. Cecilia Avilés Valdez talked about the recent works of Mexican female writers, particularly novels from the 1970s up to the present. Sarah Corona Berkin discussed Mexican children's literature as well as publication policies established by the government and those followed by Mexican publishers. Complementing these presentations was Walter Brem's paper on techniques and tools for evaluating the contemporary Mexican novel.

We were fortunate to have from the Facultad de Letras, Universidad de Granada in Spain, Angel Esteban del Campo, who spoke on the theme of death in *Doce cuentos peregrinos* by Gabriel García Márquez. Representatives from Latin American countries discussed trends in their literatures. Marta Domínguez Díaz expanded our perspectives on Chilean narrative through a historical view of the literary movements in Chile from 1842 to the present. On Uruguayan literature, Alvaro J. Risso explained its relevant themes and trends beginning with Onetti (1939) up to contemporary times. A complementary feature was an evening presentation with Clemente Padín's reading of his works on Uruguayan "concrete" poetry.

We also had the opportunity to delve deeper into areas that in the past were given less attention. Gay literature in Latin America, in general, and in Mexico and Brazil, in particular, was discussed by David William Foster, Víctor F. Torres-Ortiz, Luiz Mott, Sonia T. D. G. Silva, and Carmen Muricy. Research on sexual dissidence in Latin American cultural production was addressed by David William Foster. Specific to contemporary Mexican narrative, Víctor F. Torres-Ortiz expounded on the theme of the homosexual. Luiz Mott and Sonia T. D. G. Silva provided a listing of thirty-eight academic theses on the subject accepted at Brazilian universities; this complements a previous bibliography with 260 titles presented by the same authors at SALALM XXX (1985). Also, Carmen Muricy furnished a

selective listing of ephemeral materials on Brazilian homosexual groups
which were published from 1978 to 1994 and are available in the Library of
Congress, Rio de Janeiro Office. A review of the literature on the Brazilian
gay community published over the last decade and a select bibliography are
contributed by Robert Howes.

On another interesting topic, Gloria de Alfaro and Yolanda Maloney
gave a historical and comparative overview of the Latin American and
French literary representation of the prostitute. While both relegate the
prostitute's fate to inevitable doom and hopelessness, she is seen as a
lustful, corrupt creature in French literature while perceived as a victim of
circumstances and social injustice in Latin American narrative. In another
presentation, the same authors analyzed the portrayal of the female subject
in three Latin American films using a dual perspective: psychoanalytic and
cultural. They concluded that the existing patriarchal structure, through
unconscious and cultural mechanisms, shapes the female subject, who is
relegated to a passive position in society and is represented in this manner
in the cinematic text.

Growing Access to Latin American Resources and Information

Along with enriching our perspective on the content and quality of
Latin American literature, several presentations broadened our knowledge of
library services and resources. Luis Villar spoke about the Dartmouth
College database containing more than 30,000 poems of Sor Juana Inés de
la Cruz, which is available on the Internet. Another database was introduced
by Elsa Barberena Blásquez, which comprises reviews of the works of
about 280 contemporary Mexican writers from 1970 to 1980; this is
intended to provide information similar to that in the *Book Review Digest*.

Three participants introduced us to the microfilm project of the Family
History Library's International Genealogical Index, another resource for
religious, scholarly, and personal purposes. Kahlile Mehr explained the
project's expansion to include Latin American records, starting with Mexico
in the 1950s and now covering almost all countries of Latin America. In
turn, Frederick Graham detailed the type of documents and extent of filming
done in Spain, Portugal, Mexico, Central and South America, and the
Caribbean. Rebecca Horn discussed the scholarly use of the Latin American
collection of the Family History Library.

Newspapers have been taking on a more significant role in Brazilian
society, and efforts by the Library of Congress, Rio de Janeiro Office, to
increase access to them were discussed by Carmen M. Muricy. On another
significant endeavor, Reynaldo Ayala and Marta Stiefel Ayala provided
details about a project on public library services to the Latino community,

funded by the W. K. Kellogg Foundation. David Block supplemented the information on print media with a survey of newspaper holdings.

Emphasizing the essential role of booksellers in the development of Latin American bibliography, Howard Karno pointed out that their products are excellent references for bibliographic, historical, and biographical information. Several panelists spoke about bibliographic sources for important authors and works in Latin American literature. Nelly S. González discussed the theme of the dictator in the works of Asturias, García Márquez, and Valle-Inclán. Scott Van Jacob provided a selective annotated bibliography of works incorporating some significant aspect of Africa, written by Afro-Hispanic writers in the twentieth century. Iliana Sonntag Blay gave her view of the exhausting and cumbersome task of compiling an index to Latin American poetry in anthologies.

A number of presentations accentuated the vast resources on Latin American literature available in American libraries. Guillermo Náñez Falcón gave a historical overview of the manuscript collection at the Latin American Library at Tulane University and discussed his cataloging project, which rescued and provided access to rare Mexican archival collections. A video presentation by Jane Garner explored the assortment of Mexican and Mexican-American manuscripts at the Benson Latin American Collection and the history of this collection. The University of Miami Library houses one of the largest Cuban collections outside Cuba. Esperanza de Varona provided an excellent guide to the library's Cuban and Cuban-American bilingual archives from 1492 to the present.

Attention was also given to trends and challenges in Latin American studies and collection development in Canada. Wanda Quoika-Stanka charted the expansion of the Latin American collection at the University of Alberta to support growing academic interest on Latin American topics and an increasing Latino population in the surrounding community. The persistent growth of Latin American studies and the library collection at the University of Calgary, despite twenty-seven years of budgetary constraints, was highlighted by Nora Robins. At the University of Manitoba, a strong partnership between librarians and faculty promoted effective management and expansion of the Latin American collection, as described by Nicole Michaud-Oystryk.

Vera Cristina Neumann described library services provided at the Universidade Estadual de Campinas. Likewise, we obtained firsthand information on Central American resources. The Mellon Foundation/ Mortenson Center, sponsors of the USIA/ALA Library Program Associates, presented a panel. Following Susan Schnuer's overview of the Mellon/ Mortenson program, Laura Shedenhelm, Conny Méndez Rojas, Jeannette Alfaro Ugalde, and Josefina Castro de Roque described the Latin American library collections in Honduras, Nicaragua, Costa Rica, and El Salvador, respectively. I hope that this experience will be repeated in future meetings of SALALM.

To promote cooperative collection development, Karen Lindvall-Larson proposed a model for evaluating Chilean collections, which involves creating a core list of authors for each country, identifying important movements or genres, and listing important reference resources. Also, Russ Davidson discussed his evaluation of the University of New Mexico's Brazilian literary collection, which included a quantitative assessment of how the collection measures up to appropriate core lists and a more detailed analysis of particular segments of the collection.

ENLACE sponsored the participation of Roberto Guerra Milligan and Ricardo Reyes Hernández, who provided current sources of economic information on Mexico.

Current Challenges in Expanding Resources on Latin American Literature

New trends and challenges in the acquisition, cataloging, microfilming, and publishing of Latin American library materials is another overarching theme in the presentations. Access versus ownership is one of the increasingly persistent issues we face. To provide a balanced view on this topic, the conference engaged both librarians and publishers in two separate discussions.

Citing the dilemma of small libraries in contending with a growing demand for and supply of Latin American materials, Molly Molloy outlined a three-pronged strategy: maintain a core collection of major scholarly works on Latin America, build an area of specialization, and emphasize access over ownership. In turn, Terry Peet described the cost-saving techniques being applied and considered by the Library of Congress to maintain a proper balance in collecting for archival and access purposes. Stella Bentley and David Block provided two other viewpoints of librarians.

Publishers of Latin American materials, Peter Stern, George Elmendorf, Lynne Rienner, and Sharon Moynahan, afforded us another perspective on the access versus ownership issue. We are reminded once again that publishers and libraries have a symbiotic relationship. George Elmendorf and Sharon Moynahan caution us on the dangers of carrying access over ownership to the extreme.

A comparison of academic publishing in Chile, Ecuador, and Mexico was presented by Carl W. Deal based on his study of the publishing industry, including commercial publishers, university and academic presses, quasi-academic presses, and non-governmental organizations. A profile that is representative of the entire Latin American region could be generated from this study. Adalberto Santana presented a detailed report on the role of *Cuadernos Americanos* and Centro Coordinador y Difusor de Estudios Latinoamericanos (CCYDEL) in the dissemination of information on Latin American studies. The fifty-five years of uninterrupted publication of *Cuadernos Americanos* and its role in the Latin American literary boom were elaborated by Liliana Weinberg de Magis. Along with Santana, Micaela Chávez referred to their problems and solutions applied in the acquisition of Latin American materials for their libraries. John B. Wright, on the other hand, explained reasons for the existence of different editions and/or duplicates which results in an overabundance of books and cataloging backlogs, and recommended possible cataloging solutions to this problem.

Issues involved in the microfilming of Latin American materials was the subject of another panel. Dan Hazen, Peter Johnson, Mary Jo Zeter, and Dan Haverkamp discussed the microfilming projects for preservation of, and/or access to, materials essential for scholarly study of Latin America.

SALALM XXXIX afforded an opportunity to exchange information about our rich literary heritage. It also provided a venue to examine the challenges and explore the possibilities in the fast-changing world of libraries and literature. Latin America and the Caribbean continue to assert their strong presence in literature, starting from the literary boom in 1956 up to the present. We—librarians, publishers, bookdealers, academicians, and scholars alike—have a significant role to play in promoting greater access to and appreciation of this literature. As SALALM approaches its fifth decade, we face new challenges and opportunities. The rapid growth and utilization of modern technology in bibliographic services are profoundly affecting the ways libraries provide services to their patrons. The changing focus of cultural diversity is expanding the range of Latin American studies. Much is still ahead, but we can be encouraged by the great strides that have been made in Latin American literature, knowing that we all had a part in it.

These papers do not contain the presentations in their entirety but, rather, reflect the substance of the conference. I hope that this volume will be a source of insight and encouragement to us all.

Nelly S. González

Acknowledgments

SALALM XXXIX was an excellent conference. Many who attended have said that they found it a pleasant and rewarding experience. On behalf of SALALM, I would like to give due recognition to the people who made its success possible.

The David Kennedy Center at Brigham Young University played a key role as host of our conference; I extend my gratitude to its staff. My deep appreciation goes to Mark Grover and the Special Arrangements Committee for their special preparations for the conference. Past SALALM presidents Pat Noble and David Block provided unceasing support and guidance, and I thank them.

The conference was greatly enriched by excellent presentations by a number of invited guests. I thank professors Merlin Forster, David William Foster, Ted Lyon, Raymond L. Williams, and Carlos Guillermo Wilson for their participation in the seminar. Likewise, I express my gratitude to all the presenters, moderators, and rapporteurs for their cooperation. I appreciate greatly the cooperation of bookdealers for their excellent book exhibits, which made the conference an even more enriching experience, and helped to support us financially.

I thank Executive Secretary Sharon Moynahan, Rapporteur General Cecilia Sercan, and all members of the Executive Committee for the fine execution of their tasks. The work of Barbara G. Valk and her editorial staff is indispensable in the publication of the SALALM Papers, and I warmly acknowledge their contribution.

My deep appreciation goes to the University of Illinois at Urbana-Champaign, especially to the University Librarian, Robert Wedgeworth. Their financial support and strong commitment to excellence in librarianship facilitated the performance of my tasks as president, especially in planning for the conference and preparing the papers for publication. I take this opportunity to thank Carl W. Deal for his constant encouragement throughout my career.

Finally, I want to thank Scott Van Jacob for his able assistance in the preparation phase and during the conference, and Carmina Tolentino for following through on the post-conference work toward publication of the papers. All of us together made the SALALM XXXIX conference a very productive and fulfilling endeavor.

Nettie Lee Benson, January 15, 1905-June 23, 1993: A Personal Memoir

Laura Gutiérrez-Witt

I met Nettie Lee Benson in September of 1965, and my life was never ever the same after that meeting! So much of what I have done professionally has been molded by her presence and influence. But so much of what SALALM is about and what we all do in our daily work was also shaped by Nettie Lee Benson.

The first SALALM meeting I attended was the seminar held in San Juan, Puerto Rico, in 1969. I remember that meeting for several reasons, among them the breakdown of the air-conditioning system at the Condado Beach Hotel where the sessions were being held. The other much more vivid memory I have of that conference was seeing and hearing two very articulate women tell us *all* there was to know about Latin American books, bibliography, libraries, and acquisitions. The two, of course, were Marietta Daniels Shepard—who spoke extemporaneously, without notes, for close to two hours at several sessions, giving facts, figures, and dates about book and library matters in Latin America. The other very visible and articulate participant, who corrected practically every speaker, including Marietta at times, was Nettie Lee Benson.

Many of you had the opportunity to meet or at least hear Nettie Lee Benson at the 1992 Austin SALALM meeting. Over the years, her very lively participation and contributions to the discussions at SALALM meetings remained prominent and important. She was active in SALALM from its first meeting in 1956 to her retirement from the library in 1975. A few persons here today will recall working with her on many committees; others may remember her service as president in 1970-1971, and her organization of the Austin meetings in 1957 and again in 1974.

Many of Nettie Lee Benson's accomplishments are well documented. At the 1992 SALALM meeting John Wheat presented a wonderful synthesis of Nettie Lee Benson's life based on many hours of interviews he recorded with Dr. Benson herself.[1] I do not repeat too much of what John wrote, since his paper appears in the recently issued conference proceedings. But I would like to recall some of her experiences in her own words.

Nettie Lee's life as a librarian began in 1942 at the University of Texas. She was 37 years old, and it must not have been easy for her to assume the role of general assistant to an absent Latin American librarian.

She faced countless collections which remained uncataloged; library services were in high demand and she was the only full-time staff member; and book and serial acquisitions were dauntingly slow or, it seemed, nonexistent. In the annual report for the Latin American Collection which she wrote that first year, her flair for ferreting out missing materials is evident:

It was found that a number of serials had collected in the vault of the Catalogue Department. As these serials never came to the Latin American Collection for six months to a year after they had been received, there was no way for the general assistant [herself] to know which numbers were missing in order to make claims for same."[2]

Nonetheless, she did indeed write 544 letters that year, requesting missing issues or to be placed on mailing lists, adding 689 missing issues and 96 new serials! Obviously, she worked as hard on learning to be a librarian as she worked on her tennis game in high school, putting in long hours and incredible energy until she did it right. In addition to her serials claiming efforts, that year she also reorganized the stacks, inventoried the rare books collection, found more secure cases for rare materials, and shifted the card catalog. She also filed 7,858 catalog cards and stated, "because the general assistant [herself] had more work than she could handle, the work of filing . . . was transferred . . . to the Catalogue Department." I doubt that the Catalogue Department had much choice: "No" was not an acceptable answer for Nettie Lee Benson! Every annual report that she wrote after that year tells of her tackling new projects and badgering the administration to correct problems—the need for new typewriters, filing cabinets, sunscreens for the windows, better lighting, more stack space, additional cataloging staff, and always, "more money."

Even before SALALM began meeting in 1956, Nettie Lee Benson had begun her acquisitions trips to Mexico and South America. In 1951 she spent eight weeks in Mexico visiting libraries, archives, and bookstores in several state capitals looking for materials for the library. She loved Mexico and visited there every opportunity she had. Her first trip was in 1924 when the nineteen-year-old Nettie Lee traveled to Monterrey, Mexico, to teach at an American Methodist school. She stayed for two years despite her alarmed parents' admonitions to come home! She returned to Mexico almost yearly after that stay to renew friendships, to do research, to establish new contacts, and, in later years, to search for library materials.

Nettie Lee also traveled to Central America and South America early during her library career. The first mention of a South American trip occurs in her 1951-1952 annual report when she visited Central America, Colombia, Venezuela, and the West Indies. She reported "a marked increase in gifts to the library from those areas" as a result of her trip.[3]

When the first SALALM was organized in 1956, Nettie Lee Benson was as concerned as everyone else with the difficulties of acquiring Latin American books. In fact, she prepared the working paper "Microfilm Programs with Emphasis on Periodicals and Newspapers."[4] Though highly competitive, Nettie Lee Benson was also a team player, and she supported SALALM and Marietta Daniels Shepard. The following year, 1957, Nettie Lee organized the second SALALM meeting in Austin and invited numerous Mexican scholars, librarians, publishers, and bookdealers to participate. Her SALALM committee membership began at this time.[5]

A new challenge was presented to Nettie Lee Benson at the 1959 SALALM. At one of the more productive sessions (possibly the forerunner of the bookdealers' reception), a group of participants conceived the idea of sponsoring a traveling agent to acquire books and establish contacts in Latin America for a consortium of libraries.[6] The obvious choice was Nettie Lee Benson, who reluctantly agreed to travel to South and Central America as the agent for the Latin American Cooperative Acquisitions Program (LACAP). She persuaded the president of the University of Texas, Harry Ransom, to give her $25,000 to match the New York Public Library's allocation. Hence she imposed a condition to the LACAP organizers: one copy of every book she found was to be purchased by the University of Texas.

She traveled several times as a representative of LACAP; in 1960 she visited Ecuador, Peru, Chile, and Bolivia. The following year she traveled to Colombia, Venezuela, Paraguay, Uruguay, and Argentina, and in 1962 returned to Peru, Chile, Bolivia, and Ecuador, with short visits to Guatemala and Panama. Her reports to the LACAP steering group were clear and concise but referred to all manner of difficulties. She writes on January 31, 1960, from Quito: "I have spent a good part of this week trying to learn something about the government publications here. I have learned one thing. It is going to be extremely difficult to supply many copies of these publications. They cannot be bought and they are hard to beg."[7] She comments one week later, on February 7, 1960, still in Quito: "I have worked constantly at the job every day in the week and parts of Sundays and far into the night but the task is too big where there is such disorganization of the book trade."[8] The next month from Lima, she laments, "It is even harder to cover the assignment here than it was in Ecuador. There are more bookstores and one must visit everyone of them to find out what has been published here."[9]

She was in constant communication with Dominick Coppola of the Stechert-Hafner book company, the intermediary for LACAP transactions in the United States. He would forward to her specific requests from libraries, and she, in turn, informed him of what she collected and what was available. With her photographic memory, Nettie Lee also could remember titles that certain libraries needed: On January 31, 1960, she says, "I know that last year Cornell University was trying to buy this set [Publicaciones del Archivo Municipal de Quito] and I know that so far it has not been able to acquire it or so I heard. . . . You might inquire of Cornell about it."[10]

Through LACAP, Nettie Lee Benson assisted a number of other U.S. libraries to expand their Latin American holdings. On March 13, 1960, she writes from Lima concerning government publications: "I always express a desire to buy the materials but it is not always possible to do so. When it cannot be bought but is offered free to the institutions who want it, I can only leave their addresses and hope they get the material."[11]

Nettie Lee was faced not only with the usual acquisition difficulties, but she sometimes fell prey to events outside her control. During her second trip in 1961, she writes: "I arrived in Bogotá about one A.M. of the morning of Thursday, January 5, and to date have spent about the seven most miserable days of my life. I have what they called here *la gripa*. I supposed it was just a very severe cold, but it kept me in bed for four days straight and I had doubts that I would ever get out of bed again alive." She talks of her room as a "torture chamber" and of the noise from the kitchen where "continuous clatter" during the day and "screaming and ranting you never heard before" at four o'clock in the morning when "someone would disturb the kitchen ogre" prevented her from getting any sleep![12]

Nettie Lee also had to contend with local events that prevented her from moving around as freely as she would have liked. On February 27, 1961, she writes from Caracas: "Yesterday was the day of the national census. The whole city was under strict orders to stay at home and wait for the census takers. We were told the day before that no one would be allowed to leave the hotel from 6 A.M. to 6 P.M. and there was a guard at the door to see that no one did."[13]

After her trips in 1960, 1961, and 1962, Nettie Lee Benson traveled to Latin America less frequently. She concentrated her efforts on teaching, on SALALM activities, on research and writing, and, of course, on the Latin American Collection. Reading through her library annual reports, one finds that the perennial problems of inadequate budgets, cataloging backlogs, insufficient space, and limited staff never did go away. Through the years, Nettie Lee Benson continued to nag and, in her favorite word, to "pester" administrators and faculty until they saw things her way. She never ceased to work to improve library conditions and collections.

The Latin American Collection at the University of Texas at Austin was renamed the Nettie Lee Benson Latin American Collection in 1975 shortly after her retirement from the library. Believe me, it was a retirement she did not want, but she turned seventy in 1975 and the rules required her to step down. But she was never far away, making sure we knew what we were doing!

Naming the library in her honor was appropriate and well deserved. From 1942 to 1975, she not only brought order to countless uncataloged collections but also expanded the holdings of the library in many directions. Using ingenious methods—given the lack of acquisitions money—she searched for, identified, and actually obtained many gift and exchange materials from individual authors, government agencies, academic institutions, financial and corporate entities, and others in order to bring current publications to the library. To fill lacunae in library holdings, she gathered important retrospective collections from Central and South America, such as the Simón Lucuix Rio de la Plata Collection from Uruguay and the Arturo Taracena Flores Collection from Guatemala.

Nettie Lee Benson, the historian, is perhaps less well known to us librarians. Nettie Lee was a graduate student in Latin American Studies when she began working in the library, and through the years she often commented that history was her first love. Nineteenth-century Mexico gave her a fascinating scenario to study, and she never tired of it. Each of her publications broke new ground and raised questions about past interpretations. I firmly believe that her appreciation for both primary and secondary documentation and her concern for preserving these materials in libraries came from her love of history and the sources which permitted her to write history.

Nettie Lee began to offer her graduate history seminars in 1962, and the students soon learned that they had better be meticulously accurate in their citations because she checked and rechecked every last reference. Yet her classes were always full. The students quaked in their boots (or sandals) when she gave them mammoth reading assignments in Spanish each week or when she asked very pointed questions on their reading. Very few students failed to appreciate the unparalleled preparation she gave them for their future careers. In 1985 the Mexican government recognized her accomplishments in Mexican history and research by awarding her the Order of the Aztec Eagle. She continued to write about nineteenth-century Mexico until the last few months of her life.

Nettie Lee was mentor and teacher not only to her history students, her staff, and the library users, but also to library science students. With Robert Douglass of the University of Texas Graduate School of Library Science and John Harrison of the Institute of Latin American Studies, she initiated a Latin American library studies program beginning in 1964 with Ford

Foundation funding. She and the recently deceased Gunnar Mendoza of Bolivia taught the first courses, and she continued to offer them until 1975. Numerous library science students from the United States and Latin America took these courses, and recall spending every free moment in the library annotating yet another reference book which she found for them!

Working for her and with her was an incomparable experience. She was demanding, exasperating, single-minded, but also warm, supportive, loyal, and dedicated. One felt guilty, in fact, because she was invariably the last person to leave the library at the end of the day (or night). One could not remain uninvolved given her enthusiasm and great love for the work she was doing! Every day was exciting, but I have to admit her staff learned it was better not to make eye contact with her too frequently because that would bring yet another work assignment!

Her colleagues, associates, students, and employees learned just bits and pieces of Nettie Lee Benson's earlier life and of her family activities. Nettie Lee had strong family loyalties. One of ten children, eight boys and two girls, Nettie Lee received a strong work ethic and an appreciation for learning from her parents. She also showed a strong tendency to compete with her two older brothers in all they did. Her younger brothers she easily managed, an experience that helped her during her years of high school teaching! A family memoir calls her "strong-willed like her father."[14]

At an event celebrating her life held last September at the library in Austin, her many nieces and nephews remembered and appreciated her support during their college days when many of them lived with her in Austin or during other times of need. Two of her high school students from Ingleside High School, both aged at least sixty-five, recalled her adventurous spirit during class trips to Monterrey, Mexico, which she sponsored when she was their social studies teacher in the 1930s.

Nettie Lee was unstintingly generous with her time and even with her money. She endowed the Latin American Collection to the amount of $110,000, and she supported the Presbyterian Church Shelter for Abandoned Children with an equally large sum of money.

Remembering Nettie Lee Benson is not without its bittersweet memories. In her zeal, she was sometimes misunderstood: a student told her one day that she "needed to be more careful with people because they are more fragile than books." And indeed she took it to heart. But no one gave more of herself to the people and institutions in which she believed than Nettie Lee Benson. She has left her imprint not only on our libraries through LACAP but also our professional lives through SALALM. She may be gone but she is not forgotten.

NOTES

1. John Wheat, "Nettie Lee Benson: Beyond the Orthodox," in David Block, ed., *SALALM and the Area Studies Community,* Papers of SALALM XXXVII (hereafter 37th Seminar), Austin, Texas, May 30-June 4, 1992 (Albuquerque: SALALM Secretariat, 1994), pp. 106-112.

2. Nettie Lee Benson, "Ninth Annual Report of the Latin American Collection, September 1, 1942-August 31, 1943," Benson Latin American Collection Archives, The University of Texas at Austin.

3. Ibid., "Eighteenth Annual Report of the Latin American Collection, September 1, 1951 to August 31, 1952," Benson Latin American Collection Archives, The University of Texas at Austin.

4. Ibid., "Microfilm Programs with Emphasis on Periodicals and Newspapers," in *Seminar on the Acquisition of Latin American Library Materials, Final Report,* Working paper IV-1 (Gainesville: University of Florida Libraries, 1956).

5. Robert Vosper, ed., *Final Report of the Second Seminar on the Acquisition of Latin American Library Materials,* June 19-20, 1957 (Austin: Institute of Latin American Studies, The University of Texas, 1958).

6. Donald F. Wisdom, "The First Two Decades of SALALM: A Personal Account," in *37th Seminar,* p. 122.

7. Nettie Lee Benson to Dominick Coppola, LACAP Report no. 3, January 31, 1960, Quito, Ecuador (hereafter LACAP Report no. 3, January 31, 1960); Nettie Lee Benson Archives, Benson Latin American Collection, The University of Texas at Austin (hereafter NLB Archives); see also Nettie Lee Benson's "Report on the Latin American Cooperative Acquisitions Project," in *Fifth Seminar on the Acquisition of Latin American Library Materials, Final Report and Working Papers* (Washington, DC: Pan-American Union, General Secretariat, Organization of American States, 1961), pp. 263-284.

8. Ibid., LACAP Report no. 6, February 7, 1960, Quito, Ecuador, NLB Archives.

9. Ibid., LACAP Report no. 11, March 13, 1960, Lima, Peru, NLB Archives (hereafter LACAP Report no. 11, March 13, 1960).

10. LACAP Report no. 3, January 31, 1960.

11. LACAP Report no. 11, March 13, 1960.

12. Nettie Lee Benson [to Dominick Coppola?], January 12, 1961, Bogotá, Colombia, NLB Archives; see also Nettie Lee Benson's "LACAP Report No. 2" in *Working Papers of the Sixth Seminar on the Acquisition of Latin American Library Materials,* Working Paper No. 2 (Carbondale: Southern Illinois University, 1961).

13. Ibid., February 27, 1961, Caracas, Venezuela, NLB Archives.

14. Unsigned Benson Family biography of Nettie Lee Benson [September 25, 1993], NLB Archives.

Part One

Trends in Contemporary Latin American Literature

I

A View of Latin American Novels, Poetry, Drama, and Bibliographies from 1970 to 1994

1. Latin American Literary Bibliography since the Boom

David William Foster

To write on the so-called boom of the Latin American novel twenty-five years after its putative inception has a certain element of the archeological about it, perhaps even more so than in the case of remoter periods. I suspect that it has something to do with the fact that my own professional career is framed by two prominent sociohistorical events in Latin American history: the Cuban revolution, which came at the end of my first quarter as a freshman Spanish major, and the boom, which overlaps with the end of my doctoral training and my first teaching assignments as a regular faculty member. Indeed, for those of us who find such moments seductive, my first residence in Latin America, in Buenos Aires, corresponded to the publication and promotion of Gabriel García Márquez's *Cien años de soledad* (1967), which, as we all know, confirmed the boom phenomenon (a designation from an Anglo-American perspective) or the new Latin American narrative (the more legitimated term in Spanish and Portuguese). I recall reading in Buenos Aires in the September 1967 issue of *Primera plana*, a general news magazine that cosponsored with the Editorial Sudamericana the prize that was awarded to *Cien años*, the review signed by Tomás Eloy Martínez and Ernesto Schóó's interview, in Mexico, with García Márquez. I recovered this material this spring for the students in my seminar on the Nueva Narrativa with an odd result. On the one hand there was the pleasant nostalgia of rereading it more than twenty-five years later and recalling the circumstances of having bought the magazine at the corner newsstand, of reading the cover story, and of going out immediately to buy the novel, which I have now taught more times than I care to remember.

When I walked into the classroom last January to give the introductory lecture on a course that was to focus on Río de la Plata fiction since the boom, a course that included García Márquez's novel because of the circumstances of its publication in Buenos Aires, the role of Sudamericana in publishing major authors of the boom, and the importance of *Primera plana* as one of the commercial forums responsible for promoting and sustaining the image of a "fully modernized novel" for Latin America, I found myself, quite without having planned it, spending three hours explaining in detail what was worrisome about the project of the boom in

5

retrospect from the mid-1990s. My comments focused on why its major features now seemed so out of step with the agenda of current writing in Latin America (and this was not because I was referring with any specificity to the postmodernist critique), and why the reading of the major texts had to be undertaken from a double perspective: the creation of a consciousness of a new narrative for Latin America in the late 1960s and the problematical relationship of that consciousness to contemporary writing.

To be sure, I found the time to acknowledge what there was about the new narrative that could be seen as opening up ideological spaces that have subsequently been crucial to the literature of the 1980s and 1990s: for example, although Cortázar's fictional world is essentially heterosexist (and, on occasion, even homophobic), he engages so systematically in a deconstruction of the fixed and stable categories of the bourgeois mentality that little critical effort is required to see his writing as leading into a project of essentially queer dimensions. While we necessarily undertake such double readings in order both to account for current critical agendas and to afford cultural production the context of its originary moment, the way in which it has now become necessary to view the construction of a domain of Latin American novelistic production called the boom is the result of a hegemonic critical practice related to the midcentury project of modernization, a project that is as masculinist as is the inventory of the major writers produced under that purview. The result is that it is perhaps now no longer possible to teach a course on the Nueva Narrativa as such, just as it has now become necessary to expand the definition of Modernismo in ways that extend the primary bibliography beyond Rubén Darío and his male colleagues.

It should be obvious at this point that my interest here is less in discussing bibliographic sources as such—although I will be doing some of that—than it is in addressing more fundamental issues regarding the ways in which we understand the boom as an object of academic study, with the bibliographic sources required for such a study, and the ways in which it has made an impact on the creation of a significant domain of Latin American literary research. Moreover, however we decide to approach the boom as a field of study, we cannot escape a grounding observation: the boom both constituted the field of Latin American literary and cultural studies in the United States, with all of the institutional derivations such a constitution implies, as well as it established specific priorities for that literary and cultural criticism that are still with us, beginning with the simple fact that contemporary Latin American literature and research on it essentially imposes the centrality of narrative. Even when we try (aided or not by a postmodern stance) to escape the heavy burden of this centrality, we either must constantly reaffirm the way that narrative is statistically the major manifestation of contemporary Latin American literature or we must engage in multiple redefinitions of what we mean by "narrative," such that that genre is always central to our discussion (the inclusion of film, theater, television programming—especially soap operas—comic books, romance novels, chronicles, social science accounts, and even the very idea that everyday life is a social text to be read as a narrative).

I would like to underscore the importance of the boom/Nueva Narrativa in the constitution of Latin American studies in the United States—and in Europe, for that matter. As anyone with some sense of academic history well knows, the teaching of Spanish was a very small enterprise before World War II (and, for that matter, it was only the arrival of refugees from the Spanish Civil War and sympathies toward them in the United States that gave Spanish an initial, and peninsular-biased, impetus in the 1930s). But the Good Neighbor Policy and, more important, the far-ranging development of commercial interests by the United States in Latin America beginning in the 1940s led to the confirmation of Spanish as the basic foreign language taught in American schools (I myself profited from this circumstance, having begun the study of Spanish in 1951 at the age of ten in Seattle, a city then embarking on a major project of international trade development). Concomitantly, business and political interests provided an enormous stimulus for social science activity in Latin America, and the bibliography in the field essentially dates from the 1940s.

Chilean Arturo Torres-Rioseco is reputed to have been the first full-time professor of Latin American literature in this country, joining the U.C. Berkeley faculty in the late 1930s. His books, published by the University of California Press, established a vision of both Latin American literature in general and the novel in particular, and it is no surprise to find that his fundamental division of fiction between a narrative of the city and a narrative of the countryside (always with a romanticizing privileging of the latter as somehow more tied to abiding autochthonous roots) became two decades later the major ideological framework that writer-critics of the Nueva Narrativa sought to refute, with their emphasis on immigration from the periphery to the metropolis and the emergence of the Latin American megalopolises, with the latter as the principal domain of national identity (Buenos Aires = Argentina, Mexico City = Mexico) and the locus for the enactment of national crises, especially those of imperialist domination.

If the late 1940s and the 1950s saw the emergence of Spanish and an awareness of Latin America, the literature of the boom entered the American mainstream in a categorical fashion, both with the importance accorded this production as the basis of the development of Spanish programs that, in many large state and urban universities, vie for preeminence with English departments (at my university we have almost

8 percent of the entire university population enrolled in Spanish courses, from first-year through dissertation hours) and with the general-public recognition of Latin American literature in the form of translations with major publishers with high-profile translators, reviews in mainline literary supplements and reviews, and a sustained production in English of historical and critical works designed to record for the nonspecialist audience modern Latin American letters. There are now dozens of books in English on Jorge Luis Borges, and the bibliography of books in English on Gabriel García Márquez, Carlos Fuentes, Octavio Paz, Pablo Neruda, Julio Cortázar is without a doubt greater than that of all the rest of Latin American literature put together.

The publication in 1978 of Emir Rodríguez Monegal's *Jorge Luis Borges: A Literary Biography* was something of a landmark. Literary biography is a virtually nonexistent genre in Latin America, and the Uruguayan Rodríguez Monegal's biography, which was *subsequently* published in Spanish but which has generated little interest in that language, signaled the potential that writing about the lives of Latin American authors could have for an English-language culture for which literary biographies probably constitute half of the scholarly production at any one time, even on occasion attaining bestseller status, as in the case of Richard Ellman's biography of Oscar Wilde. Moreover, Rodríguez Monegal's biography was published by E. P. Dutton (Borges's major U.S. publisher).

In 1979, George Braziller brought out Doris Meyer's *Victoria Ocampo: Against the Wind and the Tide*, seeking to appeal to a then expanding feminist interest in Latin American women writers, stronger at that time, I might add, among American scholars than among their Latin American counterparts (for example, Alba Omil's *Frente y perfil de Victoria Ocampo* was published by Ocampo's own literary review, *Sur*, in 1980 as part of a homage by the journal to its founding editor, who died in early 1979). Both American commercial and academic presses now routinely publish literary biographies of Latin American authors, and I know of no such sustained production in Spanish; for that matter, only a few ever get translated into Spanish, the most notable example being Diane E. Marting's 1990 Greenwood Press encyclopedia *Spanish American Women Writers: A Bio-Bibliographical Sourcebook*, which was published in Mexico in Spanish translation in 1990. There is no similar project undertaken directly in Spanish. It should be noted that this circumstance is not specific to the category of women writers, but is also true of other fields of research (some of which are, for that matter, arguably only recognized as such from the perspective of American cultural ideologies): Afro-Hispanic writers, lesbian and gay writing, Chicano and Neo-Rican literature, and studies on film as narrative texts (e.g., when film gets written about in Spanish and

Portuguese, it is discussed either as a category of the sociology of culture or as part of anecdotal information about a particular director).

As one might expect, the Modern Language Association's *International Bibliography* is an excellent place to chart the sort of development I have been describing. It is only with the organization in the mid-1950s of the bibliography as a major reference tool, rather than as merely a listing of current reseach, that Latin American literature begins to achieve some critical identity. But it is obvious that Latin America is substantially overshadowed by Spain and Portugal. The compilations on the late 1960s and 1970s begin to show the geometric growth of Latin America coverage, and it is only in 1981, with the division of coverage in specific Latin American countries (confirming the need to understand that Spain is now only one of a panoply of Spanish-speaking countries and not the anchor member of a binary opposition between the Peninsula and Latin America; Brazil has now, of course, completely overshadowed Portugal), that the overall coverage for Latin America achieves the same status as that for Spain. The most recent volume of *International Bibliography* (1992) still shows more coverage for Spain (1,784 entries) than for Spanish America (1,436), but this is no longer a consequence of disproportionate efforts in the process of indexing. Rather, it is a function of the lesser economic resources available in Latin America for the publication of criticism and the fact that so much commentary appears in sources that the MLA staff is unable to index. I would venture to say that if information were available only for English-language or United States-based imprints, Latin America might well outstrip Spain in the listing. The point, certainly, is not that Latin America does or should outstrip Spain, but rather the degree to which it is possible to have access to Latin American publications to the same extent as is possible in the case of Spain.

Let us remember that, particularly in the case of contemporary writing, literary criticism is institutionalized in Spain to an extent that has never been possible for Latin America, and may never be. Although a considerable amount of bibliographic references is generated by university-based journals and presses and by official organs of other institutions, it is virtually impossible to have a sense of ongoing cultural production in any of the Latin American republics, from Argentina to Cuba, from Mexico to Paraguay, without access to bibliographic information that is not available in any printed or on-line source. You will immediately realize that I am referring to the function of the literary supplement attached to a major daily newpaper. In the case of Buenos Aires, to the extent that different newspapers represent pronouncedly different social and ideological sectors, in line with the venerable history of Latin American journalism in even its most Americanized professional dimensions, a valuable mosaic can be constructed out of commentaries published in *La Nación*, *Clarín*, *Página 12*, and *El Cronista*, to mention only the four most influential.

During the 1970s and the early years of the Proceso de Reorganización Nacional that began in 1976 before it was taken over by the military, Jacobo Timmerman's *La Opinión* was a principal source of information for the cultural movements that came to represent major forms of resistance against the tyranny. Throughout the military period between 1976 and 1983, *Clarín*, incidentally the only major Latin American daily owned by a woman and Argentina's newspaper with the greatest circulation, engaged in multiple forms of opposition to the dictatorship with its reporting on cultural activities. *Página 12*, which began publishing after the return to constitutional democracy in 1983, quickly emerged as the leading forum for a redemocratized Argentine culture, and it continues to publish indisputably some of the best coverage of culture available in Argentina. Finally, the scholar wishing to chart the details of anything like a sustained gay culture in Argentina would want to read the subtext of literary coverage to be found in the oligarchic *La Nación*, a newspaper founded, I might note with bemusement, over 125 years ago by the author, quite literally, of Argentina's official history, Bartolomé Mitre. Although a bibliography does exist, published by Argentina's Fondo Nacional de las Artes, of *La Nación*'s literary supplement during the final decades of the nineteenth century, only by going to the archives of these dailies is it possible to have systematic access to the wealth of critical opinion contained in their pages.

Since many of the authors of columns and notes in Latin American literary supplements are important academicians or renowned creative writers, often collections of their articles have been published: a considerable number of García Márquez's journalistic writings have appeared, for example, and volumes of writings by most of the major literary journalists in Argentina in this century are available. Yet these collections are often selective, and they represent only a small percentage of the material that has, during the two hundred years of Latin American national literature, been published in newspaper supplements. The comments I have made with respect to Argentina are equally applicable to other Latin American countries: Mexico is an obvious parallel case, and my comments would also extend to the large array of weekly and monthly magazines and journals that contain important critical and literary information. I mentioned before the case of *Primera plana*, and we have yet to have any interpretation, beyond anecdotal information, of that magazine's role in the confirmation of the Nueva Narrativa, much less a bibliography of the articles and reviews published during the ten years (1962-1973) of its existence.

Some of these publications do find their way into the MLA *International Bibliography*: reviews like Mexico's *Plural* and, subsequently, its breakaway *Vuelta* have routinely been indexed, but not *Proceso*, which was founded by people who were separated in the late 1970s from the daily *Excelsior* (which also published *Plural*) for important ideological reasons that bear significantly on the coverage of cultural production. Curiously, for a period of time two important Brazilian literary supplements were covered by the MLA index, *O suplemento literário de Minas Gerais* and *O suplemento literário do Estado de São Paulo*, but they are no longer listed, and I suspect that coverage was the consequence of an ad hoc personal contribution rather than because of any specific recognition of the importance of these two sources for Brazilian literature.

So far I have been reporting on the growth of Latin American literature beginning with the boom, how that growth accompanied/was accompanied by an expansion in Latin American culture studies, and how, despite increased coverage through indexes like the MLA *International Bibliography*, which is but synecdochic of multiple library resources now available, I fear that large segments of the critical opinion scholars must read are not available through the Reference Room. I turn now to another dimension of the research agenda constituted by the Nueva Narrativa, that of expansive ways of reading Latin American cultural production. I am not referring so much to the amplification of what constitutes narrative as mentioned above. Rather, I wish to call attention to the sort of scholarly information that it has now become necessary to possess in order to undertake what might be considered anything like an adequate reading of cultural production. To be sure, one has in mind the intellectual complications associated with any society's cultural production, and we are now well aware of the often highly pitched debates in American studies over the New Literary History and an assortment of considerations under the rubric of multicultural studies. In the case of Latin American studies (which have, I would venture to say, in many cases been ahead of English departments in developing new scholarly agendas, in part because of the greater national, and therefore conservative, institutionalization of English than foreign languages), we have seen a development that can be essentially epitomized by saying that the boundaries between literature and nonliterature and between criticism and sociohistorical interpretation have been weakened, if not crumbled, so severely that disciplinary divisions make little sense at all, and in many institutions departments of Spanish have become, to the extent that Latin American social scientists may be scattered among and in competition with other area researchers in the social science departments, the focal points of interdisciplinary Latin American cultural studies.

I do not wish to overstate the centrality of Spanish departments for interdisciplinary research on Latin America, nor do I wish to imply that those of us who were originally trained in language and literature back in the late 1950s and 1960s have acquired anything like an adequate competence with respect to the vast bibliography of the contemporary social sciences. What I do want to underscore is that it is virtually impossible at this time to pursue a reputable research agenda in Latin American literature without, first, understanding literature as a category of cultural production and, second, availing oneself of a theoretical arsenal that can afford a satisfactory definition of the term "cultural production" and what the sociohistorical parameters of cultural production are. There may be some continuing validity in "reading literature as literature," especially within the context of a theorization of why the cultural production of a specific society may generate a privileged domain called literature and why that domain ought to promote a privileged reading of an imminent or solipsistic sort. But such reading and critical practices have now become a minority if not an outrightly deprecated form of scholarship, at least in the recognized research centers in this country. Precisely what I want to echo here is how much this inter- and multidisciplinary agenda, although it may now serve the need to redefine the field of Latin American literary and cultural studies, is primarily the consequence of the intrinsic developments in Latin American culture as notably showcased in literature and particularly in the novel of the boom. Questions relating to a culture of resistance, both to specific historical events based on neofascist military tyrannies and to the larger panorama of a perceived social tradition based on a pattern of structural violence; questions relating to, first of all, the multiple manifestations of a feminist consciousness in the context of changing social roles—that change itself a part of shifts in both the political and economic macrostructures— and then to an examination of gender roles in general that allowed for an intelligibility regarding sexual subalternities; questions relating to demographics as part of the definitions of national/nationalist identity as it is both codified in and hypothesized from cultural production: these are all dimensions of major novels of the sixties in Latin America, and these are all dimensions that critical activity had to undertake to prepare itself to deal with on the basis of theoretical models scholars in the humanities had not previously dealt with.

Certainly, nineteenth-century literary studies depended largely on the knowledge of history, and some anthropological perspectives like professional folklore studies did impinge on scholarly accounts antedating the influence of text-based stylistics/New Criticism beginning around the 1930s. But such knowledge about history was very much in the master narrative and metahistorical mode of the period: one of Torres-Rioseco's books in English is called *The Epic of Latin American Literature*, and by today's standards it is unequivocally sexist, heterosexist, classist, and racist. Metahistory and the New Literary History are, if not qualitatively at least theoretically, far removed from the discursive underpinnings of Torres-Rioseco's book, and national literary histories like the multivolume project of Ricardo Rojas for Argentina are grounded in historical, sociological, and anthropological propositions that are virtually unrecognizable to current theoretical models. This shift is very evident when one compares the references in an early compilation such as Becco and Foster's bibliography on the Nueva Narrativa (1976) or in the articles in an early review like the eight issues of Helmy Giacoman's journal *Nueva Narrativa Hispano-americana* that appeared between 1971 and 1975 with the references and their methodological cross-references in the MLA's *International Bibliography* or the issues of the *Revista Iberoamericana, Dispositio, Hispamérica, Revista de Crítica Literaria Latinoamericana*, and *Nuevo Texto Crítico*. A check of the list of references of the articles in reviews like the five I have cited may often reveal more theoretical sources than citations of other criticism on the text or author being examined, and one of the reasons why the norms in scholarly publication now call for a list of references rather than citations scattered in the footnotes is because of the perceived value for readers in having handily available a checklist of theoretical sources for the topic being examined, sources that may in turn serve to characterize a domain of intellectual inquiry, rather than a literary tradition as such, with which the article at hand is interacting.

Such a foregrounding of theory is especially evident in those monographs in which the major point may appear to be more the development of a theoretical framework into which texts are plugged than an originating inquiry into a segment of cultural production. I realize fully that such a distinction is tenuous and even tendentious, to the extent that the identification of a segment of cultural production is necessarily based on theoretical principles, even if they are institutionalized and therefore essentially unconscious practices, that allow in the first place for that segment to suggest itself as a corpus for study. But what I am trying to get at is the proposition that a text-centered critical inquiry—at least one that monumentalizes texts and the authors that supposedly produce them—is simply no longer considered academically sophisticated. Academic sophistication may well be quite relative, and indeed even an ideal not to be taken too seriously. But the notion of such a quality indisputably underlies much of the current critical commentary being generated around the Nueva Narrativa and, from there, on Latin American literary and cultural production as a whole.

The requirements of such a sophistication involve both the incorporation of a rather staggering array of theoretical texts, many of which do not even acknowledge the existence of Latin America and routinely take as their point of departure examples drawn from American, British, and French literature (a cultural hegemony that over and over again revisits Latin America), and the assimilation of at least the high points of social science research on Latin American societies. As a consequence, it also represents the demand for the sort of bibliographic control that would not have even been conceivable twenty-five years ago. For this reason, the success of a source like the *Hispanic American Periodicals Index* (*HAPI*) is definitely a mixed one. On the one hand, *HAPI* has provided us with a level of accurate control over the central core of journals, and it has done so in a multi-disciplinary context that had never really been available before, making it clear to what an extent prior projects, because of a number of resource limitations, were very much hit-and-miss projects. But on the other hand, while one can count on *HAPI* for reliable access to bibliographic entries, the decision to make use of the Library of Congress headings, always roughly cut to begin with and in many cases even ideologically problematic, does not provide for the subtlety of content, especially in theoretical terms, that the research field now requires. Moreover, the Library of Congress system has never been adequate for Latin America, having been developed on the basis of a collection that at the time was too small a sample to provide for a nuanced division of the cultural field. This is perhaps more evident in the classification schedules than in the subject headings, but no one should be surprised by the assertion that they are both distinctly limited. In this case, the MLA *International Bibliography* is of greater utility, since the indexing protocols do, in fact, provide for an entry format that takes into account the features of both the research methodology and the topic categories of the entry's content, all in terms of multiple cross-referencing.

The compilation of the MLA index continues to be far more unwieldy than is the case with *HAPI*, journal coverage is more limited, and, of course, the emphasis is only on literature, often narrowly defined. I should note that there is a proposal under consideration to expand into the field of cultural production as a whole, but it is unlikely that "pure" social sciences will ever be included. I ought also to mention the *Arts and Humanities Citation Index*, which would in many ways appear to fulfill the requirements for a highly sophisticated level of indexing, and one that is prepared with greater consistency than the other two because of in-house indexers, which explains why it is such a much more costly publication. Nevertheless, coverage tends to be confined to Anglo-American journals, to the exclusion of most Latin American and Spanish sources, and, once again, the social sciences are not included (although social science references are accessible through the cross-referencing of citations).

The result of these limited sources and the restrictions that exist for them, within the parameters of the vast range of theoretical and social science scholarship that Latin American literary and cultural scholars are now expected routinely to cite, means that so many references are garnered in a random fashion and personal recommendations count for much in finding out about a source and in being able to track it down (one often ends up with a xerox copy lacking bibliographic data and then seeks in vain to complete that data from the reference sources available)—all of which means that, despite the technologization of the modern library, there is still much of a sense of venerable Latin American artisanship in what we are doing. I would be the last one to decry the demand for theory in contemporary Latin American cultural studies, having had many opportunities to collaborate on its imposition. But what it does mean is that if I at one time thought we might be able to generate enough primary and secondary bibliographies on Latin American literature, in some sort of grand modernist project of bibliographic control, the history of the protean development of Latin American scholarship since the period of the boom—and, as I have attempted to underscore, as a consequence of the boom—has rendered such an idea impossible and ultimately quite irrelevant.

BIBLIOGRAPHY

Becco, Horacio Jorge, and David William Foster. *La nueva narrativa hispanoamericana; bibliografía*. Buenos Aires: Casa Pardo, 1976.

Martínez, Tomás Eloy. "América: la gran novela [review of *Cien años de soledad*]." *Primera plana* 234 (June 20-26, 1967), 54-55.

Marting, Diana E. *Spanish American Women Writers: A Bio-Bibliographical Sourcebook*. Westport, Conn.: Greenwood Press, 1990. Also as *Escritoras de Hispanoamérica: una guía bio-bibliográfica*. Prólogo, coordinación y revisión de la edición en español por Montserrat Ordóñez. México, D.F.: Siglo Veintiuno Editores, 1990.

Meyer, Doris. *Victoria Ocampo: Against the Wind and the Tide*. New York, NY: G. Braziller, 1979.

Omil, Alba. *Frente y perfil de Victoria Ocampo*. Buenos Aires: Sur, 1980.

Rodríguez Monegal, Emir. *Jorge Luis Borges: A Literary Biography*. New York, NY: Dutton, 1978.

Schóó, Ernesto. "Los viajes de Simbad García Márquez." *Primera plana* 234 (June 20-26, 1967): 52-54.

Torres Ríoseco, Arturo. *The Epic of Latin American Literature*. Rev. ed. New York, NY: Oxford University Press, 1946.

2. Recent Trends in the Spanish American Novel, 1970–1994

Raymond Leslie Williams

One of the more recent books published in the period 1970-1994, *El naranjo o los círculos del tiempo* (1993) by Carlos Fuentes, evokes the problem of unity. This book appears at first to be a set of five independent stories probing the roots of Latin American culture or, as Fuentes prefers to call it, "Indo-Afro-Iberoamerican" culture. The reader of these classic Fuentes stories finds a hint of unity with the presence of an orange in each of the first three stories. The fourth story, however, titled "Apolo y las putas," seems to betray Fuentes's cultural interests and the reader's sense of unity. "Apolo y las putas" tells the story of a fifty-five-year-old Hollywood actor of "B" movies who goes on a vacation to Acapulco, where he rents a boat and contracts with seven young Mexican women for an afternoon of diversion on the boat. Once engaged in his very first *divertimiento*, however, this aging actor suffers a heart attack, leaving the seven young professionals extremely worried about the potential legal problems related to the corpse (not to speak of their professional futures). The reader becomes concerned with not only the unity of the volume but also how such a story relates to the classic Fuentes themes of the first three stories. At the end of the story, however, Fuentes solves the professional crisis of the young women as well as the problem of unity after the Mexican authorities bury the heartbroken actor: next to his tomb an orange tree sprouts up.

By the end of this eighteenth volume of Fuentes's fiction, it is evident that oranges and orange trees are the unifying element for this intriguing and entertaining book. (For Fuentes, the image of a Spaniard eating an orange is virtually paramount to a metaphor for Spanish identity.) What, then, can be our *naranjo*, our unifying element in this scattered body of fiction published over the past twenty-four years, a corpus that includes no fewer than three to four thousand novels and writers as different as Carlos Fuentes, Gabriel García Márquez, Mario Vargas Llosa, Julio Cortázar, José Donoso, Ricardo Piglia, Diamela Eltit, Salvador Garmendia, Julio Ramón Ribeyro, Isabel Allende, Enrique Medina, R. H. Moreno-Durán, Albalucía

AUTHOR'S NOTE: Several books by John S. Brushwood have informed this presentation, particularly *The Spanish American Novel* (Austin: University of Texas Press, 1975).

16

Angel, Severo Sarduy, Luis Valenzuela, Fernando del Paso, Luis Rafael Sánchez, Luis Arturo Ramos, and Laura Esquivel? The impulse to name seemingly endless lists of authors and titles can easily lead to a catalog or encyclopedia offering little insight into what has been happening in Spanish American fiction over the past quarter of a century. In order to avoid this encyclopedic impulse, I follow Fuentes's model and tell five stories of the Spanish American novel over the past quarter of a century and identify a few *naranjos*, or unifying elements, in the process.

The best-known story during this period, and our first story, is the story of a jet-setting boom. This is a narrative of great novels, of politics, of celebrities, and occasionally even of melodrama. Born out of personal friendships, the revolutionary politics of the Cuban Revolution, and several other fortunate coincidences, such as the entrance onto the scene of the superb translator of the boom, Gregory Rabassa.[1] The boom left us a set of the major novels of the century, such as García Márquez's *Cien años de soledad*, Fuentes's *La muerte de Artemio Cruz*, and Vargas Llosa's *Conversación en La Catedral*, in addition to some totalizing grand narratives published since 1970, such as Fuentes's *Terra Nostra*, Roa Bastos's *Yo, el Supremo*, Vargas Llosa's *La guerra del fin del mundo*, and García Márquez's *El amor en los tiempos del cólera*.

Someone has declared the death of the boom approximately every year since it began in the 1960s. Usually, these declarations come from writers of the next generation, such as the Colombian Gustavo Alvarez Gardeazábal, who has been declaring the literary death of García Márquez since 1974, and who has been so frustrated with the Nobel Laureate's success (and the overwhelming *sombra* it has left over Colombian letters), that he even made García Márquez a character in his novel *Pepe Botellas*— but a character whose most salient characteristic is his diminutive penis. The young and talented Mexican novelist Luis Arturo Ramos has not been any more kind to Fuentes, publishing a tongue-in-cheek essay about Fuentes in the United States and once declaring to a group of American high school students "Fuck Fuentes!"[2]

Writers of the boom have even declared their own literary death on occasion. Julio Cortázar confessed to Luis Harasses as early as the mid-1960s that his aesthetic and political objectives would probably make his novels less viable for a broad reading public, and the novels that he published after that, *62: modelo para armar* and *Libro de Manuel*, did indeed result in Cortázar's being remembered primarily as the author of short stories and *Rayuela*, and not as a novelist.[3] García Márquez also announced a literary suicide in 1975, claiming that he would not publish another novel until the fall of General Pinochet in Chile. The storyteller, nevertheless, won over the politician, and García Márquez published

Crónica de una muerte anunciada and *El amor en los tiempos del cólera* with Pinochet still in power.

As a group of writers with personal bonds and a common aesthetic and political agenda, they ended their boom in the spring of 1971, when they met for the last time as a group in the home of Cortázar in Saignon, France. After that, the personal and political tensions grew to such an extent that the animosity between García Márquez and Vargas Llosa became a public conflict. Now, Fuentes refuses to appear in public with Vargas Llosa, and the only remnants of the 1960s solidarity of the boom are the group's lasting admiration for the deceased Cortázar, and the ongoing friendship between Fuentes and García Márquez.

Despite the yearly obituaries of the boom, and despite the disintegration of the group's personal rapport, the novelists of this generation remain the most impressive group of creators in the Spanish language since the Siglo de Oro. And despite our perverse attempts to ignore them and even to kill them off, they keep sprouting up again, as unexpectedly as that orange tree, with *una crónica* here, *un naranjo* there, *una guerra* back there, and then *otra historia del amor*. And for those who might be in doubt about the creative energy still remaining in a sixty-six-year-old García Márquez and Fuentes, and a fifty-eight-year-old Vargas Llosa, let me remind you that García Márquez, now living in Colombia, is actively engaged in more writing projects than at any time in his life, that Fuentes has outlined the plans for his next ten novels (with titles and plots already planned for works such as *Aquiles o el guerrillero*, *Emiliano en Chinameca*, and *Los años con Laura Díaz*), and that Vargas Llosa has decided to spend the next two years in London writing the novel to follow his most recent work, *Lituma en los Andes*, a novel about his Sergeant Lituma from *La casa verde*.

With that resumé, let's leave the boom up there at the top of our orange tree, sitting contentedly on its highest branches, perhaps with the Nobel Laureate of the group smiling on the apex, as if he were an angel sitting on the pinnacle of a Christmas tree. They were there at the top in 1971 when they last chatted in Cortázar's home, planning to launch the magazine *Libre* (edited by Juan Goytisolo), and they are there today, two decades later.

Our second story of the period from 1970 to 1994 is a little more academic perhaps, for it consists of a chronological narrative of the Spanish American novel from 1970 to 1994, highlighting the predominant thematic concerns over the years. This brief story can be visualized as the trunk of the orange tree, providing for the background and growth of the Spanish American novel.

The year 1970 was marked by the publication of the type of novels that both academic critics and professional writers find attractive: complex and hermetic novels such as José Donoso's *El obsceno pájaro de la noche*, Humberto Costantini's *Háblenme de Funes*, Fanny Buitrago's *Cola de zorro*, and Héctor Manjarrez's *Acto propiciatorio*. This complexity and hermeticism were predominant notes throughout the early 1970s, with the appearance of novels such as Severo Sarduy's *Cobra* (1972), Ernesto Sábato's *Abbadón, el exterminador* (1974), García Márquez's *El otoño del patriarca* (1975), and Fuentes's *Terra Nostra* (1975).

By the mid-1970s, Latin American writers were concerned with the dictatorial regimes in place in much of the region, and the result was a series of *novelas de dictadores*, including Alejo Carpentier's *El recurso del método* (1974), Augusto Roa Basto's *Yo, el supremo* (1974), and García Márquez' *El otoño del patriarca* (1975). Fuentes had originally promoted the idea of a dictator by proposing in the late 1960s that he, Vargas Llosa, and Cortázar write a dictator novel together.

In the late 1970s and early 1980s the Latin American novelists seemed to write with a new acceptance that complexity was not necessarily profundity, and seriousness need not always require a sober tone. Lighter and often humorous books with clearly definable plots appeared in the form of Vargas Llosa's *La tía Julia y el escribidor* (1977), Fuentes's *La cabeza de la hidra* (1978), Gustavo Sainz's *Compadre lobo* (1978), Cabrera Infante's *La Habana para un Infante difunto* (1979), Isaac Goldemberg's *La vida a plazos de don Jacobo Lerner* (1979), García Márquez's *Crónica de una muerte anunciada* (1981), and David Sánchez Juliao's *Sigo siendo el rey* (1983), the latter a novel/soap opera that used the lines from Mexican *ranchera* music to open each chapter. This tendency toward more accessible and entertaining fiction set the stage for the cultural and commercial phenomenon of Isabel Allende, whose *La casa de los espíritus* and *De amor y de sombra* were best sellers superior in volume to many novels of the boom. The movement toward accessibility and populism also seemed to relate to the Premio Rómulo Gallegos, which was awarded to the popular Argentine writer Mempo Giardinelli, a traditional storyteller whose early novels, such as *Luna caliente* (1983), were relatively ignored by the intellectuals in Buenos Aires as well as by First World academics. His latest novel, *Santo oficio de la memoria* (1991), is a vast and lengthy historical work, and the one for which Giardinelli was accorded the Premio Rómulo Gallegos.

To complete the chronological story, several important novels appeared in the 1990s, including Ricardo Piglia's *La ciudad ausente* (1992), Fuentes's *El naranjo, o los círculos del tiempo* (1993) and *Diana, o la cazadora solitaria* (1994), García Márquez's *Del amor y otros demonios* (1994), and Héctor Libertella's *El paseo internacional del perverso* (1990).

Generally obscured among the branches and leaves of the orange tree are the writers of my third story of the period from 1970 to 1994. They are the generally ignored writers I identify as postmoderns, the radical innovators who have rejected the postulates of the grand narrative, the modern, and those totalizing projects of the boom. Rather than identify with the writers of the boom, they generally look back to the relatively obscure fiction of the *vanguardia* of the 1920s and 1930s—the novels of Jaime Torres Bodet, Macedonio Fernández, Julio Garmendia, and, later, the fiction of Borges. These young postmoderns often trace their literary genealogy from the novelists of the *vanguardia* to Borges, and then to Morelli's propositions in *Rayuela*. For the most part, they are as unconcerned with commercial success as were their literary forefathers. These radical innovators include the Argentines Héctor Libertella and Ricardo Piglia, the Chilean Diamela Eltit, the Bolivian Renato Prada Oropeza, the Colombians Albalucía Angel and R. H. Moreno-Durán, the Venezuelan José Balza, the Cuban Severo Sarduy, and several Mexican writers, including Salvador Elizondo, José Emilio Pacheco, Luis Arturo Ramos, Carmen Boullosa, and even those former *onderos*, such as Gustavo Sainz and José Agustín. Unlike their predecessors of the boom, these postmoderns tend to eschew public positions on political issues, even though most of them write novels that are just as "political" in their implications as were those of the previous generations. But these postmoderns generally do not profess total understanding of grand narratives such as national history and, consequently, their novels tend to be less grandiose in scope than the totalizing works of the boom.

And what exactly is this Latin American postmodern? The culture industry currently publishes approximately a book a week to explain postmodernism to us; no adequate discussion of the Latin American postmodern could be done in less than a book-length study.[4] Nevertheless, one of the most effective images of the postmodern is the architectural image proposed by Charles Jencks (and elaborated by Linda Hutcheon) of the "unresolved contradiction."[5] The unresolved contradiction of postmodern architecture is represented by the perfectly modern skyscraper, with its sleek, vertical lines, interrupted at the lower levels by classical Greek columns that, instead of fitting harmoniously into the architectural whole, stand in unresolved contradiction with these lines. Such postmodern architecture can be seen today in many parts of Mexico City, Buenos Aires, and Caracas, as well as the north side of Bogotá, the Miraflores neighborhood of Lima, and the center of Santiago.

The unresolved contradictions of postmodern texts differ from the old "ambiguities" of "traditional" and modern novels in their disinterest in offering rational solutions to the intrigues and doubts created in these older texts. The unresolved contradictions in the fictions of Diamela Eltit and other Latin American postmoderns are increasingly present since the late 1980s, and the key postmodern works of the late 1960s and early 1970s: Cabrera Infantes's *Tres tristes tigres*, Manuel Puig's *La traición de Rita Hayworth*, and Sarduy's *Cobra*. Their unresolved contradictions are like a ripe red apple hanging inexplicably on our orange tree.

A concept of exactly what constitutes the postmodern in Latin America is just as polemical among critics of Latin American culture as it is in First World cultures. Echoing many doubts of their North Atlantic counterparts and, more specifically, the positions of Habermas, Latin American critics such as the Chilean José Joaquín Brunner and the Mexican Adolfo Sánchez Vásquez question the viability of the postmodern. Nevertheless, Latin American society and culture have experienced the same crisis of truth that Lyotard, Baudrillard, and Jameson describe in North Atlantic nations. With the breakdown of the grand narratives of the nation-state, Latin America's traditional ruling classes now respond to the same multinational companies, corporate leaders, high-level administrators, and the like that Lyotard describes as the new rulers of the North Atlantic nations.

The discourse and concepts of First World postmodernism are now circulating in Latin America—*lo indeterminado, la problematización del centro, la marginalidad, la descontinuidad, la simulación*, and the like. One of Diamela Eltit's common terms, *precariedad*, is close to *the provisional* emphasized by many of the North Atlantic postmoderns. Perhaps the one key word North and South share most, however, with no translation, is Borges. The same Borges who was cited by the European poststructuralist theorists Barthes, Foucault, Baudrillard, and Lyotard, also planted the seeds for a Latin American postmodern fiction with his stories of the 1940s.

The Latin American postmodern writers offer radically different kinds of postmodernism—perhaps a postmodern phenomenon in itself: if Culture (with a capital C and in the singular) becomes cultures in postmodernity, as Hutcheon has suggested, then the provisionality and heterogeneity of postmodern cultures in Latin America are even more extreme than in the North Atlantic nations. For the most part, these Latin American post-moderns, like their First World counterparts, are interested in various kinds of theory and literary discourse. Sarduy's essays read like fiction and vice versa; Eltit's fiction contains the theoretical discourse of Derrida, Baudrillard, Deleuze, and others.

Latin American postmodern writers share many of the trends of the First World postmodernism noted by Ihab Hassan, Brian McHale, Linda Hutcheon, and Steven Connor. A broad range of cultural critics share the consensus that the postmoderns as a cultural phenomenon arose in the

1960s. For Hutcheon, the 1960s did provide the background, though not the definition, of the postmodern.[6]

Numerous North Atlantic critics have observed the postmodern bridging of the gap between elite and popular art. Since the 1960s, the Latin American writers who have been the object of intense academic study have, at the same time, frequently been best sellers, particularly García Márquez, Vargas Llosa, Isabel Allende, Luis Rafael Sánchez, and Manuel Puig. Three of the works that have sold particularly well to both the general public and to academe (and seemingly bridged the gap between elite and popular art) are Vargas Llosa's *La tía Julia y el escribidor*, Allende's *La casa de los espíritus*, and García Márquez's *Crónica de una muerte anunciada*—three novels that could arguably be called, for different reasons, "postmodern." For Hutcheon, postmodernism's relationship with contemporary mass culture is not just one of implication but also one of critique. This argument is perhaps stronger in the Latin American case because the historical and political have been consistently present in the entire Latin American novelistic tradition, from the traditional through the modern.[7]

My fourth story of the Latin American novel from 1970 to 1994 complicates the imagery of the orange tree considerably, for this is a story of diversity and of writers who represent marginalized sectors of Indo-Afro-Iberoamerican society. If the writers of the boom produced those large, luscious oranges ripe for commercial consumption, these are the products that tend to go unnoticed and often unpicked on the orange tree, and somehow miss the process of crating, processing, transporting, and mass-marketing of those other oranges. This is the work of Elena Poniatowska, who has given voice to the marginalized in Mexico, or the writing of Rigoberta Menchú, whose own story is the subject of her testimonial writing. The Argentine Enrique Medina has published more than ten novels dealing with different sectors of the marginalized in Argentina, beginning with *Las tumbas* in the early 1970s and continuing with novels that have not only challenged the values of Argentine society during and after the military dictatorship but also confronted official censorship. In his *Gay and Lesbian Themes in Latin American Writing* (1991), David W. Foster has pursued a topic that has no ontological status in Latin American literary criticism.[8] By venturing into this minefield of issues, ideologies, and opinions, Foster studies a group that should be included in our fourth story of the marginalized writers. It is a story of sexuality as an ideological construct of discourse. Latin American literature is especially silent about sexual themes, and even more so when it comes to lesbianism and gayness. Nevertheless, gay writers such as Manuel Puig, the Colombian Gustavo Alvarez Gardeazábal, and the Mexicans Luis Zapata, Rafael Calva, and Luis Arturo Ojeda are creating a new space for cultural production in Latin America.

The fifth story is a narrative of women writers of the period from 1970 to 1994, certainly one of the more phenomenal stories of the period. The women writers opened this period inauspiciously, as novels such as Fanny Buitrago's *Cola de zorro* (1970) and Albalucía Angel's *Dos veces Alicia* (1972) were accompanied by a general absence of fiction published by women in the early and mid-1970s. Works such as Alejandra Pizarnik's *La condesa sangrienta* (1976), something of a cult book in Argentina, were generally ignored by critics and scholars and the mainline reading public. It all changed in the 1980s, with a rearrangement of the very makeup of the orange tree, from its roots upward, a rearrangement promoted by the rise of First World feminist theory and women's studies programs, as well as by the fiction of Isabel Allende. The feminist fiction of the 1980s is characterized by new attitudes toward discourse and an ongoing questioning of dominant ideologies. For the first time in Indo-Afro-Iberoamerica, the unmasking of ideology and the social construction of gender were carried out with a self-conscious and overt understanding of ideology and feminist theory.

Many Latin American women writers share with their First World counterparts what Hutcheon calls the postmodern valuing of the margins. The women postmodern novelists' self-conscious awareness of post-structuralist theory is evident in the fiction of the Colombian Albalucía Angel, as it is in the writings of the Brazilian Helena Parente Cunha, the Chilean Diamela Eltit, and several others.

Writers such as Eltit, Angel, and the Argentine Susana Torres Molina seek to understand the social and cultural practices that clarify how gender relations are constituted, reproduced, and contested. This feminist project is being effected in Mexico by writers such as Carmen Boullosa, María Luisa Puga, Angeles Mastretta, Angelina Muñiz, Barbara Jacobs, Ethel Krauze, Aline Petterson, Silvia Molina, Margo Glantz, Luisa Josefina Hernández, and María Luisa Mendoza. These writers are currently fashionable in Mexico and among the best-selling novelists. As the Mexican writer and critic Federico Patán told me recently, "Hay que ser mujer para vender libros hoy en México, están de moda." Indeed, after the phenomenal sales of *Arráncame la vida* by Angeles Mastretta in the mid-1980s, the Laura Esquivel phenomenon is *unprecedented* in Latin America: her novel *Como agua para chocolate* has sold more copies than all the books of the boom combined. She is, in effect, her own orange tree.

This fifth story would not be complete without at least mentioning some of the other prominent women writers who have produced fiction during this period. The Puerto Rican Rosario Ferré has assumed a prominent role both as novelist and essayist, as has the Argentine Luisa Valenzuela and the Venezuelan Milagros Mata Gil. The Uruguayan Cristina

Peri Rossi is best known as a superb short story writer, but has also produced novels. A group of young women writers in Chile includes Diamela Eltit, Elizabeth Subercaseaux, and others. Other notable women novelists include the Argentine Reina Roffé, the Nicaraguan Giacondi Belli, the Colombian Fanny Buitrago, the Ecuadorian Alicia Yánez Cossío, and the Costa Rican Carmen Naranjo.

How, then, does this orange tree look after these five different versions of the Spanish American novel from 1970 to 1994? Seen in 1994, it is far more diverse than most critics would have imagined possible in the early 1970s. After Borges, *Rayuela*, *Cien años de soledad*, and *El beso de la mujer araña*, everything is now possible and to be expected from these writers. The heterogeneity of themes precludes the possibility of reduction to a few tendencies. The rise of women writers, nevertheless, is perhaps the most outstanding phenomenon of Latin American fiction since the boom. By 1994, stated quite simply, an orange tree can no longer be expected to be just an orange tree as it was known before. After a more careful perusal of the structure and foliage, we notice a diversity of oranges, that shining red oxymoron that turns out to be an apple, some semihidden fruit, and even some forbidden fruit. We also notice some postmodern oranges here and there, and begin to wonder just how many are natural, how many are hybrids, and how many are plastic. And now we suspect that at any moment a new orange tree might sprout up next to the tomb of Borges or Cortázar just as it did in Acapulco for that deceased Hollywood actor and as it did in Mexico City in the patio of Laura Esquivel.

NOTES

1. For a review of the personal relationships among the writers of the boom, see José Donoso, *Historia personal del Boom* (Barcelona: Seix Barral, 1972).

2. Luis Arturo Ramos's tongue-in-cheek article on Fuentes, "Para ver a Carlos Fuentes," appears in José Francisco Conde Ortega and Arturo Trejo Villafuerte, eds., *Carlos Fuentes: 40 años de escritor* (Mexico: Universidad Autónoma Metropolitana, 1993). Ramos's remark about Fuentes at the high school occurred in Denver in April of 1989.

3. See Luis Harasses, *Los nuestros* (Buenos Aires: Sudamericana, 1966).

4. A selection of the most recent studies of postmodernism include Herman Herlinghaus and Monika Walter, eds., *Posmodernidad en la periferia* (Berlin: Langer Verlag, 1994); *Boundary 2* 20:3 (Fall 1993); John Beverly and José Oviedo, eds., *The Postmodernism Debate in Latin America*; Zygmunt Bauman, *Postmodern Ethics* (Cambridge: Blackwell Publishers, 1993); Christopher Norris, *The Truth about Postmodernism* (Cambridge: Blackwell Publishers, 1993). I am currently preparing a book-length study of postmodern fiction in Latin America.

5. See Charles Jencks, *Post-Modern Classicism: The New Synthesis* (London: Academy, 1980), and Linda Hutcheon, *A Poetics of Postmodernism* (London: Routledge, 1988).

6. See Steven Conner, *Postmodernist Culture* (Cambridge: Blackwell, 1989); Ihab Hassan, *The Postmodern Turn* (Columbus: Ohio State University Press, 1987); Brian McHale, *Postmodernist Fiction* (London: Methuen, 1987).

7. I discuss Latin American postmodern fiction in more detail in "Western Truth Claims in the Context of the Modern and the Postmodern Latin American Novel," *Readerly/Writerly Texts*, 1:1 (Fall/Winter 1993), 39-64.

8. See David William Foster, *Gay and Lesbian Themes in Latin American Writing* (Austin: University of Texas Press, 1991).

3. Contemporary Latin American Poetry and Drama

Merlin H. Forster

An occasion such as this year's SALALM conference represents for me an honor and a challenge, and I am grateful to my friends and to the conference organizers for their confidence. I can only echo the words of Martín Fierro, the protagonist of José Hernández's nineteenth-century gaucho epic; in these opening stanzas Fierro asks for divine aid as he begins the arduous presentation of his life's story:

> Pido a los Santos del Cielo
> Que ayuden a mi pensamiento;
> Les pido en este momento
> Que voy a cantar mi historia
> Me refresquen mi memoria
> Y aclaren mi entendimiento.
>
> Vengan Santos milagrosos,
> Vengan todos en mi ayuda,
> Que la lengua se me añuda
> Y se me turba la vista;
> Pido a mi Dios que me asista
> En una ocasión tan ruda.
>
> (*Martín Fierro*, I.1.2-3)

One of my professors in graduate school, a man more noted among us students for the passion of his opinions than for the breadth of his vision, once stated scornfully in my hearing, "It isn't possible to study Latin American literature, because there isn't any." I am happy to report that my professor's view, not altogether uncommon at that time, has been radically altered in more recent years. A change in perception was beginning to be visible, really, while I was still a graduate student, but with the tremendous energy of the so-called boom of the 1960s and 1970s Latin American literature now has a firm place alongside peninsular Spanish and Portuguese literature and in relationship to other major world literatures. In short, it is now seen as a vital and established expression, with something unique to say to readers both inside and outside its primary linguistic and cultural areas. My presence at the SALALM conference should make it obvious as well that my professor's comment did not dissuade me from focusing my work centrally on Latin American literature, and now from the perspective of a number of years in the field I am pleased to be able to consider with you some of the more recent developments in what we all recognize as an increasingly mature literary expression.

Let me establish an initial context with a brief commentary on two persistent and often interrelated tensions that provide a developmental background for twentieth-century Latin American literature.* The first of these tensions is a search for independence. As we all know, modern Latin America had its beginnings in several European colonial empires, and, as Tzvetan Todorov has made clear in his insightful 1984 work *The Conquest of America*, a process of assimilation, change, and emancipation was set in motion in the early sixteenth century which has continued up to our own time. Though political independence from Europe came for most areas of Latin America in the early nineteenth century, a very real cultural dependence was much harder to set aside. In literary expression, especially, the hegemony of the standard European languages made clear, well into the twentieth century, the dominating relationship of center to periphery, of mother country to colonized area. A second tension, often intertwined with the first, is a search for modernity. Once again, this search is to be seen strongly in nineteenth-century movements such as romanticism and naturalism, in which the Latin American manifestations not only used European models but had as well a considerable delay in transmission from Europe to America. In the latter part of the century both the degree of dependence and the delay in time of transmission were greatly reduced, and by the first decades of the twentieth century literary experimentations were comparable and virtually contemporaneous. In all these manifestations Latin American literature and culture displayed their fundamental acquisitive nature. The Brazilian modernist Oswald de Andrade would insist, for example, on the concept of cultural "cannibalism," in which the European models were ingested, digested, and used as energy source for a very distinct expression.

Keeping in mind these two interrelated tensions, then, let me expand my initial context somewhat. I see four primary dimensions in the development of twentieth-century literary expression in Latin America: (1) continued experimentation in poetic discourse, (2) the establishment of

---

*Many of the ideas here are more fully developed in "Toward a Synthesis of Latin American Vanguardism," my introduction to *Vanguardism in Latin American Literature*, Merlin H. Forster and K. David Jackson, eds. (Westport, CT: Greenwood Press, 1990), esp. pp. 4-6.

the drama as a viable genre alongside the other major literary forms, (3) a veritable explosion in first-class works of prose fiction, and (4) increasingly visible feminine voices in a traditionally male-dominated literature and culture. Elsewhere in this volume (see Chapter 2) Raymond Williams approaches the extraordinary development of prose fiction over the last several decades, and I therefore leave that most significant dimension of the total picture in his hands. I identify my own task as the consideration of contemporary poetry and drama in Latin America, taking into account as well in those two genres the presence of a number of significant female figures.

Poetry has had in Latin America the most extended tradition of all the literary genres. Cultured poetic expression antedates the European arrival in the hemisphere (one might think, for example, of the brilliant poems in Nahuatl composed by Nezahualcóyotl, the fifteenth-century poet-king of Texcoco in the valley of Mexico); in the following centuries poetry in Spanish and Portuguese was the major expressive vehicle for a number of the area's leading writers. The twentieth century began with the already established values of modernism in Spanish America and symbolism in Brazil, values expressed in a profound disenchantment with mediocre surroundings, insistent use of exotic themes and settings, a studied search for perfection of form, and the development of a musical and richly sensorial figurative language. Rubén Darío's *Cantos de vida y esperanza* (1905) is a culminating work for the modernist/symbolist years, and as such provides a kind of solidity against which to measure subsequent developments.

The relative stability of modernist/symbolist poetic discourse was put under severe strain in the third and fourth decades of the century, with the appearance of a noisy avant-garde that seemed bent on the virtual destruction of form and conventional meaning. Some of the major vanguardist works are César Vallejo's *Trilce*, published in Lima in 1922, Mário de Andrade's *Paulicéia Desvairada*, which appeared in São Paulo in 1922, Vicente Huidobro's *Altazor, o el viaje en paracaídas*, published in Madrid in 1931, and Pablo Neruda's *Residencia en la tierra*, whose two parts were published together in Madrid in 1935. The rather extreme positions of the vanguardists were attenuated in the 1940s, however, and the development toward what can properly be considered contemporary poetry began with a group of poets born between 1910 and 1920 (see Appendix, I.A.1). The major figure here is the Mexican Octavio Paz (1914–), whose imposing work won him the Nobel prize for literature in 1990. *Libertad bajo palabra* (1949, expanded in 1960) is a compilation of his earlier poetry; *Blanco* (1967), *Pasado en claro* (1975), and *Árbol adentro* (1987) represent his later work. Paz is also a brilliant cultural and literary essayist; *El laberinto de la soledad* (1950), a commentary on modern Mexican culture, and *Los hijos del limo* (1974), on the interconnections between romanticism and the avant-garde, are only two of many influential works. Other important poets who are more or less contemporaneous with Paz are the Cuban José Lezama Lima (1910–1976), the Nicaraguan Pablo Antonio Cuadra (1912–), the Chileans Nicanor Parra (1914–) and Gonzalo Rojas (1917–), and the Brazilian João Cabral de Melo Neto (1920–). Lezama's anguished and self-reflective poetry found its fullest expression in *La fijeza* (1949) and *Dador* (1960); both his essays and his novel *Paradiso* (1953) reveal similar complexities. Cuadra's poetry develops a central view of his native country; *Cantos de Cifar* (1971), set in the central lake region of Nicaragua, and *Siete árboles contra el atardecer* (1980), a totemic vision of a multiple Nicaraguan reality, are examples of that view. Parra is best known for *Poemas y antipoemas* (1954), which makes effective use of a denunciatory poetic style. Rojas is passionate, irreverent, and at the same time brilliantly sensorial in his poetic language. *Materia de testamento* (1988) is an excellent collection of his recent work. Cabral's best-known work is *Morte e Vida Severina* (1956), a dramatic poem that follows the wanderings of a pilgrim figure through the Brazilian northeast.

These major postvanguardist figures, born between 1910 and 1920, establish a clear reference point from which to begin an exploration of contemporary poetic discourse, or in other words, poetry of the last twenty or thirty years. Let me borrow a term and a definitional model from the geologists, in the hope that I can thus give a certain degree of organization and direction to this exploration. I suggest looking at poetic development over the last few decades in terms of three interrelated strata, which in a kind of chronological definition and overlayering unite individuals across national boundaries in a common and successive temporality. In keeping with that vision, then, the earliest stratum of activity, and obviously by now the most firmly established, is represented by poets born in the 1920s and early 1930s (see Appendix, I.A.2). There are two first-rate figures from this group whose substantial and significant poetic production was truncated by premature death, namely Rosario Castellanos (Mexico, 1925–1974) and Enrique Lihn (Chile, 1929–1988). Still active in their sixties are Ernesto Cardenal (Nicaragua, 1925–), whose politically committed and controversial works continue to speak to his own and his country's changing circumstances, and Haroldo de Campos (Brazil, 1929–), whose name is linked to the brilliantly visual concrete poetry movement of the 1950s and 1960s but who maintains a very active role in the current literary scene. At an earlier point the ironic and often violent expression of Jaime Sabines (Mexico, 1925–) promised greater distinction, but to my mind isolation and silence have reduced his relative importance. Other well-established poets who should be mentioned as a part of this first stratum are Rubén Bonifaz Nuño (Mexico, 1923–), Álvaro Mutis (Colombia, 1923–), Ida Vitale (Uruguay, 1923–), Roberto Juárroz (Argentina, 1925–), Blanca Varela (Peru, 1926–), Carlos Germán Belli (Peru, 1927–), Juan Gelman (Argentina, 1930–), Ferreira Gullar (pseudonym of José Ribamar Ferreira, Brazil, 1930–), and Roberto Sosa (Honduras, 1930–).

A second and less firmly established chronological stratum would include poets born in the late 1930s and early 1940s (see Appendix, I.A.3). Like Castellanos and Lihn from the earlier group, Roque Dalton (El Salvador, 1935–1975), Alejandra Pizarnik (Argentina, 1936–1972), and Javier Heraud (Peru, 1942–1963) had promising careers cut short by premature death. The most active and best-established figures in this group, now in their early fifties, are Affonso Romano de Sant'Anna (Brazil, 1937–), Óscar Hahn (Chile, 1938–), José Emilio Pacheco (Mexico, 1939–), and Antonio Cisneros (Peru, 1942–), all of whom have solidly established international reputations. Other significant poets in this grouping are Carlos Nejar (Brazil, 1939–), Homero Ardijis (Mexico, 1940–), José Koser (Cuba, 1940–), Pedro Shimose (Bolivia, 1940–), Enrique Fierro (Uruguay, 1941–), Rosario Ferré (Puerto Rico, 1942–), Eduardo Mitre (Bolivia, 1943–), Nancy Morejón (Cuba, 1944–), and Iván Silén (Puerto Rico, 1944–).

A third and even more recent stratum, one really still in the process of formation in the currents of the present moment, encompasses poets born in the late 1940s and beyond (see Appendix, I.A.4). There is even less of a basis here to speak of established figures, and consequently any assessments must be open to change and the shifting of critical shoals, to insist on my central and sedimentary geological image. My readings up to this moment would lead me to mention as significant developing figures the names of Elsa Cross (Mexico, 1946–), Alurista (pseudonym of Alberto Urista, Mexico-United States, 1947), Arturo Carrera (Argentina, 1948), Néstor Perlongher (Argentina, 1948–), David Huerta (Mexico, 1949–), Alberto Blanco (Mexico, 1951–), Coral Bracho (Mexico, 1951–), Raúl Zurita (Chile, 1951–), Eduardo Milán (Uruguay, 1952–), Carlos Ávila (Brazil, 1955–), and Fernando Paixão (Brazil, 1955–). There are many, many others, I know, but the best that can be done with this most recent stratum is to make preliminary assessments that hopefully will with time turn out to be reasonably accurate.

In keeping with the openly geological image that I have been using, let me now make reference briefly in my profile to some specific texts that can at least give some small amount of detail to the three interrelated poetic strata that I have suggested. From the earliest, made up of poets born in the 1920s and early 1930s, I would mention three. For example, Rosario

Castellanos's "Valium 10" (collected in *Poesía no eres tú*, 1972) probes deeply into a feminine view of the problematic pressures of modern life: ". . . // Y tienes la penosa sensación / de que en el crucigrama se deslizó una errata / que lo hace irresoluble. // Y deletreas el nombre del Caos. Y no puedes / dormir si no destapas / el frasco de pastillas y si no tragas una / en la que se condensa, / químicamente pura, la ordenación del mundo." Also from the first stratum, Enrique Lihn's "Gallo" (from *La musiquilla de las pobres esferas*, 1969) presents death and the passage of time as part of everyday existence: "Canta este gallo, el mismo, y yo: ?soy otro? / que degollé, y a la redonda estaban / todos mis años; / el número ha crecido, pero en esto / no se distinguen entre sí, escuchándolo / sólo un poco más cerca de la muerte. // Gallo, qué insomnio, / clarín de qué batalla más perdida, / vindicativo, no, ni cruel, / pero enemigo, enemigo, enemigo." Finally, a stanza from Haroldo de Campos's "Anamorfose" (collected in *Xadrez de Estrelas*, 1974) displays the verbal and conceptual play of the Brazilian concrete poets: "dúvida / sombra / sem dúvida / na sombra / na dúvida / sem sombra / fora de dúvida / hora de sombra / hora de dúvida / fora de sombra / sem sombra de dúvida."

From a second and more recent stratum, made up of poets born in the late 1930s and early 1940s, Alejandra Pizarnik's "Un sueño donde el silencio es de oro" (from *Extracción de la piedra de locura*, 1968) presents an anguished and surrealistic vision: "El perro del invierno dentellea mi sonrisa. Fue en el puente. / Yo estaba desnuda y llevaba un sombrero con flores y / arrastraba mi cadáver también desnudo y con un sombrero / de hojas secas. / He tenido muchos amores—dije—pero el más hermoso / fue mi amor por los espejos." José Emilio Pacheco's "Those Were the Days" (from *No me preguntes cómo pasa el tiempo*, 1969) makes an especially poignant statement on the inevitable temporal process that is a part of our lives: "Como una canción que cada vez se escucha menos / y en menos estaciones y lugares, / como un modelo apenas atrasado que tan solo se encuentra / en cementerios de automóviles, / nuestros mejores días han pasado de moda / y ahora son / escarnio del bazar, / comidilla del polvo / en cualquier sótano."

The third and most problematic stratum is made up of poets born in the late 1940s and beyond, and, as I have already observed, relative values here are more difficult to establish. It is important, nonetheless, to mention a couple of representative texts. Arturo Carrera's "En más espacios" (from *Animaciones suspendidas*, 1986) takes an almost childlike approach to both the past history and the present moment of poetic creation: "El paso de la poesía eterna / como el único brío y el / último estertor, / la rosa que anuncia / la casa vacía y el recordarse / en ella // sin el bullicio del amor, / sin los pequeños amores que caen / en terrones / sobre las pequeñas momias / de Lugones y Reissig. // Sólo el pudor de poder / sustituir alguna / omnipotencia del gesto: / la libertad no es el sentido / salvo la gloria abolida, / salvo la emoción de bailar / tras unas breves lumbres." The final stanza of Coral Bracho's "Deja que esparzan su humedad de batracios" (from *Bajo el destello líquido*, 1988) opens into a humid and shadowy world from which reality can be seen only dimly: "Deja que pasen, / deja que inunden con su sombra imprecisa / los resquicios, las fuentes, los piracantos, / deja que impregnen su ansiedad de batracios / en las baldosas tibias. / Savia de lirios. / Como una oscura tajada. Las tardes brotan de los vapores / en la terraza; las noches mecen la flama. / De aquí, los arcos, / los algarrobos / y los delirios."

Let me conclude this section by suggesting several general conclusions on recent poets and poetry:

1. There is no substantial diminution of poetic production and publication across Latin America. Availability of publication resources favors certain traditional cultural centers (Mexico City, Buenos Aires, and São Paulo, for example), but groups are formed, poetry journals are published, and poets get themselves into print in both the central and peripheral areas of Latin America. Short editions, however, and the uncertain quality of communications between countries and regions make for difficult circulation and therefore problematic acquisition of the poetry materials that appear abundantly in every country.

2. The major figures of modernism and vanguardism (Darío, Huidobro, Vallejo, Neruda, and Andrade, for example) become less and less a direct influence on younger poets. They are increasingly distant figures, venerated to be sure, but not to be taken as models or sources for the present moment. On the other hand, the postvanguardists (in particular Paz, Parra, Cuadra, Rojas, and Cabral de Melo Neto), still alive and active, function as much more immediate—and on occasion more intimidating— presences for younger writers.

3. Contemporary poets obviously identify themselves with their own country/region and its problems, but there is as well a sharp sense of an international community, of being part of an ongoing "Latin American" literary expression. There is no mistaking the native areas of a Pacheco or a Cisneros, for example, but at the same time these poets, and most others, are familiar and comfortable with other cultural values and points of view.

4. The canon-formation process has been opened up considerably, and voices that not too long ago were not taken seriously into account (e.g., women, ethnic and racial minorities) are now included and studied alongside more mainstream figures. The increasing attention given to Castellanos, Pizarnik, Varela, Ferré, Morejón, Bracho, Silén, and Alurista, among others, illustrates for me this more ample degree of acceptance.

5. Thematic concerns of recent Latin American poets may at times tend toward introspection, as in the past, but just as often reflect obvious political or social concerns. At the same time, poetic structures and expressive language are more simple and direct, in contrast with the studied beauty of the modernists or the complex internalized experimentations of the vanguardists. With some exceptions, the message seems to be more important than the form in which it is expressed.

Let me turn now to the second dimension of my presentation. I should begin by saying that the drama has had in Latin America a rather different development from that of poetry. There is evidence of a pre-Columbian tradition here as well, but in contrast with poetry in the centuries following the conquest, there was relatively little theatrical activity and few significant playwrights. The period of greatest importance is clearly the twentieth century, and more especially the last four or five decades. The first major figure in the development of a modern Latin American drama is the Uruguayan Florencio Sánchez, whose 1905 masterwork *Barranca abajo* is the culmination of a series of plays on the problems of rural Argentina and Uruguay at the turn of the century. There are three important transitional figures, two Brazilian and one Mexican, who provide a link between Sánchez and the later decades of the century. The first is Joracy Camargo, whose 1932 social commentary *Deus lhe Pague* came as a bombshell in a still rather staid Brazilian society. Eleven years later, in 1943, Nélson Rodrigues's *Vestido de Noiva* was just as revolutionary in theatrical terms, and marks the real beginning of the modern Brazilian theater. The same year Rodolfo Usigli's *El gesticulador* fulfilled the same function for modern Mexican drama. Usigli comments pointedly on Mexican society by extending the basic meaning of the verb "gesticular" (to gesture) to include the playing of roles, both personal and political.

Drama has enjoyed spectacular development over the past several decades, a transformation that critics have often referred to as the "new" Spanish American theater (see Appendix, II.A). Significant initial contributions to that development were made in the 1950s and early 1960s by René Marqués (Puerto Rico, 1919–1979), Carlos Gorostiza (Argentina, 1920–), Carlos Solórzano (Guatemala, 1922–), Jorge Andrade (Brazil, 1922–), Alfredo Dias Gomes (Brazil, 1922–), and Ariano Suassuna (Brazil, 1927–). Marqués's best plays are the ever popular *La carreta* (1953), which depicts the disintegration of Puerto Rican rural life, and *Los soles truncos* (1959), in which the pressures of the modern world produce the suicide of three aging sisters. In *El juicio* (1954) and *El pan de la locura* (1958), Gorostiza uses realistic staging for pointed social commentary. *Las manos de Dios* (1956), Solórzano's best play, also carries a strong social message but one that is expressed in the more symbolic terms of traditional religious drama. Andrade is best known for *A Moratória* (1955), a modern tragedy set in the coffee-growing region of Brazil; Suassuna's best play is *Auto da Compadecida* (1956), which combines the medieval theater and the *literatura de cordel* ballad tradition of the Brazilian Northeast. Dias Gomes's best works are the immensely successful *O Pagador de Promessas* (1960), a play making effective use of Afro-Catholic syncretism, and *O Berço do Herói* (1965), on the exercise of freedom in a capitalist society.

In the mid-1960s the presence of a group of brilliant younger dramatists began to be increasingly evident, providing the central and continuing impetus for what we have termed the "new" drama. Let me mention some of the major figures. The extensive work of Emilio Carballido (Mexico, 1925–) includes such successes as *Yo también hablo de la rosa* (1970), a metatheatrical commentary on multiple reality, *Tiempo de ladrones* (1984), a long melodramatic presentation based on the bandit-hero Chucho el Roto, and *Rosa de dos aromas* (1986), a double-sided put-down of traditional Mexican *machismo*. The plays of Egon Wolff (Chile, 1926–), especially *Los invasores* (1963) and *Flores de papel* (1970), depict in chilling fashion the invasion and destruction of middle-class values. Loss of freedom and movement is the dominant theme in the plays of Griselda Gambaro (Argentina, 1928–), as seen poignantly in the two brothers of *Los siameses* (1967) and in the concentration-camp setting of *El campo* (1968). Fellow Argentine Osvaldo Dragún (1929–) has written a number of full-length plays, among them *Y nos dijeron que éramos inmortales* (1963), but is best known for his *Historias para ser contadas* (1965), a series of whimsical but often sharply critical one-act plays. *El cepillo de dientes* (1967), depicting bizarre everyday rituals by El and Ella, is an obvious incursion into theater of the absurd by Jorge Díaz (Chile, 1930–). Equally absurdist but considerably more violent is *La noche de los asesinos* (1966) by José Triana (Cuba, 1933–); the three characters act out over and over the murder of their parents. The plays of Eduardo Pavlovsky (Argentina, 1933–) deal with the violence of recent Argentine history; *El señor Galíndez* (1973), for example, is set in a well-equipped torture chamber that becomes increasingly visible as the play progresses. A dark Brazilian underworld is graphically represented by Plínio Marcos (Brazil, 1935–), particularly in *Navalha na Carne* (1967) and *Dois Perdidos numa Noite Suja* (1967). Vicente Leñero (Mexico, 1939–) makes adroit use of everyday Mexican language in his *Jesucristo Gómez* (1987), a present-day reworking of the Gospel of Luke in which Christ becomes an ordinary bricklayer, and in his *Nadie sabe nada* (1988), a searing denunciation of Mexican journalism and public life. Leilah Assunção (Brazil, 1949–) and Sabina Berman (Mexico, 1956–) are two already established female dramatists who continue to develop in remarkable fashion.

In the same way as I have suggested for the development of contemporary poetry, the overriding vision of contemporary drama in Latin America has to be one of variety, vitality, and considerable promise for the future. There are severe problems that do not afflict poetic discourse and publication, the greatest of which is the establishment and cultivation of the complex infrastructure that supports successful theatrical presentations. The struggle to maintain an ongoing tradition continues in every country, working against the inroads of television and the movies, but in spite of serious difficulties I maintain a hopeful view of things here as well. The presence of the "new" playwrights I have considered here, a selected few among many others, is a powerful indicator for me of an open canon process and a relatively healthy Latin American theater.

My purpose has been to consider some recent dimensions of a literature that over now several centuries has developed toward both maturity and a wider international recognition. I'm not sure just what "booms" may yet await us in the future, but there is no doubt that the literary processes discussed here will be carried forward with distinction and solidity into a new century. I just wish I could be around in fifty or a hundred years to follow some of the details.

APPENDIX

I. POETRY

    A. INDIVIDUAL POETS (listed by year of birth)

        1. *Born between 1910 and 1920*

            José Lezama Lima (Cuba, 1910–1976)
            Pablo Antonio Cuadra (Nicaragua, 1912–)
            Nicanor Parra (Chile, 1914–)
            Octavio Paz (Mexico, 1914–)
            Gonzalo Rojas (Chile, 1917–)
            João Cabral de Melo Neto (1920–)

        2. *Born in the 1920s and early 1930s*

            Rubén Bonifaz Nuño (Mexico, 1923–)
            Álvaro Mutis (Colombia, 1923–)
            Ida Vitale (Uruguay, 1923–)
            Ernesto Cardenal (Nicaragua, 1925–)
            Rosario Castellanos (Mexico, 1925–1974)
            Roberto Juárroz (Argentina, 1925–)
            Jaime Sabines (Mexico, 1925–)
            Blanca Varela (Peru, 1926–)

Poetry *(cont.)*

>   Carlos Germán Belli (Peru, 1927–)
>   Haroldo de Campos (Brazil, 1929–)
>   Enrique Lihn (Chile, 1929–1988)
>   Ferreira Gullar (pseudonym of José Ribamar Ferreira, Brazil,
>   1930–)
>   Juan Gelman (Argentina, 1930–)
>   Roberto Sosa (Honduras, 1930–)

> 3. *Born in the late 1930s and early 1940s*
>   Roque Dalton (El Salvador, 1935–1975)
>   Alejandra Pizarnik (Argentina, 1936–1972)
>   Affonso Romano de Sant'Anna (Brazil, 1937–)
>   Óscar Hahn (Chile, 1938–)
>   Carlos Nejar (Brazil, 1939–)
>   José Emilio Pacheco (Mexico, 1939–)
>   Homero Ardijis (Mexico, 1940–)
>   José Koser (Cuba, 1940–)
>   Pedro Shimose (Bolivia, 1940–)
>   Enrique Fierro (Uruguay, 1941–)
>   Antonio Cisneros (Peru, 1942–)
>   Rosario Ferré (Puerto Rico, 1942–)
>   Javier Heraud (Peru, 1942–1963)
>   Eduardo Mitre (Bolivia, 1943–)
>   Nancy Morejón (Cuba, 1944–)
>   Iván Silén (Puerto Rico, 1944–)

> 4. *Born in the late 1940s and beyond*
>   Elsa Cross (Mexico, 1946–)
>   Alurista (pseudonym of Alberto Urista, Mexico-United States,
>   1947–)
>   Arturo Carrera (Argentina, 1948–)
>   Néstor Perlongher (Argentina, 1948–)
>   David Huerta (Mexico, 1949–)
>   Alberto Blanco (Mexico, 1951–)
>   Coral Bracho (Mexico, 1951–)
>   Raúl Zurita (Chile, 1951–)
>   Eduardo Milán (Uruguay, 1952–)
>   Carlos Ávila (Brazil, 1955–)
>   Fernando Paixão (Brazil, 1955–)

Poetry *(cont.)*

B. WORKING CRITICAL BIBLIOGRAPHY

Barradas, Efraín. *Para entendernos: Inventario poético puerto-rriqueño*. San Juan: Instituto de Cultura Puertorriqueña, 1992.

Bruce-Novoa. *Chicano Poetry: A Response to Chaos*. Austin: University of Texas Press, 1982.

Bus, Heiner, and Ana Castillo. *Recent Chicano Poetry/Neueste Chicano-Lyrik*. Bamberg, Germany: Univ.-Bibliothek, 1994.

Cobo Borda, Juan Gustavo. *Antología de la poesía hispano-americana*. Mexico: Fondo de Cultura Económica, 1985.

Costa, Horácio. *A palavra poética na América Latina*. São Paulo: Fundação Memorial de América Latina, 1992.

Forster, Merlin H. *Historia de la poesía hispanoamericana*. Clear Creek, IN: The American Hispanist, 1981.

Massi, Augusto. *Artes e ofícios da poesia*. Porto Alegre: Artes e Ofícios, 1991.

Ortega, Julio. *Antología de la poesía hispanoamericana actual*. Mexico: Siglo XXI, 1987.

Rodríguez Padrón, Jorge. *Del ocio sagrado: Algunos poetas hispanoamericanos*. Madrid: Libertarias/ Prodhufi, 1991.

Sánchez, Marta Ester. *Contemporary Chicana Poetry: A Critical Approach to an Emerging Literature*. Berkeley: University of California Press, 1985.

Savary, Olga. *Antologia da Nova Poesia Brasileira*. Rio de Janeiro: Fundação Rio/Hipocampo, 1992.

Sefamí, Jacobo. *Contemporary Spanish American Poetry: A Bibliography of Primary and Secondary Sources*. New York, NY: Greenwood Press, 1992.

II. DRAMA

A. INDIVIDUAL DRAMATISTS (listed by year of birth)

René Marqués (Puerto Rico, 1919–1979)
Carlos Gorostiza (Argentina, 1920–)
Carlos Solórzano (Guatemala, 1922–)
Jorge Andrade (Brazil, 1922–)
Alfredo Dias Gomes (Brazil, 1922–)
Emilio Carballido (Mexico, 1925–)
Egon Wolff (1926–)

Drama *(cont.)*

> Ariano Suassuna (Brazil, 1927–)
> Griselda Gambaro (Argentina, 1928–)
> Osvaldo Dragún (1929–)
> Jorge Díaz (Chile, 1930–)
> José Triana (Cuba, 1933–)
> Eduardo Pavlovsky (Argentina, 1933–)
> Plínio Marcos (Brazil, 1935–)
> Vicente Leñero (Mexico, 1939–)
> Leilah Assunção (Brazil, 1949–)
> Sabina Berman (Mexico, 1956–)

B. WORKING CRITICAL BIBLIOGRAPHY

Albuquerque, Severino João. *Violent Acts: A Study of Contemporary Latin American Theatre*. Detroit, MI: Wayne State University Press, 1991.

Latin American Theatre Review. See esp. the 1987–1992 index included in 25/2 (Spring 1992), 211-235.

Lyday, Leon F., and George W. Woodyard. *Dramatists in Revolt: The New Latin American Theater*. Austin: University of Texas Press, 1976.

Perales, Rosalina. *Teatro hispanoamericano contemporáneo: 1967–1987*. Mexico: Editorial Gaceta, 1989. Only Vol. 1, on South America, has been published.

Quackenbush, L. Howard. *Teatro del absurdo hispanoamericano*. Mexico: Clásicos-Patria, 1987.

Taylor, Diana. *Theatre of Crisis: Drama and Politics in Latin America*. Lexington: University Press of Kentucky, 1991.

II

Contemporary Developments in Mexican Literature

4. Escritoras mexicanas de los últimos tiempos

Cecilia Avilés Valdez

Introducción

Escritoras mexicanas de los últimos tiempos constituye una semblanza de la participación de la pluma femenina, a través del relato y la novela, desde fines de los sesenta y hasta nuestros días.

No es un trabajo con fines antológicos y mucho menos exhaustivo, dado que no son todas las autoras que han aportado algo a la literatura de los últimos años, ni tampoco las obras reseñadas constituyen la totalidad de la bibliografía por ellas editada.

La idea principal del trabajo es la de destacar el papel intelectual de las mujeres en la literatura y además hacer un señalamiento a la mesurada oportunidad de editar la literatura escrita por ellas.

El antecedente de esta idea nace del reconocimiento de la relación tan desigual de la producción editorial entre mujeres y varones. El peso de la balanza se inclina hacia el varón narrador en los catálogos editoriales, en las antologías, y por consecuencia en los registros históricos de la literatura mexicana. Si la inclinación del peso ha sido legítimo, surge el cuestionamiento ¿no ha habido mujeres o suficientes mujeres sensibles a tratar temas, que al igual que al varón le atañen, si vivimos en una sociedad de hombres y mujeres? La pretención no es llegar a imitar al hombre, mucho menos convertirse en réplica de George Sand, sino que desde su perspectiva la mujer estuviera realizando su propio trabajo.

El punto en donde coinciden quiénes y cuántos son publicados es el de la oportunidad, no sólo de que los editores publiquen la obra escrita por las mujeres, sino que además las mujeres reclamen y hagan suyo un espacio en la literatura mexicana. ¿O es que acaso la literatura tiene sexo?

Este trabajo no tiene el propósito de ser un trabajo feminista. Aunque sí reconozco la imposibilidad de sustraerme a mi condición de mujer, por lo que en todo caso pudiera considerarse un trabajo femenino.

Para no dar un sentido de homenaje y en consideración a aquellas autoras que no incluí, me he abstenido de citar los premios que muchas de ellas han obtenido, producto del reconocimiento de sus obras. Por otra parte, sí emito juicios de valor en algunos de los libros reseñados, así como, aludo a sus éxitos editoriales.

Escribió Max Aub que cada país tiene la Revolución que merece y la Literatura que le corresponde. Creo que es cierto porque ambos son producto de la intelectualidad de un conjunto de individuos delimitados por su contexto social, sólo ellos pueden cambiar el rumbo de su aparente destino.

"En unas cuantas décadas el mundo se ha hecho pequeño. Lo que antes estaba aislado, separado, hoy está interrelacionado con todo. De la misma manera que el concepto de nación creó el de "tradiciones literarias nacionales, el de 'comunidades' está creando el de tradiciones continentales".[1]

Así pues, hablar de los escritores mexicanos, es como hablar de la literatura argentina o peruana, dado el concepto de literatura nacional y la circunstancia en común que rodea a las mujeres.

La mujer y su circunstancia

A partir del surgimiento de los movimientos feministas, en el siglo XIX, todo lo relacionado con la circunstancia que rodea a la mujer, empieza no sólo a cobrar interés, sino que empieza a tener relevancia. La educación formal de la mujer es un fenómeno relativamente nuevo y no sólo eso, se consideraba además un lujo para ella.

De hecho la regulación del acceso de la mujer a la educación inicia a principios del presente siglo XX, cuando la enseñanza elemental se convierte en obligatoria, tanto para mujeres como para varones, no obstante, prevalecía el criterio de que las mujeres no podían ambicionar realizar estudios superiores.

Después vino el recuento de un sinnúmero de obstáculos que las primeras generaciones de mujeres tuvieron que sortear al ingresar a la universidad y luego al incursionar en campos que "tradicionalmente" habían estado reservados para los varones.

Prácticamente desde la finalización del la Segunda Guerra Mundial hasta nuestros días, el balance de fin de siglo es, que cada vez más mujeres se encuentran integradas a la fuerza laboral, mundialmente, cada vez más mujeres, de todas las edades, ingresan a las estadísticas de estudiantes en todas las áreas del conocimiento humano.

Según datos de la Oficina Estatal Laboral de Estados Unidos en la actualidad las mujeres ocupan el 39.3% de empleos ejecutivos, administrativos y gerenciales, porcentaje que representa casi el doble al correspondiente de hace 20 años.

Juan Rámon de la Fuente en un reciente estudio sobre la educación médica en México, señala que la matrícula de mujeres estudiantes de medicina en 1970 era solamente del 21%, mientras que en 1990 fue de más del 50%.

Paralelo a la participación de la mujer en todos los órdenes de la vida social, económica, política, educataiva, etc., viene el problema de la discriminación y la misoginia (aversión u odio hacia la mujer).

Actitudes o conductas misóginas son resultantes adversos al fenómeno feminista que afirma sus posiciones ideológicas, partiendo de la consideración de la mujer como semejante al hombre y con la dignidad propia de un ser humano.

Al perder la claridad de la dimensión del ser humano, se acreditan actitudes estereotipadas para el varón y otras tantas para la mujer. De esto se derivan consecuencias tales como la de que los hombres no deben llorar y las mujeres no pueden ejercer autoridad. Sin embargo, tanto las características femeninas como las masculinas pertenecen al inventario de cualidades humanas susceptibles de desarrollarse, tanto por los hombres como por las mujeres.

"La dignidad de los seres se mide por su autonomía y la autonomía implica desarrollo y realización".[2]

En estudios realizados en los Estados Unidos e Inglaterra demuestran que mujeres con enfermedad isquémica del miocardio[*] no son estudiadas tan detalladamente como la de los hombres y las opciones terapéuticas tampoco son las mismas que las de los hombres. Un caso similar es el tratamiento del Sida en los Estados Unidos, donde en el pasado, no incluían manifestaciones específicas para las mujeres y morían más rápidamente que los hombres.

La situación en México no es distinta a la ilustrada en los ejemplos. El ejemplificar con situaciones de países desarrollados es una manera de mostrar que la subvaloración de la mujer no es privativa de una cultura en particular. La mujer no es la víctima de una misteriosa fatalidad, sino de una situación. Es, indudablemente, que si mantenemos a un ser en estado de inferioridad, permanecerá inferior.

El fin del siglo se nos presenta con una dinámica influida por cambios geopolíticos, formación de bloques comerciales, alianzas, sociedades, acuerdos, que llevan implicaciones en todos los órdenes, social, religioso, político, educativo. Tal vez esta sea la mejor condición o situación coyuntural para aprovechar la riqueza humana inexplorada de la mujer, permitiendo la operación de sumar esfuerzos —hombre y mujer— en vías de construir una sociedad mejor, reivindicando valores morales, el concepto de familia, ser antes que mujeres y hombres, humanos.

---

[*]La causa de los infartos cardiacos y causa de muerte más frecuentes en mujeres norteamericanas.

Escritoras mexicanas de los últimos tiempos

La metaficción como la define John S. Brushwood es la narración que se refiere a la narración misma. Es la observación, por parte del autor, de su propio acto creativo. Es justamente la metaficción una de las características más relevantes en la novela mexicana de la década de los setenta y alcanza su esplendor casi al finalizar la década.

Su mérito consiste en poner en relieve el aspecto creativo en el trabajo literario. Es además un fenómeno interesante dada la peculiaridad de una sociedad que reprime la inclinación creativa de sus miembros.

Es decir, la metaficción juega un rol importante en el cambio de la estructura social, haciéndose más evidente con las manifestaciones del 68. La metaficción, no es que no haya sido trabajada anteriormente, sino que es una característica frecuente en las novelas de esa época y también es oportuno señalar que hay novelas que pueden referirse a su propia narración y a la vez a otro tema. La metaficción es además una característica de índole universal.

¿Porqué hacer la distinción de empezar a hablar de la literatura a partir del año 67? Porque es el año anterior a la tragedia de Tlatelolco, también en ese año empieza a predominar el recurso de la autoconciencia en la novela mexicana. Para la literatura mexicana los sucesos de Tlatelolco tienen un gran significado, me atrevería a decir que el año 68 fue un año que nos dejó marcados a todos los mexicanos. El tema de Tlatelolco aparece en la literatura en repetidas ocasiones, y además trabajado de diferentes formas. En algunos casos como tema principal de la obra y la mayoría de las veces como un elemento de la realidad a que hace referencia la narrativa.

"El 68, además de marchar y pliegos petitorios fue también, confrontación con el autoritarismo familiar. Se viven broncas de tipos ideológico y político . . . hubo conflicto por la intolerancia familiar ante la libertad de cantidad de mujeres y hombres jóvenes sujetos a tutela".[3]

Memorial del 68: un relato a muchas voces es un libro recientemente publicado, estructurado a base de 70 relatos, de los cuales 14 fueron escritos por mujeres. Esto último le sirve de punto de partida a Marcela Lagarde para escribir un artículo que publicó hace dos meses, donde analiza y encuentra puntos convergentes en los testimonios de estas 14 mujeres que a 25 años de distancia, constituyen un segmento de la memoria colectiva de México.

"El memorial del 68 multiplica, con ello, la obstinación para que el 2 de octubre no se olvide".[4]

Largarde pone en relieve el hecho de que las 14 mujeres en cuestión, respondieran a una convocatoria que no fue hecha específicamente para mujeres. De los puntos en común encontrados, señala que no existe en esos textos, algún indicio de venganza, pero es patético comprender que son cómplices de un mismo secreto . . . todas dejan ver cómo a partir de la represión surgió otra realidad.

Otra característica que aparece en la narrativa de esta época, aunque en menor grado, es el de la identidad inestable y la vida urbana. Una de las obras más importantes y representativas de esta época es la escrita por Elena Poniatowska, *La noche de Tlatelolco*. Además de su valor literarario, el recurso testimonial lo utiliza para destacar elementos morales e históricos, es una obra de denuncia. "Texto que nace de voces múltiples, texto donde la realidad ha tomado la palabra, *La noche de Tlatelolco* cuestiona de un modo radical el papel y las funciones del narrador (¿quién habla?) sin por ello ahorrarles responsabilidades. Quizá una de las cosas más bellas de este libro sea la renuncia a la identidad de su autora . . .".[5]

La más reciente novela publicada por Elena Poniatowska (1992) es *Tinísima*, biografía novelada acerca de la fotógrafa Tina Modotti. A pesar de que la historia biográfica es ficción, está tan bién trabajada, que nos la creemos, nos convence la autora de cuanta cosa dijo, hizo y sintió la protagonista. No en balde Poniatowska dedicó diez años a la realización de esta obra, que resulta ser una obra monumental, no tan sólo por su extensión de 660 páginas, sino por el contenido y labor literario que ahí imprimió. Imaginación e investigación de hechos que rodearon a *Tinísima* y un ritmo acelerado provocan una lectura ligera.

En contraste con otras obras biográficas, éste es un trabajo muy cuidado, que se mantiene al margen del enjuiciamiento del biografiado. Poniatowska sabe sortear los peligros, probablemente por su experiencia como periodista sagaz; como autora camina por la obra sin comprometerse con el entorno que rodea la vida de la Modotti. Camina de puntas y maneja con pinzas la situación, logrando un efecto de neutralidad ideológica.

Muchas de las novelas que se publicaron a partir del año 67 son en gran medida experimentos hechos en el arte de narrar. Esta es una característica fácil de detectar a partir de esa época.

Quizá en la narrativa donde es más evidente lo puramente autorreferencial sea la de Julieta Campos en sus obras *Tiene los cabellos rojizos y se llama Sabina* (1974) y *El miedo de perder a Eurídice* (1979).

Campos también explora las posibilidades del género en obras no tan autorreferenciales como ocurre con Tita Valencia en *Minotauromaquia* (1976) donde la autora expresa conceptos muy interesantes relacionados con la naturaleza del arte, incluyendo el arte literario.

Por otra parte, "la identidad inestable remite a una condición irreal y, al mismo tiempo, aporta una dimensión a la definición de la realidad".[6] Este fenómeno de identidad inestable se encuentra en la novela de Mercedes Manero llamada *Río revuelto* (1982) en donde la temática se desarrolla en un ambiente de corrupción entre empresario y potentado.

En *Cena de cenizas* (1975) Ana Mairena utiliza un sentido del tiempo muy especial, irónico y con cierto tremendismo, utiliza el recurso de la vida moderna con un sentido augustioso. También trabaja en esta novela una relación con Tlatelolco.

Mairena al igual que Elena Garro y Amparo Dávila destacan en una época anterior a lo que en este trabajo no ocupa, junto con el grupo de los maestros modernos que nacen en la tercera década del siglo.

Luisa Josefina Hernández es autora de más de quince novelas y ha destacado ampliamente en teatro. Pocas obras permiten dar un seguimiento a su historia. En 1970 publica *Nostalgia de Troya*, considerada como una de sus mejores novelas. Utiliza muchos y distintos enfoques para caracterizar a un protagonista. Lo suyo es una narración no tradicionalista y pertenece al círculo de los llamados novelistas "intimistas".

Es válido decir "que la novela mexicana desde 1967 hasta 1982 se desarrolla siguiendo dos ejes de tensión: uno de contexto, entre la amenaza de una realidad que cambia muy rápidamente y la tendencia de asir lo conocido; otro de expresión, entre la narrativa como puro placer y la narrativa como significante de una realidad extratextual y reconocible".[7]

María Luisa Mendoza escribe su primera novela en 1971 titulada *Con él, conmigo, con nosotros tres*, el tema central es la tragedia de Tlatelolco. La primera parte de la novela la autora le llama "Cronovela", un término seguramente derivado de su profesión como periodista. Se refiere a los sucesos transcurridos precisamente en la noche de Tlatelolco. La historia se desarrolla en varias etepas de la vida de una familia que reside en ese sitio. "Este lugar sigue siendo punto de referencia, pero cuando el énfasis cae sobre la familia, el lugar y el horror se ubica en la perspectiva de experiencia nacional".[8]

La segunda novela denominada *De ausencia* (1974) de ella Vicente Leñero hace un análisis minucioso del lenguaje haciendo resaltar el valor del estilo como el recurso más relevante en la obra, porque funge como eje, controlando los otros componentes de la narrativa.

La historia *De ausencia* logra fácilmente atraer la atención del lector. La protagonista nació pobre y luego se enriqueció. "Sus relaciones sexuales son tan escandalosas como interesantes, provocan además un homicidio".[9] La novela tiene un dejo de época, la protagonista vive in Guanajuato a fines del siglo pasado y mitad de este y además realiza un viaje por Europa. Un sello característico de esta autora es el lirismo. Casi una década después publica *El perro de la escribana*, obra que, si bien, no llega a ser una novela, por su categoría de narrativa, su valor se centra justamente en la lírica.

Las características de la novela del período del 67 y cuando menos hasta 1982 es la nostalgia por un lado, y la ciudad, el ambiente urbano de la capital y el cosmopolitismo, por el otro. Es normal que toda reminiscencia, evocación de recurso, retrospección tenga un dejo de nostalgia, porque hace referencia a un tiempo que ya se fue, a una época pasada, a costumbres, olores o tal vez a experiencias conocidas por muchos lectores. Es probable que sea este el canal por donde entra el gusto por ese tipo de narración. Un ejemplo de novela de nostalgia es *Memorias de la libertad* (1979) de Martha Robles, donde el personaje central, una mujer, acepta los recuerdos pero rechaza el sentimiento negativo a que la remiten dichos recuerdos.

Los novelistas que trabajan mucho el tema de las relaciones humanas no forman una escuela, por lo contrario, son muy diferentes entre sí. Un ejemplo es Ana Ma. Puga.

Puga trabaja mucho sobre la vida de clase media urbana. Es autora de nueve libros, y en especial el primero *Las posibilidades del odio* (1978) es una novela que se desarrolla en Kenia, donde expone una denuncia del colonialismo. La obra que más tarde desarrolla, enfoca generalmente en el uso de la ciudad, como recurso de expresión.

"Puga emplea el lugar para fundar el concepto y luego consigue que éste traspase el significado de una sola ciudad".[10]

La nostalgia de la que anteriormente hablaba en algunas obras se da acompañada de una dosis de realismo. Ejemplo de ello es el libro *Las genealogías* (1982) de Margo Glatz, libro que no es precisamente una novela sino una autobiografía desarrollada a base de entrevistas, lo cual provoca en el lector un sentido de verismo, porque algunos personajes hablan de la realidad. Algo semejante sucede con el libro de Ma. Luisa Mendoza titulada *El perro de la escribana* (1982) basado en las distintas casas en que la narradora ha habitado.

Tal relación de la nostalgia con la realidad existe también en el efecto que provoca la novela histórica al tender un puente hacia la búsqueda de una estabilidad. Algunas de las características de la nueva narrativa escrita por la pluma femenina son: la mujer como personaje central, la homosexualidad de la mujer, la relación padre e hija, la denuncia, la búsqueda de la identidad, etc.

Dice Elena Poniatowska: "Me atrevo a predecir que la literatura del siglo XX en México estará marcada con un indeleble sello femenino. Esto no quiere decir que los mejores libros de este siglo han sido escritos por mujeres. . . . Quizá por una ley de la balanza o porque ya les tocaba, el lector las prefiere. Los escritores mexicanos se quejan: 'Ahora para triunfar hay que ser vieja' . . . (a lo que hay que agregar). Según las estadísticas en México, el público lector lo conforman las mujeres".[11]

En los últimos veinte años el tema de la pasión amorosa, siendo un tema fijo en la historia de la literatura, sufrió transformaciones en su percepción y forma de tratarlo. Barbara Jacobs en su obra *Las hojas muertas* (1987) deja ver la ambigüedad de la mujer ante la figura paterna. Analiza figuras sociales y familiares como el esposo, el amante, el padre. "El tono elegido por la autora para narrar la vida de Emile Jacobs (personaje central de *Las hojas muertas*) es usar ese tono prefabricado que Elena Poniatowska impuso a las escritoras mexicanas y que se ha convertido en una edulcorada cárcel retórica".[12]

Silvia Molina en su novela histórica *Ascención Tun* (1981) a través de técnicas adecuadas a la narración moderna, desarrolla un tema de gran relevancia en la cultura mexicana que es la guerra de castas. Molina utiliza el recurso de un anciano que plastica con un niño para dar a conocer al lector el punto de vista maya. Hace referencias a personas fallecidas, que no afectan a la trama. Otro recurso del que echa mano es el de la memoria de un hombre blanco para dar a conocer la otra versión. Recientemente ha publicado *Un hombre cerca* (1992). Es un libro integrado por siete relatos donde con suma maestría presenta la imagen de la mujer de hoy. Sus personajes femeninos evaden las relaciones tediosas, son seres independientes y sus destinos están decididos por ellas mismas. "Las mujeres de Molina aunque independientes, no han destruido sus temores primarios, y en ella nunca deja de asomar el fantasma de la infancia, del pasado con todos los prejuicios y tabúes inculcados".[13] De los siete relatos hay uno que sobresale por su temática, cuyo título es "Hospital", ahí expone la relación padre e hija, haciendo notar la devaluación del mito del amor filial.

El tema tratado es un tema muy poco trabajado en la literatura mexicana y esta autora lo hace muy acertadamente. Otro tema también poco manejado en la narrativa mexicana, aunque mucho en poesía, es el del homosexualismo femenino.

Ethel Krauze en su novela *Infinita* (1992) abarca el tema de la homosexualidad femenina en el triángulo que forma con Delfina, Leonor y Agustín, personajes centrales de la novela. Ethel Krauze ha dedicado una parte muy significativa de su producción literaria a la poesía y no ha de sorprendernos el encontrar en *Infinita* imágenes y frases cortas, aunado a un fino trabajo de creación de caracteres y psicología, queda como resultado un excelente producto literario.

"*Infinita* es un buen relato de la mujer contemporánea que intenta sacudirse las ataduras, así como las relacionces amorosas de hoy que responden a un apetito voraz por experimentar nuevas sensaciones y opciones, pero siempre en la búsqueda infinita de la identidad".[14]

Angeles Mastretta con *Arráncame la vida* (1985) se dio a conocer como novelista, alcanzó éxito en México y en otros países donde su obra fue traducida. Es reconocida como la autora del "nuevo realismo mexicano". *Arráncame la vida* es una historia de amor con una estructura basada en el cruzamiento de varias historias de iniciación, matrimonio, adulterio y venganza. Es una novela trabajada con mucha habilidad narrativa en "la búsqueda sin inhibición de una voz femenina que captura al mismo tiempo historia e identidad".[15]

Sin embargo, Christopher Dominguez Michael se refiere a la primera novela de Mastretta diciendo que: "La extraordinaria difusión de esa novela es una prueba de que esa amplia fracción del público internacional sigue necesitando del folletín". Y que el éxito se refiere "más a las nada caprichosas leyes del comercio que a su profundidad literaria".[16]

Carmen Baullosa es una de las escritoras que quizá posea uno de los talentos más intrincados de la nueva literatura mexicana. Ha incursionado en el género dramático, poesía y novela. De sus cualidades más sobresalientes podemos comentar su desbordante imaginación. Sus novelas *Mejor desaparece* (1987) y *Antes* (1989) "exhiben la posibilidad de un viaje, inédito por claustrofóbico y maligno por el mundo de la infancia".[17] Su novela más reciente es el *Soledumbre*.

La trayectoria de Alicia Trueba se muestra en la publicación de cuentos y relatos en los principales diarios de la ciudad de México. No es sino hasta 1992 cuando publica su primera novela *Los colores del principio* donde narra la infancia y adolescencia de una niña que formula preguntas. La historia se va tejiendo a través del simil de un rosario: Primer misterio, Inés, Nefus, la nana, su protección exacta; Segundo misterio . . . De esta su primer novela Elena Poniatowska describe "Es un libro puro en el sentido mágico de la palabra, un libro que nos pone la hostia en la boca, sin confesión".

Rosa Nissan publicó su primer libro *Novia que te veas* (1992) y antes de que la novela se presentara públicamente se agotó la primera edición, esto significa que en quince días se vendieron dos mil ejemplares. De tiempo atrás Nissan se ha venido desempeñando profesionalmente tanto en fotografía como en la elaboración de audiovisuales. Rosa Nissan es también la autora del guión de la película basada en su novela. Este acontecimiento abasallador por el interés de la adquisición de una novela escrita por una mujer, en los últimos años se ha venido presentando con cierta regularidad en México.

Un caso similar es el éxito obtenido por Laura Esquivel con su libro *Como agua para chocolate* (1989) que también fue llevado al cine con un guión escrito también por ella. Hasta el año 93 se habían producido 16 ediciones de la novela de Esquivel, se había traducido a 18 lenguas y solamente en México desde 1989 se habían vendido 200,000 ejemplares.

Laura Esquivel a la inversa que Nissan concibió primeramente el guión, la transformó en novela y de la buena acogida de su libro, se llevó posteriomente al cine. Esquivel en 1985 se inició en el medio cinematográfico con el guión de la película *Chido Guán, el taco de Oro* del cual obtuvo muy buenas críticas. *Como agua para chocolate*, vista desde una perspectiva de globalidad, se puede ubicar en el contexto de literatura de masas, entendiéndose así, aquella comprendida por cualquier lector, escrita en un lenguaje coloquial y con una estructura que no representa problema alguno para hilvanar las distintas situaciones. Abundan los personajes femeninos, los hombres en la novela se encuentran en un segundo plano. Es una novela rica en elementos literarios pero además estamos hablando también de una obra donde el arte culinario ha sido novelado. Constantes, simbolismos e imágenes como la de "todos nacemos con una caja de cerillos en nuestro interior" (pp. 119, 120) hacen que el lector se adentre tanto en la cocina de Tita, perdón, a la novela de Laura, que hasta crea percibir los olores de los ingredientes de las recetas. Dijo Laura Esquivel en una entrevista que se le hiciera el año pasado: "No me interesa la crítica a nivel literario, sino decirle algo al ser humano sin que importe su preparación académica".

En cierta forma los éxitos editoriales confirman la predicción de Elena Poniatowska, de que el siglo XX en México estará marcado por la participación de la mujer en las letras y más que eso por la oportunidad de que se les publiquen sus libros, aunque estos tengan categoría de folletín, como algunos críticos etiquetan ciertas obras comentadas en este trabajo. El asunto es que la mujer hable, escriba, diga, exponga, pregunte, venza el miedo a la equivocación, a decir lo nunca dicho, y a mostrar su feminidad a través de la literatura.

Martha Cerda escribe en 1993 *Y apenas era miércoles, crónica de un desamparo*, novela basada en la tragedia ocurrida en Guadalajara el 22 de abril de 1992, a consecuencia de la explosión de gasoductos. Es una novela de denuncia donde Cerda narra los hechos con la autoridad que le da el haber sido testigo presencial.

Siguiendo la costumbre de otros autores jaliscienses como Arreola y Rulfo, Cerda utiliza viñetas como punto de partida para expresar sensaciones y experiencias de los personajes (protagonistas y víctimas).

Entre los méritos de esta novela están el uso y manejo del lenguaje, que en obras con temática de denuncia resulta casi un requisito, que sea claro, específico y derivado en la narración de una historia contada en forma natural. "En *Apenas era miércoles* constantemente se muestra la articulación que tienen planos aparentemente tan directos entre sí como el tiempo colectivo y el tiempo personal, el placer y el dolor, la cadena de complicidades y traiciones de la vida pública y el peso aplastante de la vida histórica".[18]

Con la novela *Mami ¿jugamos a odiarnos?* (1993) de Beatriz Duarte, la autora, como lo han estado haciendo otras novelistas de los últimos tiempos, expone la situación conflictiva que vive la mujer en los tiempos actuales, desarrollándose el hilo de la narración a partir de ella misma. Duarte desvirtúa en su novela el mito de la madre abnegada y partiendo de las figuras madre e hija, desarrolla el conflicto de tal relación, donde se derivan sentimientos antagónicos. Existen en esta novela recursos interesantes como monólogo interior, un vívido lenguaje coloquial y algunas frases en prosa poética. Esta es la primera novela de Duarte y para sorpresa de muchos, logró ventas muy altas antes de haber sido presentada públicamente y como ya parece ser una predicción, actualmente se encuentra trabajando en el guión cinematográfico.

Conclusiones

El orden y el poder son dos constantes en las novelas de fines de las décadas de los años sesenta y en los setentas. Epoca en que se pone en entredicho a la familia y surge la figura de la mujer con una carga política, no vista anteriormente, y por extensión, tenemos a la política no sólo ejercida por el Estado, sino a ésta como parte de la vida cotidiana. Las novelas aunque tratan temas de la familia y lo urbano, la mujer se convierte en un reflejo crítico del contexto social mexicano. Mientras México abre sus puertas al mundo, la literatura se constriñe, llega al punto de la metaficción, a las tendencias formalistas y a esa novela que su propósito no es más que pensar en su propia creación.

En la década de los ochenta arriba al país la crisis económica y de la mano un retroceder al realismo, motivado por el derrumbamiento de los sueños de grandeza. En los ochenta se trabaja más en un personaje determinado, con una narrativa más meditada y con nuevas técnicas. Se vuelve más al realismo, se hace novela politizada, se sigue utilizando a la ciudad como un punto de referencia, pero ahora como un espacio de degradación. Hay decepción por las instituciones, en síntesis la intención de estas novelas es la crítica social.

A lo largo de la historia la novela mexicana ha cumplido con su finalidad, su misión ha sido la de dar a conocer la realidad. Pero no se ha limitado a relatar o a retratar simplemente, por el contario, ha asumido el compromiso con una conciencia crítica de enseñar y en muchas ocasiones de moralizar. Hay muchos mitos que nos determinan como mexicanos y que la literatura los observa, un afán de ser modernos, la meta de salir del tercer mundo, nuestra economía y dependencia, la miseria de muchos mexicanos y el papel de la mujer en la literatura.

A mediados de los ochenta casi en contraposición y contradictoriamente a lo que ocurría en el país, que estaba sumergido en los años más críticos de la crisis económica, surge una narrativa que recupera su facultad de distraer, de escapar, con un estilo anecdotario muy digerible, sin mucha profundidad textual, sin recursos técnicos, si se quiere, pero que tiene la virtud de romper el elitismo cultural, compliendo su función social de acercarse a las masas.

Angeles Mastretta es quien con su novela *Arráncame la vida* inicia el trayecto, seguida por otras autoras, de novelas con uno o pocos personajes, ofreciendo datos de la realidad y creando una anécdota rápida, legible en "una sentada".

La narrativa mexicana de los últimos tiempos se categoriza bajo dos tendencias que la definen, que son la totalidad y lo social. Un ejemplo del grupo de novelistas de esta categoría es María Luisa Puga. La otra tendencia es la de los novelistas que desde su perspectiva exponen y emiten un juicio como Angeles Mastretta, entre otras autoras.

Estas dos tendencias antagónicas en la narrativa, unen lo que se encontraba separado, describiendo de esta forma un cambio en la cultura mexicana, dando más fuerza a la base del objetivo de la narrativa mexicana, la de ser reflejo social del país y de los mexicanos.

NOTAS

1. Manuel Ulacia, "Confluencias de fin de siglo", *Examen* 5:55 (diciembre 1993), 36.

2. Ma. Teresa De la Garza Camino, "Identidad femenina", *Magistralis* 1:2 (enero-junio 1992), 69.

3. Marcela Lagarde, "Voces de mujeres en el memorial del 68", *La Jornada* semanal 247 (marzo 1994), 37.

4. Lagarde, "Voces de mujeres", p. 4.

5. Christopher Domínguez Michael, *Antología de la narrativa mexicana del siglo XX*, vol. 2 (México: F.C.E., 1989), p. 72.

6. John S. Brushwood, *La novela mexicana (1967–1982)* (México: Grijalbo, 1984), p. 83.

7. Ibid., p. 33.

8. Ibid., p. 64.

9. Ibid., p. 65.

10. Ibid., p. 77.

11. Elena Poniatowska, "Literatura mexicana del siglo XX", *Libros de México*, 27, 28 (abril/septiembre 1992), 27.

12. Domínguez Michael, *Antología*, p. 498.

13. Amalia Rivera, "Varias mujeres", *La Jornada* semanal 187 (enero 1993), 9.

14. Amalia Rivera, "De amores postmodernos", *La Jornada* semanal 200 (abril 1993), 13.

15. Domínguez Michael, *Antología*, p. 821.

16. Ibid., p. 498.

17. Ibid., p. 1333.

18. Laura Zavala, "Las imágenes de la tragedia", *La Jornada* semanal 226 (octubre 1993), 13.

BIBLIOGRAFIA

Brushwood, John S. *La novela mexicana (1967–1982)*. México: Grijalbo, 1984.

De la Garza Camino, Ma. Teresa. "Identidad femenina". *Magistralis* (Universidad Iberoamericana) 1:2 (enero-junio 1992).

Domínguez Michael, Christopher. *Antología de la narrativa mexicana del siglo XX*. Vol. 2. México: Fondo de Cultura Económica, 1989.

Largarde, Marcela. "Voces de mujeres en el memorial del 68". *La Jornada* semanal 247 (marzo 1994).

Ponce de León R., Samuel. "Medicina, mujeres y misoginia". *La Jornada* semanal 230 (noviembre 1993).

Poniatowska, Elena. "La literatura mexicana del siglo XX". *Libros de México*, 27, 28 (abril/septiembre 1992).

Rivera, Amalia. "Varias mujeres". *La Jornada* semanal 187 (enero 1993).

———. "De amores postmodernos". *La Jornada* semanal 200 (abril 1993).

Ulacia, Manuel. "Confluencias de fin de siglo". *Examen* 5:55 (diciembre 1993).

Zavala, Laura. "Las imágenes de la tragedia". *La Jornada* semanal 226 (octubre 1993).

5. Los libros para niños en México: Las políticas editoriales de 1956 a 1993

Sarah Corona Berkin

La literatura infantil en México tiene una larga tradición que está ligada a la vida cotidiana y al aprecio que nuestra cultura tiene por los niños. La tradición oral, los cantos, las leyendas, los cuentos de horror y espanto, están llenos de poesía y juego. Por otro lado, la edición de libros de texto y su distribución gratuita son parte de una política cultural institucionalizada. De esta manera los libros infantiles pueden considerarse una consecuencia natural del desarrollo editorial aunado a una tradición cultural.

Este trabajo ofrece una descripción de las políticas editoriales para niños, en México, de 1956 a la fecha, haciendo un especial hincapié en la enorme influencia que el gobierno ha tenido a lo largo de estos años. Las políticas editoriales seguidas por cada administración educativa en México, han reflejado, de manera fiel, la situación política general del país. Podemos ver que los esfuerzos que se le dedican a las publicaciones infantiles corresponden a políticas más amplias que no sugieren una preocupación igual por la niñez y que cada seis años, duración de un período presidencial en México, varía el interés, según las circunstancias políticas generales.

Se observa (Cuadro 1) que el aumento de nuevos títulos no va en aumento progresivo con los años. La voluntad política de publicar corresponde a otros factores. Revisemos, en cuanto a políticas editoriales, los cinco períodos que nos corresponden.

Muy poco le debe la literatura infantil al período llamado "Desarrollo estabilizador" que se inicia en 1946. Entre la tecnología y los libros, se opta por las máquinas. En 1955, el entonces presidente Adolfo Ruiz Cortines declara que la mitad de la población en México no sabe leer ni escribir. Sin embargo se elige apoyar la educación superior. Entre lo poco que se publica para niños en este período están 20,000 ejemplares de *Nuestro canto patrio* y de *Canto a la bandera*, que reflejan el fervor patrio que cultivó Ruiz Cortines a cambio de no ofrecer recursos económicos para la educación primaria.

El período que le sigue, 1958-1964, se caracterizó por una voluntad política para fomentar la educación básica. En este sexenio, cuyo presidente fue Adolfo López Mateos, se produjeron millones de libros de texto para las escuelas primarias de todo el país.

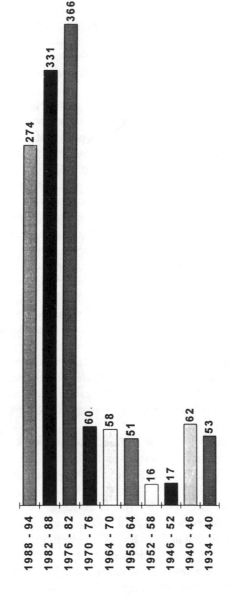

Cuadro 1. Publicaciones infantiles SEP
Títulos por sexenio
(Cálculo aproximado hasta 1992)

Fuente: Cálculo del autor a partir del *Catálogo de publicaciones infantiles en México 1921–1993* (libro en preparación), cuadro 1.

Un espacio especial merece este programa ya que ha sido fundamental en la relación que tienen los niños con los libros en México. En 1959 se creó la Comisión Nacional de los Libros de Texto Gratuito. Esta comisión tuvo su aniversario número 30 en el año de 1989 y durante este lapso de tiempo se han publicado y distribuido gratuitamente cerca de 2 mil millones de ejemplares de libros de texto para los niños mexicanos. La política inaugurada en este sexenio continúa hasta la fecha, pues con la edición millonaria de libros de texto se garantiza un instrumento para uniformar la educación de los mexicanos.

Por otra parte, se reconoció oficialmente, durante estos años, la mestización o síntesis de las diferentes herencias nacionales. Se ratificó la educación bilingüe y como publicaciones representativas encontramos 20,000 ejemplares de *Los números* y *Animales* en lenguas indígenas.

Sin duda, el gran esfuerzo de edición y distribución gratuita de los textos escolares para la primaria absorbió la atención del gobierno de tal manera que poco espacio quedó para la literatura recreativa.

Sin embargo, es tan importante esta labor, que los libros llegaron por primera vez a muchos hogares mexicanos y brindaron entonces, como aún hoy, la posibilidad a esos niños de aprender a leer y escribir.

En una investigación realizada en 1990,[1] se encontró que, para muchos niños en México, el concepto de lo que es un libro se define por el único que conocen: el libro de texto gratuito.

Los años de 1964 a 1970 corresponden al gobierno de Gustavo Díaz Ordaz. Hablar de libros para niños en este período es de nuevo, referirse a los libros de texto. La política del desarrollo estabilizador y crecimiento económico genera un interés en programas educativos basados en "aprender haciendo" así como en el uso de tecnología audiovisual. Surgió la telesecundaria en 1965 así como la alfabetización por televisión y la radioprimaria. Desafortunadamente no partieron de teorías pedagógicas sólidas ni experimentadas.

Más grave resultaba la situación de la educación indígena, de los más de tres millones de indígenas monolingües entre los 6 y 14 años, el sistema educativo atendía sólo a 23,248.[2] De nuevo quedó poco espacio para la lectura recreativa.

La educación como tarea política fue la consigna de Luis Echeverría Alvarez, presidente de México de 1970 a 1976. Frente a la necesidad de permitir los cambios que demandaba la sociedad como consecuencia del movimiento de 1968 y su violenta represión, este gobierno condenó el desarrollo estabilizador. Se apartó del programa económico de los gobiernos anteriores y propuso un "desarrollo compartido" y una retórica oficial que censuraba al imperialismo y al capitalismo.

Se desarrollaron nuevos planes de estudio que requirieron nuevos libros de texto. La "Reforma Educativa" transformó totalmente los libros de texto. Estos cambiaron de ser asignaturas a las llamadas áreas de conocimiento. Curiosamente los libros en Braile para niños, se siguieron editando con los antiguos contenidos. La reforma educativa no llegó a este público.

En relación a obras infantiles en lenguas indígenas encontramos cuentos tradicionales de grupos Choles y Chinantecos en ediciones bilingües, y libros para aprender a contar el dinero o leer el reloj en el idioma de la comunidad y en español.

El interés por los niños indígenas es patente. La Secretaría de Educación Pública informó que mientras en 1971 egresaron de primaria sólo 72 niños indígenas, cuatro años después, la cantidad aumentó a 7,300 niños, con base en métodos bilingües de contenido bicultural.

Los años 1976-1982 marcan un nuevo período de gobierno. José López Portillo fue presidente en este sexenio que navegó en las aguas de la abundancia petrolera para llegar al mismo punto de partida: la devaluación monetaria y la crisis del endeudamiento.

A la vista de mayores ingresos para el país, el gobierno mostró interés por la tarea educativa. Entre los lineamientos básicos se incluyó el promover la lectura y el libro como vehículo de cultura. El interés por editar libros recreativos y publicaciones periódicas para los niños significó una nueva etapa para el desarrollo de la literatura en nuestro país. A diferencia de regímenes anteriores y que desde 1960 concentraron casi todos sus esfuerzos editoriales en los libros de texto, en este sexenio se diversifican en forma notable los títulos (ver Cuadro 1).

En 1978 apareció la colección *Clásicos de la literatura*. Fueron 13 títulos editados dos o tres versiones cada uno, para niños de 6 a 9 años, de 9 a 12 años y para jóvenes. Uno de los más grandes aciertos en publicaciones infantiles en México también corresponde a esta época. La *Enciclopedia Infantil Colibrí* apareció en los puestos de periódico en forma de fascículos coleccionables. Se editó también *Colibrí preescolar* y *Colibrí en lenguas indígenas*: maya, náhuatl, otomí y purepecha.

La colección *Pájaro Bandera* integra textos prehispánicos y de tradición oral con un tiraje de 10 a 13 mil ejemplares por título. Vemos que a partir de estas fechas la literatura infantil gana terreno. Prueba de ello es que en el período que sigue, 1982-1988, la edición de libros para niños se continuará a pesar de coincidir con la crisis económica de estos años.

En este período de gobierno se publican cuentos para iluminar, colecciones sobre fauna y flora, así como un proyecto de recopilación de juegos infantiles y narrativa oral tradicional en comunidades rurales mestizas. De este trabajo surgió la colección *Así Cantan y Juegan* en distintas regiones del país. Este material impreso estuvo acompañado de cassettes de audio de las canciones grabadas. El periódico *Tiempo de Niños* se convirtió sin duda en uno de los programas editoriales principales. Se editaron 137 millones de ejemplares en cuatro años.

Durante este período se consolidó la producción editorial adecuada a las distintas lenguas de nuestro país. La serie *Tradición oral indígena* y los libros de texto en lenguas indígenas produjeron más de 50 títulos. La recuperación de la tradición continuó con fuerza durante estos años. Se editaron en forma facsimilar las *Lecturas clásicas para niños* editadas por primera vez en 1923. Se editaron los *Cuentos mexicanos para niños* de Pascuala Corona originalmente publicados a partir de cuentos contados por nanas en 1945.

Este período se caracteriza por el aumento cuantitativo en su producción editorial para niños así como por la importancia que se le reconoce a los niños mexicanos indígenas. El pasado cultural se recupera reeditando cuentos de autores e ilustradores de este siglo así como la historia oral y tradicional del pasado indígena de nuestro país. De esta forma se descubre una literatura infantil mexicana de gran calidad.

Es curioso notar que el auge editorial de este período contrasta con la situación económica de México. En 1982 nos entramos en una crisis de la que todavía no salimos, sin embargo parecería que la industria editorial infantil hubiera escapado. Revisemos con más detalle la política del gobierno con respecto a sus ediciones (ver Cuadro 2). De sus 276 títulos, 243 fueron coeditados con empresas privadas, fenómeno que puede explicarse como un apoyo brindado por el gobierno a las editoriales privadas para apoyar su economía, en compensación a que el negocio del libro de texto les está vedado. Según un estudio del Banco Mundial, con la nacionalización de los libros de texto la industria editorial perdió 60% del mercado.[3] Esta política está aún vigente (ver Cuadro 3). De los 796 títulos publicados por la Secretaría de Educación Pública en los últimos 16 años, 614 son en coedición. Aclaramos que más de la mitad de los 2,640 libros de 23 editoriales privadas corresponden a dos grandes editoriales: Trillas y Fernández Editores. Los temas de estos libros, dirigidos a niños y publicados por las principales editoriales privadas, son las que aparecen en el Cuadro 4.

Cuadro 2. Ediciones del gobierno y coediciones con casas privadas
(Cifras aproximadas)

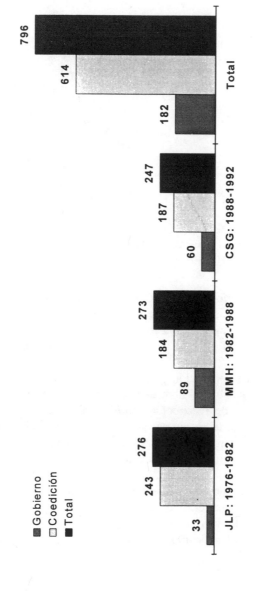

Fuente: Arnulfo Santiago, "Libros recreativos para niños en español", 1ª Reunión Internacional de Investigadores de la Cultura del Libro, Guadalajara, diciembre 1992, cuadro 2.

Cuadro 3. Ediciones por sectores: Gobierno, editores
privados y coediciones, 1976–1992

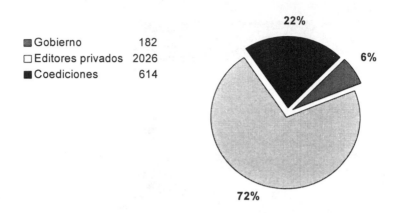

■ Gobierno   182
□ Editores privados 2026
■ Coediciones   614

Fuente: Arnulfo Santiago, "Libros recreativos para niños en español", 1ª
Reunión Internacional de Investigadores de la Cultura del Libro,
Guadalajara, diciembre 1992, cuadro 6.

Llegamos al período actual. Cambio e identidad son los términos
básicos para entender las políticas de los últimos años en México. Tiempos
de negociación del Tratado de Libre Comercio (TLC) con los Estados
Unidos y Canadá, control de la inflación, privatización, sacrificio social y
modernización.

En esta meta la educación juega un papel importante. Entre nuevas
disputas, se decide cambiar el libro de texto vigente hasta entonces. Pero las
críticas provenientes de reconocidos intelectuales por la calidad de los
nuevos textos obliga a la Secretaría de Educación a no volver a utilizar los
libros de texto que circularon en 1992. La enseñanza de la historia no
ha dejado de ser centro de la discusión pública y esta historia no se
acaba aún.

A pesar de que hemos hablado del impacto de los libros de texto,
debemos aclarar que en el transcurso de los años que nos ocupan, el
gobierno le ha dado una importancia especial a la edición de libros
recreativos. En cantidad de títulos podemos observar en el Cuadro 5 la
importancia de este género.

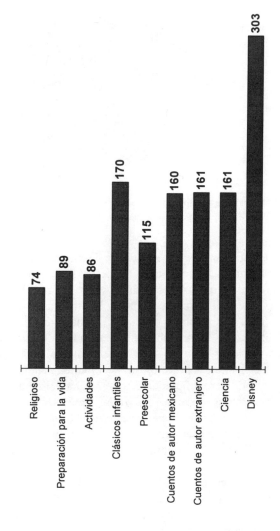

Cuadro 4. Tipografía del libro infantil privado

Categoría	Valor
Religioso	74
Preparación para la vida	89
Actividades	86
Clásicos infantiles	170
Preescolar	115
Cuentos de autor mexicano	160
Cuentos de autor extranjero	161
Ciencia	161
Disney	303

Fuente: Arnulfo de Santiago, "Datos sobre la edición infantil privada", 1ª Encuentro Internacional de Escuelas para Editores y Libreros, cuadro 5.

Cuadro 5. Títulos por género, 1958–1993

■ Libros de texto   320
■ Libros recreativos   929
■ Publicaciones periódicas   9

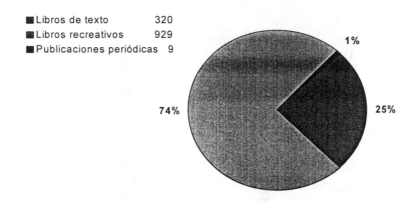

Fuente: Cálculo del autor a partir del *Catálogo de publicaciones infantiles en*
México 1921–1993 (libro en preparación), cuadro 3.

Como sucede en otras partes del mundo, la literatura infantil, quizás
por su prestigio de literatura menor, no se ha desarrollado como debería.
Los autores consagrados, algunas veces dedican unas líneas a la literatura
infantil. En México aparecen obras de Octavio Paz adaptadas por Elena
Poniatowska, quien a su vez colabora con otros cuentos. Escritores como
Silvia Molina o poetas como Jaime Sabines y Fernando del Paso, también
han participado en versiones para niños. Existen autores como Marinés
Medero, el Tío Patotas, Francisco Hinojosa y Gilberto Rendón con una
amplia producción infantil, pero difícilmente podemos hablar de una escuela
dedicada a producir literatura moderna para niños. Parecería más bien que
los editores arman ciertas colecciones que consideran importantes y
encargan los textos. De esta manera encontramos intelectuales, científicos
y público en general que experimenta en el campo de la edición
infantil.

Tampoco podemos decir que existe una crítica literaria especializada
que pudiera dar pautas para definir las características de la literatura que se
ofrece a los niños en México. En el mejor de los casos encontramos reseñas
con objetivos mercadotécnicos o comentarios informales con buenas inten-
ciones que buscan fomentar la lectura en los niños, pero no llegan a aportar
en el conocimiento literario de la obra.

La evaluación es otra importante etapa ausente de las políticas editoriales. Las empresas comerciales poseen un balance económico que les ofrece pistas sobre las preferencias del mercado. En cuanto al Estado, en cada sexenio surgen nuevas políticas y se sepultan las viejas sin hacer diagnósticos educativos y culturales.

Ahora bien, con respecto a la ilustración, que ha llegado a ser parte indisociable de los libros infantiles, encontramos que en México tiene una larga trayectoria de éxitos. Para sólo nombrar algunos de los grandes artistas mexicanos que en su momento dedicaron su arte a la niñez están: Roberto Montenegro y Gabriel Fernández Ledesma, Diego Rivera, José Guadalupe Posada, Julio Prieto, José Chávez Morado, Arnaldo Coen, Alberto Beltrán y Francisco Toledo.

En 1987 la Secretaría de Educación invitó a notables pintores para que se hicieran cargo de ilustrar las portadas de todos los libros de texto gratuito. Acudieron al llamado: Leonora Carrington, Rafael Coronel, José Luis Cuevas, Miguel Felguérez, Vicente Rojo, Tamayo y Gironella entre otros muchos.

Actualmente podemos hablar de ilustradores especializados en libros infantiles que han cosechado aplausos en México y en el extranjero. Embellecen las páginas de estos libros: Felipe Dávalos, Carlos Dzib y Martha Avilés.

La ancestral tradición plástica en México se deja ver en el aspecto icónico del libro, quizás falte un propósito mayor por convertir la riqueza oral de México en libros de literatura para niños.

Ahora bien, la pregunta obligada, ¿dónde se encuentran estos libros? El problema de la distribución quizás sea uno de los mayores obstáculos con los que se enfrentan los libros para niños. Las librerías en México son muy escasas, se reducen a unas pocas en las grandes ciudades y las especializadas en niños o que contengan una dotación importante para ese público son aún más limitadas. Las bibliotecas públicas y escolares tienen algunas colecciones, pero tampoco son una opción real para quienes desean leer libros infantiles. Curiosamente en el Centro para el Estudio de la Literatura Infantil en Español, de la Universidad del Estado de California, en San Marcos, se encuentra una biblioteca y un importante centro de documentación sobre libros en español para niños. Finalmente, como resultado de la modernidad, son las tiendas de autoservicio, las que ofrecen, junto con la comida y los artículos del hogar, una selección comercial de libros para niños.

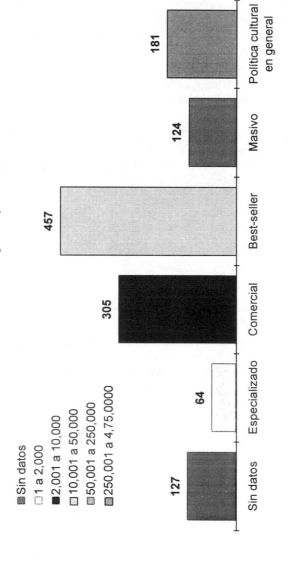

Cuadro 6. Políticas editoriales por tirajes, 1958–1993

Fuente: Cálculo del autor a partir del *Catálogo de publicaciones infantiles en México 1921–1993* (libro en preparación), cuadro 4.

Otro gran obstáculo del libro son los medios masivos de comunicación. Las condiciones sociales han favorecido el desarrollo de la comunicación electrónica. Considerando el crecimiento desmedido de las ciudades, la gran inmigración rural-urbana y los problemas de integración de esta nueva sociedad, los medios masivos funcionaron mejor. Estos correspondieron mejor a las necesidades populares, se adecuaron a los requisitos de los recién llegados, ofreciendo, de forma simplificada, modelos de comportamiento social. El libro se queda atrás. Primeramente por que para acceder a él, es necesario saber leer, condición que no todos cumplían en el momento de la aparición del cine, la radio y la televisión. El libro debió ocuparse casi exclusivamente de la educación, rezagándose así en los estantes escolares.

Reconocemos el enorme esfuerzo de los libros de texto gratuito y la posibilidad real de que todos los niños en México tengan acceso a ellos. Y aunque parezca contradictorio, también vemos el esfuerzo que representan los tirajes muy limitados (ver Cuadro 6). Creemos que la cantidad de títulos en este rubro debe aumentar, ya que los libros especializados aportan a las necesidades específicas de grupos pequeños de niños, como lo son los niños de lenguas indígenas y los niños minusválidos. Esta sería una especificidad del libro frente a los medios masivos, que en aras de llegar a públicos cada vez más amplios, homogeneizan y empobrecen sus contenidos.

Vemos la lectura como un derecho social. La política del Estado persigue el cumplimiento de ese derecho, pero no basta. Las condiciones de nuestro país lo hacen difícil, pero insistimos en que el apoyo al libro debe mantenerse y debe acercarse a los niños con buenos precios, buena distribución y cuidado y calidad en los contenidos.

NOTAS

1. Sarah Corona y Evelyn Díez Martínez, "El concepto de libro en niños de dos grupos sociales", *Comunicación y Sociedad* 18-19 (1994).

2. Ernesto Meneses Morales, *Tendencias educativas oficiales en México 1964-1976* (México: Centro de Estudios Educativos, 1991), pp. 31-35.

3. Peter H. Neumann y Maureen A. Cunningham, *Los libros de texto gratuito de México: El nacionalismo y la urgencia de educar*, Serie Documentos de Trabajo del Personal del Banco Mundial, No. 541 (Washington, DC: Banco Mundial, 1984), pp. 10-11.

6. Evaluating Mexican Literature: Sources and Uses

Walter Brem

Introduction

In carrying out evaluations of literature, application of the American Library Association publication *Guide to the Evaluation of Library Collections* is a useful starting point. The sections titled "Planning" and "Guide to Collection-Centered Measures," in which the "evaluator selects titles of works appropriate to the subjects collected," are helpful. For this paper, a portion of the suggested list of possible sources was used. They are as follows: specialized bibliographies, reference works, periodicals, and tangentially publishers lists. Included in these works are citations from current journals and other evaluated works at the forefront of current research.[1]

My specific intentions and assumptions herein are as follows: One, to provide Latin American specialists with a small and accessible number of sources for the purposes of the design of evaluation instruments. It is written for librarians and institutions from the largest to smallest collections. Two, to employ the concept of bibliographical layers, that a few sources can open up the whole panorama of materials useful for collection evaluations from the complementary publishing and scholarly universes of Mexican literature. Sources can be used to develop broad evaluations as well as small, specialized "boutique" surveys of any kind of holdings. Finally, to emphasize that there is a continuum in evaluation work. Long-term and short-term evaluations, from the most historical to the most current, bear the assumption that collection evaluations have an inherent objective of acquisition at some point, especially for more recent and current materials of all kinds. These assumptions and needs are addressed.

Genre and Subject

Until recently, a librarian would have had to do extensive library catalog, index, abstract, and database searching to find and put together an array of appropriate tools to plan, design, and carry out any kind of evaluation of Mexican literature. Fortunately, David William Foster has created a work that cuts through such an extensive effort. His *Mexican Literature: A Bibliography of Secondary Sources* is one of the more extensive and well-organized works for beginning an evaluation. For our purposes, "Part I: General References" is immensely valuable. It comprises twenty-eight chapters of bibliographies, reference works, and critical sources on all genres, periods, and special topics. Besides monographs and journal articles, it has chapters from anthologies. Foster also includes historical and critical works on eighty historical and modern authors, but for our purposes, the use is negligible because the selection of contemporary writers is very small.

Bio-bibliographies

Literature collection and evaluation are strongly author-driven, as are literary reference sources. Of the many dictionaries of authors available, two are especially useful for modern Mexican literature. In keeping with the theme of this work in focusing on literature published since 1956, the first is Josefina Lara Valdez's *Diccionario biobibliográfico de escritores contemporáneos de México*, which hones in on the younger literati. Charged by the writer Gustavo Sainz, then Director of Literature of the Bellas Artes, Lara Valdez compiled a listing of 407 writers of all genres writing in Mexico in the latter 1980s, including many born outside Mexico. Her universe of writers is wide, including critics, essayists, and historians. All the writers were born between 1930 and 1960.

For each entry, she includes basic biographical information, institutional affiliations, and genre. She lists monographic titles and publishers; titles of the cultural supplements, magazines, and journals to which they have contributed; titles of creative works published in serials with the institution of the publication; and prizes won. On the whole, it is an excellent source for identifying the younger generation of authors, their output, and with whom they have published.

From my perspective, the major weakness of the work is that it omits many writers born before 1930, many of whom are still living and productive. To fill such a gap, the *Dictionary of Mexican Literature*, edited by Eladio Cortés, is an excellent source. Both historical and contemporary in its coverage, it is a work of scholarship and bibliographical depth. It covers older contemporary writers as well as the most prominent younger authors.

After excellent biographical sketches, Cortés's work includes precise and full bibliographical entries of the authors' original works in all forms of publications and genres. This is especially valuable, as many works are published in magazines, supplements, and even scholarly journals. To this latter point, Cortés provides one of the most comprehensive lists of those kinds of periodicals published in Mexico, as well as selected titles for other Latin American countries. For each writer, there are also full lists of criticisms in all forms of publications.

These three works by Lara Valdez, Foster, and Cortés form an excellent core to begin any evaluation design. Lara Valdez's is most useful for any compilation of young authors whose newer works can be followed closely from current sources mentioned below. The two works by Foster and Cortés complement each other well.

Foster's structural approach toward criticism interacts with Cortés's author orientation. Much of the same critical information emerges from both works, but in different organizational forms. Foster has relied heavily on database searching for his journal listings, all of which are listed in Cortés's. The latter's scholars have gone beyond that and include much information from cultural supplements, one of the most elusive sources for the librarian to identify. Both of these sources cover imprints to roughly 1990, thus providing an excellent base from which to delimit searching of library catalogs and the appropriate databases.

National Serials

For recently published literature, long-term evaluation and short-term collection development become indistinguishable in the effort to develop information about authors, genres, themes, and topics. As one leaves the subject bibliographies, dictionaries, and the indexing and abstracting services—what to do? From those sources, there is considerable built-up information about literature publishing, including such objective information about publishers and series which can be followed in current serials. In one sense, designing short-term evaluation projects becomes more like the reference problem of what to recommend to students when the indexing runs out. Instead of following the obvious scholarly journals, one turns to current serials to fill the author and subject indexing void.

Three magazines are especially useful in creating a current biblio- graphical universe with critical information necessary to know for whom or what you may want to survey. The most useful for bulk bibliographical information is *Libros de México*, put out by the Cámara Nacional de la Industria Editorial Mexicana. In its early years, it periodically printed large ISBN lists of books and serials both by author/title and by international decimal classification. More recently, it has moved to printing lists by publisher and classification in every issue. Its substantive articles about books and printing are broad and historical but lack the kind of critical surveys or reviews useful for evaluation. Nevertheless, *Libros de México* is an essential catalog tool for constructing lists.

For currency, cultural magazines seem to be more useful than strictly literary periodicals. Current literary periodicals reproduce works but with little or no critical information about the author or genre. There are many cultural magazines, especially academic products, and newspaper supplements published, but their accessibility for most librarians is limited, their coverage spotty, and they are unindexed.

For reviews and periodic surveys of literature, two well-known cultural journals are sufficient to provide the intellectual basis of evaluating design. They are the monthlies *Nexos* and *Vuelta*, the dueling popular magazines of the Mexican intelligentsia. *Nexos* is considered leftist and nationalist, and *Vuelta* liberal and cosmopolitan. Together they blanket the mainstream national literary scene with regular reviews and occasional author or topical surveys. Moreover, unlike the academic journals, they are widely available in U.S. academic libraries.

Regional Serials

As we have seen since 1980, and especially the years since the 1985 earthquake, administrative and fiscal decentralization has created a tremendous flow of literature from the states, especially those away from the core. This is attested to by the prodigious amount of literature listed by bookdealers providing regional coverage of Mexico.

Foster's chapter on "Local and Regional Literature" contains only twenty-seven entries for the whole country. The state volumes in the series República de Letras of Consejo Nacional para la Cultura y las Artes cover long chronological periods with the briefest selection of writers of all genres. These volumes would be useful for the most selective of coverage of state literature, however.

Because extensive regional literature output is a relatively recent phenomenon, evaluation and collection building blur again. Some effort is required to put together evaluative materials, but the universe selected again employs serials as tools for evaluation or building.

The best overview source and that with the longest duration is *Tierra adentro*, possibly best translated as the "land within" rather than "inland," which started publication in the fall of 1974. Winner of the 1992 Premio Nacional de Periodismo for cultural journals, it has strong current literary coverage supplemented by topical and genre articles covering the whole country.

More focused are two bimonthly cultural magazines that cover the northern and southern frontiers. They are *Cultura Norte* and *Cultura Sur*, respectively. Typically copublished, *Norte* is put out by the Programa Cultural de las Fronteras del Consejo Nacional para la Cultura y las Artes and the state governments of Baja California, Baja California Sur, Chihuahua, Coahuila, Nuevo León, Sonora, and Tamaulipas. *Sur* covers Campeche, Chiapas, Quintana Roo, Tabasco, and Yucatán. Very formulaic, they are produced in Mexico City and are similarly organized. I emphasize

Cultura Norte because of the more obvious interest among North American university libraries.

For evaluative purposes, *Cultura Norte* includes several useful features. Besides broad coverage, the magazine occasionally has wholly thematic issues, focusing on a state or topic. In its regular features, one can expect to find anthological articles of various writers by genre, and brief surveys such as "La narrativa en Baja California: breve recuento," which historically surveys authors, titles, and genres of literature in the state.[2] The most useful section is "Mirador fronterizo," which emphasizes culture, serials, and books. It details varieties of cultural expositions, meetings, festivals, and competitions, many of which revolve around literary gatherings. It alerts readers to published proceedings from conferences and reviews new periodicals and books. Also included are publishing developments in the region. Especially important is the listing of state literary prizes and the winning works, a major category of material in all levels of collection plans.

This paper presents a new generation of reference and bibliographical sources that provide breadth, depth, and sophistication for the librarian surveying modern and contemporary Mexican literature. Used with the selections of serials, the librarian is faced with minimal supplementary updating work, as these sources easily and rapidly open up the vistas of all aspects of Mexican literary output and criticism that may want to be evaluated and collected.

NOTES

1. *Guide to the Evaluation of Library Collections* (Chicago, IL: American Library Association, 1989), pp. 4-6.

2. Humberto Felix Berumen, "La narrativa en Baja California," *Cultura Norte* 5:19 (August/September 1992), 11-16.

BIBLIOGRAPHY

Subject Bibliographies

Foster, David William. *Mexican Literature: A Bibliography of Secondary Sources.* 2d ed. enlarged and updated. Metuchen, NJ: Scarecrow Press, 1992.

Bio-bibliographical Dictionaries

Cortés, Eladio, ed. *Dictionary of Mexican Literature.* Westport, CT: Greenwood Press, 1992.

Lara Valdez, Josefina. *Diccionario biobibliográfico de escritores contemporáneos de México.* Mexico: Instituto Nacional de Bellas Artes, 1988.

National Serials

Libros de México. No. 1– , 1985–.
  Mexico: Cámara Nacional de la Industria Editorial Mexicana.
Nexos. Año 1, no. 1– , 1978– .
  Mexico: Centro de Investigación Cultural y Científica.
Vuelta. Vol. 1– , 1976– .
  Mexico: Vuelta.

Regional Serials

Cultura Norte. Año 1, vol. 1– , 1987- .
  Mexico: Programa Cultural de las Fronteras de la Secretaría de
  Educación Pública.
Cultura Sur. Año 1, vol. 1– , 1989– .
  Mexico: Programa Cultural de las Fronteras.
Tierra adentro. No. 1– , 1974– .
  Aguascalientes, Mexico: Consejo Regional de Bellas Artes.

III

Current Themes and Movements in Latin American Literature

7. Una nota bibliográfica sobre la nueva narrativa chilena

Marta Domínguez Díaz

Es difícil establecer qué se entiende por generación literaria, pués no existen parámetros de validez universal. Según los especialistas una generación literaria se produce sólo como respuesta a condiciones determinadas, estímulos que pueden ser históricos, sociales o puramente estéticos. Conforme este principio en Chile se han producido cuatro generaciones indiscutidas: el Movimiento Literario de 1842, la Generación Costumbrista Vernacular de 1900, la Generación Poética de 1920, a la que pertenecieron la Mistral, Huidobro y Neruda, y la Generación Realista Popular de 1938, la más numerosa y homogénea de nuestra historia literaria pués reúne a una cincuentena de escritores que publican sus obras entre 1938 y 1950. Luego viene una promoción de escritores, que se ha llamado Generación del 50, cuyos componentes quisieron identificarse más bién con la alta burguesía. Nombres importantes de la narrativa actual se formaron como discípulos de una cofradía de amigos de esta generación del 50, integrada por José Donoso, Jorge Edwards, Enrique Lafourcade, Guillermo Blanco, Claudio Giaconi, Enrique Lihn y Luis Alberto Heiremans, en los talleres literarios que en el tiempo ellos fueron dirigiendo.

La generación que eran adolescentes para el estremecedor año 1973 en Chile, más o menos cuarenta narradores, conoció y vivió fundamentales alteraciones históricas tales como la Revolución Cubana, la Guerra de Vietnam, la Revolución Cultural China, la Guerra Arabe-Israelí, la muerte del Che Guevara, el Movimiento de Mayo en París, el Gobierno Popular de Salvador Allende y el Golpe Militar de 1973.[1] Este último hecho produjo la diáspora de los escritores que comenzaban a conocerse en Chile y que transformaron su discurso literario, en testimonios desde el exilio: Guillermo Atías, *La sangre por las calles*; Volodia Teitelboim, *La guerra interna*; Luis Enrique Délano, *Veladas del exilio*; Fernando Alegría, *El paso de los gansos* y *Coral de guerra*; Efraín Barquero, *Bandos*; Luis Armando Uribe, *El libro negro*; Jaime Valdivieso, *Lamento por Chile*; José Donoso, *El jardín del lado*; Ariel Dorfman, *Viudas, la última canción de Manuel Sendero* y la obra teatral, *La muerte de la doncella*; Antonio Skármeta, *No Pasó Nada y otros Relatos, Soñé que la nieve ardía, Ardiente paciencia, La insurrección*; Carlos Cerda, *La noche del soldado* y *Lo que está en el aire*, llevada al teatro en Chile; Poli Délano, *Piano Bar de Solitarios* y *Como si no muriera nadie*; así también los destacados escritores Eduardo Carrasco, Isabel Allende y Luis Sepúlveda, se desarrollaron literariamente en el exilio. Los que se quedaron, se mantuvieron silenciados y dispersos. Esta generación se conoce en Chile como la generación N.N. o Generación Marginal. Ellos se formaron y produjeron sus obras durante un régimen de censura y persecución que marcó a la literatura como a otras formas de expresión y que contrariamente a lo esperado, fue material fértil para ellos. Su hábitat fue la violencia y el miedo. Esta prolongada convivencia con un drama colectivo, dio como resultado innumerables novelas y cuentos, muchos testimoniales, los más comprometidos políticamente, pero que en conjunto asumieron una actitud crítica e interpretativa de esta realidad.

Hacia los 80 surge una generación cuyo mayor rasgo es la desdramatización de la realidad circundante y un culto a lo frío, generación que según Skármeta está asimilada a la desarticulación de los grandes espacios sociales, lo que hace imposible detectar en ella un estilo común. Tiene muchas estéticas y muchas influencias. No son una ruptura como la que significó la generación del 50 con respecto al criollismo. En esta generación nueva se advierte una cierta poética de lo cotidiano, del lenguaje popular creativo y juvenil, del permanente cuestionamiento del orden establecido, de la actitud irreverente de los adolescentes, del erotismo. Ellos incorporan a sus relatos, elementos paródicos, el humor y la ironía, la música popular como bagaje cultural, el deporte, las historietas, la alienación de la publicidad, del consumismo y la TV, la apología de las drogas, la desacralización de mitos impuestos por una sociedad pacata y aburguesada, en fin, una generación que abjura del narrador como profeta.

Entre sus figuras podemos destacar a: Jaime Collyer, joven escritor, discípulo de José Donoso, como otros tantos, bien dotado como cuentista, lo demuestra en *Gente al Acecho* (Planeta, 1992), una quincena de relatos breves, amenos y penetrantes. Ya antes había mostrado su talento narrativo en las novelas *El infiltrado* (Mondadori, 1989) y *Los años perdidos* (Madrid, 1986). Collyer se remonta a los años de la dictadura militar en que se quedaron solos, crecieron solos y se formaron solos porque sus maestros tuvieron que exiliarse, y ellos leían a Skármeta a escondidas, siguiendo desde Chile, los textos de sus dilectos.[2] Sobre su generación afirma que tienen una nueva forma de pensar Chile y los espacios urbanos. Que ellos escriben desde un todo, no de los espacios privados como lo hacía Donoso o de ciertos barrios, como lo hacía Skármeta. Sus pares, Ramón Díaz Eterović, aborda con soltura el género policial y presenta por tercera vez a su personaje el inspector Heredia en la novela *Nadie sabe más que los muertos* (Planeta, 1993). Gonzalo Contreras, actual director de la revista *Reseña* de la Cámara Chilena del Libro, ganador del Premio Novela Revista de Libros El Mercurio 1991 con su obra *La ciudad anterior* (Planeta, 1991), una metáfora de la vacuidad existencial que imperaba en el Chile de los 80 y que ya alcanza más de seis ediciones. Además su volumen de cuentos *La Danza Ejecutada* (1985) acaba de aparecer en una segunda edición de Planeta 1993 con algunos relatos agregados. Discípulo de José Donoso, opta por una literatura de la imaginación inspirada en su maestro. Alberto Fuguet se presenta con dos obras candentes que denuncian lo que está ocurriendo con la juventud chilena, *Sobredosis* (Planeta, 1990), con varias ediciones agotadas, y *Mala onda*, cuentos, Premio Municipal de Literatura 1991, novela llevada al teatro con gran éxito de taquilla. Se comenta que la influencia de la nueva literatura norteamericana lo tiene al borde del colapso. Sobre su generación opina que es una generación lectora, que sabe mucho de literatura, pero poco de la vida, ha leído más que vivido. Este joven escritor se siente más cercano a los mayores que a sus pares, porque son sus referentes literarios y los encuentra más civilizados y menos competitivos.[3]

Roberto Ampuero, ganador del Premio Novela Revista de Libros El Mercurio 1993 con su obra de género policial, *¿Quién mató a Cristián Kustermann?* (Planeta, 1993), que alcanzó dos ediciones en 1993 y que pone de relieve el talento que ya había demostrado Ampuero en el cuento. Luis Sepúlveda publicó el primero de sus 10 libros a los 20 años. Ha recibido, entre otros, el Premio Rómulo Gallegos de novela 1978 y el Premio Tigre Juan de Oviedo en 1989 por su obra best seller *Un viejo que leía novelas de amor* (Emisión, 1990, y Tusquets, 1993), que ya alcanzó 11 ediciones desde febrero 1993 a enero 1994 y ha sido traducida a 14 lenguas. La novela cuenta la historia de un hombre que vive en un pueblo remoto de la selectiva Amazónica relacionándose con sus animales e indígenas, dentro de un absoluto respeto por ambos, descrita en un lenguaje escueto, claro y emotivo. Sepúlveda es un escritor que recupera la perdida gracia de narrar con hechizo, imantando al lector, llevándolo novela adentro. Antes se conocía de él, *Mundo del fin del mundo* (Emisión, 1992; Colección V Centenario), novela sobre la caza de la ballena en mares australes de Chile, de moraleja ecologista. Darío Osses ingresa a la narrativa ganando el Premio a la Narrativa Joven Andrés Bello 1992 con su obra *Rockeros celestes*, cuya temática aborda las pandillas juveniles de rock y spots publicitarios y luego presenta la vigorosa novela *Machos tristes* (Planeta, 1992), en la que desmitifica la uniformidad social del régimen militar pasado, su pragmatismo consumista, su pobreza cultural, todo con una certera dosis de humor. Prosa tan flexible como poética, rigurosa en su decir, secuencia de capítulos breves, casi siempre incisivos y bien ensamblados entre si. En esta novela estructura muy bién el desencanto político y de la universidad militante, a través de sus dos protagonistas

antagónicos, el uno fascista y el otro marxista. Según Darío Osses la nueva
literatura apunta a desmitificar y desacralizar lo que se vivió en los años 70
y se enriquece con el boom económico de los 80, los "Chicago boys", el
consumismo y el desencanto hacia la política.

Arturo Fontaine Talavera, discípulo también de Donoso, se destaca con
su obra best seller *Oír su voz* (Planeta, 1992), de gran rigor de estilo, de
argumento inteligible y claro; una historia pasional, un crimen político, los
devaneos del mundo pseudo intelectual de Chile, adulterios y sensualidad.
"Un Balzac a la chilena, sazonado con Proust, Tolstoi y Verlaine", dice
Marco Antonio de la Parra en crónica periodística.[4] Carlos Franz se presenta
con su novela premiada *Santiago cero* (Editorial Nuevo Extremo, 1990),
enmarcada en una realidad reciente. Además prologa y edita *Nuevos cuentos
eróticos* (Grijalbo, 1991), una radiografía de la realidad erótica de Chile.
Francisco Simón Rivas, pseudónimo que tuvo que usar durante la dictadura
para su verdadero nombre Francisco Rivas, ganador del Premio Quimera a
la mejor novela chilena 1988 con *Todos los días un circo* (Planeta, 1988),
antes habíamos conocido su hermosa novela *Martes tristes* (Bruguera,
1985). La violencia es su género junto a una ternura que le es muy propia.
Marco Antonio de la Parra, en su novela *Cuerpos prohibidos* (Planeta,
1991), revela la tragedia de Edipo en los barrios marginales de Santiago,
profundizando en las claves de la sexualidad local y la mitología criolla
sobre el tema. Antes conocíamos su novela *La secreta guerra Santa de
Santiago de Chile* (Planeta, 1989), en la que el autor reconstruye los mitos
de la clase media chilena integrando elementos cultos y populares que
delatan la clara tendencia posmodernista del escritor. Sobre la nueva
narrativa él opina que se les pasaron las fiebres revolucionarias y que ahora
sus ideas políticas difieren alegremente. Dice creer en una literatura hecha
con el lector y que el lector completa.[5] Reinaldo Edmundo Marchant,
escritor muy galardoneado por su obra literaria. Sus obras más recientes
El hombre de la mano seca, novela, *Un ave de prodigiosos colores*, novela,
e *Imaginaciones*, cuento (Red Internacional del Libro, 1993, las tres obras).
De él dice el escritor Enrique Lafourcade que será uno de los grandes
escritores de Hispanoamérica, y otros lo aprecian como el García Márquez
chileno. Carlos Cerda también ha ocupado por tiempo los primeros lugares
del ranking con su novela *Morir en Berlín* (Planeta, 1993), historia
conmovedora, retrato de un mundo desencantado, muy aplaudida por la
crítica. Cerda es doctor en literatura (U. de Humboldt, Berlín), y escritor
muy fecundo en ensayos políticos, literarios, cuentos y novelas.

En cuanto a la creatividad de la mujer chilena en el campo de la
narrativa hay representantes destacadas. En una breve crónica el escritor
Gonzalo Contreras se refiere al boom femenino latinoamericano representado por Isabel Allende, quien vende en Europa más que García Márquez, y

Laura Esquivel, la escritora mexicana autora de *Como agua para chocolate*, que triplica en ventas a Carlos Fuentes, y además está Angeles Mastretta. Contreras lo atribuye a que las mujeres han encontrado por fin narradoras que interpretan su sensibilidad y por eso están leyendo mucho más. Tal vez el 35% de incremento, que según la Cámara Chilena del Libro, ha experimentado la literatura, se deba a ellas.[6] Los fuertes relatos de Lucía Guerra C. abordan derechamente los problemas del ser femenino en un contexto social. Sus cuentos *Frutos extraños* (1993) tratan el violento destino de la mujer marginal. Su última novela *Muñeca brava* obtuvo el segundo lugar en el Concurso "Sor Juana Inés de la Cruz", 1993, certamen auspiciado por la Feria Internacional del Libro de Guadalajara y otra entidad. Lucía Guerra ejerce la docencia en los Estados Unidos, tal como muchos otros escritores chilenos, entre ellos Marjorie Agosin, escritora y ensayista chilena, profesora asociada en el Wellesley College, Massachusetts, investigadora de la escritura femenina, como lo muestra en su obra *Violeta Parra Santa de Pura Greda: Un estudio sobre su obra poética*, junto a Inés Dolz B. (Planeta, 1988); después nos ofrece *Las hacedoras, mujer, imagen y escritura* (Cuarto Propio, 1993) y luego *Sagrada memoria* (Cuarto Propio, 1993), conmovedora historia sobre lo que significa ser judía en Chile. Agosin cree que la participación de la mujer en la defensa de los derechos humanos en los 70, les ha ayudado a abrirse paso como escritoras.

Ha habido un movimiento paralelo de mujer política y mujer literaria. La escritora Ruth González Vergara presentó recientemente dos obras muy interesantes: *Teresa Wilms Montt: Un canto de libertad* (Grijalbo, 1993) y *Nuestras escritoras chilenas: Una historia por descifrar*, I tomo, un estudio y examen extenso de la literatura femenina en Chile, que agrega un Diccionario Bio-bibliográfico de las Escritoras Chilenas (Hispano-Chilena, 1993). La obra citada primero es una acabada biografía de la trágica vida de una escritora chilena que vivió entre los años 1893 y 1921. La joven representante Ana María del Río tiene varias obras premiadas: su novela *Tiempo que ladra*, ganadora en 1991 del Concurso Letras de Oro, auspiciado por la Universidad de Miami. Sus novelas *Oxido del Carmen* y *De golpe Amalia en el umbral*, han ganado respectivamente el Premio María Luisa Bombal 1986 y el Premio Novela Andrés Bello 1990. Su reciente novela *Siete días de la Señora K*, de controvertido erotismo, de más atrevida temática sobre la sexualidad asumida y jactada, se ha mantenido por meses en el ranking de los libros más vendidos y leídos y ya alcanza la tercera edición, de abril a septiembre 1993. Otra de las autoras muy leídas es Marcela Serrano Pérez, cuyas obras *Para que no me olvides* y *Nosotras que nos queremos tanto* (Editorial Los Andes, 1992 y 1991), alcanza 5 ediciones la primera y 10 ediciones la segunda, ambas con una perspectiva femenina chilena de los últimos años, y con una adecuada cuota de ternura y humor. Brillante narradora promete ser Andrea Maturana, quien ya ha dado señales a través de sus cuentos incluidos en varias recientes antologías y con su propia antología titulada *(Des) Encuentros (Des) Esperados* (Los Andes, 1992), trece relatos en atmósfera urbana, escritos en prosa sencilla y vigorosa y que ya tiene una segunda edición. Mención aparte merece Isabel Allende, cuyas obras *La casa de los espíritus, De amor y de sombra, Eva Luna, Cuentos de Eva Luna* y *El plan infinito*, son universalmente conocidas por traducción a más de 25 lenguas y las dos primeras llevadas ya al cine. Este año 1994, Isabel Allende será condecorada en Chile con la "Orden al Mérito Docente y Cultural Gabriela Mistral", el 8 de marzo, Día Internacional de la Mujer.

Y en este recuento quedan muchos, muchos más: Pia Barros, *A horcajadas* (Mosquito, 1992); Adolfo Couve, *Balneario* (Planeta, 1993); Diamela Eltit, *Vaca sagrada* (Planeta, 1992); Martín Faunés, *Tranvía equivocado* (Cuarto Propio, 1992); Sergio Gómez, *Adios Carlos Marx: nos vemos en el cielo*, 2 ed. (Planeta, 1993); Jaime Hagel, *El amor de Noemí* (Sinfronteras, 1993); Carlos Iturra, *Otros cuentos* (Pehuén, 1987); Silverio Muñoz, *Tenure Track* (Ediciones Arauco, 1992); Diego Muñoz Valenzuela, *Todo el amor en sus ojos* (Mosquito, 1990); Francisco Ortega, *60 kilómetros*, obra premiada (Los Andes, 1993); Fidel Sepúlveda Llanos, *Aventuras estelares de Zoom el Aveser*, una fábula ecológica (Planeta, 1992); Alejandra Rojas, *Legítima defensa* (1993); José Leandro Urbina, *Las malas juntas*, 2 ed. (1986) y *Cobro revertido*, varias ediciones (Planeta, 1992). Interesante es agregar lo que sus maestros dicen de los escritores jóvenes: Jorge Edwards estima que la orfandad les ha hecho bien, pero que parece que buscan apoyo en el poder; Poli Délano dice que reconoce que esta generación creció sin paternidad y que él desde el exterior hizo los esfuerzos por estar cerca. Así conoció los primeros textos de Gregory Cohen, Ramón Díaz Eterović, Antonio Ostornol, Alvaro Cuadra, y una vez en Chile, formó junto con Fernando Jerez y Ramiro Rivas talleres de amistad para relacionarse con los jóvenes y como integrante de jurado le ha correspondido premiar a varios de ellos. Los considera un grupo generacional vital de este momento, con capacidad, talento, vocación y energía; Skármeta dice haberse vinculado también a su regreso, a través de un taller al que postularon 184 jóvenes y uno de guionistas al que accedieron 282 jóvenes, de manera que es una generación a la que conoce cotidianamente; José Donoso, el Maestro, como lo llaman cariñosamente, les ha abierto en su taller, un camino único, dicen ellos. Los menos afortunados con la acogida editorial participan en antologías, recitales, concursos, talleres.

Lo que sí parece seguro es que los lectores están empujando a los editores a arriesgarse con los escritores jóvenes. Se puede apreciar cómo las editoriales han creado premios y han fundado colecciones especiales para acogerlos: señalamos a Editorial Planeta con Planeta Biblioteca del Sur y Planeta Veintiuno; a editorial Universitaria con Nueva Narrativa, Colección Antologías y Generación Espontánea; a editorial Sudamericana con Narrativas Latinoamericanas; a Editorial Mosquito con Colección Narrativa; a Editor Zig-Zag con Novelas de Hoy; a Editorial Grijalbo con Colección Mondadori Narrativa; a Editorial Documentas con Colección Documentas/ Literatura; a Editorial Contrapunto con La Máquina de Leer; a Editorial Cuarto Propio con Serie Narrativa; a Editorial Emisión con Narrativa Contemporánea (esta editorial dejó de existir); a Editorial Melquíades con Serie Ficción; a Editorial Los Andes con La Otra Narrativa; a LAR (Literatura Americana Reunida) con Biblioteca de Autores Chilenos; a Editorial Bruguera con Colección Narradores de Hoy (esta editorial dejó de existir como tal); Editorial Nowadays con un Programa para Difundir a Jóvenes Novelistas Chilenos.

Para un futuro no lejano se perfilan excelentes narradores que quieren contar buenas historias, pero siempre frente al peligro de que el "marketing" les haga perder calidad, ya que el mercado acarrea la lucha por el éxito y son muchos los escritores jóvenes que sueñan con estar entre los más vendidos. La voz disidente de generaciones anteriores, sentencia que se editan obras de éxito inmediato, aptas para venderlas en los supermercados, como si fueran analgésicos. Se agrega la voz del joven escritor Francisco Véjar que dice:

... Ahora, cuando veo que nace la nueva ola de escritores en Chile, amparados por el "marketing" y por falsos lectores, yo miro para atrás y me encuentro con novelas como *Mejor que el vino* de Manuel Rojas, con narrativa a la altura de *Cuentos militares*, de Olegario Lazo Baeza. Ahora, que la gente no quiere leer sino la "sobredosis" de un consumismo destinado a perecer, recuerdo *Un domingo en provincia*, de Augusto D'Halmar. Veo tantos falsos "Bukowskis" frente a un vaso de whiskey, que prefiero el *Ayer* de Juan Emar, quien inventara San Agustín de Tango, antes de que García Márquez no deleitara con su Macondo.[7]

NOTAS

1. Gonzalo Drago, *Muestra de literatura chilena*, Juntémonos en Chile, Congreso Internacional de Escritores (Santiago de Chile: SECH-PRED, agosto 1992), p. 10.

2. Elena Irarrázabal, "¿Sigue el boom de la narrativa chilena? Lo que vendió, lo que vende, lo que venderá", *La Segunda* (22 de octubre, 1993), pp. 76-77.

3. Faride Zerán, "Nueva narrativa: El cascabel al gato", *La Época* 4:207 (marzo 1992), pp. 4-5.

4. Marco Antonio de la Parra, "La novela que vi", *La Época* 1:53 (16 de abril, 1989), pp. 4-5.

5. Ana María Larraín, "1993: Un año prolífico en literatura chilena", *Revista de Libros El Mercurio* (26 de diciembre, 1993), pp. 4-5.

6. Gonzalo Contreras, "Boom femenino", *Que Pasa* 1193 (19 de febrero, 1994), p. 48.

7. Francisco Véjar, "La agonía de la actualidad", *Entrevista* (octubre 1993).

BIBLIOGRAFIA

Bibliografía Consultada

Brito, Eugenia. *Campos minados*. Santiago: Editorial Cuarto Propio, 1990.

Díaz Eterović, Ramón, y Diego Muñoz V. *Contando el cuento: Antología joven narrativa chilena*. Santiago: Sinfronteras, 1986.

Domínguez D., Marta, comp. *Biobibliografía de nuevos escritores chilenos*. Santiago: Servicio de Extensión de Cultura Chilena, SEREC, 1992.

————. *El libro chileno en venta*. Santiago: SEREC, 1985–1994.

González Vergara, Ruth. *Nuestras escritoras chilenas: Una historia por descifrar*. Santiago: Ediciones Hispano Chilenas, 1993.

Merino Reyes, Luis. "Humanidad y literatura". *Simpson* 7 (1993), 14-28.

Piña, Juan Andrés, ed. *Conversaciones con la narrativa chilena*. Santiago: Editorial Los Andes, 1991.

Promis, José. *La novela chilena del último siglo*. Santiago: Editorial La Noria, 1993.

Skármeta, Antonio, y Alberto Fuguet, eds. *Santiago pena capital*. Santiago: Documentas, 1991.

Entrevistas

Mario Ferrero, escritor y ensayista, diciembre 1993.

Darío Osses, joven escritor, enero 1994.

Ana María del Río, joven escritora, diciembre 1993.

8. Tradición y modernidad en la poesía latinoamericana: El Concretismo

Clemente Padín

No fue casual que este XXXIX Seminario de SALALM se fijara el año 1956 como límite inicial del período a considerar acerca del desarrollo de la nueva literatura en Latinoamérica. Precisamente, en 1956, ocurren las históricas exposiciones de Arte Concreto en el Brasil que harían conocer públicamente las primeras obras poéticas concretas comenzando así uno de los movimientos poéticos de mayor predicamento en el mundo en esta segunda mitad de siglo. Para evitar malentendidos trataremos de precisar los alcances de los conceptos de "poesía" y de "vanguardia". Entendemos por "poesía" no el sentido estricto de género literario caracterizado por el empleo del verso, sino el sentido amplio de objeto artístico capaz de provocar la "emoción" poética", al decir de Jean Cohen (1978), dejando de lado la concepción estrecha de literatura estrictamente definida por el uso determinante de la significación verbal por una concepción no tan limitante basada en la Semiótica (Pierce) o en la Semiología (Saussure), esto es, una literatura que admita la expresión de sus contenidos a través de otros sistemas de signos o a través de otros medios, con o sin exclusión de la significación verbal. Por "vanguardia" entendemos toda aquella corriente que proponga elementos informacionales nuevos o inéditos al repertorio de conocimiento social. Esta nueva información disrumpe violentamente en primera instancia en esos fondos del saber social, primero al referido a la poesía, luego al referido a la literatura y al arte para, finalmente, volcarse al repertorio total de la sociedad. Todos los conocimientos ya aceptados socialmente deben reubicarse a la luz del nuevo saber hasta ese momento ignorado. Así, por ejemplo, ocurrió con la Física Clásica de Newton frente a la novedad de la Teoría de la Relatividad de Einstein.

El Concretismo literario surge, más o menos simultáneamente, en Europa y en Latinoamérica. A comienzos de los 50 se funda el Grupo Noigrandes de São Paulo (1952); aparece el manifiesto "For Concrete Poetry" (1953) en Suecia, de Oyvind Fahlstrom, curiosamente nacido en São Paulo, Brasil, en 1928; y sobre todo, aparecen, en 1953, las "Constelaciones" de Eugen Gomringer, también curiosamente nacido en Latinoamérica, en 1925, en Cachuela Esperanza, un pueblo boliviano. Fueron precisamente Gomringer y Decio Pignatari, pertenecientes al Grupo

Noigrandes, los que acuerdan llamar "Poesía Concreta" al naciente movimiento poético, en 1955.

Al principio fue la estructura

Desde sus comienzos la Poesía Concreta brasileña no fue una propuesta monolítica sino que ya, en 1956, aparecen sutiles diferencias que definirían, más tarde, tres vertientes claramente diferenciadas. La tendencia más importante, sobre todo por su irradiación mundial, fue el Grupo Noigrandes de São Paulo. Fundado en 1952 en torno a la revista *Invenção*, se integró con Decio Pignatari y los hermanos Haroldo y Augusto de Campos a los cuales se sumarían, más tarde, Ronaldo Azeredo, José Lino Grunewald y otros. Los mayores aportes vanguardistas de esta tendencia "estructural" de la Poesía Concreta fueron la descalificación del verso en tanto soporte de la poesía (para centrarse en la palabra) y la valorización del "espacio gráfico como agente estructural" procurando la expresión "directa-analógica, no lógica-discursiva", según se lee en el *Plan Piloto para la Poesía Concreta*, manifiesto del Grupo Noigrandes editado en 1958.

Para esta tendencia centrarse en la palabra significa estudiarla en todas sus dimensiones: en tanto significación, en tanto sonido y en tanto forma gráfica que establece relaciones estructurales junto a otras palabras en el blanco de la página. Esta interrelación se expresa en lo que en el *Plan* se denomina "verbivocovisualidad", suerte de unidad expresiva que atiende la totalidad comunicativa de la lengua.

Históricamente, en una primera etapa, la estructura se organiza siguiendo la figura o forma del objeto expresado verbalmente, a la manera de un Apollinaire (fase orgánico-fisonómica). En la siguiente, decididamente no-figurativa, se concreta en un isomorfismo entre la estructura visual y la estructura verbal (fase geométrico-isomórfica) dando cuenta, así, de la creciente influencia de la Psicología de la Gestald. Como ejemplo de este etapa, específicamente "concreta", veamos el poema "Tensão" de Augusto de Campos (1956):

com   can
som   tem

con   ten   tam
tém   são   bem

         tom   sem
         bem   som

No en vano, según el *Plan*, "el poema concreto, valiéndose del sistema fonético (dígitos) y de una sintaxis analógica, crea un área lingüística específica —verbivocovisual— que participa de las ventajas de la comunicación verbal". La nueva estructura visual se interrelaciona con la estructura semántica, coincidiendo las informaciones provenientes de ambos campos.

Fónicamente las sílabas se comportan como unidades de significación en sí mismas y como unidades rítmicas, pudiendo agruparse en cadencias o en ritmos según el énfasis que se ponga en la lectura. Obsérvese la contínua aliteración que provocan las nasales *m* y *n*. Asimismo las oposiciones consonánticas y el juego intervocálico completan la solidez de la estructura fónica acorde con la visual.

Semánticamente el polo central "tensão" nuclea las diversas unidades de significación, ya sean monosilábicas ("bem") o las generadas por condensación ("tambem") o condensadas a distancia ("contentam") en una pluritopía que impone imprevisibilidad y ambigüedad significativa, bases de la sugestión poética y consecuencia de la riqueza estética del poema de Augusto de Campos. A nivel profundo la verdadera "tensão" ocurre entre los polos semánticos "com som" y "sem som", es decir, entre la palabra y el silencio, entre la comunicación o el vacío.

Esta vertiente de la Poesía Concreta, también conocida como del "rigor estructural", generó una corriente poética tangencial, la "Poesía Praxis", desarrollada, entre otros, por Mario Chamie quien, en el postfacio de su libro *Lavra Lavra* (1962) propone una vuelta al verso lineal, valorando las posibilidades expresivas que permiten la semejanza y la proximidad de las palabras, sobre todo, en su índole fónica.

La vivencia de lo inefable

El Neoconcretismo, tendencia impulsada por Ferreira Gullar, según sus propias palabras, surge en reacción al excesivo "objetivismo de los poetas racionalistas del Grupo Noigrandes que intentan imitar a la máquina". Y, más adelante: "En lugar de acentuar las relaciones mecánicas entre las palabras, busqué acentuar el vacío entre ellas, el silencio. La página se tornó, a mis ojos, silencio materializado" (Crespo, Bedate y Gómez, 1963).

Es en su texto básico, *Teoría del No-Objeto* (1960), en donde mejor define lo "no-dicho", la única fuente de la poesía que se trasmite a través del no-objeto que "no es un anti-objeto, sino un objeto especial en el cual se pretende realizada una síntesis de experiencias sensoriales y mentales: un cuerpo transparente al conocimiento fenomenológico, íntegralmente perceptible, que tiende a la percepción sin dejar resto. Una pura apariencia". Su formulación poética se sustenta no en la destrucción del verso como en Noigrandes, sino en el replanteo de la sintaxis visual. Las palabras rodeadas por el blanco de la página, aún siendo silencio, funcionan "como un espacio simbólico de ampliación de lo significado. . . . El espacio vivencial de la palabra se suma al espacio existencial" (Alvaro de Sá, 1977).

Así al concitar la participación del espectador como co-gestor y actualizador del poema y, al establecer la preeminencia del tiempo, la duración en la cual se produce la vivencia transcendental del no-objeto, se fundan las premisas del arte y la poesía de los años siguientes, sobre todo, las formas expresivas que habría de popularizar el Conceptualismo en su doble vertiente: las artes de la acción, el "happening", la "performance", el evento, las ambientaciones o instalaciones, etc. y las artes del lenguaje, volcadas al estudio de las posibilidades expresivas del lenguaje verbal, a través del metalenguaje, las paradojas y las autorreferencias.

Veamos someramente un poema neoconcreto de Ferreira Gullar, "Verde Erba", tomado de su libro *Poemas* (1958):

verde	verde	verde	
verde	verde	verde	
verde	verde	verde	
verde	verde	verde	erba

La preocupación por la sintaxis visual se superpone a la mera destrucción del verso. Con sus propias palabras: ". . . el poema deja de fluir como una frase para concretizarse en el espacio de la página, según las fuerzas del campo visual y conforme a las leyes descubiertas por la Psicología de la Gestald" (Gullar, 1957). El blanco no como pausa, a la manera del blanco mallarmeano, sino como silencio que corresponde a la realización vivencial del momento poético, como espacio existencial. Así, el "verde" se organiza sintácticamente en el espacio para permitir que "erba" trasmita su carga expresiva. El "verde" no sólo en tanto representación del color "verde", propio, además, del objeto "erba" sino, como dijera el propio Gullar, "una presencia concreta que se percibe sobre el espacio real del mundo", una suerte de presentación física del objeto a través de su representación lingüística, la palabra "verde" adjetivando a "erba" que irradia toda su carga expresiva como si nunca la hubiéramos visto u oido.

La fisicalidad del poema

La tercer vertiente de la Poesía Concreta brasileña se relaciona con la obra de Wlademir Dias-Pino, quien presentó, en la histórica exposición del 56, los poemas *A Ave* y *Sólida*. *A Ave* (1956) es un libro-poema en el sentido de que el poema sólo existe gracias a la existencia del libro. La fisicalidad, la índole objetual del libro, las páginas, etc. son partes integrantes e intransferibles del poema: es imposible transponer el poema a otros lenguajes o a otros soportes sin que pierda totalmente su índole.

El poema se construye, se lee en tanto se manipulea: la textura del papel, su grosor y tamaño, su transparencia y color, el número y forma de las páginas, las perforaciones, las líneas que intentan orientar la lectura, etc., son elementos primordiales, custodios de la significación que el "lector" (entre comillas) debe descubrir o, mejor dicho, recrear a partir de su repertorio de conocimientos y vivencias. La información poética está íntimamente ligada a las propiedades físicas del libro y ello hace que éste sea su exclusivo canal o soporte.

Veamos someramente una de las primeras versiones de *A Ave* (1954), expuesta en la Exposición Nacional de Arte Concreta de 1956, base del libro homónimo de Dias-Pino editado en 1956:

```
              cor
           cor cor
       cor cor cor
           cor a s a
               a s a
               a s a   cor
               a s a   cor cor
               a s a   cor cor cor
           cor a ve

               a ve
               a ve a ve
               a ve a ve a ve
           ave voo
               voo a ve
               voo a ve a ve
               voo a ve a ve a ve
           ave vae


               vae
```

El espacio ni significa por sí mismo ni regula la sintaxis del poema como en las otras tendencias de la Poesía Concreta brasileña, sino que organiza el proceso de la numeración ordinal mediante palabras que asumen el carácter de número en código romano clásico. Así, *cor* corresponde a I (1), *asa* a V (5), *ave* a X (10), *voo* a C (50) y *vae* a M (100). Sin olvidar el propio poema conlleva su expresión semántica generada por la significación verbal, también connota el proceso del conteo mediante recursos lingüísticos, por ejemplo, para decir 48 diríamos *cor cor voo*. Dias-Pino, ya en 1956, preanunciaba los algoritmos que habría de utilizar la naciente computación. Importa la visualización del proceso y no la cristalización estructural.

Veamos ahora, brevemente, la versión didáctica de *Solida* (1956) de Dias-Pino:

Una de sus traducciones pudiera ser: "Soledad/única/contienda/sol/que surge/de la/lectura/del día". Compárese este poema con las siguientes versiones, gráfica, estadística y tipográfica:

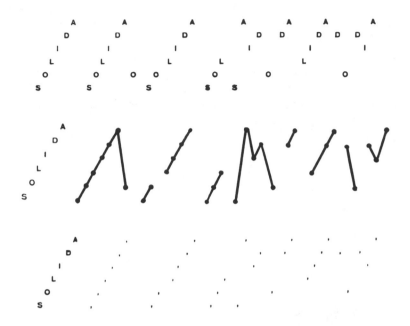

Las letras de *Solida* se ubican de acuerdo a las relaciones estadísticas establecidas de acuerdo a la frecuencia de su uso en el poema. Una vez establecido el código espacional se pueden sustituir por otras gráficas, por ejemplo, las líneas rectas del gráfico siguen las correspondientes a la posición de las letras de *Solida*. Idem las comillas del tercer gráfico. La lectura crítica que la generación siguiente hiciera de estos poemas daría lugar a un nuevo movimiento poético: el Poema/Proceso.

Icono versus palabra

El paso siguiente en la evolución que venimos observando lo constituye el Poema Semiótica, la bisagra que articularía la poesía que se vale de la palabra de aquella otra que, sin desterrarla totalmente, prefiere valerse de

otros lenguajes. En el Poema Semiótico la palabra es sustituida por figuras
o íconos que se ordenan serialmente de tal manera que pudieran configurar
un texto poético, para el cual se dispone un código lingüístico traductor.

El Poema Semiótico fue descubierto por Wlademir Dias-Pino en 1962
y divulgado por Angelo Aquino y Decio Pignatari, a partir de 1964 en
Invenção 4. Al Poema Semiótico que suele ser, visualmente, analógico a la
manera de los ideogramas chinos, le es necesario una sintaxis o un
ordenamiento en unidades discretas para poder ser entendido. A veces la
relación entre el orden de los íconos y el orden del código lingüístico es
mecánica, sobre todo, en los primeros poemas. El ícono es traducido por la
palabra y repite la sucesividad del lenguaje verbal sin que los órdenes
puedan mezclarse. Como en el siguiente Poema Semiótico "Hambre" de
José de Arimathéa (1970) en donde cada ícono se adiciona a otro generando
una narración:

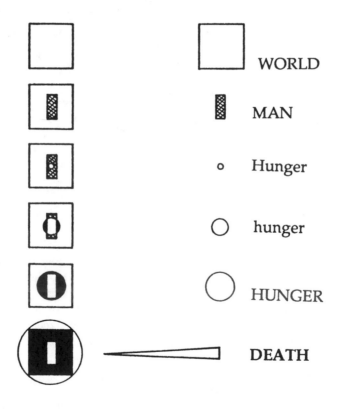

Más adelante el código "traductor" interviene insólitamente en el texto iconográfico, generando insospechables posibilidades expresivas. En otras la manipulación del poema genera textos imprevisibles. Pero, en última instancia el Poema Semiótico requiere, para su comprensión, de claves léxicas: la palabra sigue siendo insustituible.

Observemos brevemente este Poema Concreta de Neide Sá (1967), perteneciente a la etapa en la cual la relación mecánica ícono-palabra había sido superada dando lugar a innúmeras interacciones entre ambos órdenes, es decir, los elementos del código no sólo traducen los íconos sino que, también, intervienen en el texto:

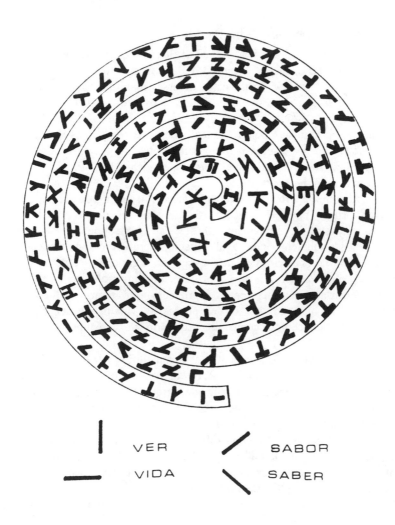

Por una parte el código lingüístico, impuesto por la autora, impone cierta lectura, pero, la espiral al cambiar la dirección de los íconos también altera su significación, con lo cual aumenta la ambigüedad. Por otra parte las conjunciones de íconos hacen estallar significaciones totalmente ajenas a la lengua. Por ejemplo, "ver-vida-sabor" es una expresión que no tiene formulación lingüística, es decir, no existe el concepto que pudiera expresar esa situación. En cambio sí tiene expresión visual o gráfica. Otra lecturas serían posibles según se comience la lectura por el principio o el final de la figura. Obsérvese que basta girar la espiral sobre sí misma para que las significaciones intercambien sus valores en una suerte de semiosis incontrolada.

El proceso se superpone a la estructura

El Poema/Proceso nace a raíz de la lectura crítica de las obras de Wlademir Dias-Pino, poeta concreto del movimiento inicial en 1956. Oficialmente surge en 1967 a través de diversas manifestaciones públicas y de los manifiestos "Proceso: Lectura de Proyecto" (1967) y "Poema/ Proceso: Situación Límite" (1968) y cierran sus actividades en 1972 con otro manifiesto "Parada: Opción Táctica", luego de cinco años de intensa y proficua actividad, en la cual participaron cientos de poetas brasileños tal cual ha quedado documentado en el libro de Wlademir Dias-Pino, *Processo: Linguagem e Comunicação* (1971).

Los mayores aportes del Poema/Proceso pueden agruparse en cuatro ítems: en primer lugar el concepto de proceso, el punto inicial de la creación, opuesto al inmovilismo de la estructura poética del Grupo Noigrandes y, también, opuesto al espacio metafísico y existencial del Neoconcretismo de Ferreira Gullar. En segundo lugar el concepto de matriz y el concepto de versión que se establecen como una solución al consumo pasivo y elitista. Luego la idea de proyecto que permite el consumo colectivo de la obra de arte o del poema y, finalmente, el concepto de contraestilo, concebido como una solución al consumo y creación individualista.

El proceso, núcleo de la creación, está constituido por las relaciones de devenir e intercambio entre los elementos de una estructura dada, es decir, la forma que adopta depende en la forma en que los elementos del poema interactúan entre sí. El poema debe trasmitir esos procesos y no estructuras estáticas e inamovibles.

La versión aparece como una solución al consumo individualista de la obra única, tal cual lo definió Walter Benjamin (1973), expresión de un privilegio, mejor dicho, expresión de una sociedad que hace posible la existencia de privilegiados. La versión permite al consumidor operar sobre el poema que se le ha propuesto creando, así, su propia poética. Como ejemplo veamos este Poema/Proceso de Alvaro de Sá (1967), llamado "12 x 9":

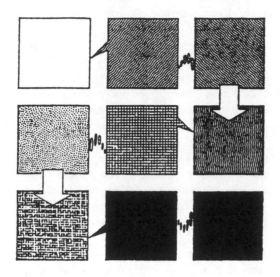

Y la versión de Moacy Cirne (1968):

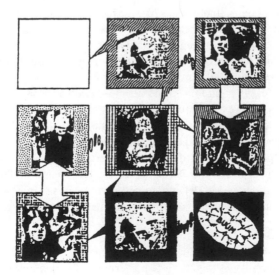

La historieta autorreferente de de Sá señala el proceso típico del "comic", la direccionalidad de los cuadros, la ubicuidad de los balones, etc. La versión de Cirne incluye una narración visual de fuerte contenido dramático (bastante común en Latinoamérica). Se constituye, asimismo, en una nueva matriz que en manos de otro consumidor puede asumir otras formas.

El tercer aporte teórico-práctico del Poema/Proceso que rompe finalmente con las limitaciones de material y de concepción es el proyecto. Ahora sólo es preciso describir la matriz del poema, a la manera de un arquitecto que dibuja su proyecto en un plano y deja en manos de los constructores la ejecución de la obra de acuerdo a los materiales e instrumentos que posean. Por última, el contraestilo trata de oponerse al individualismo que genera el estilo, formas y maneras del hacer y del decir fácilmente reconocibles que los artistas y poetas van concretando en el correr del tiempo en la medida en que van redundando y copiándose a sí mismos. El contraestilo tiende a romper ese círculo vicioso propiciando, no meras copias y reproducciones seriadas, sino obras realmente nuevas, que aportan elementos formales inéditos y desconocidos al fondo social del saber.

En relación a la conocida expresión de Dias-Pino: "Poesía para ser vista y sin palabras", conviene agregar que, también, según Dias-Pino: "El Poema/Proceso no pretende terminar con la palabra, así como no tiene la necesidad exclusiva de afirmar que el libro, hoy, es un objeto obsoleto. Lo que el Poema/Proceso reafirma es que el poema se hace con el proceso y no con palabras". Para completar esta parte veamos un Poema/Proceso sin palabras de José de Arimathéa (1970). La lucha entre la huella digital, ícono de la ignorancia y el analfabetismo y la letra "a", ícono del conocimiento y la civilización. La paulatina aparición/desaparición de un ícono coincide con la entrada/salida del otro así como la entera presencia de uno coincide con la entera desaparición del otro.

Obsérvese que, para la comunicación poética, son innecesarias las palabras. También es observable que los contenidos, en este caso la *ignorancia* y el *conocimiento*, pueden ser sustituidos por otros sin que la esencia del poema se modifique. Incluso esta matriz, en manos de cualquier consumidor, puede ser alterada de tal manera que pudiera constituirse en otra matriz en un desarrollo permanente. De tal manera el Poema/Proceso antepone el dinamismo del proceso creativo a la inmovilidad de la estructura, inaugurando vías informaciones nuevas en cada versión.

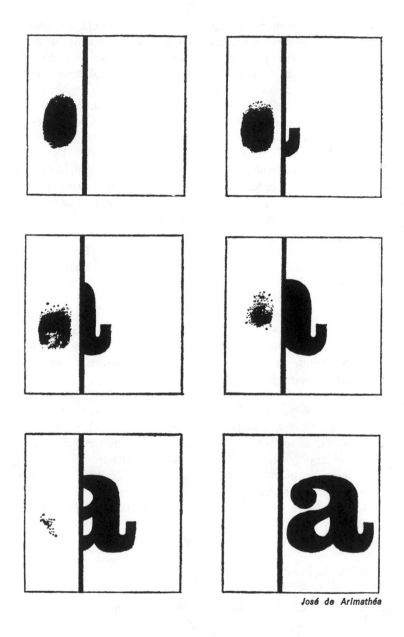

José de Arimathéa

Conclusión

Luego de este breve panorama de la Poesía Concreta brasileña y de sus derivaciones, parecería que sobran los argumentos que harían de estos movimientos poéticos piedras angulares del modernismo en el sentido en que han constituido vanguardia, es decir, han apostado al desarrollo de la humanidad desde su campo específico, la literatura.

Sin embargo, desde otras tiendas, se sostiene que la Poesía Concreta (al abolir el verso) y el Poema/Proceso (al abandonar a la palabra en tanto único soporte del poema) provocan un quiebre irreversible en el desarrollo de la poética, lo que comportaría un "cambio de paradigma" (Kuhn, 1971) y los alejaría del modernismo y los acercaría, concomitantemente, al posmodernismo. Estas tendencias críticas se refuerzan con la conocida afirmación de F. Jameson (1986) para quien "la aparición de nuevos rasgos formales en la cultura (provoca) un corte radical", es decir, el quiebre modernismo/posmodernismo, al cual, además, hace datar en la década de los 50, precisamente cuando nace el concretismo poético brasileño.

Para otros, Argañaraz (1992), la formación poética latinoamericana que se inicia con la Poesía Concreta brasileña (1956) y se continúa con el Poema/Proceso (1967), para concluir en la Argentina con la Poesía para y/o a Realizar (1970) y la Poesía Inobjetal (1971) en el Uruguay, al decidirse por "la muerte del arte", provocada por "el abandono de todos los lenguajes . . . puede ser vista como ejemplo o alegoría de uno de los caminos y destinos del arte de la modernidad", lo cual, parecería, confirmar la sustitución del modernismo por otra formación poética.

Pero, si no hay consenso entre los críticos literarios, menos lo hay entre los sociólogos: aún no se sabe si la modernidad es un constructo que habría de ser sustituido por otro llamado posmodernismo o si el modernismo en tanto macroformación cultural admitiría una nueva faceta de sí, fruto de su propio desarrollo, llamado posmodernismo.

Para terminar, quedémosnos con la Poesía Concreta, esta erupción creativa sin parangón, nacida también en Latinoamérica, en el marco de una sociedad empobrecida y expoliada cuya respuesta ante la violencia ha sido este riquísimo y efervescente *corpus* poético que ha dado y dará cuenta de nuestra realidad y de nuestra época.

BIBLIOGRAFIA

Argañaraz, N. N. 1992. *Poesía latinoamericana de vanguardia*. Montevideo: Ed. O Dos.

Benjamin, Walter. 1973. *Discursos interrumpidos I*. Madrid: Taurus.

Chamie, Mario. 1962. *Lavra-Lavra*. São Paulo: Ed. Massao Ohno.

————. 1963. *Palavra*. Rio de Janeiro.

Cirne, Moacy. 1975. *Vanguarda: Un projeto semiológico*. Petrópolis: Vozes.

Cohen, Jean. 1978. *Estructura del lenguaje poético*. Madrid: Gredos.

Crespo, A., Bedate y P. Gómez. 1963. *Situación de la Poesía Concreta*. Separata de la *Revista de Cultura Brasileña* (Madrid), no. 5 (junio).

De Campos, Augusto. 1979. *Poesía 1949–1979*. São Paulo: Duas Cidades.

De Sá, Alvaro. 1977. *Vanguarda: Produto de Comunicação*. Petropólis: Vozes.

Dias-Pino, Wlademir. 1956. *A Ave*. Cuiba: Ed. Igrejinha.

————. 1962. *Solida*. Rio de Janeiro: Ed. del autor.

————. 1971. *Processo: Linguagem e Comunicação*. Petropólis: Vozes. 2da. ed. 1973.

Fahlstrom, Oyvind. 1993. "Manifiesto for Concrete Poetry". En *Literally Speaking*, antología de Bo Ejeby, ed. Goteborg.

Garnier, Pierre. 1968. *Spatialism and Concrete Poetry*. París: Gallimard.

Gomringer, Eugen. 1953. *Constellations*. Berna.

————. 1955. "Du Vers a la Constellation". *Revista Augenblick* (Berna).

Gullar, Ferreira. 1959. *Teoría del No-Objeto*. En Suplemento de *Jornal do Brasil* (Rio de Janeiro).

————. 1958. *Poemas*. Rio de Janeiro: Ed. Espaço.

Jameson, Friedrich. 1986. "El posmodernismo o la lógica cultural del capitalismo tardío". En *Revista Casa de las Américas* (La Habana), no. 155-156 (marzo-junio).

Kuhn, Thomas. 1971. *La estructura de las revoluciones científicas*. México: Fondo de Cultura Económica.

Padín, Clemente. 1975. *De la représentacion a l'action*. Marsella: Ed. Polaires.

Pignatari, Decio. 1979. *Semiótica e literatura*. São Paulo: Ed. Cortez e Moraes.

Pignatari, Decio, y Augusto y Haroldo de Campos. 1958. "Plan Piloto para la Poesía Concreta". En *Revista Noigrandes* (São Paulo), no. 2.

————. 1965. *Teoria de la Poesia Concreta*. São Paulo: Invenção.

Vigo, Edgardo Antonio. 1970. *De la Poesía/Proceso a la Poesía para y/o Realizar*. La Plata: Diagonal Cero.

9. La muerte en los doce cuentos peregrinos

Angel Esteban del Campo

El tema de la muerte domina toda la obra narrativa de García Márquez, desde sus primeros relatos, escritos allá por los años cuarenta, hasta la última novela, publicada en abril del 94. Los *Doce cuentos peregrinos*, por tanto, no son ajenos a esta obsesión, y se puede decir que es el motivo real que unifica la colección, por encima del cambio de perspectiva espacial. El escritor colombiano ha salido del ámbito mítico de Macondo y alrededores, y se sitúa en una Europa convertida en escenario propicio para el desarrollo del mito. Los personajes demostrarán que la idiosincrasia, producto de la tierra, genera unos mecanismos interiores de conducta que saltan las fronteras nacionales e incluso continentales, determinando comportamientos vitalicios, independientes del suelo en el que se asientan.

Cuando en el prólogo se propone explicar por qué los doce cuentos son peregrinos, se limita a afirmar que se trata de "las cosas extrañas que les suceden a los latinoamericanos en Europa".[1] Pero la intención es mucho más compleja: la misma vida es un peregrinaje, en el sentido bíblico, de un alfa hasta un omega. La simbología telúrica y apocalíptica proclamada a los cuatro vientos en *Cien años de soledad*, los cuentos de finales de los sesenta, *Crónica de una muerte anunciada*, etc., tiene sentido en los últimos cuentos desde el propio título. *Peregrinos* significa, en este contexto, el camino de América a Europa que desemboca en la muerte, como el pueblo elegido peregrinaba para encontrar la tierra prometida o los hombres del medievo lo hacían, desde los puntos más recónditos de Europa, para venerar la imagen del Apóstol Santiago. El presidente exiliado del primer relato ha llegado a Ginebra procedente de América con una victoria, la mayor de su vida, lograr que le olviden (p. 32), y aventurando su próxima muerte (p. 33). Olvido, exilio y premonición son tres formas típicas de muerte en la narrativa de G. Márquez, que aquí ofrecen un paralelismo evidente con *El otoño del patriarca*. Por su parte, en el último cuento, Nena Daconte, la recién casada colombiana que llega a Madrid, rumbo a París, para celebrar con su esposo la luna de miel, muere después de una larga, fría y penosa peregrinación, de un modo inesperado e insólito. Entre esos dos polos, las demás escenas suponen viajes correspondientes de alfa a omega, de América a Europa, para morir, imaginar que se muere, toparse con alguna muerte, caer en el olvido o establecerse en un sueño que es como la muerte. "Tramontana" es la muerte anticipada de un joven que sucumbe ante el terror que le produce el viento de Cadaqués. La fuerza destructora del vendaval conecta este relato con el final apocalíptico de otras obras de G. Márquez, como *Cien años de soledad*, donde el viento es símbolo de desolación y acompaña a la desaparición de la estirpe, de la sociedad por ella creada y de todo rastro de vida. "Espantos de agosto" rememora una antigua historia ligada a un lugar. El suicidio de un caballero en la habitación donde previamente había asesinado a su amada estimula la imaginación del narrador y determina sus reacciones, al tener que alojarse en el mismo castillo varios siglos después. "Me alquilo para soñar" contempla la muerte de una mujer colombiana al estrellarse su coche contra el muro de un famoso hotel habanero. Los poderes de adivinación de la difunta, sobre todo para sucesos desagradables, contrastan con una tragedia tan poco previsible, y son el punto de partida que el escritor utiliza para recordar los momentos que pasó con ella en Europa. Así podríamos repasar uno a uno los doce cuentos y llegar a una misma conclusión: el hilo conductor no es tanto el motivo del viaje mismo como el tema, constante, de la muerte.

La obsesión por el mundo de los muertos en G. Márquez tiene unas raíces culturales y personales bastante bien definidas desde la infancia. En un famoso texto citado por Vargas Llosa describe la impresión que le producía, cuando era un adolescente, visitar la casa de los abuelos:

En esa casa había un cuarto desocupado en donde había muerto la tía Petra. Había un cuarto desocupado donde había muerto el tío Lázaro. Entonces, de noche, no se podía caminar en esa casa porque había más muertos que vivos. A mí me sentaban, a las seis de la tarde, en un rincón y me decían: "No te muevas de aquí porque si te mueves va a venir la tía Petra que está en su cuarto, o el tío Lázaro, que está en otro".[2]

La ambivalencia de los dos mundos, el de los vivos y el de los muertos, ligados a espacios concretos, es el motor de la dicotomía realidad/ficción, y es consecuencia del terror a la muerte, la incertidumbre personal con respecto al más allá y el desequilibrio entre esta incertidumbre del narrador y las creencias y supersticiones del pueblo que describe. De ahí la ironía constante y los rasgos de humor que sazonan los relatos. García Márquez propone dos tipos de miradas: la del mundo real hacia el vacío de la muerte, y la del mundo de los muertos, más real en ocasiones que la primera, hacia el de los infortunados peregrinos. La mejor demostración de que es éste el verdadero sustrato de la obra es el empeño por aclarar, en el prólogo, que la idea de escribir un libro tan cohesionado —el único libro de relatos con unidad interna— surgió de la imagen de su propio entierro. El mismo lo explica:

La primera idea se me ocurrió a principios de la década de los setenta, a propósito de un sueño esclarecedor que tuve después de cinco años de vivir en Barcelona. Soñé que asistía a mi propio entierro, a pie, caminando entre un grupo de amigos vestidos de luto solemne, pero con un ánimo de fiesta. Todos parecíamos dichosos de estar juntos. Y yo más que nadie, por aquella gran oportunidad que me daba la muerte para estar con mis amigos de América Latina, los más antiguos, los más queridos, los que no veía desde hacía más tiempo. Al final de la ceremonia, cuando empezaron a irse, yo intenté acompañarlos, pero uno de ellos me hizo ver con una severidad terminante que para mí se había acabado la fiesta. "Eres el único que no puede irse", me dijo. Sólo entonces comprendí que morir es no estar nunca más con los amigos. (pp. 13-14)

El narrador de esta historia ha pasado de un mundo a otro. En las primeras líneas, el punto de vista pertenece a la realidad del otro mundo, el que está más allá de la muerte, y es tan real como el de los mortales, tan real que asiste como los demás a su propio entierro. Pero al final del texto el universo del revés gira hacia la inexorable realidad, con un guiño irónico y una conclusión desproporcionada. No hay patetismo en las palabras del colombiano, sino una especie de melancolía focalizada, puntual, que no se toma en serio o no repara lo suficiente en el alcance de la propia muerte. Ese ir y venir de la vida en la muerte a la vida en la vida, tomando como pretexto el vicio de escribir (p. 13), sirve al artista de catarsis momentánea frente al terror de la muerte, y constituye una solución mítica para el escéptico ante sus dudas. Lévy-Bruhl, en su obra *El alma primitiva*, descubría en el hombre antiguo interpretaciones míticas en torno a los fenómenos inexplicables, aclarando que en el reino de los muertos "tout y est a l'envers . . . tout s'y fait a rebours",[3] todo se ve y se hace al revés. De ahí la sorpresa del narrador cuando le explican que debe quedarse y no puede volver con los demás. Para profundizar en este rasgo existencial del colombiano, que pone del mismo lado la cara y la cruz en el juego entre ficción y realidad, vamos a comparar dos textos significativos: su primer relato, de 1947, "La tercera resignación", y uno de los más eficaces de los doce peregrinos, "María dos Prazeres". Se trata de dos fases distintas en una misma secuencia: la primera es aventurar su propia defunción y someter a lo que hay alrededor a un proceso de educación, para preparar el trato del medio exterior con el futuro muerto. Es el caso de María. La segunda fase es más sutil, más fantástica e irónica: el muerto vive dentro de su ataúd e intercambia experiencias con el medio. Mientras María parece muerta en vida, el muchacho muerto vive. Y es una vida como las demás vidas, llena de sensaciones e incertidumbres. Constantemente se hace referencia a los olores, al tacto, a la manera en que el joven siente sus miembros, sus huesos, su piel, al tiempo que ha transcurrido desde la primera muerte, etc., así como a los azares de la vida dentro de la muerte. El título "La tercera resignación" habla de una posible tercera muerte, después de haber pasado, ese cuerpo, por el mismo trance dos veces. Aparte de no saber cuándo ni cómo acaecerá, ni el narrardor ni el personaje son capaces de averiguar si el estado en el que se encuentra el protagonista es la vida o la muerte. Casi al final del relato salta la duda con una virulencia también inesperada:

De pronto el miedo le dio una puñalada por la espalda. ¡El miedo! . . . ¿A qué se debía? El lo comprendía perfectamente y se le estremecía la carne: probablemente no estaba muerto . . . ¡lo iban a enterrar vivo![4]

La duda persiste en la descripción que el narrador hace de los pensamientos del protagonista, y en las líneas siguientes la obsesión continúa pero, como siempre, contenida, sin emotividad, sin rasgos de desequilibrio, dolor o desesperación. Primero el lenguaje discursivo del razonamiento: "No podía estar muerto porque se daba cuenta exacta de todo; de la vida que giraba en torno suyo, murmurante . . . Se daba perfecta cuenta del lento caer del agua en el estanque . . ." (p. 19). Luego, el asombro frío ante las apariencias que se presentan del revés:

Todo le negaba su muerte. Todo menos el "olor". Pero, ¿cómo podía saber que ese olor era el suyo? Tal vez su madre había olvidado el día anterior cambiar el agua de los jarrones, y los tallos estaban pudriéndose. O tal vez el ratón, que el gato había arrastrado hasta su pieza, se descompuso con el calor. No. El "olor" no podía ser de su cuerpo. (p. 19)

Y es la paradoja desconcertante de ese mundo del revés la que desestabiliza una posible sensación de alegría y plenitud en el espacio de los muertos, ya que "un muerto puede ser feliz con su situación irremediable. Pero un vivo no puede resignarse a ser enterrado vivo" (p. 19). Antes de plantearse la duda "estaba feliz con su muerte, porque creía estar muerto" (p. 19), pero ahora, el mayor problema es la visión de su propio entierro:

Lo enterrarían vivo. Podría sentir. Darse cuenta del momento en que le clavaran la caja. Sentiría el vacío del cuerpo suspendido en hombros de los amigos, mientras su angustia y su desesperación se irían agrandando a cada paso de la procesión. (p. 19)

La situación es muy parecida a la que narra García Márquez en el prólogo a los *Doce cuentos peregrinos*, y que nunca pudo terminar en cuento, a pesar de todos sus esfuerzos. La voz del narrador es no sólo omnisciente, sino también ubicua, entendiendo por tal la capacidad trascender espacios físicos y espirituales, anteriores y posteriores, animados e inertes, del mundo de los vivos en vida y del de los vivos en la otra orilla de la muerte. De ahí la carencia de gravedad, la trivialización de una realidad inexorable, a la que sólo se puede hacer frente mediante la catarsis del placer de escribir y la ironía. No hay horror hacia la muerte porque su umbral se traspasa o, más bien desaparece, pero sí lo hay hacia otras realidades a las que el sentido común da una importancia relativa. La ironía, muy fina pero sumamente eficaz, aumenta su poder destructivo al comparar las verdaderas causas del terror del muchacho con aquéllas que provocan la muerte:

Lo que más horror le producía no era exactamente que se lo comieran los ratones. Al fin y al cabo podría seguir viviendo con su esqueleto. Lo que le atormentaba era el terror innato que sentía hacia esos animalitos. Se le erizaba la piel con sólo pensar en esos seres velludos que recorrían todo su cuerpo, que penetraban por los pliegues de su piel y le rozaban los labios con sus patas heladas. (p. 14)

En el cuento de "María dos Prazeres" la ironía va por otro lado. Una mujer de 76 años recién cumplidos presiente su muerte en un sueño, al estilo de los personajes bíblicos del Antiguo Testamento, capaces de interpretar sin error el contenido profético de los sueños. Pero este dato no aparece hasta que la trama del cuento está ya consolidada, cuando ha pasado el episodio del encuentro con el vendedor de entierros, que termina con una anécdota rebosante de humor:

—¿Puedo hacerle una pregunta indiscreta? —preguntó él.
Ella lo dirigió hacia la puerta.
—Por supuesto —le dijo—, siempre que no sea la edad.
—Tengo la manía de adivinar el oficio de la gente por las cosas que hay en su casa, y la verdad es que aquí no acierto —dijo él—. ¿Qué hace usted?
—Soy puta, hijo. ¿O es que ya no se me nota?
El vendedor enrojeció.
—Lo siento.
—Más debía sentirlo yo —dijo ella, tomándolo del brazo para impedir que se descalabrara contra la puerta—. (pp. 142-143)

A continuación se describe la preparación para su muerte y entierro, con una sola obsesión: tener alguien que vaya a llorarle a su tumba. Para ello educa al perro con el fin de que sepa ir, cada domingo, solo, desde la casa al mismo lugar donde debe ser enterrada, y llore durante un rato. A partir de ahí, el colombiano se las ingenia para colocar, en los momentos claves de los cambios de escena, los signos inequívocos de la muerte. En primer lugar, la lluvia que, junto con el viento, es inmediato señalizador de las grandes catástrofes destructoras. Viento, lluvia, o ambos fenómenos aparecen en "Buen viaje, señor presidente" y "La santa" en varias ocasiones con el mismo sentido devastador; en "Me alquilo para soñar" una tromba de agua causa la muerte violenta a la misma intérprete de los sueños; "Sólo vine a hablar por teléfono" presenta la lluvia pertinaz en el momento de producirse el equívoco fatal que llevará a la protagonista hasta la desolación del manicomio; en "La luz es como el agua" la interpretación fantástica de la frase que da título al cuento provoca la muerte de unos niños, ahogados en una casa inundada de luz, como si fuera agua, etc. En "María dos Prazeres" la "llovizna de vientos sesgados" (p. 137) primaveral sirve para presentar al vendedor de entierros, y poco más tarde para poner en escena al perrito de aguas, que "entró . . . empapado por la llovizna, y con un talante de perdulario que no tenía nada que ver con el resto de la casa" (p. 141). Por último, la lluvia es el marco y el objeto inductor del desenlace, aunque en este caso representa el guiño que se le hace a la muerte. Es el instante del signo definitivo, aunque anteriormente ha habido otros, estratégicamente colocados. En pleno proceso educativo del perro, un día observa la llegada de un trasatlántico blanco con la bandera de Brasil, y "deseó con toda su alma que le trajera una carta de alguien que hubiera muerto por ella en la cárcel de Pernambuco" (p. 147). En ese momento mágico, observa G. Márquez, "superó el terror de no tener a nadie que llorara sobre su tumba" (p. 147). Y en el siguiente otoño "empezó a percibir signos aciagos que no lograba descifrar" (p. 147), "y en todas partes encontró señales inequívocas de la muerte" (p. 148). Esa Navidad, al presenciar frente a su ventana un asesinato, reacciona así: "¡Dios mío —se dijo asombrada— es como si todo se estuviera muriendo conmigo!" (p. 148), y llega a la conclusión de que sólo había sentido una inquietud semejante hacía muchos años, contemplando en Manaos un amanecer, cuando "la selva amazónica se sumergía en un silencio abismal que sólo podía ser igual al de la muerte" (p. 148). El día que cortó las relaciones con el conde de Cardona, "tuvo la certidumbre de que el último ciclo de su vida acababa de cerrarse" (p. 151) y preparó los últimos detalles para su tumba y para prevenir la reacción de su perro. Es decir, entre los dos ciclos de la lluvia (el primero con el descubrimiento del vendedor de entierros y el perro, y el último con el pasaje del desenlace) que son premonitorios, se distribuyen equidistantemente los demás signos claros de la muerte. Sin embargo, de aquí hasta el final el cariz de los signos cambia por completo, puesto que pasamos de la obsesión por la muerte al sentimiento de la supervivencia y la felicidad. Así pues, si volvemos a los postulados de Lévy-Bruhl, el territorio entre lluvias es el de la muerte, y todos los signos tienen la misma dirección, y el episodio del desenlace es el de la vida, y en él los signos también son unívocos, pero de sentido contrario. María dos Prazeres ha sido recogida, en medio de la tormenta de noviembre, por un adolescente con un coche de lujo, "cuando ya parecía imposible hasta un milagro" (p. 152). De ese modo, dentro del coche la "lluvia se convirtió en un percance irreal, la ciudad cambió de color, y ella se sintió en un mundo ajeno y feliz donde todo estaba resuelto de antemano" (p. 153). La incertidumbre sobre los presagios del sueño ha desaparecido, e incluso los objetos que antes recordaban la muerte, ahora aparecen envueltos en una atmósfera mágica de benignidad. Una vez acomodada en el coche, María comenta:

—Esto es un trasatlántico —dijo, porque sintió que tenía que decir algo digno—.
  Nunca había visto nada igual, ni siquiera en sueños. (p. 153)

Estamos ahora frente al portal de la casa. El joven ha llevado a la prostituta hasta el mismo umbral de su guarida, y el viraje en el universo de los presagios se confirma cuando hace además de subir con ella. Insiste hasta que María le da vía libre. El adolescente la sigue y ella, de modo instantáneo, "volvió a examinar por completo el sueño premonitorio que le había cambiado la vida durante tres años, y comprendió el error de su interpretación" (p. 155). No era la muerte de María, sino la vida de él. En la narrativa de G. Márquez, el problema del mito no estriba en su credibilidad, sino en la interpretación, porque las fronteras entre la vida y la muerte son vulnerables en los dos sentidos. Hay quien es capaz de "vivir su muerte" o vice-versa, estar muerto en vida. El joven resignado que siente dentro del ataúd se prepara para su tercera muerte, la definitiva, mientras María, muerta desde la primera premonición, deja de visitarse a sí misma en el cementerio cuando pasa de nuevo a la vida. Con estos trasvases, a menudo envueltos en una fina capa de ironía, la ficción logra suavizar el único terror real, ineludible, inequívoco: el de la verdadera muerte.

NOTAS

1. Gabriel García Márquez, *Doce cuentos peregrinos* (Madrid: Mondadori España, 1992), p. 14. A partir de ahora, cada vez que se cite la obra, se hará dentro del texto, con referencia a esta edición, indicando el número de página entre paréntesis.

2. Mario Vargas Llosa, *García Márquez: Historia de un deicidio* (Caracas: Monte Avila, 1971), p. 23.

3. Lucien Lévy-Bruhl, *L'ame primitive* (París: F. Alcan, 1927), cap. XI.

4. Gabriel García Márquez, *Ojos de perro azul*, 4 ed. (Madrid: Mondadori España, 1992), pp. 18-19. A partir de ahora, los textos de esta obra se citarán con el número de página de esta edición entre paréntesis.

BIBLIOGRAFIA

Arroyo, Francesc. "El amor, la vejez, la muerte". *El País* (Libros) 7:321 (12 diciembre 1985), 1-3.

Campos, Jorge. "Una nueva fábula americana: *El otoño del patriarca*". *Insula* 348 (noviembre 1975), 11.

―――. "Una novela y un cuento de Gabriel García Márquez". *Insula* 420 (noviembre 1981), 11.

García Márquez, Gabriel. *Ojos de perro azul.* 4 ed. Madrid: Mondadori España, 1992.

―――. *Doce cuentos peregrinos.* Madrid: Mondadori España, 1992.

Gullón, Ricardo. *García Márquez o el arte de contar*. Madrid: Taurus, 1970.

Lévy-Bruhl, Lucien. *L'ame primitive*. París: F. Alcan, 1927.

Mallett, Brian J. "Los funerales del patriarca que no quiere morir". *Arbor* 97:377 (1977), 47-58.

Palencia Roth, Michael. *Gabriel García Márquez: la línea, el círculo y las metamorfosis del mito*. Madrid: Gredos, 1983.

Triviño, Consuelo. "La escritura errante." *Cuadernos Hispanoamericanos* 513 (1992), 40-44.

IV

Emerging Themes: Homosexuality, Prostitution, Women

10. De la clandestinidad a la legitimidad: El homosexual en la narrativa mexicana contemporánea

Víctor F. Torres-Ortiz

El 20 de noviembre de 1901 un grupo de policías irrumpe en una residencia ubicada en la calle La Paz de la capital mexicana y arresta a cuarenta y un individuos que celebraban una fiesta privada. El escándalo constituyó la comidilla de la sociedad mexicana por largo tiempo a tal punto que el número 41 se convirtió en sinónimo inequívoco de homosexual para los mexicanos.[1]

El incidente sirvió de pretexto para que cinco años más tarde Eduardo A. Castrejón publicara *Los cuarenta y uno* (1906), primera novela que trata el tema homosexual en la narrativa mexicana. La aparición, sin embargo, no pudo ser más funesta. La novela recoge el discurso médico de la época empeñado en catalogar al homosexual como un ser híbrido, un tercer sexo que pretende asumir una identidad femenina.

Junto a estas imágenes distorcionadas, encontramos los propios prejuicios del autor para quien la homosexualidad es ". . . ese vicio que rebaza en la copa de la prostitución más desenfrenada"[2] al tiempo que los homosexuales son "monstruos" (p. 24) con "instintos criminales y bastardos" (p. 30) que habitan "una inmunda cloaca" (p. 74).

La homofobia de Castrejón no es producto de una moral cristiana, sino el reflejo de su orientación socialista. Esto lo conduce a establecer una oposición entre los valores de la clase obrera y los vicios de la aristocracia y la burguesía, entre los que destaca la homosexualidad. Castrejón afirma que ésta es el resultado del ocio y de la riqueza, presenta al homosexual como la escoria de la humanidad y lo hace acreedor de los castigos más atroces.

Este intento de condenar y rechazar al homosexual no se repitió, por fortuna, en los años siguientes. Al calor del machismo y de la tradición católica, el homosexual como personaje literario desaparece. Sin embargo, el homoerotismo seguiría manifestándose a través de las obras de algunos de los intelectuales más notables del país: poetas como Salvador Novo, Xavier Villaurrutia y, sobre todo, Elías Nandino o pintores como Manuel Rodríguez Lozano, Roberto Montenegro, Chuco Reyes Ferreira, Abraham Angel y Agustín Lazo.[3]

El mutismo alrededor del tema homosexual es común a toda la narrativa latinoamericana dominada por la novela de la tierra durante las primeras décadas del siglo. Donald Shaw señala que no sólo se evitó representar la homosexualidad, sino que la sexualidad en general fue parca y discreta durante este período.[4] Las escasas apariciones del homosexual están regidas por el signo de lo patológico.[5]

En los años 50 y comienzos de los 60, el homosexual se incorpora a la narrativa mexicana como figura secundaria o de fondo que oscila entre lo cómico y lo trágico. Autores como Arreola (*La feria*), Fuentes (*Cambio de piel*, *La víbora de la mar*), Castellanos (*Album de familia*) y, particularmente, Sergio Fernández y Luisa Josefina Hernández registran la presencia del homosexual en la sociedad mexicana. En los relatos de estos autores la homosexualidad es circunstancial, no hay un análisis ni un conocimiento profundo del tema.[6]

Dos textos publicados en 1964, a escasos meses de diferencia, rompen con esta tendencia y pueden considerarse los pioneros de la literatura "gay" mexicana: *El diario de José Toledo* y *41 o el muchacho que soñaba en fantasmas*. Si bien ambas obras salen a la luz pública en una época de transformaciones que se caracterizó por el cuestionamiento del orden social y político, es innegable que todavía median restricciones.

Las circunstancias que rodean la publicación de ambos textos evidencian cómo el tema acarrea un riesgo tanto para el autor como para la casa editora. El autor de *41* recurre al uso de un seudónimo, Paolo Po, y hasta el día de hoy su identidad resulta desconocida. La obra, además, se publica bajo el sello de Costa-Amic, casa editora de poco prestigio. Por su parte, el autor de *El diario*, Miguel Barbachano Ponce, se ve obligado a publicar su obra por cuenta propia, a pesar de gozar de renombre como periodista, ya que "los editores comerciales la consideraron peligrosa y contraria a las buenas costumbres y al pudor".[7]

Los factores extraliterarios condicionan la publicación y la divulgación de estas obras de tal manera que ambas circulan subterráneamente. Con el paso del tiempo, *El diario* corre mejor suerte gracias a una edición comercial en los años 80 a cargo de Premiá Editores lo que permite su rescate y valoración. Uno de los críticos que se ha ocupado de esta novela es David Foster quien la designa ejemplo de "homosexualismo trágico".[8]

Esta designación se puede hacer extensiva a *41* o *El muchacho que soñaba en fantasmas* ya que en ambas novelas persiste la idea de que la homosexualidad conduce inevitablemente a la desgracia. La represión y la homofobia están presentes a tal extremo que los protagonistas perciben su homosexualidad como algo vergonzoso y ambos internalizan los consabidos estigmas. Es revelador el empleo del número 41 como parte del título de *41* o *El muchacho que soñaba en fantasmas*. El título refleja la oposición entre lo perverso, lo amoral, representado por el número 41 y aquéllos, como el protagonista, que intentan reivindicarse a través del amor genuino. *El muchacho que soñaba en fantasmas* termina por condenarse a sí mismo y a los suyos a quienes llama: "una raza de prostituidos que se depravan en los lechos"[9] al descubrir que el amor está vedado, no sólo por la sociedad, sino por el propio estilo de vida que fomenta las relaciones furtivas.

En oposición a la auto-destrucción, en *El diario de José Toledo* encontramos la auto-censura, la secretividad a toda costa. La homosexualidad se convierte aquí en "lo que no se dice" y el temor a ser descubierto obliga a su joven protagonista a permanecer en el clóset con el fin de ser tolerado. Manifestarse abiertamente como "gay" está asociado a la vergüenza, al deshonor, a romper el arreglo tácito que José tiene con su familia. Su sexualidad, su intimidad, se manifiesta únicamente a través del diario que se convierte en su confidente y "testimonio de su pesadumbre".[10]

Barbachano Ponce se aproxima al personaje con demasiado paternalismo y José Toledo resulta un sujeto débil, un estereotipo del homosexual enamorado. Todo su accionar gira en torno a Wenceslao, el amante evasivo que lo abandona sin mayores explicaciones. En el suicidio del personaje, se evidencia la fidelidad a los patrones literarios que exigen que el transgresor pague con la muerte.

No será hasta 1969 que surge un protagonista que asume sin temores ni culpabilidad su homosexualidad. Javier Lavalle, narrador-protagonista de la novela *Después de todo* de José Ceballos Maldonado, es el primer protagonista homosexual de la narrativa mexicana que no se autocompadece ni se flagela. "He vivido de acuerdo con lo que quiero y con lo que soy"[11] escribe Lavalle postulando así su derecho a ejercer su sexualidad libremente.

En *Después de todo* presenciamos el surgimiento de una voz contestataria que no busca ni perdón ni aceptación: "He vivido así y no me siento amargado a pesar de los reveses" (p. 195), de un homosexual que no recurre al engaño ni a la discreción. Se trata de un personaje que se acepta tal cual es: "Seré como soy hasta la ausencia del apetito sexual o hasta la muerte" (p. 95). Esta reafirmación de su "diferencia" está ligada a la formación de una minoría que justamente en esos años comienza a reclamar su legitimidad. Por esto, *Después de todo* se considera una "obra pivote que abre la actual perspectiva de la literatura homosexual mexicana".[12]

En los siguientes diez años se publican varias novelas pero ninguna recibe la divulgación para suscitar el interés entre el público ni el respaldo de los críticos o de la industria del libro.[13] Ese logro le corresponde a *El vampiro de la colonia Roma*, publicada en 1979. En la publicación de esta novela convergen dos factores que van a ser determinantes en la acogida y el impacto que suscita. Por un lado, el autor, Luis Zapata, obtiene el Premio Juan Grijalbo de Novela. A su vez, la Editorial Grijalbo la publica lo que le aseguró un mercado y mayor receptividad por parte de los críticos. *El vampiro* logra generar interés desde un principio al extremo de que surge un debate entre sus detractores y defensores y en el aspecto estrictamente comercial establece un precedente al demostrar la viabilidad del tema. Acertadamente, la novela ha sido consignada "punta de lanza de la temática homosexual" ya que a partir de su aparición surge un corpus literario sostenido que enfoca abierta y exclusivamente la experiencia homosexual.

Así como el homosexual mexicano comienza a manifestarse públicamente a finales de la década del 70 a través de grupos, publicaciones, marchas e, inclusive, una Semana Cultural Gay,[14] surge un personaje literario que revela, sin inhibiciones, su orientación sexual y que reclama, con naturalidad, la aceptación y los derechos del homosexual. "Cada uno tiene derecho a hacer con su vida sexual lo que se le pegue la gana"[15] declara Adonis García, el vampiro de la colonia Roma. Este chichifo —joven proletario dedicado a la prostitución masculina— es un pícaro moderno y su narración, que es la transcripción de su testimonio, sirve como una apología de la vida homosexual.

Con *El vampiro* Luis Zapata establece las pautas para que se formalice la narrativa gay mexicana. Entre los rasgos de esta literatura encontramos que el homosexual se desmitifica, se aleja de lo patológico, lo exótico, para convertirse en un sujeto normal. Se privilegia al homosexual al convertirlo en protagonista indiscutible y, en muchos casos, narrador de su propia historia. Por otro lado, se deja de cuestionar la homosexualidad —ya no se condena ni justifica— lo que le permite a los narradores abordarla como una dimensión de la sexualidad.

En lo que concierne estilo y estructura, presenciamos un rompimiento con los convencionalismos de tiempo, espacio y género para abordar diferentes perspectivas, puntos de vista y enfoques narrativos.[16] Se emplea un lenguaje homoerótico donde el sexo se plasma sin inhibiciones o se recrea el argot homosexual. En ambas instancias se logra proyectar un discurso gay, un discurso alterno que se opone a la tradición literaria dominante.

Este discurso servirá para legitimar las relaciones íntimas entre personas del mismo sexo a través de dos vertientes: la exploración del fenómeno amoroso o la celebración del estilo de vida homosexual. Tres novelas ejemplifican la primera vertiente: *Octavio* (1982) de Jorge Arturo Ojeda, *Las púberes canéforas* (1983) de José Joaquín Blanco y *En jirones* (1985) de Luis Zapata. En las tres encontramos a un protagonista que reconoce y vive plenamente su homosexualidad en oposición a otros que asumen una actitud ambigua en lo que respecta su orientación sexual. Por debajo de esta ambivalencia subyacen el machismo, la represión, y la homofobia.

El protagonista de *Octavio*, un hombre maduro, un pensador de amplia cultura, narra su relación con un joven vano, práctico, "carente de vida intelectual"[17] cuyo nombre le da título a la novela. Mientras el narrador procura una relación afectiva intensa y declara que "el mejor amor es entre dos hombres" (p. 16), Octavio se debate entre sus impulsos sexuales y el disimulo: "Pero yo tengo a una amiga, a mi novia. Yo todo lo cifro en una mujer" (p. 14).

Con esta postura Octavio cumple con el código de la hombría, aunque en realidad está dispuesto a traspasar las barreras de la heterosexualidad a cambio del dinero adecuado. Prostituirse se convierte así en una forma de autojustificarse para satisfacer sus inclinaciones homoeróticas. Esto resulta inaceptable para el narrador quien termina la relación no sin antes consignar aspectos íntimos de la misma en un texto titulado precisamente *Octavio*.

Al igual que *Octavio*, *Las púberes canéforas* es una novela auto-referencial, una novela que se alude a si misma a través del libro que el narrador está empeñado en escribir: "una novela que se llamaría *Las púberes canéforas* nomás para que tanta loca ignorante preguntara: ¿Las qué?".[18] Sin embargo, *Las púberes canéforas* va más allá de la auto-referencia para aproximarse a la metaliteratura, a la exploración de la propia escritura. El libro que Guillermo, el protagonista, quiere escribir es el que estamos leyendo. Se trata de la historia que Guillermo hilvana a medida que deambula por las calles de Ciudad México, "para contarse una novela a si mismo" (p. 21), aunque en la misma narración cuestione su capacidad de escritor insinuando que "no llegaría más allá de los primeros esbozos, de algunas notas y tres o cuatro piezas de diálogo" (p. 104).

El punto de partida de su relato son los acontecimientos recientes en la vida de Felipe, el amante que acaba de abandonarlo por una prostituta. La historia, sin embargo, dista mucho de ser el "sobado melodrama del puto que se derrumba en llanto" (p. 33) por el abandono de su amante. Por el contrario, *Las púberes canéforas* trasciende la anécdota amorosa y adquiere implicaciones sociales.[19]

La novela se inscribe en un contexto urbano, violento, donde convergen una gama de homosexuales de todas las capas sociales. El resultado es una multiplicidad de estilos de vida y visiones de la homo-sexualidad destacándose la actitud de comercializar con el sexo tal y como lo ejemplifica Felipe.

A diferencia de Octavio, Felipe se dedica de lleno y abiertamente a la prostitución masculina. Es significativo cómo a pesar de su prolífica actividad homoerótica el personaje no se considera homosexual. Esto es así

porque Felipe se beneficia de los patrones sociales que le aplican el estigma
de homosexual al individuo que desempeña el papel pasivo. Como ha
señalado acertadamente Octavio Paz, la sociedad mexicana condona al
individuo que ejerce el papel activo en los actos homosexuales y le permite
llevar una vida heterosexual libre de prejuicios.[20] Felipe puede coquetear
con Guillermo y con Analía, su novia, al mismo tiempo sin que se cuestione
su virilidad. Es justamente cuando un individuo insinúa penetrarlo al
conocer su oficio que se pone en entredicho su heterosexualidad.

Otra estrategia para enfrentar la homosexualidad, aun entre aquéllos
con una intensa actividad homoerótica, es ocultarla a la familia, los amigos
y la sociedad heterosexual en general. Este es el caso del personaje
identificado únicamente por la inicial de su primer nombre, A., en la novela
de Luis Zapata *En jirones*. Nos encontramos con una oposición binaria:
Sebastián, el homosexual liberado versus A., empeñado en ocultar, inclusive
negar, su orientación sexual. "Mientras no tenga que nombrar sus actos,
decir sus sentimientos, no hay problema: su homosexualidad no existe"[21]
anota Sebastián en el cuaderno donde registra con detalle los primeros
diecinueve días de su relación con A.

A. encierra la personalidad conflictiva, ambivalente, de los individuos
que se debaten entre sus "inclinaciones" y las presiones de la sociedad. Las
contradicciones del personaje se evidencian al desaparecer cuando la
relación con Sebastián parece estable para anunciar a su regreso que va a
casarse. El personaje justifica su matrimonio con las siguientes palabras:
"quería sentirse en paz consigo mismo, con su familia; quería reducir las
presiones que estaban minando su salud y su tranquilidad" (pp. 165-166).

La vida heterosexual, sin embargo, no trae la paz deseada. Por el
contrario, A. regresa a Sebastián con más deseo, con más vehemencia,
dando inicio a una relación regida por el sexo. El título *En jirones* consigna
la auto-destrucción de la pareja, la relación marcada por el deterioro físico
y emocional de Sebastián y la desesperación de A. quien, además de
enfrentarse a su homosexualidad, ahora lleva una vida doble que lo obliga a
decir: "me está llevando la chingada" (p. 268).

En jirones es la crónica de una pasión tan obsesiva que se torna
destructiva. El propio Zapata ha indicado que al escribirla tuvo la intención
de establecer un paralelo entre una pasión intensa y el proceso de
enloquecimiento.[22] No toda la locura proviene del enamoramiento, gran
parte de la misma es el resultado de la lucha entre permanecer en el closet
o enfrentarse a los obstáculos y prejuicios de la sociedad.

Estas tres novelas transgreden la moral dominante al reflexionar
sobre el amor homoerótico desde una perspectiva íntima. Otros textos, en
cambio, van a abordar la misma problemática adoptando una actitud
irreverente, subvirtiendo y burlándose de los propios estigmas y de los

convencionalismos. La parodia y la sátira van a constituir la punta de lanza para reivindicar el amor que ahora se atreve a decir su nombre.

En *Melodrama* (1983), Luis Zapata utiliza los elementos arquetípicos del género que encumbró al cine mexicano de los años 40 y 50 para crear la primera novela rosa de tema homosexual en la narrativa mexicana.[23] Como corresponde a este género la anécdota es simple; la tragedia se inicia cuando una madre escucha que su hijo emplea el género femenino al referirse a si mismo: "es que estoy muy desvelada, manita"[24] le dice a su interlocutor. La madre sospecha que el hijo es homosexual y contrata a un detective para que lo persiga. El detective, que es casado, termina abandonando mujer e hijos para establecer una relación con el joven perseguido.

En *Melodrama* hay una ruptura con los esquemas tradicionales del género.[25] La pareja de enamorados se compone de dos hombres que no ocultan su relación. "Soy homosexual, que es muy distinto, y estoy enamorado" (p. 91) le dice el joven a su madre. La oposición viene por parte de la madre quien lejos de ser la mujer sufrida o abnegada del melodrama es una señora patética. La esposa engañada pierde a su marido en brazos de otro hombre, pero se consuela con el compadre quien la alienta a chantajear a la madre adinerada de su "rival". La subversión de los papeles arquetípicos la completa el padre del joven homosexual quien, para consternación de su mujer, es el único personaje heterosexual que declara: "La homosexualidad puede ser una elección" (p. 81).

En un final nada convencional, el joven, luego de robarle dinero y prendas a la madre, regresa con su amante y es recibido con beneplácito por sus padres que invitan a los enamorados a la cena de Nochebuena con lo que la pareja homosexual se ve finalmente integrada a la institución familiar.

Al igual que Zapata, Luis Montaño recurre a la parodia en *Brenda Berenice o el diario de una loca* (1985). A través de su diario, Gerardo Urbiñon Campos, alias Brenda Berenice, rescata al marginal por excelencia, al homosexual denominado "loca". El personaje subvierte los estigmas de tal suerte que la loca surge como una ser único, dotado de una sensibilidad especial. Una loca es, según su definición, "una poesía, una quimera, un sueño".[26]

La novela incorpora el gusto por lo superfluo y chabacano tan típico del "camp". Brenda Berenice recrea el romanticismo a ultranza de la novela rosa a lo Corin Tellado. Su mundo se caracteriza por recurrir a la teatralidad y la fantasía propia del traestí.

El extremo de la parodia se logra con la inversión gramatical, el empleo del argot homosexual, particularmente aquél que practica el travestí, y la invención de un vocabulario propio. Brenda Berenice se apropia de la lengua para establecer un distanciamiento entre el homosexual y el hombre heterosexual.[27] Así, un joto es "un hombre feliz" (p. 20), y un pervertido es "un hombre que sabe hacer el amor" (p. 20). En cambio, el heterosexual es un "hombre que reprime sus deseos homoeróticos" (p. 20) y el buga que ejerce la violencia contra el homosexual "una aberración de la naturaleza" (p. 20).

El macho, el buga, es objeto de burlas incontables. Brenda Berenice se refiere a su padre como "una perra", "una loba" (p. 111) que lo ataca cuando descubre su homosexualidad. Al respecto escribe: "no creo que pueda existir mayor ofensa para un macho que se jacta de serlo, que tener una hija como yo" (p. 106). La loca representa una agresión a la masculinidad por lo que el macho recurre muchas veces a la violencia. Brenda Berenice utiliza la sátira para condenar esta ira irracional y asociarla a la insatisfacción, a la represión sexual que oculta el machismo.

Una propuesta a la violencia, al rechazo y a la homofobia consiste en contemplar la idea de alejarse del mundo tal y como lo concibe Adonis García al final de su testimonio en *El vampiro de la colonia Roma*.[28] Este deseo llega a su máxima realización en *Utopía gay* (1983) de José Rafael Calva. Los protagonistas, Carlos y Adrián, deciden abandonar la Ciudad de México para hacer una casita en Baja California Sur frente al Mar de Cortés con el fin de "vivir como ermitaños del huerto y el trabajo de la tierra".[29] Paralelo a este retiro, está la idea de crear un espacio propio, un espacio aparte donde "la homosexualidad será el establishment" (p. 182).

La creación de esta arcadia obedece a un hecho más insólito: Adrián espera un hijo de Carlos con lo que la novela logra institucionalizar al homosexual por partida doble. Carlos y Adrián van a legitimar su relación con este hijo y a fundar una nueva institución familiar, "siempre unidos los tres hasta que tengamos que ayudar a Carlos Adrián a conseguirse un hombre que lo ame" (p. 181). Esta utopía que propone Calva, la total realización del amor entre dos hombres, constituye la amenaza más radical del texto. Como ha señalado Foucault lo que más perturba a la sociedad heterosexual, más que el propio acto sexual, es que las personas del mismo sexo comiencen a amarse.[30]

En un mundo que le niega al homosexual la capacidad de amar, *Utopía gay* reafirma el amor homoerótico concediéndole fuerza creativa y liberadora. A través de sus monólogos, Carlos y Adrián deconstruyen el mito, la "leyenda negra" (p. 55) que ha difundido la imagen de promiscuidad, concupiscencia, e inmoralidad en torno al homosexual. Carlos y Adrián rechazan el estereotipo, los papeles tradicionales impuestos por la sociedad-masculino/femenino, activo/pasivo-para proponer un modelo que se fundamenta en la igualdad: "Tú y yo somos maridos los dos y llevamos partes intercambiables" (p. 86).

Si hasta la publicación de *Utopía gay*, se percibe en el tema gay un dominio del hombre, tanto en la fase autorial como en la de sujeto narrativo, y el vehículo por excelencia es la novela, los años subsiguientes evidencian la diversificación del tema como lo atestigua la antología de cuentos compilada por Mario Muñoz. Junto a nombres conocidos como Jorge Arturo Ojeda, Luis González de Alba y el inevitable Luis Zapata, se destaca la presencia de escritoras: Inés Arredondo, Dolores Plaza, Ana Clavel. Estos cuentos abordan la homosexualidad desde diferentes épocas, clases y culturas.[31]

Con la incorporación de escritoras, el lesbianismo surge como tema literario válido. *Amora* (1989) de Rosamaría Roffiel, es la primera novela en abordar el homosexualismo femenino en la narrativa mexicana. Este cuadro confirma la vigencia de la narrativa homosexual en la literatura mexicana, una narrativa que ha ganado espacio y reconocimiento desde que aparece tímidamente en los años 60. Aunque todavía no logra su inscripción en el canon, ya es imposible mantenerla al margen. La aparición ininterrumpida de títulos, la mayoría a cargo de editoriales de prestigio como Grijalbo, Posada, Cal y Arena y Planeta, y el grupo de autores que abordan el tema homosexual indican que en las últimas tres décadas, el homosexual mexicano ha dejado de ser objeto de risa o condena para legitimar su presencia en la sociedad mexicana.

NOTAS

1.   Uno de los artículos más completos sobre estos acontecimientos es el que ofrece Miguel Capistrán, "Los auténticos 41", *Contenido* (febrero de 1974), 64-68.

2.   Eduardo A. Castrejón, *Los cuarenta y uno* (México: s.n., 1906), p. 165. Todas las citas posteriores corresponden a esta edición y se indicarán directamente en el texto.

3.   Sergio González Rodríguez ofrece un panorama de esta época en "Los amores del joven Novo", *Nexos* 165 (septiembre de 1991), 9.

4.   Donald L. Shaw, "Notes on the Presentation of Sexuality in the Modern Spanish-American Novel", *Bulletin of Hispanic Studies* 59:3 (1982), 275.

5.   Así lo sugiere Kessel L. Schwartz en "Homosexuality as a Theme in Contemporary Spanish American Novels", *Kentucky Romance Quarterly* 22:2 (1975), 247-257.

6.   Entre los críticos que coinciden en esta apreciación, cabe mencionar a Claudia Rodríguez-Schaefer, "The Power of the Subversive Imagination: Homosexual Utopian Discourses in Contemporary Mexican Literature", *Latin American Literary Review* 17:33 (January 1989), 32.

7.   Ignacio Trejos Fuentes, "La 'literatura homosexual': A propósito de *Utopía gay*", *Excelsior* (Sección Cultural), 31 de julio de 1983, p. 1.

8.   David W. Foster, *Gay and Lesbian Themes in Latin American Writing* (Austin: University of Texas Press, 1991), p. 58.

9.   Paolo Po, *41 o el muchacho que soñaba en fantasmas* (México: Costa-Amic, 1964), p. 27.

10. Miguel Barbachano Ponce, *El diario de José Toledo* (México: Premiá Editores, 1988), p. 118. La primera edición se publicó en 1964.

11. José Ceballos Maldonado, *Después de todo* (México: Premiá Editores, 1986), p. 195. Todas las citas posteriores corresponden a esta edición y se indicarán directamente en el texto. La primera edición se publicó en 1969.

12. Gonzalo Valdés Medellín, "*Después de todo*, de José Ceballos Maldonado, un clásico de la literatura gay mexicana", *Sábado* suplemento de *Unomásuno*, no. 601 (8 de abril de 1989), p. 6.

13. Las novelas de este período incluyen *Los inestables* (1968) de Alberto X. Teruel, *El desconocido* (1977) de Raúl Rodríguez Cetina, y *Muchacho solo* (1976) de Jorge Arturo Ojeda.

14. Esta actividad se celebra anualmente desde 1982 en el mes de junio y coincide con la celebración a nivel mundial del inicio del movimiento de liberación homosexual.

15. Luis Zapata, *El vampiro de la colonia Roma* (México: Editorial Grijalbo, 1979), p. 31.

16. Mario Muñoz, *De la onda gay: Doce cuentos mexicanos*, inédito, p. 11.

17. Jorge Arturo Ojeda, *Octavio* (México: Premiá Editores, 1982), p. 58.

18. José Joaquín Blanco, *Las púberes canéforas* (México: Cal y Arena, 1991), p. 77. Todas las citas posteriores corresponden a esta edición y se indicarán directamente en el texto.

19. Vicente Francisco Torres, "Gay Life: Las ¿qué?", *Sábado* no. 293 (11 de junio de 1983), 11.

20. Octavio Paz, *El laberinto de la soledad* (México: Fondo de Cultura Económica, 1987), p. 35.

21. Luis Zapata, *En jirones* (México: Grijalbo, 1985), p. 51. Todas las citas posteriores corresponden a esta edición y se indicarán directamete en el texto.

22. Reinhard Tiechmann, *De la onda en adelante: Conversaciones con 21 novelistas* (México: Editorial Posada, 1987), p. 366.

23. Luis Mario Schneider, "El tema homosexual en la nueva narrativa mexicana", *Casa del tiempo* (febrero 1985), p. 86. Esta apreciación se puede hacer extensiva a toda América Latina.

24. Luis Zapata, *Melodrama* (México: Editorial Posada, 1985), p. 19. Todas las citas posteriores corresponden a esta edición y se indicarán directamente en el texto.

25. José Luis Benavides, "Melodrama", *El Gallo Ilustrado* suplemento de *El Día* 1133 (11 de marzo de 1984), p. 15.

26. Luis Montaño, *Brenda Berenice o el diario de una loca* (México: Editorial Domés, 1985), p. 36. Todas las citas posteriores corresponden a esta edición y se indicarán directamente en el texto.

27. Timothy Compton, *Mexican Picaresque Narratives*, Diss., University of Kansas, 1989, pp. 197-198.

28. Adonis expresa el deseo de irse con marcianos gayos o que seres de otro planeta lo lleven a Marte.

29. José Rafael Calva, *Utopía gay* (México: Editorial Oasis, 1983), p. 50. Todas las citas posteriores corresponden a esta edición y se indicarán directamente en el texto.

30. René de Ceccaty, "Un modo de vida: Conversación con Michel Foucault", *La Jornada Semanal* 65 (15 de diciembre de 1985), p. 7.

31. Muñoz, *De la onda gay*, p. 14.

11. Teses acadêmicas sobre a homossexualidade no Brasil

Luiz Mott
Sonia T. D. G. Silva

Data de 1853 a primeira publicação acadêmica brasileira onde faz-se referência à homossexualidade masculina —condenada violentamente sob os eufemismos de *libertinagem* e *onanismo*. Apesar do étimo *homossexual* ter sido cunhado pela primeira vez em 1869 na Alemanha, pelo ativista-gay disfarçado de médico, Karol Maria Kertneby,[1] no Brasil, ainda no final do século XIX, os intelectuais preferiam o termo clássico *pederasta*, alguns poucos adotando o neologismo *andrófilo* e *uranista*. Salvo erro, somente em 1906 foi publicado pela primeira vez no português do Brasil o termo *homossexual*, na antológica obra *O homossexualismo: A libertinagem no Rio de Janeiro*,[2] de autoria de José Ricardo Pires de Almeida. A palavra *lésbia* (sic) precedeu em nosso país ao termo *homossexual*; já em 1894 o jurista Francisco José Viveiros de Castro escrevia "lésbia" como sinônimo de *tríbade*, no seu não menos famoso livro *Atentados ao pudor*.[3] Também são registrados os termos "*lésbica*" e "*lesbiana*".

Em nossa comunicação "A Homossexualidade no Brasil: Bibliografia", apresentada em 1985 no XXX Seminar on the Acquisition of Latin American Library Materials (SALALM), na Princeton University,[4] arrolamos 268 títulos, dentre os quais, 12 dissertações acadêmicas. Nos últimos anos, ampliamos para 38 as dissertações de Mestrado e Doutorado consagradas aos homossexuais do Brasil, incluindo três no século XIX. No século XX temos uma na década de 20, duas nos anos 30, duas nos anos 40, uma datada de 1959, cinco da década de 70, quatorze nos anos 80 e dez nos primeiros anos da década atual. Tais números evidenciam um interesse crescente na Universidade pelo estudo da homossexualidade, pois 2/3 destas dissertações concentram-se a partir dos anos 80.

O enfoque ideológico e teórico da questão homossexual demonstra igualmente salutar evolução, pois deixa de ser tratada como vício abominável, patologia e desvio, para tornar-se variável neutra da sexualidade humana, estudada nos últimos anos como sub-cultura socialmente construída. Enquanto as teses mais antigas abordavam a *pederastia* sobretudo em seus aspectos médico-legais, os trabalhos

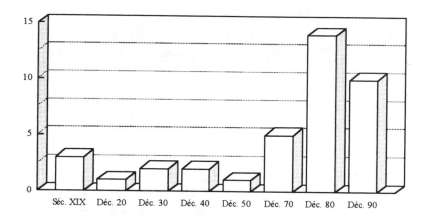

Distribuição das teses no tempo

contemporâneos enquadram-se sobretudo na área das ciências humanas, totalizando 27 monografias distribuídas nas seguintes sub-áreas: Antropologia, Sociologia, História, Psicologia, Letras e Literatura, sendo 11 as teses na área da Medicina e Direito.

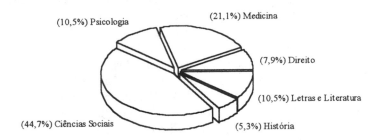

Distribuição das teses por áreas do conhecimento

Dentre os temas abordados por estas 38 dissertações, apenas 4 são consagradas ao *lesbianismo*, predominando os estudos de diferentes aspectos da sub-cultura homossexual masculina: os "casos" homossexuais; o erotismo gay; a prostituição viril; a sub-cultura dos travestis; o movimento homossexual brasileiro; e o impacto na Aids na comunidade gay. São Paulo e Rio de Janeiro concentram cerca de 2/3 das dissertações acadêmicas, seguidos pela Bahia, Ceará, Rio Grande do Norte, Minas Gerais, Paraná, Santa Catarina e Rio Grande do Sul, acrescentado-se a estas, duas monografias defendidas nos Estados Unidos, uma na França e uma na Holanda. Quase 1/4 desta bibliografia chegou a ser impressa quer por editoras comerciais, quer pelas próprias instituições universitárias onde foram primeiramente defendidas, permanecendo as demais mimeografadas e disponíveis para consulta nas respectivas faculdades.

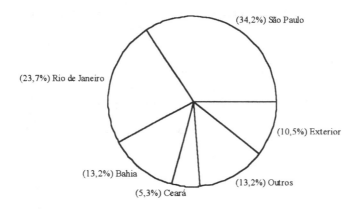

Distribuição das teses por áreas geográficas

Apesar do número ainda diminuto de teses consagradas à homossexualidade masculina e feminina no Brasil, no cômputo geral podemos ser otimistas, pois trata-se de uma área em franca expansão quantitativa e qualitativa, com maior volume de publicações do que os demais países da América Latina. E desde 1982, graça à iniciativa do autor deste trabalho, a Sociedade Brasileira para o Progresso da Ciência (SBPC) aprovou uma resolução que garante aos estudos e pesquisas sobre a Homossexualidade o mesmo status acadêmico das demais temáticas científicas, a saber: "Considerando a pequena produção científica no Brasil de pesquisas e trabalhos relativos à sexualidade humana em geral, e à homossexualidade em particular, diferentemente do que já acontece nos países mais desenvolvidos; considerando que os projetos de pesquisas sobre estes temas têm sido mal recebidos, discriminados e considerados irrelevantes ou faltas de interesse científico, apesar da inquestionável qualidade científica e relevância social; RESOLVE a SBPC: usar de todo o empenho, através de ofícios às Fundações, Institutos de Pesquisas e Orgãos Financiadores, para que sejam acolhidos com idêntica objetividade e sem discriminação os projetos que tratem de temas relacionados à sexualidade e à homossexualidade, incluíndo-se prêmios e estímulos aos projetos sobre esses temas."[5]

122   LUIZ MOTT / SONIA T. D. G. SILVA

Nossa esperança e objetivo ao divulgar tal bibliografia é despertar a curiosidade científica de novos pesquisadores a fim de que escolham a homossexualidade no Brasil como tema de suas futuras teses acadêmicas.

NOTAS

1. Wayne Dynes, ed., *Encyclopedia of Homosexuality* (New York, NY: Garland, 1990).

2. J. R. Pires de Almeida, *O homossexualismo: A libertinagem no Rio de Janeiro; estudo sobre as perversões e inversões do instinto genital* (Rio de Janeiro: Laemmert, 1906).

3. F. J. Viveiros de Castro, *Atentados ao pudor: Estudos sobre as aberrações do instinto sexual*, 2 ed. (Rio de Janeiro: Freitas Bastos, 1934).

4. Luiz Mott, "A Homossexualidade no Brasil: Bibliografia", in D. C. Hazen, ed., *Latin American Masses and Minorities: Their Images and Realities* (Madison, WI: SALALM Secretariat, 1985), v. 2, pp. 592-609.

5. "Os direitos dos homossexuais defendidos pelas associações científicas", in *Cadernos de texto do grupo gay da Bahia* (Salvador: Editora do GGB, 1990).

BIBLIOGRAFIA

Almeida, Sérgio Alves. "Michê". Dissertação de Mestrado em Psicologia Social, Pontifícia Universidade Católica de São Paulo, 1984. 220 p.

Aquino, Luís Otávio Rodrigues. "As derivas do desejo: Processo de construção, manutenção e manipulação de identidades lésbicas em um conjunto de mulheres de Porto Alegre, RS". Dissertação de Mestrado em Antropologia Social, Universidade Federal do Rio Grande do Sul, 1992. 311 p.

Bellini, Lígia. "A coisa obscura: Mulher, sodomia e Inquisição no Brasil Colonial". Dissertação de Mestrado em História, Universidade Federal da Bahia, 1989. [São Paulo: Brasiliense, 1989. 101 p.]

Bello da Motta, Antonio. "Homossexualismo em Medicina Legal". Tese de Concurso à Cátedra da Faculdade de Direito do Ceará, 1937. [Rio de Janeiro: Tipografia do Jornal do Commércio, 1937.]

Brito, Marinômio. "Dissertação sobre a libertinagem e os seus perigos relativamente ao físico e moral do homem". Tese de Doutorado em Medicina, Faculdade de Medicina da Bahia, 1853. [Salvador: Tipografia V.C.O. Chaves, 1853. 33 p.]

Daguer, Pedro J. "Transexualismo masculino". Tese de Mestrado em Psiquiatria, Universidade Federal do Rio de Janeiro, 1977.

Dantas, Antonio Ribeiro. "A representação da homossexualidade: A leitura da imprensa escrita". Dissertação de Mestrado em Ciências Sociais, Universidade Federal do Rio Grande do Norte, Natal, 1989. 210 p.

Endermann, Regina Maria. "Reis e rainhas do Desterro: Um estudo de caso". Tese de Mestrado em Ciências Sociais, Universidade Federal de Santa Catarina, Florianópolis, 1981.

Ferraz de Macedo, Francisco. "Da prostituição em geral e em particular em relação ao Rio de Janeiro". Tese de Doutorado, Faculdade de Medicina da Universidade do Rio de Janeiro, 1872. 115 p.

Grootendorst, Sapê. "Literatura gay no Brasil?: Dezoito escritores brasileiros falando da temática homo-erótica". Tese de Qualificação da Universidade de Utrecht, Holanda, set. 1993. 90 p.

Guimarães, Carmen Dora. "O Homossexual visto por entendidos". Dissertação de Mestrado em Antropologia Social, Museu Nacional da Universidade Federal do Rio de Janeiro, 1977.

Guimarães, Celeste Maria Baitelli Zenha. "Homossexualidade: Mitologias científicas". Tese de Doutorado em História, Universidade Estadual de Campinas, 9 maio 1994.

Klabin, Aracy A. L. "Aspectos jurídicos do transexualismo". Tese de Mestrado, Faculdade de Direito da Universidade de São Paulo, 1977. 53 p.

Jaime, Jorge. "Homossexualismo masculino". Tese de Medicina Legal, Universidade do Brasil, Rio de Janeiro, 1947. 105 p.

Leite, Rommel Mendes. "Acasos, casos e ocasos: O relacionamento homossexual masculino e a ideologia sexual dominante". Tese de Mestrado em Sociologia, Universidade Federal do Ceará, Fortaleza, 1986.

————. "Les jeux et les masques: L'ambigusexualité dans la région Nordeste du Brésil". Dissertação-Diploma d'Etudes Approfondies, Université René Descartes, Sorbonne, Paris. 1987.

Lobert, Rosemary. "A palavra mágica: Uma resposta difícil de perguntar". Tese de Mestrado em Antropologia, Universidade Estadual de Campinas, 1979.

Lutz, Adolfo G. "Auto-acusação, homossexualismo e transvestismo: Contribuição à prática da criminologia psicoanalítica". Tese de Doutorado, Faculdade Nacional de Medicina da Universidade do Brasil, Rio de Janeiro, 1939.

Macrae, Edward J. B. "A construção da igualdade, identidade sexual e política no Brasil da abertura". Tese de Doutorado em Antropologia, Universidade de São Paulo, 1986. [Campinas: Editora UNICAMP, 1990. 321 p.]

Nunes, Viriato. "As perversões sexuais em medicina legal". Tese Inaugural, Faculdade de Direito de São Paulo, 1928.

Oliveira, Neuza Maria. "As Monas da Casa Amarela: Os travestis no espelho da mulher". Dissertação de Mestrado em Ciências Sociais, Universidade Federal da Bahia, 1986. 229 p.

Pacheco e Silva, A.C. "As origens psicológicas da homossexualidade masculina". Tese de Doutoramento em Neurologia, Universidade de São Paulo, 1971. 165 p.

Parker, Richard. "Bodies, Pleasures and Passions: Sexual Culture in Contemporary Brazil". Tese de Doutorado em Antropologia, Universidade da California, Berkeley; Boston: Beacon, 1991. Tradução em Português: "Corpos, prazeres e paixões: A cultura sexual no Brasil contemporâneo". Rio de Janeiro: Bestseller, 1991. 295 p.

Pereira, Ricardo Calheiro. "O desperdício do sêmen: Um estudo do erotismo entre rapazes". Dissertação de Mestrado em Ciências Sociais, Universidade Federal da Bahia, 1988. 262 p.

Perlongher, Nestor. "O negócio do michê: A prostituição viril". Tese de Mestrado em Antropologia Social, Universidade Estadual de Campinas, 1986. [São Paulo, Brasiliense, 1987. 275 p.]

Pinheiro, Domingos Firmino. "O androfilismo". Tese de Doutoramento, Faculdade de Medicina da Bahia, 1898. 216 p.

Portinari, Denise. "O discurso da homossexualidade feminina". Tese de Mestrado em Psicologia Clínica, Pontifícia Universidade Católica do Rio de Janeiro, 1989. [São Paulo, Brasiliense, 1989. 127 p.]

Queiroz, Luiz Gonzaga Morando. "Transgressões e transviados: A representação do homossexual na literatura brasileira do século XIX (1870-1900)". Mestrado em Letras, Universidade Federal de Minas Gerais, 1993.

Sell, Tereza Adada. "Identidade homossexual e normas sociais: Histórias de vida". Tese de Mestrado em Psicologia, Universidade de São Paulo, 1987. [Florianópolis, Editora da Universidade Federal de Santa Catarina, 1987. 182 p.]

Silva, José Fábio Barbosa. "Aspectos sociológicos do homossexualismo em São Paulo". Tese de Mestrado, Escola de Sociologia e Política de São Paulo, 1959. [*Sociologia* (São Paulo) 21:4 (outubro 1959).]

Silva, Hélio R. S. "O travesti: A invenção do feminismo". Tese de Mestrado em Antropologia Social, Museu Nacional da Universidade Federal do Rio de Janeiro, 1989. [Rio de Janeiro: Edit. Relume Dumará-ISER, 1993. 176 p.]

Silva, Lindinalva Laurindo. "AIDS e homossexualidade em São Paulo". Dissertação de Mestrado em Antropologia, Pontifícia Universidade Católica de São Paulo, 1986. 204 p.

Souza, Pedro de. "Confidências da carne: O público e o privado na enunciação da sexualidade". Tese de Doutorado em Literatura, Universidade Estadual de Campinas, dezembro 1993.

Stuckelmam, Joey. "Intercourse, Discourse and Identity: A Study of the Formation of Homosexual Identities under Authoritarianism in Argentina and Brazil". Senior Thesis, Latin American Studies, University of California, Santa Cruz, Spring 1992. 63 p.

Teixeira, Maria Lina Leão. "Transas de um povo de santo: Um estudo sobre as identidades sexuais". Dissertação de Mestrado em Sociologia, Universidade Federal do Rio de Janeiro, 1986.

Terto Junior, Veriano. "No escurinho do cinema: Sociabilidade orgiástica nas tardes cariocas". Dissertação de Mestrado em Psicologia, Pontifícia Universidade Católica do Rio de Janeiro, 1989.

Venturelli, Paulo Cesar. "A carne embriagada: Uma leitura em torno de João Silvério Trevisan". Dissertação de Mestrado em Letras, Universidade Federal do Paraná, Curitiba, 1993. 22 p.

Vieira Filho, Joaquim. "Contribuição para o estudo clínico e médico legal do hermafroditismo". Tese de Livre-Docência, Escola Paulista de Medicina, São Paulo, 1941.

12. Literature of the Contemporary Brazilian Gay Community: A Review

Robert Howes

This paper is an updating of a paper I originally wrote for SALALM XXX in 1985 on the literature of the gay community in Latin America, this time referring only to Brazil.[1] Here I divide the literature into nonfiction and fiction. In the intervening years, three major worldwide phenomena have affected the literature of the Brazilian gay community. One is the development of gay studies as a serious academic discipline. Another is the spread of literary theories of deconstruction and postmodernism whose ideas of transgression and cultural diversity have had a particular resonance for gay writers and readers. Permeating everything is the impact of the AIDS epidemic which, in Brazil as in many other countries, has taken a disproportionately high toll among gay men.

Nonfiction

This section considers research-based works and polemical and informational publications issued by members of the gay movement. Whereas in the past, academic works dealing with homosexuality were mainly written by doctors, psychiatrists, and the proponents of forensic medicine, the major players now are anthropologists, sociologists, and historians. Some cover the whole range of sexuality. A notable example is the American anthropologist Richard G. Parker, whose *Bodies, Pleasures and Passions: Sexual Culture in Contemporary Brazil* analyzes the structure of the sexual universe and the ideology of the erotic in Brazil, with its emphasis on bodies and pleasures, and the interrelated, sometimes contradictory, discourses of sexuality with their formal rules and delight in transgression. The book is a tour de force, with its emphasis on the social origins and diversity of Brazilian sexual experience. The main shortcoming is that while Parker manages to recreate the entire galaxy of Brazilian sexual culture, he fails to draw out those elements which make it unique. He also has written extensively on the relationship between sexual culture

AUTHOR'S NOTE: I should particularly like to thank João Antônio Sousa de Mascarenhas and Luiz Mott for their help over the years in bringing much of this material to my attention.

and AIDS prevention. This book helps to set present-day Brazilian homosexual experience in its wider context.

Under the influence of the writings of Michel Foucault, many writers have looked to the past and adopted a historical approach to the changes in the interpretation of the social meaning of homosexuality. Brazilian historians have a rich source of documents in the archives of the Holy Office or Inquisition, which have survived from colonial times in Lisbon. Ronaldo Vainfas's monograph *Trópico dos pecados: moral, sexualidade e Inquisição no Brasil* uses this source to analyze the sexual morality of colonial Brazil, covering marriage, concubinage, and extramarital sexual relations as well as the *nefando* or sodomy. Male sodomy was the most frequent offense after Judaizing, with particular attention being paid to incorrigible sodomites, who would probably nowadays be identified as confirmed homosexuals. In defense of the Inquisition, Vainfas notes that its procedures were more scrupulous and its punishments less cruel than those of contemporary secular legal institutions or some Protestant churches, though this does not seem to have diminished the fear of its victims. Its bureaucratic methods have left us, however, a detailed insight into the thought processes of the past. Vainfas disagrees with Gilberto Freyre's picture of total sexual license, concluding that there were both popular and religious norms of sexual morality, although less rigidly enforced than in Europe.

Confessions and denunciations to the Inquisition during its visitation of Bahia and Pernambuco in 1592 are the subject of Ligia Bellini's *A coisa obscura: mulher, sodomia e Inquisição no Brasil colonial*. Ronaldo Vainfas has also edited a collection of historical papers entitled *História e sexualidade no Brasil*, which covers the whole range of sexuality from religious sexual morality through marriage and illegitimacy to prostitution in the nineteenth century.

The Brazilian scholar who has concentrated particularly on those accused by the Inquisition of homosexual behavior is the anthropologist and president of the Grupo Gay da Bahia, Luiz Mott. Mott contributed a paper on slavery and homosexuality, "Escravidão e homossexualidade", to Vainfas's *Historia e sexualidade no Brasil* mentioned above. More papers by Mott on episodes of gay history based on research in the archives of the Inquisition and other aspects of sexuality in colonial Brazil are collected in his *Escravidão, homossexualidade e demonologia* and *O sexo proibido: virgens, gays e escravos nas garras da Inquisição*.

Another source for analyzing the mental pictures of the past is the confessional or confessor's manual. These works, which were a popular literary genre in the sixteenth and seventeenth centuries, detailed the sexual misdemeanors that had to be confessed in order to obtain absolution. The light they throw on religious and popular concepts of marriage, the family, and illicit sexual relations has been analyzed by Angela Mendes de Almeida in *O gosto do pecado: casamento e sexualidade nos manuais de confessores dos séculos XVI e XVII*, which includes a short section on sodomy and masturbation. Although based mainly on European sources, there is a chapter on Brazil.

By the nineteenth century, the main problem was considered to be prostitution, whose links to the spread of syphilis attracted the attention of the increasingly science-based medical profession. Besides a number of works which deal solely with female prostitution, Luiz Carlos Soares's *Rameiras, ilhoas, polacas . . .: a prostituição no Rio de Janeiro do seculo XIX* has a chapter on homosexuality and male prostitution, which is largely based on the works of doctors Francisco Ferraz de Macedo, *Da prostituição em geral*, 1872, and José Ricardo Pires de Almeida, *Homossexualismo (a libertinagem no Rio de Janeiro)*, 1906, together with Adolfo Caminha's novel *Bom-Crioulo*, 1895.[2]

Coming up to the present day, the Argentinian anthropologist Nestor Perlongher describes the different categories, life stories, and self-images of the male hustlers in the center of São Paulo in *O negócio do michê: prostituição viril em São Paulo*. Also based on fieldwork, although the results are less well organized, is the sympathetic portrait of the transvestite prostitutes of Rio's Lapa district by an anthropologist attached to the Museu Nacional, Hélio R. S. Silva, in his *Travesti: a invenção do feminino*. Travestis have a notable place in popular culture as well as the sexual world, and it notable that Adir Sodré's explicit portrait of the transvestite Roberta Close was included in the exhibition of Brazilian art, *Modernidade*, held in Paris in 1987–1988.[3]

A more traditional area of anthropological interest is described in Peter Fry's article "Male Homosexuality and Spirit Possession in Brazil," which analyzes the role of the *bicha* in Afro-Brazilian cults in Belém do Pará. On the other hand, *O pecado de Adão: Crimes homossexuais no eixo Rio–São Paulo* is a work by two journalists, Márcio Venciguerra and Maurício Maia, which attributes a spate of murders of homosexuals to hustlers who wanted to rob their customers rather than to a politically motivated death squad.

The above works refer mainly to male homosexuals and transvestites. The most comprehensive work on female homosexuality is Luiz R. B. Mott's *O lesbianismo no Brasil*. Mott's work ranges widely over historical references to lesbianism, lesbian characters in Brazilian literature (mostly written by male authors), and the present-day situation of lesbians in Brazil, including social life, the lesbian movement and scene, lesbian singers, characters in *telenovelas* and advertisements, lesbians in popular music, the cinema, the Church and Afro-Brazilian religions, lesbian involvement in crimes, and lesbian role-playing. Mott stresses his role as an out gay activist and his solidarity with lesbians, despite being a man, and notes that he has only referred by name to contemporary lesbians who have publicly identified themselves as such. There is no bibliography, but the footnotes and references in the text are a valuable bibliographic source.

Lesbian and Gay Movement

The Brazilian gay movement enjoyed a rapid rise in the late 1970s in the days of "Abertura," inspired by the foundation of the first regular gay newspaper *Lampião*. Once the initial euphoria had passed, however, and *Lampião* had ceased publication following internal dissension, the number of groups declined dramatically. The movement is now enjoying a renaissance, and by early 1994 there were forty-four lesbian and gay groups in Brazil.

A general view of gay life in Brazil written from the perspective of a gay activist is João Silvério Trevisan's exuberant *Perverts in Paradise*, which also appeared in Portuguese as *Devassos no paraíso*. Academic books are more soberly written. Teresa Adada Sell's *Identidade homossexual e normas sociais (histórias de vida)* bases an analysis of the question of homosexual identity on a series of interviews with gay men. Edward Macrae's account of the history of the Somos gay liberation group in São Paulo in the late 1970s, *A construção da igualdade*, is based on a doctoral thesis. A recent master's thesis analyzing the development of a gay group, this time in Rio de Janeiro, is Cristina Luci Câmara da Silva's *Triângulo Rosa: a busca pela cidadania dos "homossexuais"*.

The Grupo Gay da Bahia or GGB produced a commemorative *Textos do Grupo Gay da Bahia: em comemoração ao 10.o aniversário, Fundação do GGB: 28 de Fevereiro de 1980*, photocopied from typescript to mark its ten years of activism. Of more immediately practical interest is the visitor's guide to gay Salvador, *Guia gay da Bahia: roteiro turístico & cultural dos locais, datas & assuntos de maior interesse na Bahia para gays, lésbicas, & etc.*, also published by the Grupo Gay da Bahia.

The most striking and professionally produced of the gay serial publications is *Nós por exemplo*, published in Rio de Janeiro, containing articles, letters, news items, lists of gay groups, and AIDS help facilities, illustrated with a sophisticated layout and tasteful black-and-white nude photographs. The Grupo Gay da Bahia continues to publish its *Boletim do GGB* at intermittent intervals in a mimeographed or xeroxed format. The list of murdered gays which it regularly features is an important antidote to the image of Brazil as an uninhibited sexual paradise. Other gay groups that produce serials from time to time include Triângulo Rosa in Rio de Janeiro, which produced a *Boletim informativo* in the late 1980s; Lambda, Movimento pela Livre Orientação Sexual in São Paulo which also produced a *Boletim informativo* in 1988; Atobá, Movimento de Emancipação Homossexual in Rio which was producing *O Caso* in tabloid format in 1992; Dignidade, Grupo de Conscientização e Emancipação Homossexual in Curitiba, Paraná, which issues the *Folha de Parreira: jornal* and, in English, *News from Brazil*; and the Comunidade Fratriarcal in Natal, Rio Grande do Norte, which is producing a journal xeroxed from typescript entitled *O Grito*. Recent publications are *Journal des Amis*, published by Les Amis Club in São Paulo, *Ent&*, and *SuiGeneris*, a new glossy consumerist magazine; the latter two are published in Rio de Janeiro.

AIDS

Brazil has been badly hit by the AIDS epidemic. The two authors who have written most widely on the social and cultural implications of AIDS are Herbert Daniel and Richard Parker. Herbert Daniel has described his life as a left-wing guerrilla in the late 1960s and early 1970s and the repercussions of his coming out as a gay man in his autobiographical *Passagem para o próximo sonho*. His *Vida antes da morte*, with text in Portuguese and English, written shortly after he discovered that he had AIDS, is a courageous and moving affirmation of his determination to make the most of life. A number of papers written by Daniel and Parker separately and jointly are collected in two works, *AIDS: a terceira epidemia* and *Sexuality, Politics and AIDS in Brazil*. The latter has a bibliography which includes more strictly medical articles discussing AIDS in Brazil.

The Grupo Gay da Bahia has waged a long campaign to promote AIDS awareness and prevention by distributing leaflets and condoms, which has resulted in its official recognition as a body of public utility. There are a number of AIDS prevention groups, referred to as GAPA or Grupo de Apoio à Prevenção a Aids, which were publishing a bimonthly *Previna-se* in 1990. *Nós por exemplo* also carries a strong AIDS awareness message.

Fiction

Homosexuality as a theme in Brazilian literature dates back to the naturalists Aluiso Azevedo in his *O cortiço* of 1890 and Adolfo Caminha with his celebrated *Bom Crioulo* of 1895. The second main wave of books in which writers dealt openly with homosexual subject matter started in the 1960s, with writers such as Walmir Ayala, Gasparino Damata, and Darcy Penteado. These writers have all died in the last ten years, and a new generation of writers has now come to the fore.

The study of gay writing has flourished worldwide in recent years under the influence of theorists such as Barthes, Derrida, Foucault, and

Lacan and the later generation of gay scholars who have followed them, developing the critical theories of deconstruction, postmodernism, and, now, queer theory. This has been reflected in Brazil by a number of works that analyze gay writings and discourse. Jurandir Freire Costa's *A inocência e o vício: estudos sobre o homoerotismo* is concerned almost exclusively with the analysis of foreign writers, especially André Gide and Marcel Proust, and the impact of AIDS on the notion of gay identity. Denise B. Portinari's *O discurso da homossexualidade feminina*, as the title states, is a mainly theoretical work dealing with the discourses of lesbianism and relies heavily on foreign sources. Paulo Hecker Filho, a prolific writer who in 1951 published an interesting novella about adolescent gay passions in a boarding school, *O internato*, has collected his critical writings and reviews of gay works in *Um tema crucial*, subtitled on the cover *Aspetos do homossexualismo na literatura*. This again deals mainly with foreign writers but also includes reviews of works by Gasparino Damata (*Os solteirões*), Silviano Santiago (*Nas malhas da letra*), Darcy Penteado (*A meta*), and João Guimarães Rosa (*Grande sertão: veredas*). A final article entitled "Que é o homossexualismo" argues in a downbeat way that homosexuality should be tolerated but not accepted as the proponents of gay liberation demand.

Among works of literary history, we should mention particularly Gentil Luiz de Faria's *A presença de Oscar Wilde na "Belle Époque" literária brasileira*, which deals with the influence in Brazil of the writer who has become the symbol of the international gay movement, though in this case Faria concentrates more on the concept of decadentism. General works about gay life in Brazil which include significant references to literary works are João Silverio Trevisan's *Perverts in Paradise* and Luiz Mott's *O lesbianismo no Brasil*.

Foreign scholars have also written in depth about homosexuality in Brazilian literature. David William Foster's *Gay and Lesbian Themes in Latin American Writing* analyzes the following Brazilian works: Adolfo Caminha's *Bom Crioulo*, Aguinaldo Silva's *No país das sombras* and *Primeira carta aos andróginos*, Darcy Penteado's *Nivaldo e Jerônimo*, Marcia Denser's story "Ladies First," and Cassandra Rios's *A borboleta branca*. Professor Foster's book provides an overview of the themes, theories, and concerns of Latin American gay literature covering both Brazilian and Spanish American writers, and gay men and lesbians. Published by the University of Texas Press, it has brought Latin American gay literature into the mainstream of academic publishing and concerns. Foster's forthcoming *Latin American Gay Literature: A Biographical and Critical Sourcebook* includes articles on many Brazilian writers.

The most complete guide to contemporary Brazilian gay writers is a recent thesis by a Dutch student, Sape Grootendorst, *Literatura gay no Brasil? Dezoito escritores brasileiros falando da temática homoerótica*, presented to the Portuguese Department of the University of Utrecht in September 1993. Grootendorst's thesis is based on interviews with gay writers in which he tries to establish whether there is such a thing as gay literature in Brazil. Generally, the writers reject the idea, fearing ghettoization. The writers interviewed were Caio Fernando Abreu, Amylton de Almeida, Manoel Amorim, Antônio Bivar, Gilmar de Carvalho, Nelson Carvalho, Marcelo Costa, Fernando Gabeira, Getúlio Grigoletto, José Honório, Francisco Caetano Lopes Júnior, Geraldo Markan Ferreira, Valdo Motta, Jomard Muniz de Britto, João Gilberto Noll, Silviano Santiago, Aguinaldo Silva, and João Silvério Trevisan. The list includes not only established writers living in Rio and São Paulo but also, interestingly, much lesser known writers living in the provinces whose ambit is purely local. Although the thesis is based mainly on interviews rather than textual analysis, there is an extremely useful bibliography and one hopes that this thesis will soon be published.

Grootendorst makes a distinction between high and low literature, noting the gay writer's desire not to be associated with pornography. Another distinction worth making is between popular and intellectual literature. Of the writers listed above, probably the one who is best known nationally is Aguinaldo Silva, who is the author of a number of highly successful *telenovelas* broadcast by the Rede Globo, and several police novels, drawing on his experience as a newspaper reporter. Silva has a background in political and gay activism, having been the principal editor of the gay newspaper *Lampião* in the late 1970s, a background that he draws on heavily in the autobiographical novel *Lábios que beijei: o romance da Lapa*. In this book, which itself is a reworking of an earlier collection of chronicles entitled *Memórias da guerra*, the narrator recounts his traumatic relationship with a young petty criminal, O Alemão, during the period 1968–1970 when he lived in the old bohemian district of Lapa in Rio, as it was being demolished to make way for a grandiose urban redevelopment scheme. The novel includes descriptions of various aspects of the gay milieu in the city at that time and the effects of the repression unleashed by the military regime. The narrator is completely open and matter of fact about his homosexuality but notes the patronizing attitude of other political prisoners while he was imprisoned in the Ilha das Flores. From this he specifically concludes that the only way to be free in a capitalist society is to have money. Despite a weak attempt at a bit of magical realism with a flying *bicha*, the novel relies on straightforward realistic narrative.

A writer who has incorporated homosexual themes into writing with a clear intellectual and theoretical concern is João Silvério Trevisan. Trevisan has previously published a collection of stories, some with gay content, *Testamento de Jonatas deixado a David*, and a notable account of adolescent love and budding male sexuality set in a seminary in the novel *Em nome do desejo*. His *Vagas notícias de Melinha Marchiotti* is a consciously literary work comprising a mixture of experimental novel and autobiography. The narrator describes his attempts to write a novel about the fictional character of the title against the background of his passionate love affair with a man named Pepo. Intensely written pieces of prose contain explicit descriptions of gay sexual activities, parts of the body and bodily functions, fantasies of homosexual desire, and the narrator's physical and emotional love for Pepo. In deliberate contrast to this, there are frequent erudite allusions to literary authors and themes, literary critical theory, and the cinema. The two come together when a poetic description of a visit to a sauna ends with the sentence, "Enfim, o escritor transgredia [At last, the writer was transgressing]."[4]

Herbert Daniel also makes use of sophisticated wordplay in his attempt to come to terms with AIDS in *Vida antes da morte*. Daniel is clearly aware of the political dimension of AIDS, and his involvement in radical politics and the guerrilla movement as well as in sexual politics forms the basis of two earlier works, the autobiographical *Passagem para o próximo sonho: um possível romance autocrítico* and *Meu corpo daria um romance*. The latter is a mixture of autobiography, memoirs, personal reflections, and fiction structured in eleven parts and inspired by an incident on a bus in which he was objectified as a *bicha* by the other passengers. He reflects on his growing sexual awareness as an adolescent, promiscuity, active and passive roles, his relationship to other men and masculinity, his sense of otherness, his relationships with women, Brazilian attitudes toward homosexuality, especially during Carnaval, and love, passion, and long-term relationships. A later novel about gay life is his *Alegres e irresponsáveis abacaxis americanos: romance*.

Perhaps the major contemporary writer with an established reputation who deals with gay subjects is Caio Fernando Abreu. Scattered through his collections of short stories such as *Morangos mofados*, *O ovo apunhalado*, and *Os dragões não conhecem o paraíso* are stories with a gay theme, for example, "Sargento Garcia," where the narrator recounts his rough initiation by an Army sergeant, "Natureza viva," recounting voluptuously the dilemma of whether to tell another man of his love, "Visita," where the narrator is filled with nostalgia for a dead friend, and "Linda, uma história horrível," a restrained, understated narrative describing a gay man with AIDS returning home to his mother. *Triângulo das águas (noturnos)* includes a novela, "Pela noite," in which two middle class gay men with very different personalities and life stories begin a relationship. Abreu has also broached the topic of AIDS in the novel *Onde andará Dulce Veiga?*, a work based loosely on the detective novel and B movie genres in which the narrator discovers halfway through that he has AIDS. The narrator does not think of himself as gay, although he has had an affair with another man. The impact of AIDS is also underplayed, as is so much in Abreu's work. Some of Abreu's work has been translated, for example, *Os dragões não conhecem o paraíso* has been published in English as *Dragons*.

The above gives merely a taste of the increasing range and sophistication of contemporary Brazilian gay literature. Although the theoretical label may be disputed, there is much available material, both in serious literature and in the vast field of popular culture, which reflects the vitality and influence of the gay community in Brazil.

Postscript

In July 1994, the Coletivo de Lésbicas Feministas issued a report entitled *Lésbicas no Brasil: contribuição para avaliação da Década da Mulher, 1985/1995*. This gives a detailed account of the Brazilian lesbian movement over the last ten years, with lists of groups and their publications, a chronology of meetings and workshops, a review of public opinion, legislation, health aspects, violence, religion, and politics, and a list of current groups with their addresses.

The serial *Ent&* suspended publication on December 5, 1994 after publishing six issues (nos. 00 to 05).

NOTES

1. Robert Howes, "The Literature of Outsiders: The Literature of the Gay Community in Latin America," in Dan C. Hazen, ed., *Latin American Masses and Minorities: Their Images and Realities*, Papers of SALALM XXX, Princeton, New Jersey, June 19-23, 1985, 2 vols. (Madison, WI: SALALM, 1987), vol. 1, pp. 288-304; vol. 2, pp. 580-591.

2. Francisco Ferraz de Macedo, *Da prostituição em geral* (Rio de Janeiro, 1872); José Ricardo Pires de Almeida, *Homossexualismo (a libertinagem no Rio de Janeiro). Estudo sobre as perversões e inversões do instincto genital* (Rio de Janeiro, 1906); Adolfo Caminha, *Bom Crioulo* (Rio de Janeiro, 1895).

3. *Modernidade: art brésilien du 20.e siècle, Musée d'Art Moderne de la Ville de Paris, 10 décembre 1987–14 février 1988* (Paris: Association Française d'Action Artistique, 1987), pp. 296-297.

4. João Silvério Trevisan, *Vagas notícias de Melinha Marchiotti* (São Paulo: Global, 1984), p. 37.

BIBLIOGRAPHY

Nonfiction

Almeida, Angela Mendes de. *O gosto do pecado: casamento e sexualidade nos manuais de confessores dos séculos XVI e XVII*. Rio de Janeiro: Rocco, 1992.

Bellini, Ligia. *A coisa obscura: mulher, sodomia e Inquisição no Brasil colonial*. São Paulo: Editora Brasiliense, 1989.

Daniel, Herbert. *Passagem para o próximo sonho: um possível romance autocrítico*. Rio de Janeiro: Codecri, 1982.

————. *Vida antes da morte. Life Before Death*. Rio de Janeiro: Tipografia Jaboti, 1989.

Daniel, Herbert, and Richard Parker. *AIDS: a terceira epidemia. Ensaios e tentativas*. São Paulo: Iglu Editora, 1991.

————. *Sexuality, Politics and AIDS in Brazil. In Another World?* London: Falmer Press, 1993.

Fry, Peter. "Male Homosexuality and Spirit Possession in Brazil." In Evelyn Blackwood, ed., *The Many Faces of Homosexuality: Anthropological Approaches to Homosexual Behavior*. New York, London: Harrington Park Press, [1986?]. Pp. 137-153.

Grupo Gay da Bahia. *Textos do Grupo Gay da Bahia. Em comemoração ao 10.o aniversário, fundação do GGB: 28 de fevereiro de 1980*. Salvador: Editora Grupo Gay da Bahia, 1990.

Guia gay da Bahia. Roteiro turístico & cultural dos locais, datas & assuntos de maior interesse na Bahia para gays, lésbicas & etc. Salvador: Editora Grupo Gay da Bahia, 1993.

Machado, Luiz Carlos. *Descansa em paz, Oscar Wilde*. Rio de Janeiro: Editora Codecri, 1982.

Macrae, Edward. *A construção da igualdade: identidade sexual e política no Brasil da "Abertura"*. Campinas: Editora da Universidade Estadual de Campinas, 1990.

Mott, Luiz R. B. "Escravidão e homossexualidade". In Ronaldo Vainfas, org., *História e sexualidade no Brasil*. Rio de Janeiro: Graal, 1986. Pp. 19-40.

————. *Escravidão, homossexualidade e demonologia*. São Paulo: Icone Editora, 1988.

————. *O lesbianismo no Brasil*. Porto Alegre: Mercado Aberto, 1987.

————. *O sexo proibido: virgens, gays e escravos nas garras da Inquisição*. Campinas: Papirus Editora, [1989?].

Parker, Richard G. *Bodies, Pleasures, and Passions: Sexual Culture in Contemporary Brazil.* Boston, MA: Beacon Press, 1991.

————. *Corpos, prazeres e paixões: a cultura sexual no Brasil contemporâneo.* Tradução de Maria Therezinha M. Cavallari. São Paulo: Editora Best Seller, [1991/2?].

Perlongher, Nestor Osvaldo. *O negócio do michê: prostituição viril em São Paulo.* São Paulo: Editora Brasiliense, 1987.

Sell, Teresa Adada. *Identidade homossexual e normas sociais (histórias de vida).* Florianopolis: Editora da UFSC, 1987.

Silva, Cristina Luci Câmara da. *Triângulo Rosa: a busca pela cidadania dos "homossexuais."* Dissertação de Mestrado apresentada ao Mestrado em Sociologia do Instituto de Filosofia e Ciências Sociais da Universidade Federal do Rio de Janeiro, sob a orientação da Profa. Dra. Paola Cappellin Giuliani. Rio de Janeiro, 1993.

Silva, Hélio R. S. *Travesti: a invenção do feminino.* Rio de Janeiro: Relume-Dumará; ISER, 1993.

Soares, Luiz Carlos. *Prostitution in Nineteenth-Century Rio de Janeiro.* Occasional papers, 17. London: University of London, Institute of Latin American Studies, 1988.

————. *Rameiras, ilhoas, polacas . . . A prostituição no Rio de Janeiro do século XIX.* São Paulo: Editora Atica, 1992.

Trevisan, João Silvério. *Devassos no paraíso: a homossexualidade no Brasil, da colónia à atualidade.* 2 ed. [São Paulo]: Editora Max Limonad, 1986.

————. *Perverts in Paradise.* Trans. Martin Foreman. London: GMP, 1986.

Vainfas, Ronaldo, org. *História e sexualidade no Brasil.* Rio de Janeiro: Edições Graal, 1986.

————. *Trópico dos pecados: moral, sexualidade e Inquisição no Brasil.* Rio de Janeiro: Editora Campus, 1989.

Venciguerra, Marcio, and Mauricio Maia. *O pecado de Adão: crimes homossexuais no eixo Rio–São Paulo.* São Paulo: Icone Editora, 1988.

Serials

Boletim do Grupo Gay da Bahia. Grupo Gay da Bahia, Caixa Postal 2552, 40022-260, Salvador, BA.

Boletim informativo. Lambda, Movimento pela Livre Orientação Sexual, Caixa Postal 8692, 01051-970, São Paulo, S.P.

Boletim informativo. Triângulo Rosa, Rio de Janeiro, R.J. [suspended].

O Caso. Atobá—Movimento de Emancipação Homossexual, Rua Professor Carvalho de Melo, no. 471, Magalhães Bastos, 21735-110, Rio de Janeiro, R.J.

Ent&. 2AB Editora Ltda., Largo de São Francisco, 26/403, 20051-070, Rio de Janeiro, R.J.

Folha de Parreira: jornal. Dignidade—Grupo de Conscientização e Emancipação Homossexual, Caixa Postal 1095, 80001-970, Curitiba, PR.

O Grito. Comunidade Fratriarcal, Caixa Postal 346, 59001-970, Natal, RN.

Journal des Amis. Les Amis Club, Caixa Postal 9919, CEP 01065-970, São Paulo, S.P.

News from Brazil. Dignidade (see above under *Folha de Parreira*).

Nós por exemplo. Editora Leviatã Ltda., Rua Visconde de Pirajá, 127/201, Ipanema, 22410-001, Rio de Janeiro, R.J.

Previna-se. Grupo de Apoio à Prevenção a AIDS, Caixa Postal 04106, 01051, São Paulo, S.P.

SuiGeneris. Tribo Editora, Rua da Lapa, 120, Grupo 801, CEP 20021-180, Rio de Janeiro, R.J.; Caixa Postal 48031, CEP 20512-970, Rio de Janeiro, R.J.

[N.B. If requesting publications from a group, please remember to offer to pay or make a donation.]

Fiction

Abreu, Caio Fernando. *Os dragões não conhecem o paraíso.* São Paulo: Companhia das Letras, 1988.

———. *Dragons . . .* Trans. David Treece. London: Boulevard, 1990.

———. *Morangos mofados.* 4. ed. São Paulo: Editora Brasiliense, 1983.

———. *Onde andará Dulce Veiga? Um romance B.* São Paulo: Companhia das Letras, 1990.

———. *O ovo apunhalado.* 3. ed. revista. Rio de Janeiro: Salamandra Editora, 1984.

———. *Triângulo das águas: noturnos.* Rio de Janeiro: Editora Nova Fronteira, 1983.

Costa, Jurandir Freire. *A inocência e o vício: estudos sobre o homo-erotismo.* Rio de Janeiro: Relume-Dumará, 1992.

Daniel, Herbert. *Alegres e irresponsáveis abacaxis americanos: romance.* Rio de Janeiro: Espaço e Tempo, 1987.

———. *Meu corpo daria um romance: narrativa desarmada.* Rio de Janeiro: Editora Rocco, 1984.

Faria, Gentil Luiz de. *A presença de Oscar Wilde na "Belle Époque" literária brasileira*. São Paulo: Editora Pannartz, 1988.

Foster, David William. *Gay and Lesbian Themes in Latin American Writing*. Austin: University of Texas Press, 1991.

Grootendorst, Sape. "Literatura gay no Brasil? Dezoito escritores brasileiros falando da temática homoerótica." Utrecht, The Netherlands: Utrecht University, 1993. Tese de qualificação entregue ao Departamento de Português da Universidade de Utrecht.

Hecker Filho, Paulo. *Internato: novela*. [Porto Alegre?]: Edição Fronteira, 1951.

————. *Um tema crucial. [Aspetos do homossexualismo na literatura]*. Porto Alegre: Editora Sulina, 1989.

Lésbicas no Brasil: contribuição para avaliação da Década da Mulher, 1985/1995. São Paulo: Colectivo de Feministas Lésbicas, 1994.

Mautner, Jorge. *Sexo do crepúsculo*. São Paulo: Global Ground, 1983.

Portinari, Denise B. *O discurso da homossexualidade feminina*. São Paulo: Editora Brasiliense, 1989.

Silva, Aguinaldo. *Lábios que beijei: o romance da Lapa*. São Paulo: Editora Siciliano, 1992.

————. *Memórias da guerra*. Rio de Janeiro: Editora Record, 1986.

Trevisan, João Silvério. *Em nome do desejo: romance*. Rio de Janeiro: Editora Codecri, 1983.

————. *Testamento de Jonatás deixado a David*. São Paulo: Editora Brasiliense, 1976.

————. *Vagas notícias de Melinha Marchiotti*. São Paulo: Global Editora, 1984.

13. Homosexual Groups in Brazil: Ephemeral Material Acquired for Brazil's Popular Groups Collection on Microfilm

Carmen M. Muricy

This is a selective list of ephemeral material on Brazilian homosexual groups, acquired by the Library of Congress Office, Rio de Janeiro, and available through the *Brazil's Popular Groups Collection on Microfilm, 1966–1986*; Supplement 1987–1989; Supplement 1990–1992 (ongoing). The titles cited in this list, published in 1993–1994, will be included in the next supplements. It covers 16 pamphlets, 6 posters, and 14 serial titles, published from 1978 to 1994. It also includes material related to AIDS. Some titles are mimeographed and the serials are very irregular.

There are some 44 homosexual groups in Brazil today. They are difficult to contact. Most can be reached only through a post office box.

Pamphlets

ARCA. Rio de Janeiro: Instituto de Estudos da Religião—ISER. 2 p.

Declaração dos direitos fundamentais da pessoa portadora do vírus da AIDS. Porto Alegre: Rede Brasileira de Solidariedade, 1989. 2 p.

Dia Internacional do "Orgulho Gay". Aracaju: Grupo Dialogay de Sergipe, 1991. 4 p.

Dia Mundial da AIDS: Boletim Informativo. Brasília: Ministério da Saúde, 1989. 16 p.

Encontro Brasileiro de Homossexuais (5th, 1991, Recife). Recife: n.p., 1991. 32 p.

Encontro Brasileiro de Homossexuais (6th, 1992, Rio de Janeiro). Relatório Final. Rio de Janeiro: n.p., 1992. 27 p.

Encontro Regional Sul de Homossexuais (1st, 1993, Florianópolis). Relatório. Florianópolis: n.p., 1993. 13 p.

GGB: Sindicato dos gays. Salvador: Centro Baiano Anti-AIDS; Grupo Gay da Bahia—GGB, 1990. 1 leaf.

Grupo pela Vidda. Grupo pela Vidda. N.d. 2 p.

Guia dos serviços de assistência e orientação: AIDS. Rio de Janeiro: Instituto de Estudos da Religião—ISER; Apoio Religioso contra a AIDS—ARCA, 1993. 131 p.

Guia Gay da Bahia: Roteiro turístico e cultural dos locais, datas e assuntos de maior interesse na Bahia para gays, lésbicas & etc. 2 ed. Salvador: Grupo Gay da Bahia—GGB, 1993. 24 p.

Homossexual: Defenda-se da violência! Aracaju: Grupo Dialogay de Sergipe, n.d. 1 folded leaf.

Igrejas: AIDS. Rio de Janeiro: Instituto de Estudos da Religião—ISER; Apoio Religioso contra a AIDS–ARCA, Programa Protestantismo, 1989. 6 folded leaves.

Ousadia!: Projeto Mulher e AIDS. São Paulo: Coletivo Feminista Sexualidade e Saúde, 1992. 30 p.

Seminário de Ativismo Lésbico/Gay da Região Sul (1st, 1993, Curitiba). Relatório. Curitiba: Associação Sul Brasileira de Gays e Lésbicas—ASBRAGEL, 1993. 13 p.

Textos do Grupo Gay da Bahia. Salvador: Grupo Gay da Bahia—GGB, 1990. 106 p.

Posters

Carnaval 84: Oxum, dia 1-03; Gala Gay, dia 2-03; Coringa, dia 3-03; Diabo, dia 4-3. 1984. Col.

E na bunada, num vadinha? Se for, só com camisinha. Rio de Janeiro: Núcleo de Orientação em Saúde Social—NOSS, 1993. B&W: 56,5 x 39,8 cm.

Homossexuais: Quem cala sobre teu corpo consente na tua morte (Milton Nascimento) . . . / Roberto Moraes. Aracaju: Dialogay, n.d.

Não importa com quem. Rio de Janeiro: Grupo pela Vidda; São Paulo: Grupo pela Vidda, 1993. Col.: 64,0 x 46,0 cm.

Prevenção é não discriminação. São Paulo: Secretaria Municipal de Saúde, Programa de DST/AIDS. Col.: 43 x 31 cm.

Transe numa boa: Sexo é bom, não deixe a AIDS acabar com isso. São Paulo: Grupo de Apoio à Prevenção à AIDS—GAPA, [1987]. Col.

Serials

ABIA Boletim. Rio de Janeiro: Ação Brasileira Interdisciplinar de AIDS—ABIA.
6-7 (1989); special issue (1994).

Boletim do Grupo Gay da Bahia. Salvador: Grupo Gay da Bahia—GGB.
1-8:1-16 (1981–1988); 9:19 (1989); 10:21 (1990); 12:23 (1992); 13:27 (1993).

Boletim pela Vidda. Rio de Janeiro: Grupo pela Vidda—RJ.
18 (1994).

Caso, O. Rio de Janeiro: ATOBA—Movimento de Emancipação Homossexual.
0-1:1-5 (1991–1992).

ChanacomChana. São Paulo: Grupo Ação Lésbica Feminista—GALF.
10 (1986).

Deusa Terra. São Paulo: Deusa Terra.
1-2:1-2 (1991–1992).

Do Mesmo Sexo. São Paulo: Grupo de Homossexuais do Partido dos Trabalhadores.
1-2 (1993).

Dossiê/Grupo pela Vidda-RJ. Rio de Janeiro: Grupo pela Vidda-RJ.
2 (1992).

Folha de Parreira. Curitiba: Dignidade—Grupo de Conscientização e Emancipação Homossexual.
1-3:1-12, 14 (1992–1994).

GAPA-RJ Notícias. Rio de Janeiro: Grupo de Apoio e Prevenção à AIDS—GAPA/RJ.
1:1 (1989).

Informativo/Secretariado Latino-Americano de Grupos Homosexuales. Salvador: Secretariado Latino-Americano de Grupos Homosexuales.
1 (1984).

Lampião da Esquina. Rio de Janeiro: Esquina Editora de Livros, Jornais e Revistas.
1:1-4, 6, 8 (1978–1979); 2-3:13, 16-17, 19-34 (1979–1981).

Nós por Exemplo. Rio de Janeiro: Núcleo de Orientação em Saúde Social—NOSS.
1-3:1-12 (1991–1994).

Triângulo Rosa. Rio de Janeiro: Grupo de Defesa dos Direitos dos Homossexuais.
3:11, 13-15/16 (1988).

Um Outro Olhar. São Paulo: Rede de Informação Lésbica.
10, 12-15 (1990–1991).

14. Representation of the Prostitute in Latin American Narrative

Gloria de Alfaro
Yolanda Maloney

The prostitute is portrayed differently in Latin American literature than in other Western cultures. Although trends in the French novel supplied the patterns for much of Latin American fiction until the latter half of this century, the treatment of the prostitute diverged from the French model early on and has continued to evolve in a style unique to the region.

The prostitute in Latin American literature is more often portrayed realistically than in Europe, which might not be the contrast one would expect between Catholic countries and secular ones. All European literary traditions are represented in Latin American fiction (particularly the French, because from 1880 to 1920, Hispanic America embraced Modernism and, with it, French Parnassianism and Symbolism). However, overall, the latter is more pragmatic about prostitution than the symbolic and judgmental representations of the Europeans.

Western literature shows a "lust-and-disgust" ambivalence toward the prostitute; on the one hand reveling in the glamor and fascination of sexual attraction and, on the other, recoiling in revulsion toward animality and disease. Latin American literature views the prostitute more as a victim of circumstances or an unimportant fact of life, never going to the extremes of the French model that presents her as intensely erotic or the embodiment of corruption.

In some French novels like Zola's *Nana*, the whore is definitely the protagonist of her own story and, for a time, is almost frightening in her power over men, perhaps reflecting a broader fear of women in general. In Latin America, prostitutes do not have such a hold over the imagination because they are more dismissed than feared, largely seen as powerless. Ibero-America's more matter-of-fact practical view of the whore looks at prostitution in relation to money and powerlessness, not in terms of desire or the erotic.

Most of the Latin American characters are not represented as whole people; some are just plot devices in stories of male protagonists. While some are victims in sentimental tearjerkers, others are symbols of social problems or of the underclass and the exploited.

In the French model there are always these elements: (1) at some point in her career, the woman has fancy trappings and high social standing (although she usually loses them); (2) she has the power to ruin men through manipulating their desires: woman the destroyer; and (3) she always comes to a bad end, no matter whether she is a sympathetic character or not. French novels do not make all fallen women whores, but they are all doomed in the end. Emile Zola's *Nana* is an example of the complex relation between the French attitudes toward sex, gender, power, and pleasure and the prostitute. In *The Image of the Prostitute in Modern Literature*, Nana is referred to as "the bitch-witch symbol of wickedness."[1] Zola portrays Nana as a dissipated mother who ruins everything she touches and whose evil is in her blood.

Alexandre Dumas's prostitute Marguerite in *La Dame aux Camelias* is a different stereotype: the whore with a heart of gold, whose meteoric rise to notoriety is only surpassed by the rapidity of her fall and her tragic death.

In the Latin American model the prostitute is characterized by the following: (1) the girl is poor or middle class; (2) she is seduced or raped, then abandoned; (3) she is rejected by family and society and has to leave home; (4) her chance at a new life proves illusory; and (5) she comes to a bad end, whether the life was her choice or was forced upon her (this, at least, she has in common with the French counterpart). No distinction is made in this model between a disappointed lover and a whore. In reality, in both societies, it was actually possible for prostitutes to marry and lead conventional lives (in Latin America, only in the lower classes), but never in literature. The vast majority of real prostitutes actually went into the life for economic reasons. In Mexico in 1908, it is estimated that 80 percent of prostitutes had been servants or washerwomen looking for an "easier," better-paying job.[2] This element of choice is rarely represented in the literature.

The image of the prostitute as developed in three novels, *Juana Lucero* (1902),[3] *Santa* (1903),[4] and *Nacha Regules* (1919),[5] is an indictment of contemporary social conditions existing at the turn of the century. The big city provides the anonymity in which a woman goes to a life of prostitution in preference to earlier responses to her disgrace, such as suicide or entering a convent.[6] The fallen woman moves from the colonial, Catholic Spanish culture to the anonymity of the big city. *Juana Lucero*, written by the Chilean Augusto D'Halmar, follows the formula: Juana is a pure and innocent girl who, at the death of her mother, goes to live with her aunt. The aunt, a staunch Catholic, treats her as a servant and "lends" her to a friend while she goes on a holiday. At the friend's house, Juana is raped by the husband. She accepts the invitation of another man to move in with him.

When she tells him of the pregnancy, he dumps her in a brothel. Juana
Lucero's fall from innocence into prostitution is told by a sympathetic,
omniscient narrator.

Females in this kind of fiction, and to some extent in real life, are
enslaved to male power. The patron and his son claim seigneurial rights to
deflower their virgin servants. The question of power or lack thereof is
further complicated by the interplay of the social classes. Juana, obviously
from the upper middle class but reduced to the level of a servant by the evil
aunt, is seen as a competitor by the other servant-concubines who see their
power, which is exercised through illicit sexuality, threatened by the
newcomer. She is made to feel all their maliciousness and vindictiveness.
The parallelism between the brothel where Juana finds herself at the end
and the house where she was raped by the patron is plain. Both are
marketplaces where the women are bought or exchanged under the eye of
the madam in the whorehouse or of the "lady of the house." Juana takes
refuge in insanity to break away from the hopelessness of her situation.
Following the convention, there is no salvation or redemption for the
prostitute, although in this case the punishment is insanity, not death.

In 1903, one year later, Mexico produced *Santa* by Federico Gamboa,
where the image is similar to that of the Chilean one. Both characters are
beautiful, impregnated (Juana against her will, Santa seduced by a soldier),
and have abortions. Both come from homes where the religious fervor
dictates that a transgression against the teachings of the church and the
social conventions cannot be forgiven, so that both are thrown out and
irrevocably doomed. Santa is meted out a worse fate than Juana. She is
loved by Hipolito, a blind musician, but is repulsed by his physical
appearance. She goes from one man to the next until finally, with nowhere
to turn, she accepts Hipolito's love. Punishment comes to her nevertheless—
she gets cancer and dies.

In 1919, the Argentinian writer Manuel Gálvez portrayed his *Nacha
Regules* as the "whore with a heart of gold,"[7] so dear to the French novels.
Nacha is seduced by one of the students in her mother's boardinghouse,
who persuades her to run away with him, and abandons her when she
becomes pregnant. The child is stillborn, and Nacha commences her descent
into prostitution. At this point, the story takes on variations. In the first
place, Nacha is not the protagonist of her own story; this is the story of
Fernando Monsalvat, the man who loves her. Second, in this case she
doesn't actually die. She doesn't thrive either. Monsalvat, her redeemer, has
to be blighted and undesirable (he is ill, poor, and blind) before his union to
Nacha can be sanctioned, but they do end up getting married.

Long after the French abandoned the sentimental novel for modernism,
Latin American writers followed the old patterns. In 1934, the Venezuelan

Guillermo Meneses wrote *La balandra Isabel llegó esta tarde*,[8] in which the prostitute Esperanza has had a relationship with a sailor, who has promised to take her out of the life. The sailor has second thoughts about becoming a fisherman and abandoning his free life with women in every port and, at the last minute, sails away. Esperanza pays a witch doctor to call him back, but when the boat arrives, she is told that the sailor is now captain of a ship that only travels to the Orient. She goes with her sailor's friend to get drunk and, presumably, repeats the cycle. Another view of prostitution as a grim fate is in *Es que somos muy pobres*,[9] written in 1953 by Juan Rulfo, where the twelve-year-old Tacha sits with her brother by the river after a flood and cries at the sight of her cow floating by. Her parents had given her this cow to keep her from having to sell herself like her two sisters who became whores to avoid starving to death. These stories are all different, but they share a vision of the hopelessness, doom, and inevitability of a prostitute's fate.

The boom movement, fueled by the North American writers Faulkner and Dos Passos, by the European Joyce, Proust, Woolf, Musil, Camus, and Sartre, and by the commercial expansion of the publishing companies in Spanish America, had an everlasting impact on Latin American letters. When Miguel Angel Asturias and Pablo Neruda won the Nobel Prize, some of the old patterns were broken forever. Some of the representatives of the boom, Jorge Luis Borges, Alejo Carpentier, Mario Vargas Llosa, and Gabriel García Márquez, moved away from regional stories and adopted universal themes. In this literary movement, some prostitutes became people and sometimes gained control over their own fates, or their fates are left open.

The Chilean writer José Donoso was a main player in the boom. In his 1966 work *El lugar sin límites*,[10] his prostitute Manuela is a transvestite.[11] The madam of the brothel and Manuela win ownership of the brothel from a friendly landlord who bets that she can't get Manuela to have sex with her. When the madam dies, the daughter takes over the brothel. It is never clear whether Manuela is her father. She is celibate and she prospers. The "lugar sin límites" is Hell, which also describes the miserable village, where the men are brutal and the animals are treated better than people. In this case, Manuela appropriates the role of the prostitute and suffers the typical literary fate of the whore. He/she dies a brutal and violent death.

In *Erendira*,[12] by the Colombian Gabriel García Márquez, a girl's fourteen-year-old body is a commodity exchanged for money by her grandmother.[13] The latter has herself been a prostitute and has been conditioned to think of the commerce of the flesh as a normal way to make a living. She decides how long Erendira will work and how much she will charge, and where and who will have her. It is notable that García Márquez's most intelligent literary critic, Angel Rama, says that there is no graphic violence in his books about violence.[14] In this work not ostensibly about violence, Erendira's rape, which marks the beginning of her career as a traveling whore, is depicted graphically.

Like all the prostitutes in fictional works from the 1900s to 1991, Erendira has no voice of her own, but she also literally does not speak, except to her savior Ulises, whom she incites to kill her grandmother, thus setting her free. She runs away, never to be heard from again, and Ulises is left behind to face the music. This at least makes a change from tradition.

In 1945, the Argentinian scriptwriter Homero Manzi discovered a letter addressed to the dictator Rosas. The letter asked for a contingent of women to go to service soldiers who were in the desert. Manzi wrote a script for a movie based on this letter.[15] Mario Vargas Llosa took the same idea, but in his work *Pantaleón y las visitadoras*,[16] instead of the desert he made it the Amazon. In all his works, the prostitute is a plot device, in this case a ludicrous one, set in to bring in relief the true protagonist, who is often himself. In *La ciudad y los perros*,[17] the student Alvaro goes to visit a prostitute called "Pies Dorados" who serves as the young boy's rite of passage. With Vargas Llosa, women are not real people; they are a narrative artifice.

In the 1991 *Hoy está solo mi corazón*, by the Chilean Enrique Lafourcade,[18] Malena is a prostitute more in the European style than the Spanish American one. She is a beautiful singer with whom the narrator falls in love; she gets pregnant by an aristocrat who dies and would never have married her anyway. The narrator takes her in, but when she has the child she leaves them both and joins a brothel. He ends up poor and maimed and her son is killed, but he still hopes she will return to him. This is a very European-style novel in the style of *Of Human Bondage*, even more than *Nana*.

The ambivalence toward the whore did not begin in nineteenth-century France. The earliest appearance of the whore in literature is considered to be in *The Epic of Gilgamesh*, a Sumerian epic of the third millennium B.C., where Enkidu, the King's companion, first curses her for taking his strength and then blesses her for giving him solace,[19] just the reverse of the modern formula of lust first, then disgust. The standard Latin American version seems to skip the lust altogether; one might pity a prostitute for her fate, but it never appears either glamorous or exciting. Until recently, she is not even herself, a real person. She is a public convenience and a symbol of social injustice, an unpleasant fact of life. She has no magic, no power, and no future.

NOTES

1. Pierre L. Horn and Mary Beth Pringle, eds., *The Image of the Prostitute in Modern Literature* (New York: Frederick Ungar, 1984), p. 3.

2. Bettina Gutiérrez-Girardot, *Prostituierte in der lateinamerikanischen Literatur: das Bild der Prostituierten in der lateinamerikanischen Literatur der Jahrhundertwende* (Frankfurt am Main: Peter Lang, 1990), p. 15.

3. Augusto D'Halmar, *Juana Lucero* (Santiago de Chile: Sur del Mundo, 1988).

4. Federico Gamboa, *Santa* (Mexico: Ediciones Botas, 1948).

5. Manuel Gálvez, *Nacha Regules* (Buenos Aires: Losada, 1960).

6. Enrique Amorim, "Un fabricante de felicidad en 1918," in Enrique Amorim et al., *Prostibulario* (Buenos Aires: Editorial Merlin, 1967), p. 33.

7. See Horn and Pringle, *The Image of the Prostitute in Modern Literature*.

8. Guillermo Meneses, *La balandra Isabel llegó esta tarde* (Caracas: Editorial Elite, 1938).

9. Juan Rulfo, "Es que somos muy pobres," in *El llano en llamas* (Mexico: Fondo de Cultura Económica, 1953), pp. 31-36.

10. José Donoso, *El lugar sin límites* (Mexico: Joaquín Mortiz, 1966).

11. Years later, Manuel Puig would mistakenly be credited with having been the first to introduce a homosexual character in his book *El beso de la mujer arana* (Barcelona: Seix Barral, 1976).

12. Gabriel García Márquez, *Candida Erendida* (Bogotá: La Oveja Negra, 1982).

13. In the world of the Latin American prostitute, virginity or extreme youth brings a higher price than experience. Catulo Castillo, in his essay "Prostíbulos y prostitutas" (*Prostibulario*, 1967, p. 29), narrates his experiences in Buenos Aires, where a young girl carries a prize of 100 pesos, almost double what the older whores bring. In *Los hombres de a caballo* (Mexico: Siglo XXI, 1968) by David Viñas, two Argentinians refuse to avail themselves of a prostitute not because she is barely ten years old but because she comes from the same city as they do.

14. Angel Rama, *García Márquez: edificación de un arte nacional y popular* (Montevideo: Universidad de la República, Facultad de Humanidades y Ciencias, 1987), p. 60.

15. Jorge Miguel Couselo, "Los autores en el sistema de estudios," in *Cine Latinoamericano: Años 30-40-50* (Mexico: Dirección General de Actividades Cinematográficas, Coordinación de Difusión Cultural, UNAM, 1990), pp. 121-122. The movie whose script Homero Manzi wrote is *Pampa barbara* (Demare-Fregonese, 1945).

16. Mario Vargas Llosa, *Pantaleón y las visitadoras* (Barcelona: Seix Barral, 1973).

17. Mario Vargas Llosa, *La ciudad y los perros* (Barcelona: Seix Barral, 1968).

18. Enrique Lafourcade, *Hoy está solo mi corazón* (Santiago de Chile: Zig-Zag, 1991).

19. Khalid Kishtainy, *The Prostitute in Progressive Literature* (London: Allison and Busby, 1982), pp. 13-15.

BIBLIOGRAPHY

Amorim, Enrique. *Eva Burgos*. Montevideo: Editorial Alfa, 1960.

Barrios, Eduardo. *Un perdido*. Buenos Aires: Editorial Patria, 1921.

Bernheimer, Charles. *Figures of Ill Repute: Representing Prostitution in Nineteenth-Century France*. Cambridge, MA: Harvard University Press, 1989.

Bullough, Vern, and Bonnie Bullough. *Women and Prostitution: A Social History*. Buffalo, NY: Prometheus Books, 1989.

Cabrera Infante, Guillermo. "Josefina atiende a los senores." In *Así en la paz como en la guerra*. Barcelona: Seix Barral, 1971. Pp. 70-75.

Carlos, Alberto J. "Nacha Regules y Santa: Problemas de intertextualidad." *Symposium* 36:4 (Winter 1982/83), 301-307.

Carrión, Miguel de. *Las impuras*. Havana: Editora Latinoamericana, 1959.

Edwards Bello, Joaquín. *El roto*. Santiago de Chile: Soc. Imp. y Lit. Universo, 1929.

Evans, Hilary. *Harlots, Whores, and Hookers: A History of Prostitution*. New York, NY: Tanlinger Publishing Company, 1979.

Guy, Donna J. "Tango, Gender, and Politics." In *Sex and Danger in Buenos Aires: Prostitution, Family and Nation in Argentina*. Lincoln: University of Nebraska Press, 1991. Pp. 141-174.

Ibieta, Gabriela. "El personaje de la prostituta según Manuel Gálvez: Aproximaciones a Dostoievski." *Revista de Estudios Hispánicos* 21:3 (October 1987), 11-19.

Kaminsky, Amy Katz. "Inhabitants, Visitors, and Washerwomen: Prostitutes and Prostitution in the Novels of Mario Vargas Llosa." *Inti* 8 (Fall 1978), 45-56.

———. "Women Writing About Prostitutes: Amalia Jamilis and Luisa Valenzuela." In Pierre L. Horn and Mary Beth Pringle, eds., *The Image of the Prostitute in Modern Literature*. New York, NY: Frederick Ungar, 1984. Pp. 119-131.

Méndez, José Luis. "La dialéctica del amo y el esclavo en la *Candida Erendira* de Gabriel García Márquez." *La Torre* 1:1 (1987), 58-68.

Méndez Rodena, Adriana. "'Este sexo que no es uno': Mujeres deseantes en *Las honradas* y *Las impuras*, de Miguel de Carrión." *Revista Iberoamericana* 56:152-153 (July-December 1990), 1009-1025.

Meneses, Guillermo. *La mano junto al muro*. Caracas: Consejo Municipal del Distrito Federal, 1972.

Mercado Romero, Jairo. *Cosas de hombres y otros cuentos*. Bogotá: Punto Rojo, 1971.

Moriyon Mojica, Carlos. "Asedio a la figura del narrador. Un ejemplo práctico: *La mano junto al muro* de Guillermo Meneses." *Castilla* 13 (1988), 79-118.

Onetti, Juan Carlos. *Juntacadaveres*. Madrid: Editorial Alianza, 1964.

Schwartz, Kessel. "The Whorehouse and the Whore in Spanish American Fiction of the 1960s." *Journal of Interamerican Studies and World Affairs* 15:4 (1973), 472-487.

Speck, Paula K. "Underworld: Sexual Satire in Three Latin American Novelists." *New Scholar* 8:1-2 (1982).

Vargas Llosa, Mario. *La casa verde*. Barcelona: Seix Barral, 1965.

———. *Conversación en La Catedral*. Barcelona: Seix Barral, 1969.

Viñas, David, and others. *La putería*. Bogotá: Latina, 1977.

15. Latin American Visions: Through the Eye of the Camera

Yolanda Maloney
Gloria de Alfaro

This paper examines the vision of Latin American women as represented in three films: *María* from Colombia, *Portrait of Teresa* from Cuba, and *Danzón* from Mexico. The female subject in Latin America is shaped by the existing patriarchal structure which establishes a position of passivity and a conditioning that is reactivated in the representations of women in the cinematic text.

Subjectivity is a condition that reflects cultural values: these values are first and foremost patriarchal and they organize subjectivity along sexual differences.[1] The emergence of subjectivity in Latin American women is determined not only by the cultural patterns in place but also by the unconscious. The place assigned to women in the three film texts provides three options for subjectivity: passivity as exemplified by María, rebellion in Teresa, or joyful acceptance in Julia.

Through the presentation of these three movies: *María*, *Portrait of Teresa*, and *Danzón*, I show that the female subject is determined by two axes: the unconscious and the cultural.

The unconscious axis—According to Freud, the unconscious is "a part of the mind not accessible to consciousness except in disguised forms: dreams, parapraxes, daydreams, neuroses and hysterical symptoms."[2] Later on, Lacan reworked Freud's theories of the unconscious and determined that the unconscious is not "an inarticulate and chaotic region but a signifying network." For Lacan, the unconscious is the discourse of the Other; its desires are those of an already constituted social order and it is organized as a language.

The cultural axis—For Lévi-Strauss, in any culture the most recurrent prohibition is the incest taboo. This is present in the relations between father/daughter and mother/son, and less so, in the Latin American culture, between brother/sister. The unconscious desire of the daughter to replace the mother in the father's affections or the unconscious wish of the son to kill the father and marry his mother takes normally an Oedipal form. The incest taboo helps to shape the individual as an obedient subject ready to take its place in the society that predates him. Foucault's view also reinforces Lévi-

Strauss theories by calling into question the values of autonomy and stability which define the position of the individual within the humanist tradition and says we must reconstruct the concept of unity in the individual. He arrives at the conclusion that human reality is a construct, the product of signifying activities which are both culturally specific and generally unconscious. My reading of the three excerpts of the cinematic texts is determined by the two axes: cultural and unconscious.

The first film is *María* (Colombia, 1971). María is an orphan who comes to live at the ranch of a noble and wealthy family. She falls in love with the oldest son, but before she can marry him she dies of epilepsy.

The film opens with an image of the hero galloping through a sterilized and colorized Colombian countryside, and we see through his eyes the unfolding of the narrative. The first shot shows María as a child standing next to Father and facing the son, thereby establishing tension between desire and patriarchal Law. This close-up is followed by a long shot that points to the minor characters: the mother, younger brother, and sisters of the hero.

I want to stay with this shot for a minute since it explains the ideological basis of the narrative. For both male and female the mother is the first love-object; but while the male makes her the object of desire, he can later on replace her with members of the same sex. This is what the hero does at this point; María becomes the locus of his desire and the Oedipus tie to Mother is broken. But for the female the Oedipus complex makes her replace one parent with the other; she turns to Father. By doing this María accepts not only her anatomical difference—her castration—as a lack, but she also takes on the burden of the mother: the mother's secondary place, her inferiority, and her powerlessness become hers.

Although the film is called *María*, and indeed María appears in almost every frame of the film, it is the socialization of the male, his subjectivization that the movie depicts. In Lacanian terms, the hero has emerged from his passage through the Oedipus complex and has been produced and constituted as subject.[3]

The next frame shows María as the embodiment of the Romantic heroine: in this scene the younger sister asks what they (her older sister and María) are reading; María replies "Atala."[4] This answer sets the film in the midst of the Latin American myth of female virginity: the ever present dichotomy of the virgin and the prostitute.

The next scenes show María in a daydream sequence: María and the hero dancing in the moonlight, María holding the hands of two infants and running in slow motion—in an unbearably corny shot—toward the hero. In these scenes the congruence between the main character's unconscious and the patriarchal ideology inscribes María twice as a mere appendage to the male.

Another shot that exemplifies the way that patriarchal Law is imposed is the gaze. The scene here shows how the gaze is another way to keep María in her space—a very restricted space. While the lovers are on the balcony, the Father intercepts the glance exchanged by the two lovers; the Father directs his gaze at María, and María returns the gaze.

In this film the cuts from one scene to the next are carefully covered. In the window sequence the male protagonist—the Romantic hero—is looking out; we the audience participate of this film "plenitude," looking with the hero onto wide opening vistas. At that moment he, as well as the spectator, sees María and her dog running outside; there is not an obvious "eye" of the camera doing the filming: the reverse shot anchors the vision to the fictional gaze by the window.

A very different film is *Portrait of Teresa* (Cuba, 1979). The film tells the story of a Cuban couple and their three children living under communism, and the ensuing breakup of their marriage. It centers mainly on the feminine character: Teresa. Unlike María, the heroine of the preceding film, who is happy in the reduced space allotted to her by the patriarchal structure, Teresa wants to break out of her suffocating milieu.

In this film there is not the pseudo "intimacy" that the use of the shot/reverse shot provides us with in *María*. The Cuban film opens with a shot of Teresa being photographed by her husband: long, windswept black hair almost covering her face; and ends with another closeup of Teresa, her hair covered, the feminine soft look replaced by a severe, resolute masculine stance. The director next sets the background by shooting the textile factory where Teresa works, cuts to the husband picking up the kids at his mother's, cuts to the husband at home waiting for Teresa to arrive. Unlike the previous film, there is no intent here to cover or hide the "eye" of the camera; the narrative is episodic, so each frame tells of a detail in the decomposition of the couple's relationship. The cinematic text carefully depicts the relative freedom and choices that the husband enjoys as opposed to the drudgery of Teresa's homemaking duties. Teresa is torn apart by the role assigned to her by the prevalent patriarchal system, and physically endorsed by the husband.

One of the most significant scenes in the film: Teresa is in the kitchen with her back turned to the camera; the husband eats in the dining room, facing the camera. The husband takes his dishes to the kitchen and sets them by her. Very calmly Teresa picks up the dishes and dumps them in the garbage can. She says: "No more washing. At least for today." The next rebellious moment occurs in the bedroom when Teresa shouts: "I want to be me, not a slave like your mother and mine." This declaration elicits a violent answer from the husband and he leaves the house. He tries to effect a reconciliation, but Teresa questions now the "double standard" that exists at the base of her society, and the final shot shows her in charge, a phallic sign.

The last film is *Danzón* (Mexico, 1991). It tells the story of a woman who works for the telephone company and holds the championship title for best Danzón performer with her partner. Julia, the protagonist of *Danzón*, tries to break out of her assigned place. She succeeds but returns to it. She looks for something that is missing, for an object lost. The sudden disappearance of her dancing partner serves as the impulse that sends her in her search.

Traditionally, in Latin America the role of the male has not been challenged. It is seemingly challenged in the film, but in the last instance, the ending puts the power back in the hands of the Father. The parallel here between her "real" quest for her partner and her discursive travel from mirror stage to imaginary to symbolic is validated by dotting the stages of her search with cultural traces. At one point in Mexico City, the "eye" of the camera enters the ladies' room and focuses on Julia and her two friends in front of the mirror. The camera does not pick up the reflection of the women, instead the viewer is made to experience Julia's absence and the interruption of the narrative. The next shot picks up Julia coming out of the bathroom and the exchange: "Lo más importante es encontrar a Carmelo" (the missing partner), Julia says. Her friend asks: "¿Por qué? No es nada tuyo." Here we experience the first sign of anxiety in the cinematic text, a tearful Julia explaining why it is necessary to find the Father. Her friend asks: "And all that was in the telegram?" "Yes," Julia says, "It was in code." Her friends then encourage her to begin her search.

The opening of her vision (in Mexico City, she is either at the Telefónica, at the apartment, or at the ballroom) is marked by the "eye" of the camera which gives a sweeping view of the street, the men for whom she is very attractive, and her entrance in the Pension Rex (Oedipus Rex?). In an interesting sequence at the Pension Rex, the camera slowly shows the body of Julia's young lover semicovered by a sheet, lying on the bed while the ventilator blows softly on his body. The feminine audience, I am sure, clamors for the breeze to blow a little harder.

In the cultural axis stand two instances that provoke anxiety in the female in quite different ways. The first scene shows a woman dancing by herself, which increases the loss in the female viewing audience: "Aha! This is how I will be if I don't find my partner." The other scene shows a man dancing by himself; this seems alright in this newer, freer environment, and the viewer is challenged to think why it is alright for a man to dance alone but provokes anxiety when a woman does so.

In the film, there are glimmers of hope: Julia's daughter does not want to learn to do the Danzón nor to understand the complex protocol attached to it; she will defy the conventions that assign a fixed place to the female.

In the film the uncanny and subtle trap is that in our Indian culture, music and dancing are inherent in our identity, the expression of our soul; this expression is deployed throughout our society through the operation of power/knowledge networks, cementing our place in the Imaginary. In *Danzón*, Julia comes to an understanding but chooses—and I think this is important—to continue to be inserted in the Imaginary and to continue the pretense that she is inserted in the Symbolic.

The very satisfactory ending for the female audience is that she finds the Father. At the end of the quest, she reencounters her dancing partner; but something has changed, and she reaches plenitude as evidenced by the fact that now they stare in each other's eyes in open defiance of Danzón's conventions.

My question to the audience is then: Can we never liberate ourselves from the tyranny of the Father?

NOTES

1.   Kaja Silverman, *The Subject of Semiotics* (New York, NY: Oxford University Press, 1983), p. 222.

2.   Sigmund Freud, *A General Introduction to Psychoanalysis* (New York, NY: Permabooks, 1953), pp. 119-120.

3.   Terry Eagleton, *Literary Theory: An Introduction* (Minneapolis: University of Minnesota Press, 1983), p. 165.

4.   François-René Chateaubriand, *Atala* (Paris: J. Corti, 1950).

Part Two

Library Services
and Resources

I

Accessing Latin American Resources through Database, Microfilm, and Print Media

16. La poesía de
Sor Juana Inés de la Cruz
Vía Internet

Luis M. Villar

En abril de 1995, el universo de las letras hispánicas conmemorará el tricentenario de la muerte de Sor Juana Inés de la Cruz. Con el propósito de celebrar la vida y la producción literaria de Sor Juana hemos creado un banco de datos el cual contiene su obra completa. Esta primera parte que hoy introducimos al público contiene la lírica personal, los villancicos y las letras sacras. Los ensayos y las comedias están en la última etapa de reproducción en forma electrónica.

La poesía de Sor Juana Inés ha sido objeto de estudio por dedicados comentaristas de la cala de Ermilo Abreu Gómez, Octavio Paz y Georgina Sabat de Rivers. La popularidad de la poesía de la Décima Muestra y la extraordinaria abundancia de ensayos de crítica e interpretación dedicados a su estudio atestiguan la popularidad de Sor Juana en la vertiente de las letras hispánicas como la primera gran poetisa del Nuevo Mundo. La expresión lírica de Sor Juana cubre una diversidad de composiciones poéticas las cuales incluye romances, endechas, décimas, glosas, sonetos, liras, ovillejos, silvas, villancicos y letras. La mayor parte de esta poesía son poemas de naturaleza profana, aunque también se encuentran poemas de temas sagrados. La poesía secular es, en su mayoría, poesía de ocasión. Muchos de ellos fueron poemas escritos para acompañar un regalo a una persona de posición, poemas compuestos en celebración de eventos públicos y privados y elegías. Estos poemas, según Sor Juana, fueron escritos para satisfacer a otros. El único poema lírico escrito para sí misma fue *El sueño,* el cual encaja en la más intricada vertiente de la tradición lírica barroca y, sin dejar a menos, la tradición hermética de Hermes Trimegisto. En general, la producción lírica de Sor Juana contiene más de 30,000 versos; aunque extensa es muy manejable en nuestra edición electrónica. Esta edición permite un acceso simultáneo a la totalidad del cuerpo poético de Sor Juana.

La edición electrónica

La edición electrónica de la poesía incluye los dos primeros volúmenes de las *Obras completas,* edición de Miguel Méndez Plancarte. Los críticos y estudiantes dedicados al estudio de Sor Juana encontrarán esta edición como un conveniente vehículo para la investigación y el análisis de léxico, trazar

Sor Juana Inés de la Cruz

el uso de vocablos e imágenes, estudiar el arte de la expresión popular, establecer relaciones intratextuales y estudiar la función poética de lenguaje en la poesía completa de Sor Juana. El texto electrónico abre nuevas fronteras para la investigación y permite la formulación de nuevas preguntas que la lectura y comentario tradicional de textos no ha permitido.

Para facilitar el acceso al banco de datos hemos preparado el *Thesaurus of the Poetry of Sor Juana Inés de la Cruz* (Hanover, NH: Dartmouth College, 1994) el cual sirve de guía e introducción al texto electrónico. El *Thesaurus* incluye tres índices, dos listas de palabras y una guía para realizar las búsquedas. Los índices son: (a) composición poética, primer verso, número de página; (b) composición y primeros versos en orden alfabético; (c) índice de nombres y epítetos. Las listas de vocablos son: (a) orden alfabético de todas las palabras utilizadas por Sor Juana, (b) lista de vocablos en forma descendente según la frecuencia de su uso en el texto.

Este *Thesaurus* atestigua en su contenido que la edición electrónica ofrece diferentes niveles de entrada o acceso al corpus poético. La poesía de Sor Juana cesa de ser fija y lineal. Los poemas y villancicos se pueden organizar en la forma, modo o manera en que el investigador desee sin ningún tipo de barreras. Esta capacidad de acceso al texto ofrece una ilimitada posibilidad de relaciones textuales a nivel del vocablo, la frase, la imagen o la figura retórica. Lo que es distante en el texto impreso se hace contiguo en la edición electrónica, eliminando el espacio entre las diversas composiciones poéticas. Las relaciones intratextuales así creadas son ilimitadas. Se establecen, además, nuevas asociaciones y se descubren nuevas e importantes relaciones intertextuales no fácilmente percibidas en el discurso poético impreso. La adyacencia creada en la edición electrónica permite un acercamiento diferente al corpus poético de Sor Juana, considerando que cada signo se relaciona con otros signos tanto sintagmáticamente, por contigüidad, como paradigmáticamente. Mas, sobre todo, el lector o investigador tiene acceso instantáneo a la poesía completa de la Décima Muestra. Y, si existe una ventaja que va más allá de todas las posibilidades combinatorias, ésta radica en el hecho de que el investigador tiene acceso instantáneo a la poesía de Sor Juana con sólo transcribir mecanográficamente uno o dos vocablos.

Formato del texto electrónico

Composition: Soneto   I. 277
First Stanza: Este, que ves, engaño colorido
Introduction:

Procura desmentir los elogios que a un retrato de la Poetisa inscribió la verdad, que llama pasión.

Text:

>   Este, que ves, engaño colorido,
>   que del arte ostentando los primores,
>   con falso silogismos de colores
>   es cauteloso engaño del sentido;
>   éste, en quien la lisonja ha pretendido
>   excusar de los años los horrores,
>   y venciendo del tiempo los rigores,
>   triunfar de la vejez y del olvido,
>   es un vano artificio del cuidado,
>   es una flor al viento delicada,
>   es un resguardo inútil para el hado:
>   es un necia diligencia errada,
>   es un afán caduco y, bien mirado,
>   es cadáver, es polvo, es sombra, es nada.

La composición poética *[composition]* y primer verso *[first stanza]* son índices que se pueden buscar en el banco de datos. Las composiciones poéticas representadas incluyen: romances, anagramas, endechas, redondillas, décimas, glosas, sonetos, villancicos, letras y *El sueño*. Los primeros versos, como es común, se recuerdan, mas no así el poema en su totalidad. Por tanto, el usuario tiene la facultad de traer a la pantalla el poema en su totalidad a partir de sólo el primer verso.

La notación numérica, I.277, corresponde al volumen y número de página en la edición de Méndez Plancarte. Si el usuario desea, puede consultar tanto el texto como las notas preparadas por Méndez Plancarte.

La introducción, la cual es producto de lecturas posteriores y redactada por los editores, clarifica la temática de algunos poemas, identifica al receptor del mensaje poético, define el propósito original de algunas composiciones, establece la aproximada fecha de redacción de algunas composiciones y clarifica la importancia de personajes y eventos históricos para el lector o investigador no versado en el momento histórico en que vivió Sor Juana.

Finalmente, el giro "text" introduce cada poema, anagrama o villancico. Cada uno es fiel reproducción de la edición impresa. Hemos hecho un esfuerzo de preservar las unidades léxicas según el texto de Méndez Plancarte. Sin embargo, hemos realizado una serie de correcciones con el propósito de registrar el uso moderno de algunos vocablos según el *Diccionario de la Real Academia Española*. Por ejemplo, *són, pára,* y *sér* se transcriben como *son, para,* y *ser*. Otros vocablos aparecen en la edición de Méndez Plancarte con y sin acento. Las mismas se han standardizado siguiendo el uso de *Diccionario*. Por ejemplo, *abate/ábate; redito/rédito; fulgida/fúlgida*. El banco de datos es fiel a los preceptos de la ortografía y prosodia española. Los signos de interrogación y exclamación inversos se registran como tales. La *ñ* aparece con su tilde. Toda palabra acentuada y todo vocablo con diéresis se registra como el uso lo dicta con el fin de observar los leyes del arte de la composición poética. Así, se pueden encontrar en los diversos textos vocablos como: *celestiales, celestïales; crió, crïó; juicio, juïcio, jüicio*. La riqueza del vocabulario de Sor Juana en los textos incluye no sólo el castellano sino también giros en diversos idiomas. Los textos contienen vocablos en latín, nahuatl, portugués, viscaíno y la lengua popular utilizada por los negros mexicanos del siglo XVII.

Terminal y programas necesarios para tener acceso al banco de datos

Para tener acceso al banco de datos necesitan un terminal Macintosh y tres programas básicos: DCIS_Navigator_1.3.1E.hqx, InfoSpeak.hqx y Online_Library_1.5.3.hqx. Éstos se pueden adquirir vía *ftp* o a través del *gopher* de Dartmouth. Las instrucciones para adquirir los programas y para acceso al banco de datos, se pueden obtener del autor. En caso de que tengan dificultad en la transferencia de los programas, deben consultar a un especialista en ordenadores en su institución académica.

17. RESEÑAS: Libros sobre narrativa y poesía mexicanas contemporáneas

Elsa Barberena Blásquez

Antecedentes

Son pocos los escritores mexicanos contemporáneos de narrativa y poesía que se conocen, la mayoría pasan desapercibidos. Se pueden nombrar Octavio Paz, Carlos Fuentes, Manuel Capetillo, Eduardo Lizalde entre los primeros, y René Avilés Fabila, Jesús Gardea, Jorge López Páez, David Martín del Campo, Francisco Prieto, entre los segundos.

A partir de los años setenta la crítica sobre literatura mexicana del siglo XX ha de buscarse en las publicaciones periódicas al ser éstas más abundantes y particularmente mayores en número los suplementos culturales y las revistas independientes. No sólo los títulos son comentados sino también hay referencia de las presentaciones de los libros e inclusión de entrevistas con los autores.

No existe una fuente de información que señale únicamente las reseñas de libros publicados ni la crítica literaria que éstas presupone.

Por lo anterior resulta indispensable contar con una guía y una información en especie que permitan consultar y emplear de manera inmediata aquella que consigna y valora el desarrollo de las letras nacionales. Si ello no ocurre, habrá que esperar a que eventualmente aparezca la bibliografía especializada, la que, según se observa, es limitada y de lenta producción.

Se necesita un tipo de obra similar al "Book Review Digest", para señalar las reseñas de libros en éstas y otras áreas. La base de datos RESEÑAS tiene este objetivo principal. Otro el difundir la creación de los escritores menos conocidos para conocer la poesía y narrativa contemporáneas de México.

Se utilizó el archivo del Prof. Jaime Cortés que consiste en información sobre aproximadamente 280 escritores. La documentación es de recortes periodísticos únicamente. Este formato no se ha incluido en índices como el *Hispanic American Periodicals Index (HAPI)* o el *Handbook of Latin American Studies.*

La elaboración de la base de datos RESEÑAS es un esfuerzo de los estudiantes de la maestría en bibliotecología, Joel Estudillo García, Fernando E. González Moreno, Shoki Goto Takashima en el curso Usuarios y Fuentes de Información en las Humanidades impartido por la que esto escribe.

Objetivos

Los objetivos de la base de datos son los siguientes:
1. Recuperar la información sobre reseñas de literatura mexicana contemporánea de 1970 a 1980 en artículos y recortes periodísticos
2. Analizar esta información y buscar los descriptores adecuados para su recuperación
3. Elaborar una base de datos útil para la difusión entre los usuarios
4. Ofrecer en especie la crítica literaria en sus diversos tipos: reseña, artículo, ensayo, entrevista
5. Establecer eventualmente un centro difusor de literatura mexicana contemporánea inexistente en México para dar a conocer las obras, creadores y crítica.

Metodologia

La metodología consiste en:
1. Elaborar el listado de publicaciones periódicas que contienen significativamente crítica literaria sobre literatura mexicana contemporánea tanto en México como en el extranjero
2. Seleccionar aquellas fuentes de crítica literaria exclusivamente dedicadas a la literatura mexicana contemporánea
3. Seguir los pasos conducentes al establecimiento de una base de datos según el programa computarizado PROCITE. Se determinó utilizar el programa PROCITE ya que permite: la captura e impresión de información bajo una amplia variedad de formatos; la recuperación de información se puede realizar por distintas llaves; la corrección o modificación de información es sumamente sencilla; es un sistema amistoso, en el que se puede trabajar casi en forma inmediata; y el sistema está siendo adquirido por varias dependencias de la Universidad Nacional Autónoma de México.

Infraestructura y apoyo técnico

El proyecto cuenta con:
1. Las revistas en la Hemeroteca de la Facultad de Filosofía y Letras de la UNAM
2. Los recortes periodísticos del archivo de Jaime Cortés Arellano
3. El programa PROCITE
4. Una PC e impresora
5. La asesoría de un jefe de sección en la Biblioteca "Samuel Ramos" de la Facultad

6. La asesoría de las Direcciones Generales de Servicios de Cómputo Académico y Administrativo a través del Grupo de Interés en bases de datos sobre Ciencias Sociales y Humanidades de la UNAM
7. La asesoría de Cortés Arellano en cuanto a la identificación de autores, obras y crítica
8. Los índices a publicaciones periódicas en la Hemeroteca de la Facultad.

Se puede obtener del autor una guía detallada al uso de la base de datos.

18. Latin America and the Family History Library: Historical Overview of Microfilming

Kahlile Mehr

Perusing the proceedings of SALALM, one finds a report written in 1957 by L. Garrett Myers, then a director of the Genealogical Society of Utah, titled "The Acquisition of Latin American Library Materials." A few things have happened in the thirty-five years since that report. I now cover the rest of the story.

As a refresher, let me review the purpose of the Family History Library and its parent organization, the Genealogical Society of Utah (for convenience I refer to both as the Library).* It promotes the gathering, preservation, and use of genealogical records on an international scale. Since 1938, it has sent microfilm cameras to many corners of the globe and over time has established a collection of genealogical sources amounting to 1.8 million rolls of film. It makes these films available at the Library in Salt Lake City, Utah, and in more than 2,000 family history centers, branches of the main library located around the world. In recent years it has promoted the extraction of information from the films and made it available to the public through computer databases.

The primary purpose of the Library is to provide guidance and assistance for members of the Church of Jesus Christ of Latter-day Saints (LDS) to identify their ancestors. The Church teaches that families can be established for eternity. To accomplish this, members perform proxy baptisms and other ordinances for deceased ancestors in the temples of the Church. The ancestors living in the next world either accept or reject the ordinances performed in their behalf. Ultimately, the Church proposes to perform these ordinances for all who have lived on earth, beginning with those we can identify through the extant records of the world.

Secondarily, the Library makes its sources available to the genealogical and research community. Dr. Robert W. Fogel, Nobel Prize winner in Economics and famed economic historian, recently lectured at the Library and commented that he considers himself and his research to be among the

---

*The Genealogical Society of Utah is a corporation operated by the Family History Department of the Church of Jesus Christ of Latter-day Saints.

greatest beneficiaries of the records gathered by the Library. Many other scholars have made use of the Library's collections for a wide spectrum of research projects.

The Library filmed extensively in North America, the British Isles, Northern Europe, and Scandinavia through 1950. A number of projects were completed in the early 1950s, freeing up funds for filming elsewhere. Filming in Mexico was of particular interest to the Church. It was the land of the "Lamanite," a term used in the Book of Mormon to identify ancient Israelite immigrants to this continent.

Even though Mexican filming was of interest to the Library, it still represented a substantial investment of time and money. Mexican filming got under way in August 1952, but only after the LDS mission president, Lucian M. Mecham, Jr., had pressed the Society for over a year to do something about the threatened loss of records. When a local attorney and a history professor took him to see the nation's census records, he later reported, he found them in a deplorable state. Located in an abandoned Catholic church, they were stacked over six feet high, covered with dust, and soiled with droppings from pigeons roosting in the attic. He also took time to visit Catholic churches as well as the Mexican National Archives where other records were stored. He continued to complain to Salt Lake City, reminding the Society that some records were being lost because of flooding and other elements simply through neglect.

Finally, the Society sent representatives and a filming project was negotiated. The United Nations Educational, Scientific, and Cultural Organization (UNESCO) had a camera at the archive which was not always in use, and the Society was able to borrow it for a period of time. The first records filmed were pedigree charts from the files of the Mexican Inquisition. Apparently, these records were created because it was beneficial for a defendant to prove his descendancy from Spanish stock. The filming in the National Archives established the Library's filming credentials. The Catholic Diocese in Mexico City readily consented to having its records filmed. In 1954 the operation in Mexico was expanded and in the following year operators were sent outside of Mexico City to copy the many outlying genealogical records of the country.

Here, as elsewhere in Latin America, we have primarily filmed church, civil registration, and census records. These are the basic Latin American sources for genealogy.

One problem that hindered the filming effort for several years was the lack of facilities to process the exposed films. It was solved in 1960 with the installation of a film lab in Mexico. At that point there were 10,000 rolls (a three-year backlog) waiting for donor prints to be made and the master sent then to Salt Lake City. With regard to donor prints, the Library has traditionally given a free print to the institution that has granted it permission to film. It also provides replacement copies at cost.

While filming continued in Mexico during the 1960s, in 1965 the Library looked farther south. Society representatives were sent to ascertain filming possibilities in South America. In May 1965, an initial project of filming parish registers was commenced in Buenos Aires, Argentina. The filmer was a native of Argentina, María Rachel Sulé. Library policy has normally been to hire filmers locally. This project lasted for a year and produced three hundred microfilm rolls.

Filming resumed in 1968 when the filming of the 1869 Argentine census began in 1968 at the National Archives. Filming was hindered here because of a misunderstanding. The person who negotiated the project, a local member of the LDS church, failed to tell the archive that the Library was part of the church. After several months the archive discovered this fact and considered it a matter of deception. Society representatives were able to visit and resolve the problem, and filming continued. The Library does not hide the fact that it is connected with a church, even though this usually creates a stir when the local press learns about it. Inevitably, the press will run articles about the LDS stealing the souls of ancestors by baptizing them in proxy.

During the same visit, Library representatives were able to make a presentation to the Society of Argentine Archivists concerning the Granite Mountains Record Vault. Completed in 1963, the vault is a permanent storage site for the master negatives created by Library cameras. Blasted from the interior of a granite mountain south of Salt Lake City, it provides a temperature- and humidity-controlled environment that augurs well for the long-term preservation of the films gathered by the Library.

The early representatives to Latin America did not speak Spanish or Portuguese. Usually they were able to find someone who could interpret. For instance, the duo of James Black and Hugh Law visited the National Archives of Brazil in 1969. There they found Victor Filler, of Stanford University, working on a doctorate. He served as interpreter. They were not so lucky at restaurants, where they were on their own. Jim Black writes, "On one occasion we ordered what we thought was chicken on the menu of one of the restaurants, and discovered while we were eating that it was baby octopus."

In contrast, our representative at this writing, Jim Streeter, who has been in charge of the filming since 1978, is fluent in Spanish. He directs the filming operation from Caracas, Venezuela.

In Guatemala the Society began in 1970 to film the notarial records of colonial Guatemala. Then it included Honduras, El Salvador, Nicaragua, and Costa Rica. Panamanian filming began in 1972. In Chile, the program got under way in 1973, only after a complicated series of negotiations with the Catholic Church regarding permissions, and with the government regarding import duties (for cameras and film). Beginning in 1975 the Society rapidly expanded microfilming into many countries of Central and South America. Filming began that year in Costa Rica; 1976 in Peru, Brazil, and El Salvador; 1977 in Bolivia; and 1979 in Honduras, Paraguay, and Ecuador. To better train the new corps of camera operators, the Society held the first Latin American filming seminar in November 1979 with sessions held in Guatemala City and Lima. In 1981 filming in the Caribbean began with a project in the Dominican Republic.

Political instability, geographic circumstances, and religious antagonisms hindered but never completely stopped the progress of projects in Latin America. Camera operators were regularly searched at gunpoint in El Salvador during 1979, prior to the temporary cessation of filming there in 1980. Similar problems were encountered in Colombia and Peru in the early 1990s as film operators occasionally encountered terrorists or drug traffickers. Geographic circumstances have also been daunting. Rudolfo Becerra, filming in Mexico in 1979, transferred his equipment from jeep to donkey in order to film a parish register in Amixtlan Puebla. In the Andes microfilming often involves hauling radio equipment (at times the only form of communication is shortwave radio) and generators as well as food, water, and camera equipment on horseback or llamas to a village church. If the priest cannot be found filmers must move on. Opposition based on religious grounds has occurred less frequently. Carlos Ferrari, filming in Bolivia in 1980, was halted by local peasants who objected to the filming and was doused with water as he scurried to leave. Filming of church records in Brazil was halted in 1983 when, in response to an inquiry from the bishops of Brazil, the Vatican objected to the program.

The Library has persisted in spite of temporary setbacks. In more recent years filming coverage has extended to virtually all countries in Latin America. Colombian filming began in 1985 and filming projects were completed in most of the Caribbean countries between 1990 and 1992. By 1991 the only major South American country in which filming had not occurred was Venezuela. Then several Catholic bishops granted permission. One became an archbishop, a position that enabled him to exert broader positive influence for the program. The first films from Venezuela were received in 1992. In Central America, Nicaragua has not yet been filmed, nor in the Caribbean has Cuba. In both cases the political situation has not permitted negotiations to proceed. Yet, the Library continues to seek permission and hopes to film in these places.

This group may also be interested in the filming of records in Spain and Portugal. In Spain, negotiations were conducted with Catholic officials rather than civil authorities because the civil records were too recent. Beginning in 1975, the initial filming was conducted in Barcelona. The microfilming program was temporarily stalled when a convocation of Spanish bishops voted against it. But by 1979 permissions were again being received. Along with Italy, Spain was the most widely filmed country in Europe during the 1980s.

Political unrest in Portugal during the early 1970s made negotiations impossible. In 1976 filming permission was granted in Madeira, a Portuguese island. By 1979 political stability had returned and filming began on the mainland. A majority of the church records in Portugal were filmed by four to five cameras in operation from 1979 to 1989.

In addition to filming the records, church members since 1978 have been extracting and data entering names, dates, and places from the filmed records. Much of this extraction work has focused on the records of Mexico. The result is a multimillion name index to the historic population

Collection Size, April 1994

Place	Rolls[a]	Place	Rolls[a]
Mexico	143,852	Honduras	1,046
Spain	29,469	Puerto Rico	932
Brazil	11,123	Dominican Republic	799
Portugal	8,297	Bahamas	633
Argentina	8,737	Uruguay	487
Guatemala	8,589	Paraguay	460
Chile	8,045	Panama	430
Peru	2,878	Guadeloupe	377
Bolivia	2,366	Martinique	306
Colombia	1,954	Venezuela	223
El Salvador	1,901	Haiti	216
Ecuador	1,462	Barbados	171
Costa Rica	1,390	Virgin Islands (U.S.)	144
Jamaica	1,321		

Other countries: Grenada, Guiana, Bermuda, Belize, Dominica, Cuba, Suriname, Turks and Virgin Islands (U.K.), Netherlands Antilles, Anguilla, Antigua, Saint Lucia.

[a]A roll of film has from 600 to 3,000 exposures, which equates as two to ten 300-page volumes.

of Mexico, which is part of the 200 million name database called the International Genealogical Index. This is available in the Library, family history centers, and selected libraries in the United States and Canada. Currently, it is also being tested for distribution to home users.

This brief summary of Latin American acquisitions is but a piece of a filming program that purports to provide a safe haven for the genealogical archives of the world. For the church it provides records for a millennium of work in which the families of the world will be identified and the familial order of eternal worlds established. For others it provides resources to pursue scholarly and personal inquiry into the past of mankind. In a quiet, unassuming fashion the Society has pursued a records gathering effort with few parallels in the history of the world.

APPENDIX

Family History Service Centers in Latin America

For information on the addresses of family history centers in Latin America, please contact the appropriate family history service center.

Mexico

Centro de Servicios de Historia Familiar de Monterrey
Concha Espino 303
Colonia Roma Sur
Monterrey, N.L.
64700 México

Telephone: 597-750

Centro de Servicios de Historia Familiar de México
Fuente de Pirámides, n. 1, p. 9
Lomas de Tecamachalco
México, D.F.
53950 México

Telephone: 760-0603

Central America

Centro de Servicios de Historia Familiar de Guatemala
24 Avenida 2-20, Zona 15
Vista Hermosa 1
Guatemala, Guatemala

Telephone: 358-982

Argentina, Uruguay, Paraguay

Centro de Servicios de Historia Familiar de Buenos Aires
Caracas 1289
1416 Buenos Aires, B.A.
Argentina

Telephone: 584-2971

Chile

Centro de Servicios de Historia Familiar de Santiago
Av. Pedro de Valdivia 1423
Clasificador 54
Santiago 9
Chile

Telephone: 225-7712

Brazil

Centro de Serviços de História da Família
Av. Prof. Francisco Morato, 2430
05512 São Paulo, S.P.
Brasil

Telephone: 814-2277

The Caribbean

Centro de Servicios de Historia Familiar
A-14 Ronda Street
Villa Andalucía
Río Piedras, Puerto Rico 00926

Telephone: 748-7240

19. Sharing the Heritage: The Latin American Collection of the Family History Library

Frederick W. Graham

Imagine with me the first waves of migration from the Old World to the New, from Europe to territory that would come to be called Latin America: the subsequent centuries of population movement from east to west; pageantry and bluster, armor and steel, robes and ritual, banners and *bandeirantes,* filibusterers and colonizers, miners and majors, landowners and tenant farmers; the indigenous peoples exploited and expropriated; imported labor, enslaved souls, a new race; the blood of Europe, the blood of America, the blood of Africa, a new people, *el pueblo, o povo.*

Consider with me the generations of persons who were born, married, had children, lived, and died in the lands we call Latin America. The majority of them have done so virtually anonymously, their lives noticed by few outside the small sphere of their household, their village, their community. The passage of time dims memory, the vital presence of individuals is transitory, *passageiro,* their lives a brief spark.

Traditionally, historians and genealogists concentrated their efforts on studies of noble or prominent families. The science of genealogy was inevitably associated with the elites of society. In recent decades, however, there has been an awakening of awareness regarding so-called common men and women. While acknowledging the essential role of the ruling elite in the leadership of nations, the fundamental position of the common people in the history of nations is now widely recognized and much better appreciated.

In a curious reversal, because of current political and social philosophy, there may well be now a higher degree of pride and pleasure in tracing one's ancestry to the common people than to the elites. Indeed, there may be at least a trace of romantic mythology in the modern exaltation of "the common people." Nonetheless, despite the laudable accomplishments of societal leaders in the history of nations and communities, many of us are now far less interested in kings and presidents, ministers and barons, and much more appreciative of those who lived and died in relative anonymity, who struggled a great deal and triumphed on occasion, who settled the land, built communities, raised families, and gave reason and meaning to civilization.

Throughout centuries of history the common people left few, if any, records of their existence, leaving us, their descendants, unable to identify their rightful place in our ancestry. It was only toward the end of the sixteenth century in European society that the existence of the common people as well as the elites of society was systematically recorded, due primarily to ecclesiastical direction from the Council of Trent. We must give our lasting thanks to the Catholic Church, which established a policy of registering the sacraments performed by the clergy. As parishioners received the sacraments of baptism, christening, and marriage, or in the hour of their death or burial received blessing, these sacraments were recorded. The ecclesiastical books of baptismal, marriage, and burial records created a generally comprehensive record of the lives of the common folk as well as the leading members of local communities.

With the worldwide exploration and colonization activities of Catholic Spain and Portugal during the sixteenth, seventeenth, and eighteenth centuries, the clergy accompanied the conquistadors and colonizers. In the territory that would come to be known as Latin America the same practice of registering the sacraments received by parishioners was instituted. We are fortunate today to have a record of many of the adherents of the Catholic faith in Latin America during the past nearly four centuries.

By the nineteenth century new ideas and a spirit of independence swept Latin America. New nations and secular governments were established, and the practice of civil registration of citizens was instituted. In local civil registry offices the births, marriages, and deaths of persons were registered, providing an additional invaluable record of the lives of ordinary people. Civil registration generally began in Latin American countries by the 1870s and 1880s. About that same time new waves of immigration reached Latin American shores, including many non-Catholic national and ethnic groups—persons who would not appear in the registers of the Catholic Church. Civil records are especially valuable in that they contain information on all residents in a community.

Both civil records and Catholic parish registers offer a wealth of personal and generational information for researchers. Parish records typically include the name of the individual being baptized or buried, or the couple being married, the parents of the individual or individuals, and in many cases, the grandparents of the couple being married, as well as the town of residence of all the persons mentioned in the records. Civil records are nearly as complete. Together, Catholic parish registers of baptisms, marriages, and burials, and civil records of births, marriages, and deaths provide the best available resource for historians, genealogists, and other researchers interested in the social and family history of Latin American nations.

There is a predictable regularity associated with parish and civil records. Parish priests used established form and phrasing in their records as they registered the sacraments offered to their parishioners. Typically only the names of the individuals and the places of residence change in the entries. By the nineteenth century, when civil registration was instituted, both civil and parish records were generally entered on printed forms that included the standard phrasing, requiring simply the entry by the registrar or priest of the individual information relating to the specific birth or baptism, marriage, or death. As one scans the records, there may be a certain monotony as name after name goes by, the wording varying but little. Yet as the names go by in regular patterns, one senses the fundamental nature of the records, of the people. Much like building blocks, the entries in the record books in their regularity represent the common people, the foundation of their society.

Because of the general availability and high value of parish and civil records for genealogical research in Latin America, the Family History Library has concentrated its efforts on acquiring film copies of these records. On a lower priority basis, we do film other genealogically valuable records, including national and local censuses, immigration records, notarial records, land records, and testamentary records or wills.

Census records list the inhabitants of a given locality or political entity. Censuses often include specific information about the individual listed, according to a variety of sociological or economic categories. Notable examples of national censuses in Latin America include the 1895 Argentine census and the 1930 Mexican census. Census records help researchers locate an individual in a specific locality and may indicate additional family members and other factual and descriptive information about the individual. The entire census for the locality in which an individual lived places him or her in a context, helping a researcher better understand the life experience of the individual. Church parishes also customarily took a census of local parishioners. Ecclesiastical censuses are not as detailed as later governmental censuses, but they do list the inhabitants of the local parish.

Because of significant international immigration to Latin America during the nineteenth and twentieth centuries, immigration records, such as ship passenger lists, are valuable for tracing the movement of individuals and groups. Typically, ship passenger lists indicate only the country of origin of an immigrant rather than the person's birthplace, so the genealogical value of the lists is somewhat limited. Still, they can provide a fascinating picture of the dynamics of international population movement and Latin American settlement. Unfortunately, we have not found available many collections of Latin American immigration records. One major collection we have filmed are the records of passenger arrivals at the ports of Santos and Rio de Janeiro, Brazil.

Notarial records, usually known as *protocolos,* were maintained in notarial books by *notarios* and *escribanos.* These officials recorded public documents and legal transactions. The records range from the very important to the relatively inconsequential, but taken as a whole they present a fascinating picture of the society of the day. The records include wills, land deeds, commerce, the exchange of goods, payments, contracts, mortgages, and dowries. The records are often not easy to read and do not necessarily include most of the residents of a locality, but where record of one's ancestors is found in notarial records one can discover a wealth of interesting information.

Although notarial records can be useful for serious genealogical and historical researchers, they are comparatively difficult to use, and most persons likely will not find their ancestors recorded in the records. The Family History Library has filmed some notarial records, and we also try to film census records where they are available. By far, however, the most useful records for the typical genealogical researcher are parish and civil records, and these records are our highest priority.

We have filmed approximately 20 percent of the available parish registers in Spain, and there is much work left to do. We are also filming Spanish notarial records. The archives of Spain are particularly rich with records of interest to family history researchers. Some of the Spanish records of interest to Hispanic family researchers of which we have acquired film copies are registers of *pasajeros a Indias* in the Archivo General de Indias in Seville; *probanzas de hidalguía* in the Real Chancillerías of Granada and Valladolíd; *expedientes y pruebas* in the Real Consejo de Ordenes Militares; and *hojas de servicios de América* in the Archivo General de América. Among the oldest Spanish records in the Family History Library collection are *expedientes matrimoniales* from the Archdiocese of Barcelona, dating from the year 1331.

In Portugal, we have filmed approximately 70 percent of the available parish registers to 1920, primarily in districts outside of Lisbon. We have virtually completed filming the parish records of Madeira and the Azores.

We have been filming for decades in Mexico, and we have significant parish register coverage and significant civil record coverage to 1920, as well as major portions of the 1930 federal census. We are currently filming civil death records, civil birth records to 1930, and civil marriage records to 1950. We also have filming projects that include land and marriage records in the Archivo General de la Nación, as well as civil records in the Distrito Federal.

Our work in Central America over the years has depended in large measure upon local conditions, and in some countries we have been much more successful than in others. In Guatemala and Panama, we have good coverage of available parish registers. Some land records and wills have also been filmed in Guatemala, where filming is currently being done in the Archivo General de Centroamérica. In Honduras, Belize, and Costa Rica, we have good coverage of both available church and civil records. Because of civil strife during past years, we have been much less successful in El Salvador, where we have approximately 25 percent of the records in which we are interested, and in Nicaragua, where we have not yet been able to film.

We have filming projects currently under way in some Caribbean island nations, including Jamaica and Puerto Rico. In the Archivo Nacional de Puerto Rico we are filming vital records and some census records. We have filmed some census, immigration, passport, and vital records in the Archivo Histórico de Ponce in Puerto Rico. We have also done filming in Antigua, Aruba, the Bahamas, Barbados, Bermuda, Dominica, Grenada, Guadeloupe, Haiti, Martinique, the Dominican Republic, St. Christopher and Nevis, St. Lucia, St. Vincent, Turks and Caicos Islands, and the British and U.S. Virgin Islands.

Filming is slow but steady in the Andean countries. Conditions are sometimes difficult and at times dangerous. Parish registers are being filmed in Peru and Colombia. We have good coverage of church records in Ecuador and Bolivia. We have also filmed census records in Ecuador and Bolivia, and land and testament records in Ecuador. We have just begun within the past two years filming in Venezuela. While we have virtually complete coverage of parish registers to 1920 in Paraguay, we are just beginning our filming efforts of civil registration in Uruguay. In Chile and Argentina, we have wide coverage of both church and civil registers. We also have film copies of the 1869 and 1895 national censuses of Argentina.

In Brazil we have approximately 60 percent of available parish registers and civil records, principally from southern states. At present we are filming civil records in several northeastern Brazilian states. We have also filmed copies of registers of immigrants from the port cities of Rio de Janeiro and Santos, a very valuable resource relating to the great period of European and Asian immigration during the late decades of the nineteenth century.

The Family History Department makes copies of its microfilm collection available to family history researchers in the Family History Library in Salt Lake City and in the more than 2,000 family history centers established throughout the world. The family history centers function as branch facilities of the Family History Library, and for a nominal fee researchers can order copies of almost any microfilm in the Family History Library for use in the family history centers. I must note here that at present, due to interpretation of our original filming contracts, many of our films of parish registers from Spain are currently restricted to use in the Family History Library in Salt Lake City only. We are hoping to renegotiate with Spanish archivists to allow greater circulation of the Spanish films.

There are presently approximately two hundred family history centers in Latin America. The centers are located in meetinghouses of the Church of Jesus Christ of Latter-day Saints. In major metropolitan areas, such as Mexico City, Guatemala City, Santiago, Buenos Aires, São Paulo, and Rio de Janeiro, there are several family history centers available for research activities. Although established in order to allow members of the Church of Jesus Christ of Latter-day Saints to research their ancestry for religious reasons, the centers are open to nonmembers of the church as well, and all patrons are welcome to use the family history centers.

In Latin American family history centers, researchers can use the Family History Library Catalog on microfiche. The catalog lists the holdings of the Family History Library in Salt Lake City, including our collection of microfilms that can be circulated to family history centers. The Library also has a number of books of genealogical interest to Latin American researchers, including compiled genealogies, geographical dictionaries, and national and local histories. Although the books do not circulate to family history centers, many of the older books have been preserved on microfilm or microfiche, and these can be circulated to family history centers.

Family history centers are administered by local church leaders and staffed by volunteers from local church congregations. Latin American family history centers are supported by and receive microfilm circulation from major regional family history service centers, located in Monterrey and Mexico City, Mexico; Guatemala City, Guatemala; Santiago, Chile; Buenos Aires, Argentina; São Paulo, Brazil; and San Juan, Puerto Rico. For information on family history centers in specific areas, we recommend that researchers contact the appropriate family history service center. A list of service centers in Latin America is found in the appendix.

It was while I was cataloging a microfilm of a Catholic parish register book from Três Corações, Minas Gerais, Brazil, a few years ago that I found a memorable baptismal record. In that particular filming project we had agreed to film parish records to the year 1930, but in the case of the entry to which I am referring our microfilmer chose to film one page of records from 1941. The entry was dated April 6, 1941, and was for the baptism of the son of João Ramos Nascimento and Celeste Arantes. Their son, born on October 23, 1940, was named Edson—Edson Arantes do Nascimento. In the margin of the entry for Edson's baptism a priest wrote some years later, presumably in 1962, "Este é Pelé, campeão mundial de football, 1958 — Bi campeão em 1962." A later clerical note, presumably written in 1970, says "Tricampeão mundial 1970."

Indeed, parish and civil registers can offer intriguing and interesting surprises. From parish registers we can learn that even Catholic priests are soccer fans, and justifiably proud of national sports heroes. The registers provide insights that enliven research and enrich our perspective on the past.

It is our hope that by collecting and making available microfilmed copies of original records from throughout the world, we can enable interested persons to research their family history and strengthen familial bonds. By preserving the records of the past, we can help ensure that not only the prominent or elite figures of society will be remembered but also that the multitudes of humble, nearly anonymous souls who have lived in the villages and urban centers of Latin America will not be forgotten, but indeed will be remembered and found and cherished by their descendants, and by all of us who share in their rich heritage.

APPENDIX 1

Family History Service Centers in Latin America

For information on the addresses of family history centers in Latin America, please contact the appropriate family history service center.

Mexico

Centro de Servicios de Historia Familiar de Monterrey
Concha Espino 303
Colonia Roma Sur
Monterrey, N.L.
64700 México

Telephone: 597-750

Centro de Servicios de Historia Familiar de México
Fuente de Pirámides, n. 1, p. 9
Lomas de Tecamachalco
México, D.F.
53950 México

Telephone: 760-0603

Central America

Centro de Servicios de Historia Familiar de Guatemala
24 Avenida 2-20, Zona 15
Vista Hermosa 1
Guatemala, Guatemala

Telephone: 358-982

Argentina, Uruguay, Paraguay

Centro de Servicios de Historia Familiar de Buenos Aires
Caracas 1289
1416 Buenos Aires, B.A.
Argentina

Telephone: 584-2971

Chile

Centro de Servicios de Historia Familiar de Santiago
Av. Pedro de Valdivia 1423
Clasificador 54
Santiago 9
Chile

Telephone: 225-7712

Brazil

Centro de Serviços de História da Família
Av. Prof. Francisco Morato, 2430
05512 São Paulo, S.P.
Brasil

Telephone: 814-2277

The Caribbean

Centro de Servicios de Historia Familiar
A-14 Ronda Street
Villa Andalucía
Río Piedras, Puerto Rico 00926

Telephone: 748-7240

APPENDIX 2

Family History Library Latin American Film Collection
(As of April 1994)

Country	Number of films	Country	Number of films
Mexico	143,852	Barbados	171
Brazil	11,123	Virgin Islands (U.S.)	144
Argentina	8,737	West Indies	80
Guatemala	8,589	Grenada	61
Chile	8,045	Guiana	59
Peru	2,878	Bermuda	43
Bolivia	2,366	Belize	28
Colombia	1,954	Dominica	18
El Salvador	1,901	Cuba	17
Ecuador	1,462	Suriname	13
Costa Rica	1,390	Turks and Caicos Islands	12
Jamaica	1,321	Virgin Islands (British)	9
Honduras	1,046	Netherlands Antilles	7
Puerto Rico	932	Anguilla	5
Dominican Republic	799	Antigua and Barbuda	3
Bahamas	633	Santa Lucia	1
Uruguay	487	Guyana, Saint Kitts, Nevis,	0
Paraguay	460	Saint Christopher, Neth.	
Panama	430	Antilles, Nicaragua, Cayman	
Guadeloupe	377	Islands, West Indies, Leeward	
Martinique	306	Islands, Montserrat, Windward	
Venezuela	223	Islands, Trinidad and Tobago,	
Haiti	216	Saint Vincent, Aruba	

NOTE: Some films are of lesser genealogical value. Not all films are of key record types such as parish and civil records, census records, public records such as notarial or land records, or immigration records.

Family History Library Filming of Key Record Types
for Genealogical Research in Latin America
(As of 1994)

The numbers below reflect the extreme ranges of years of records
available for the listed countries. The range of years indicated does not
signify that records are available for all localities in the country for the
entire range of years. For specific information on records available for a
specific locality and time period, it is essential to consult the Locality
Section of the Family History Library Catalog.

Country	Parish records	Civil records	Census records	Public records (including notarial, probate, tax, land, court)	Immigra- tion records
Argentina	1700-1930		1869, 1895	1584-1756 (notarial)	
Aruba, Nether- lands Antilles		1923-1966			
Bahamas				1788-1955 (land deeds)	
Barbados	1637-1931		1678-1679, 1715		
Belize		1881-1957	1816-1840		
Bermuda	1755-1958			1640-1913 (probate)	
Bolivia	1609-1940		1575-1808		
Brazil	1635-1940	1875-1950			1808-1922
Chile	1580-1935	1895-1930			
Colombia	1619-1945			1508-1950 (notarial, probate)	

Costa Rica	1738-1970	1860-1975		1508-1898* (notarial, probate)
Dominica	1869-1934	1901-1991		1765-1927 (land deeds)
Dominican Republic	1590-1939	1824-1944		
Ecuador	1676-1945		1776, 1861-1871	1579-1915 (notarial, land, wills)
El Salvador	1688-1947	1865-1930	1746-1787	1508-1898* (notarial, probate)
Grenada	1784-1971	1866-1940	1669-1776	1764-1931 (land)
Guadeloupe	1679-1794	1792-1870	1665-1802	
Guatemala	1599-1937	1877-1948	1662-1827, 1887	1508-1898* (notarial, probate, tax)
Guiana	1677-1830	1791-1870		
Guayana	1758-1811			
Haiti	1666-1803	1790-1803	1730-1749, 1776, 1800	1704-1803 (notarial)
Honduras	1694-1960	1906-1936	1758-1869	1508-1898* (notarial, probate)
Jamaica	1664-1880	1878-1930		
Martinique	1666-1830	1803-1874	1675-1786	
Mexico	1545-1970		1752-1865, 1930	1523-1822 (probate, land)
Nicaragua				1508-1898* (notarial, probate)

Panama	1742-1973				
Paraguay	1767-1978				
Peru	1556-1990	1874-1920		1537-1869 (notarial)	
Portugal	1540-1910				
Puerto Rico	1730-1960	1778-1988	1801-1900, 1920		1745-1900
St. Christopher, Nevis		1859-1932	1665-1701		
St. Lucia	1751-1788		1730-1789		
St. Vincent			1732		
Spain	1331-1978		1752-1754	1504-1867 (notarial, court)	1509-1701
Turks and Caicos Islands	1864-1991			1849-1954 (probate)	
Uruguay	1771-1982	1879-1930			
Venezuela	1731-1959		1756-1798		
Virgin Islands (British)	1815-1934	1859-1966			
Virgin Islands (U.S.)	1666-1979		1841-1911, 1920	1672-1860 (court, probate)	

*Records filmed in the Archivo General de Centroamérica in Guatemala.

20. Brazilian Newspapers

Carmen M. Muricy

After twenty years of dictatorship, Brazil is living a special moment of freedom and independence in mass media. In the last several years, Brazilian newspapers have had a remarkable participation in the country's history, retrieving their credibility. As the facts were made public and analyzed, and opinions expressed, newspapers were demonstrated to be necessary instruments in investigating the episodes that shocked the country. They acted as society's monitor, participating actively in one of the most difficult capters of Brazilian contemporary history: President Fernando Collor de Mello's impeachment in 1992, and CPI do Orçamento (Parliamentary Investigative Commission for the Budget) in 1993.

Modernization and Market Leadership

Aiming at increasing readership and advertisements, newspapers have been changing their layout, with creativity. They are becoming more modern, both in editorials as well as in technology employed, with automation in all major newspapers. There is a greater concern with investigation and deeper analysis.

According to Instituto de Verificação de Circulação-IVC (Institute for Circulation Checking), *Folha de São Paulo, O Globo, O Dia, O Estado de São Paulo, Zero Hora,* and *Jornal do Brasil* rank as newspapers with the highest circulation.

The *Folha de São Paulo* was the first newspaper to automate its editorial room. It was the pioneer in creating separate sections when it launched the *Caderno Ilustrado* in 1958. It continued this process, creating the Economy Section in 1986, followed by several others, such as sections for different cities of São Paulo state. With a daily average circulation of 300,000 issues, it is the leader in the country.

O Globo, published by the powerful Globo communication network, maintained a leadership position from its beginning in 1925, when it started to circulate in Rio de Janeiro. From 1990 on, it offered new products, publishing supplements for eleven city neighborhoods.

Since its first issue in 1951, *O Dia,* from Rio de Janeiro, has had the highest newsstand circulation. Basically, it reaches workers, students, and small business owners.

O Estado de São Paulo (Estadão), recognized as one of the twenty most important newspapers in the world, commemorated in January its 115th anniversary. It publishes the *Clipping do Estadão,* a monthly publication with a summary of the principal facts of the day. It has been printed in four colors since 1991 when it launched *Caderno Informática* (Computers).

Another important title is *Zero Hora* from Porto Alegre, RS. It is the most important newspaper in Southern Brazil, ranking fifth among the country's papers.

Since 1891, *Jornal do Brasil* has been known and respected for its independence and critical positions. In 1960, it launched *Caderno B,* followed by *Revista de Domingo* and several others. Its average circulation is 138,000 copies.

Diário Catarinense from Florianópolis, SC, launched in 1986 by Rede Brazil Sul, was the first automated newspaper in Brazil. It integrates regions of diversified culture in the state of Santa Catarina and ranks among the top twenty in Brazil.

Current Newspapers Acquired by the Library of Congress Office, Rio de Janeiro

The Rio de Janeiro Office of the Library of Congress acquires Brazilian newspapers on a selective basis. From the seventeen titles collected, eight are from São Paulo and four from Rio de Janeiro. The remaining titles are from the cities of Brasília, Belo Horizonte, Porto Alegre, Curitiba, and Recife. All the titles are acquired in hard copy and in microfilm, with the exception of *Jornal do Commercio* and *Tribuna da Imprensa,* acquired in microfilm only.

In 1977, the Biblioteca Nacional (BN) and the Library of Congress (LC) established a successful microfilm exchange of Brazilian newspapers. This program enabled both libraries to acquire at much reduced costs important collections of Brazilian newspapers, enriching library resources in Brazil and the United States. Under the agreement, LC and BN exchanged positive microfilm of the titles each institution had filmed. One of the most important filmings done at that time was the *Jornal do Commercio* from Rio de Janeiro, founded in 1827, the oldest continuously published newspaper of South America.

Presently, LC provides positive film stock to Fundação Biblioteca Nacional (FBN) (formerly Biblioteca Nacional) and receives from FBN reels of positive microfilm newspapers. About ten current newspaper titles have been microfilmed for LC.

The Fundação Biblioteca Nacional publishes a microform catalog: *Periódicos Brasileiros em Microformas: catálogo coletivo*. The latest published is the fourth edition in 1989. Earlier editions appeared in 1976, 1979, and 1981. It lists 2,700 current and retrospective serial titles available in 42 Brazilian institutions and elsewhere. It includes a special collection of government reports: province presidents, state governors, and ministerials (from the Empire to the First Republic), microfilmed with the support of the Center for Research Libraries (CRL)/Latin American Microform Project (LAMP) in Chicago. The Library of Congress, Rio de Janeiro Office, also participated in this cooperative program between LAMP and FBN, forwarding correspondence and films through its office.

Cooperative Acquisitions Program

In January 1990, the Library of Congress, Rio de Janeiro Office, began a program of supplying Brazilian serials to interested libraries. From a membership of 20 in its first year of activities, the program grew to 41 participants in FY94. A total of 206 serials titles were offered, resulting in approximately 800 subscriptions.

Daily newspapers have become increasingly in demand. The office supplies the four major daily newspapers: *Jornal do Brasil, O Estado de São Paulo, Folha de São Paulo*, and *O Globo*.

A preliminary list of 228 serials for 1995 is available at this SALALM meeting.

Nonstandard Newspapers and Brazil's Popular Groups Collection from the Library of Congress on Microfilm

In 1984, the Library of Congress Office began to collect ephemeral material (serials, pamphlets, and posters) published by popular groups in Brazil. The collection makes accessible to researchers a body of primary source material, which is basic to the study of grassroots political and social movements in Brazil. It is organized into twelve subject categories (Agrarian Reform, Blacks, Children's Issues, Ecology, Education and Communication Issues, Human and Minority Rights, Indians, Labor and Laboring Classes, Political Parties and Issues, Religion and Theology, Urban Issues, and Women). The material is gathered and organized by the Library of Congress, Rio de Janeiro Office, and microfilmed by the Library of Congress Photoduplication Service. The first collection covered materials published from 1966 to 1986 (2,271 pieces, preserved in 32 reels). It was followed by Supplement 1987-1989 (1,049 pieces in 43 reels) and Supplement 1990-1992 (4,271 pieces, in the process of microfilming at Library of

Congress). Henceforth, supplements will be compiled annually. A fourth collection, the 1993 supplement, is being organized at the Rio Office.

The Rio Office acquires regularly 347 serial titles for the popular groups collection. The newspapers, mostly in tabloid format, are published weekly, monthly, and many times, irregularly. For this reason, it is difficult to make a distinction between the newspapers and the magazines.

There is a great variety of titles covering the activities of the groups in all segments of society: *Folha do Aposentado* came out in 1992 in the midst of the famous "147% payment struggle" by the retired workers; *Brazil Agora*, one of the various publications of the Labor Party, voices the opposition party, PT; *Ombro a Ombro* is published by a nonofficial military group; *Folha Universal*, from Reino de Deus Universal Church of Bishop Macedo; *Maioria Falante*, from a Black Movement in Rio; *Rumos*, published by a group of former Catholic priests (now married); *Folha do Meio Ambiente*, one of the many publications on ecology; and *Nós por Exemplo* is the newsletter of homosexuals. All states are covered, from Acre (*Yuimaki*, a Comissão Pro-Indio do Acre publication) to Rio Grande do Sul (*Jornal do Amencar*, supporting the child in need).

BIBLIOGRAPHY

Jornal ANJ. v.1–. April 1985–. Brasília: Associação Nacional de Jornais. Monthly.
    75–76 (December 1993–January 1994).
Musikman, Felicia, and Maria José da Silva Fernandes. "Catálogos de microformas de periódicos brasileiros." In Ann Hartness, ed., *Continuity and Change in Brazil and the Southern Cone: Research Trends and Library Collections for Year 2000.* Papers of SALALM XXXV, Rio de Janeiro, June 3-8, 1990. Albuquerque, NM: SALALM, 1992. Pp. 270-279.
Propaganda. v.1–. no.1–. 1956–. São Paulo: Editora Referência. Monthly.
    38:483 (July 1993). Special ed.
Sullivan, Robert, "Five Decades of Microforms at the Library of Congress." *Microform Review* 17:3 (1988), 155-158.

II
Bibliographic Surveys of
Latin American Literature

21. El hecho se convierte en ficción: El dictador latinoamericano visto a través de las obras de Asturias, García Márquez y Valle-Inclán

Nelly S. González

En el transcurso de mi investigación sobre la extensa bibliografía del escritor colombiano Gabriel García Márquez, un artículo periodístico llamó mi atención por comparar a éste novelista latinoamericano con otros dos grandes escritores españoles uno de los cuales, Ramón del Valle-Inclán, no había sido mencionado en ninguno de los ensayos que sobre el escritor de *Cien años de soledad* había yo leído hasta entonces. Posteriormente, al tener noticia del XXIX Congreso del Instituto Nacional de Literatura Iberoamericana a celebrarse en la Universidad de Barcelona busqué el artículo mencionado el mismo que lastimosamente se entrepapeló entre la voluminosa colección de artículos que poseo sobre García Márquez y sus obras, y no pude encontrarlo.

Decidí entonces ponerme en contacto con el prestigioso crítico y estudioso del escritor colombiano Dr. Michael Palencia-Roth quien me aseguró que probablemente el artículo que yo mencionaba, estuviese comparando la figura del "dictador" descrita tanto en *El otoño del patriarca* de García Márquez como en *Tirano Banderas* del escritor gallego Ramón del Valle-Inclán, y *El señor presidente* del escritor guatemalteco Miguel Angel Asturias.

Como no logré encontrar siempre el artículo origen de ésta relación, decidí investigar la valiosa idea que mi amigo Palencia-Roth me había regalado. Este trabajo representa el resultado de dicha búsqueda.

Ramón del Valle-Inclán, Miguel Angel Asturias y Gabriel García Márquez tienen mucho en común, no solamente por su exquisito don de expresión literaria, sino también en sus caracteres y personalidades y en las circunstancias de la vida que les tocó vivir. Mas aún, especialmente comparten la vivencia de haber vivido bajo sistemas políticos controlados por dictadores, como el de Miguel Primo de Rivera en España, Manuel Estrada Cabrera en Guatemala, y Juan Vicente Gómez en Venezuela. Por sus fuertes convicciones, ellos no tuvieron miedo de oponerse a la situación política de sus tiempos, siendo fieles a sus principios y sistemas de valores, duros e indomables.

Los tres escritores han padecido las consecuencias de sus posturas y tendencias políticas teniendo que sufrir prisión y exilio. Así García Márquez, quien tuvo que exiliarse en Méjico, dejó una honda huella, hasta el punto de que hoy en día se identifique completamente con el pueblo mejicano de la misma manera que el propio Valle-Inclán responde a Alfonso Reyes durante una conversación sostenida por ambos, afirmando que "ama profundamente la tierra mejicana y por extensión toda la América Latina".[1] Miguel Angel Asturias, junto con su familia, primero tuvo un exilio interno, habiendo sido forzados a vivir varios años en una zona rural guatemalteca. El también tuvo que salir al exilio hacia Londres primero y después a Paris. Durante sus años en el exilio, al igual que García Márquez, tuvo que ganarse la vida colaborando con diversos periódicos mejicanos y centroamericanos como corresponsal extranjero.

Estos tres escritores tienen el don de recrear la ficción a partir de la realidad, sin ofrecer, sin embargo, un marco geográfico preciso que podría situarse en cualquier lugar de Latinoamérica. Esto ocurre también en cuanto a los personajes que representan en sus obras. El propio Miguel Angel Asturias declaró que el principal personaje de su novela *El señor presidente* está basado en alguien real, Manuel Estrada Cabrera, el dictador guate-malteco.[2] La república que el *Tirano Banderas* tiraniza es Santa Fe de Tierra Firme "pais imaginario —pero que— todos los indicios señalan a Méjico como el que Valle-Inclán tuviera presente"[3] al escribir su obra y; *El otoño del patriarca* donde "no hablan ni el dictador ni el pueblo, ni desde luego un narrador individual sino una persona imposible, incoherente hecha de retazos de distinta procedencia pronominal".[4]

Otra característica común a los tres escritores es la de disponer de una tremenda capacidad de fabulación. Miguel Angel Asturias muestra preocupación por la realidad afirmando que su creación literaria "no es una deformación de la realidad sino una nueva realidad".[5] En el caso de Valle-Inclán, la máxima expresión de su genio artístico se manifiesta en sus famosos esperpentos, de los que no me voy a ocupar aquí, pero que son sin duda, significativos en cuanto a que nos dan idea de la interpretación de la realidad que el escritor gallego realizara. García Márquez concretiza en su característico estilo que tradicionalmente ha sido denominado realismo mágico. Los tres escritores fueron prolíficos aún antes de producir sus obras cuyo tema es "el dictador". Todos ellos habían escrito para periódicos y revistas y experimentado en varios géneros literarios. Su producción es extensa y más aún todavía, los tres declaran que contrariamente a sus críticos literarios, ellos piensan que sus mejores obras son para Asturias *El señor presidente* (1946) y para García Márquez *El otoño del patriarca* (1975). Unicamente *Tirano Banderas* de Valle-Inclán, es aclamada por la crítica literaria como la mejor obra de Valle-Inclán, en concordancia con el propio Valle-Inclán, quien dijo al publicar su magistral obra, que sus anteriores trabajos "eran nada más que musiquillas" y que su primera obra de escritor era *Tirano Banderas* (1926).[6] Y así, la crítica literaria responde positivamente a *Tirano Banderas* pero *El otoño del patriarca* no la considera la mejor obra de García Márquez, y más bien aclama a *Cien años de soledad* y; para Asturias, la crítica literaria se pronuncia en favor de *El hombre de maíz* (1949).[7]

A diferencia de Miguel Angel Asturias y Gabriel García Márquez, quienes participan activamente en la política durante su juventud y presentan una definida conciencia social y espíritu combativo, Valle-Inclán toma conciencia social tardía, talvez como resultado de la efervescencia en los acontecimientos públicos cambiando espectacularmente en su forma literaria produciéndose así una "escisión inexplicable entre uno y otro Valle-Inclán".[8] Es así, que reconoce en Méjico, el lugar de su imaginación y su encuentro con su vocación literaria. Es alrededor de este tiempo, que toma su nombre literario de "Don Ramón María del Valle-Inclán"[9] volviéndole a su apellido de forma compuesta usando el guión entre Valle e Inclán.

Tanto Valle-Inclán como García Márquez, tuvieron su cita con el destino, al verse ambos reseñados e interpretados por Guillermo de Torre, aunque en diferente apreciación. Este crítico le descubre a Valle-Inclán "su verdadero rostro" indicando que es posible que "el rostro de Valle-Inclán no fuera otra cosa que su máscara",[10] y a García Márquez le rechaza la publicación en Editorial Losada, de la ya famosa obra *Cien años de soledad*, aconsejándole al entonces mostrenco literario García Márquez, que se retirara de la literatura, por no tener aptitud para ella. Fue un verdadero "torrechazo" el que Guillermo de Torre diera a García Márquez y a *Cien años de soledad*.

Finalmente, tanto Valle-Inclán como García Márquez, fracasaron en su intento de consagración en el arte de la cinematografía. Ambos escribieron guiones cinematográficos, pero sin alcanzar la gloria que la narrativa literaria les brindó.

Todas estas consideraciones, son nada más que interrogaciones que me vinieron a la mente mientras realizaba mi búsqueda bibliográfica de estos tres grandes maestros, dos de los cuales son ganadores del tan codiciado premio Nobel de literatura y referidos aquí únicamente en las tres obras citadas cuya temática es la del "dictador".

Concluyo transcribiendo la impresión causada por estas obras en las palabras de algunos de sus críticos. Así por ejemplo, Francisco Madrid dice de *Tirano Banderas*:

Apareció *Tirano Banderas*. Las gentes en cuanto lo vieron en los escaparates de las librerías agotaron la primera y la segunda edición. Fué uno de los más grandes éxitos literarios que ha habido en España en lo que va de siglo.[11]

Arturo Uslar Pietri dice así sobre Asturias:

El señor Presidente no fué solo un gran libro de literatura, sino un valiente acto de denuncia de llamada a la conciencia. Más que todos los tratados y análisis históricos y sociológicos, plantea con brutal presencia inolvidable lo que ha sido para los hispanoamericanos, en muchas horas, la tragedia de vivir.[12]

Y George R. McMurray dice que:

El otoño del patriarca es la novela mas política hasta la fecha.[13]

Martha Canfield concluye que:

La novela sobre el dictador sucita opiniones encontradas y aunque algunos la valoran en seguida (por ejemplo, Angel Rama o Julio Ortega), a otros los desconcierta hasta empujarlos a juicios negativos (Jaime Mejía Duque) o reductivos (Mario Benedetti y, en parte, Ernesto Volkening). Hoy en día se ha uniformado la valoración de esta obra y del extraordinario trabajo que hay en ella, tanto a nivel de lenguage como de elaboración mítica (el mito del dictador).[14]

Terminaré esta modesta contribución diciendo que Valle-Inclán, aunque español, tuvo corazón de hispanoamericano, porque supo identificarse con la tierra, y captar la esencia de sus dictadores, al igual que Miguel Angel Asturias y Gabriel García Márquez quienes tuvieron la suerte de sufrirlos.

La bibliografía selectiva que sigue representa monografías y tesis doctorales sobre una o más de las tres obras tratadas en este ensayo y sobre temas importantes que tienen directa relación con el núcleo literario de las tres novelas. No están incluidos artículos de periódicos, revistas, ni capítulos individuales publicados en libros. Esta bibliografía se obtuvo en las siguientes fuentes:

MLA International Bibliography. [CD-ROM] (Modern Language Association of America). Bronx, NY: H.W. Wilson Co., 1981-1991.

Illinet Online. University of Illinois Library at Urbana-Champaign.

    (Nota: Este es el catálogo conjunto del acervo bibliográfico de más de 800 bibliotecas del Estado de Illinois, USA, que están incluidas en esta base de datos.)

Dissertation Abstracts Ondisc: Literature and Language Arts Section. Ann Arbor, MI: University Microfilms, 1989-1991.

    (Nota: Esta base de datos incluye tesis presentadas en universidades de los Estados Unidos y el Canadá para la obtención del título de Master y Doctorado.)

NOTAS

1. Obdulia Guerrero Bueno, *América en Valle-Inclán* (Madrid: Albar Editorial, 1984), p. 13.

2. Ricardo Navas Ruíz, "El señor presidente: de su génesis a la presente edición", en Miguel A. Asturias, ed., *El señor presidente*, Edición crítica (México: Fondo de Cultura Económica, 1978), p. xxii.

3. Ricardo Gullon, "Técnicas de Valle-Inclán", en Ricardo Deménech, ed., *Ramón del Valle-Inclán* (Madrid: Taurus, 1988), p. 364.

4. Gonzalo Díaz Migoyo, *Guía de Tirano Banderas* (Madrid: Editorial Fundamentos, 1985), p. 200.

5. *Coloquio con Miguel Angel Asturias* (Guatemala: Editorial Universitaria Guatemala, 1968), p. 31.

6. Díaz Migoyo, *Guía*, p. 20.

7. Francisco Madrid, *La vida altiva de Valle-Inclán* (Buenos Aires: Poseidon, 1943), p. 113.

8. Díaz Migoyo, *Guía*, p. 23.

9. Roberto Barrios, "Entrevista con Valle-Inclán publicada en *El Universal* de México y reproducida en *Repertorio Americano*" (San José, Costa Rica, noviembre 28, 1921), p. 173.

10. Guillermo de Torre, *La difícil universalidad española* (Madrid: Gredos, 1965), p. 114.

11. Ireneo Paz, *Porfirio Díaz*, vol. 2 (México: Imprenta de Ireneo Paz, 1911), p. 39.

12. Arturo Uslar Pietri, "Testimonio", en Miguel A. Asturias, ed., *El señor presidente*, Edición crítica (México: Fondo de Cultura Económica, 1978), p. xvi.

13. George R. McMurray, *Gabriel García Márquez: Life, Work, and Criticism* (Fredericton, Canada: York Press, 1987), p. 19.

14. Martha L. Canfield, "Gabriel García Márquez", en Gloria Zea, ed., *Manual de literatura colombiana*, vol. 2 (Bogotá: Procultura y Planeta, 1988), p. 278.

BIBLIOGRAFIA

Tirano Banderas

Alonso, Antonio. "Sobre la estructura de *Tirano Banderas*". *Cuadernos Hispanoamericanos: Revista Mensual de Cultura Hispánica* 438 (diciembre 1986), 45-53.

Bělič, Oldřich. *La estructura narrativa de "Tirano Banderas"*. Madrid: Editora Nacional, 1968.

Berg, Walter Bruno. "Erkennen als 'Schreibe': ein beitrag zur esperpento-diskussion in Valle-Inclán's *Tirano Banderas*". *Archiv fur das Studium der Neueren Sprachen und Literaturen* 220, 2 (1983), 323-342.

Bruce-Novoa, Juan. "*Tirano Banderas* y la novela de dictadura latino-americana". En Harald Wentzlaff-Eggebert, ed., *Ramón del Valle-Inclán (1866-1936)*. Tubingen: Niemeyer, 1988. Pp. 219-232.

Campos Harriet, Fernando. "Trascendencia americana de Valle-Inclán". *Atenea: Revista de Ciencia, Arte y Literatura de la Universidad de Concepción* 447 (1983), 143-148.

Cano, Ana María. "La figura de Lope de Aguirre en su contexto literario". Tesis, Florida State University, 1983.

Cornejo-Parriego, Rosalía Victoria. "Historia, mito y ficción en novelas de dictadura". Tesis, Pennsylvania State University, 1991.

Díaz Migoyo, Gonzalo. *Guía de "Tirano Banderas"*. Madrid: Fundamentos, 1985.

————. *"Tirano Banderas* o la simultaneidad textual". *Revista Hispánica Moderna* 41, 1 (June 1988), 61-68.

Espinoza, Herberto. "Lope de Aguirre y Santos Banderas: la manipulación del mito". *Maize: Notebooks of Xicano Art and Literature* 4, 3-4 (primavera-verano 1981), 32-43.

————. "Síntesis vs. análisis: un problema de historicidad en las novelas de las dictaduras". *Maize: Notebooks of Xicano Art and Literature* 6, 1-2 (otoño-invierno 1982-1983), 7-27.

Finnegan-Smith, Pamela. "The Complementary Roles of Satire and Irony in Valle-Inclán's *Tirano Banderas"*. *Hispanic Journal* 8, 10 (otoño 1986), 31-46.

Kirschner, Teresa J. "La descripción subversiva del jardín de la virreina en *Tirano Banderas"*. *Boletín de la Biblioteca de Menéndez Pelayo* 57 (1981), 361-372.

Kloepfer, Rolf. "Der gemischte Schrecken des Erkennens: Sympraxis in Valle-Inclán's *Tirano Banderas"*. En Harald Wentzlaff-Eggebert, ed., *Ramón del Valle-Inclán (1866-1936)*. Tubingen: Niemeyer, 1988. Pp. 197-217.

Larsen, Kevin S. *"Tirano Banderas* y *Aguirre, der Zorn Gottes*: diapositivas en un continuum cinematográfico". En Juan Fernández Jiménez et al., eds., *Estudios en Homenaje a Enrique Ruiz-Fornells*. Erie, PA: Asociación de Licenciados & Doctores Españoles en Estados Unidos, 1990. Pp. 376-382.

Liano, Dante. "El problema del héroe en *Tirano Banderas"*. *Quaderni Ibero-Americani: Attualita Culturale nella Penisola Iberica e America Latina* 57-58 (1984-1985), 36-49.

————. "Valle-Inclán: los sitios de la imaginación: el espacio en *Tirano Banderas"*. *Studi dell'Istituto Linguistico* 6 (1983), 155-184.

Mejía Ruiz, Carmen. *"Tirano Banderas* y *El señor presidente"*. *Beitrage zur Romanischen Philologie* 29, 1 (1990), 51-64.

Orbe, Juan. "Una inspección de *Tirano Banderas* como 'síntesis.' En John P. Gabriele, ed., *Genio y virtuosismo de Valle-Inclán*. Madrid: Orígenes, 1987. Pp. 79-87.

Ouimette, Víctor. "El centro patético en *Tirano Banderas*". *Letras de Deusto* 19, 44 (mayo-agosto 1989), 233-249.

Rehder, Ernest C. "Historical Antecedents for the Vate Larranaga and the Baron de Benicarles in Valle-Inclán's *Tirano Banderas*". *Romance Notes* 22, 1 (otoño 1981), 37-41.

———. "Raza y racismo en *El militarismo mejicano* de Blasco Ibáñez y *Tirano Banderas* de Valle-Inclán". *Discurso Literario: Revista de Temas Hispánicos* 6, 1 (otoño 1988), 235-244.

Salgues Cargill, Maruxa. "*Tirano Banderas*". *Estudio Crítico-Analítico*. Jaén: Gráficas Nova, 1973.

Salmon, Russell O. "The Structure of Personal Power Politics and the Hispanic World". En Gene H. Bell-Villada et al., eds., *From Dante to García Márquez*. Williamstown: Williams College, 1987. Pp. 297-312.

Smith, Verity. *Valle-Inclán: "Tirano Banderas"*. Londres: Grant and Cutler, 1971.

Speratti Piñero, Emma Susana. *La elaboración artística en "Tirano Banderas"*. México: El Colegio de México, 1957.

Tietz, Manfred. "Valle-Inclán und die spanische 'novela del dictador'". En Harald Wentzlaff-Eggebert, ed., *Ramón del Valle-Inclán (1866-1936)*. Tubingen: Niemeyer, 1988. Pp. 233-242.

Varela Jacome, Benito. "El mundo narrativo de *Tirano Banderas*". *Revista de Occidente* 59 (abril 1986), 67-78.

Velasco, Juan. "Lo fantástico y la historia: la polémica entre *La sombra del caudillo* y *Tirano Banderas*". *Mester* 19, 2 (otoño 1990), 71-81.

Vélez Serrano, Luis. "Apuntes para una gramática del personaje en las novelas del dictador, I: el 'estudiante' en *Tirano Banderas*". En Jean-Claude Bouvier, ed., *Stylistique, rhétorique et poétique dans les langues romanes*. Provence: Université de Provence, 1986. Pp. 173-182.

———. "Estudio del personaje 'estudiante' en las novelas del dictador". En Miguel Angel Garrido Gallardo, ed., *Crítica semiológica de textos literarios hispánicos*. Madrid: Consejo Superior de Investigaciones Científicas, 1986. Pp. 877-886.

Wentzlaff-Eggebert, Harald. "Ramón del Valle-Inclán: *Tirano Banderas*, novela de tierra caliente". En Volker Rolof y Harald Wentzlaff-

Eggebert, eds., *Der spanische Roman vom Mittelalter bis zur Gegenwart*. Dusseldorf: Schwann Bagel, 1986. Pp. 308-329.

Wong Savioni, Khena. "Elementos estridentistas en *Tirano Banderas*". *La Palabra y el Hombre: Revista de la Universidad Veracruzana* 75 (julio-septiembre 1990), 111-122.

El otoño del patriarca

Anadón, José. *Power in Literature and Society: The Double in Gabriel García Márquez's "The Autumn of the Patriarch"*. Notre Dame, IN: Helen Kellogg Institute for International Studies, University of Notre Dame, 1989.

Aronne-Amestoy, Lida. "El mito contra el mito: narración e ideografía en *El otoño del patriarca*". *Revista Iberoamericana* 52, 135-136 (abril-septiembre 1986), 521-530.

Barsy, Kalman. *La estructura dialéctica de "El otoño del patriarca"*. Río Piedras: Editorial de la Universidad de Puerto Rico, 1989.

————. "Retroactividad del discurso en *El otoño del patriarca*". *Sin Nombre* 13, 1 (octubre-diciembre 1982), 36-49.

Beason, Pamela Sue. "The Dictator in *Yo, el Supremo, El recurso del método* and *El otoño del patriarca*". Tesis, University of Oklahoma, 1979.

Bedoya M., Luis Iván, y Augusto Escobar M. *Elementos para una lectura de "El otoño del patriarca"*. Medellín: Ediciones Pepe, 1978.

Bell-Villada, Gene H. "Pronoun Shifters, Virginia Woolf, Bela Bartok, Plebeian Forms, Real-Life Tyrants, and the Shaping of García Márquez's Patriarch". *Contemporary Literature* 28, 4 (invierno 1987), 460-482.

Bhalla, Alok. "'Power, like a Desolating Pestilence': Dictatorship and Community in *The Autumn of the Patriarch*". En Alok Bhalla, ed., *García Márquez and Latin America*. New York: Envoy, 1987. Pp. 29-42.

Borinsky, Alicia. "Avatars of Intelligence: Figures of Reading in the Work of Gabriel García Márquez". *University of Dayton Review* 18, 1 (verano 1986), 5-12.

Buchanan, Rhonda L. "The Cycle of Rage and Order in García Márquez's *El otoño del patriarca*". *Perspectives on Contemporary Literature* 10 (1984), 75-85.

————. "*El otoño del patriarca*: A Jungian Interpretation". Tesis, University of Colorado, Boulder, 1982.

Calvino Iglesias, Julio. *Historia, ideología y mito en la narrativa hispanoamericana contemporánea.* Madrid: Ayuso, 1987.

Canfield, Martha L. "El patriarca de García Márquez: padre, poeta y tirano". *Revista Iberoamericana* 50, 128-129 (julio-diciembre 1984), 1017-1056.

Castro de Lee, Cecilia. "Génesis y destrucción del poder en *Cien años de soledad* y *El otoño del patriarca*". *Boletín Cultural y Bibliográfico* 19, 1 (1982), 87-99.

Cazarré, Lourenço. "O general veste a griffe de García Márquez: *O general em seu laberinto* x o *Outono do patriarca*". *Minas Gerais, Suplemento Literario* 24, 1161 (febrero 1991), 4-6.

Cornejo-Parriego, Rosalía Victoria. "Historia, mito, y ficción en novelas de dictadura". Tesis, Pennsylvania State University, 1991.

Cuervo Hewitt, Julia. "'Nuestra América' en *El otoño del patriarca*: ecos populares y textos históricos en la invención de América". *Discurso Literario: Revista de Temas Hispánicos* 1, 2 (primavera 1984), 143-158.

Daruwalla, Keki N. "The Shadow of Power: Dictatorship and Human Destiny in the Novels of García Márquez and Carpentier". En Alok Bhalla, ed., *García Márquez and Latin America.* New York: Envoy, 1987. Pp. 68-80.

Díaz Arenas, Angel. *Folklore Iberoamericano en "El otoño del patriarca" de Gabriel García Márquez: letras, partituras, y estudio histórico-comparativo.* Bonn: Romanistischer Verlag, 1988.

———. *El realismo mágico en "El otoño del patriarca" de Gabriel García Márquez: claves para una lectura codificada.* Bonn: Romanistischer Verlag, 1987.

Dravasa, Maider. "El boom y Barcelona: literatura y poder". Tesis, Yale University, 1992.

Espinoza, Herberto. "Síntesis vs. análisis: un problema de historicidad en las novelas de las dictaduras". *Maize: Notebooks of Xicano Art and Literature* 6, 1-2 (otoño-invierno 1982-1983), 7-27.

Gil López, Ernesto. "El espacio en *El otoño del patriarca* de Gabriel García Márquez". *Revista de Filología de la Universidad de La Laguna* 2 (1983), 65-70.

Ginther, April, y Daniel Iglesias. "Vida en la muerte: presencia y efectos de la atrocidad en *El otoño del patriarca*". En Ana María Hernández de López, ed., *En el punto de mira: Gabriel García Márquez.* Madrid: Pliegos, 1985. Pp. 187-198.

Hazera, Lydia D. "La desmitificación del patriarca". En Ana María Hernández de López, ed., *En el punto de mira: Gabriel García Márquez*. Madrid: Pliegos, 1985. Pp. 199-206.

Hernández, Rafael E. "La imaginería del poder en *El otoño del patriarca*". *South Eastern Latin Americanist* 36, 1 (verano 1992), 1-8.

Holt, Candace K. "*El otoño del patriarca*: una perspectiva hegeliana". *Discurso Literario: Revista de Temas Hispánicos* 1, 1 (otoño 1983), 23-35.

————. "*Rayuela, El obsceno pájaro de la noche* y *El otoño del patriarca*: nuevas formas de estructura narrativa". Tesis, University of Iowa, 1979.

Hozven, Roberto. "Horda, ejército e iglesia en *El otoño del patriarca*". *University of Dayton Review* 18, 1 (verano 1986), 47-58.

————. "El otoño . . . la horda y sus patriarcas". *Cuadernos Americanos* 258, 1 (1985), 225-240.

Labanyi, Jo. "Language and Power in *The Autumn of the Patriarch*". En Bernard McGuirk y Richard Cardwell, eds., *Gabriel García Márquez: New Readings*. Cambridge, MA: Cambridge University Press, 1987. Pp. 135-149.

López Mejía, Adelaida. "Burying the Dead: Repetition in *El otoño del patriarca*". *MLN* 107, 2 (marzo 1992), 298-320.

Maldonado-Denis, Manuel. *La violencia en la obra de García Márquez*. Bogotá: Ediciones Sudamérica, 1977.

Martínez Ruiz, Juan. "Hacia una distinción gramatical de las voces en la novela iberoamericana: a propósito de *El otoño del patriarca* de Gabriel García Márquez". En *Estudios ofrecidos a Emilio Alarcos Llorach: con motivo de sus XXV años de docencia en la Universidad de Oviedo*. Vol. 4. Oviedo: Servicio de Publicaciones, Universidad de Oviedo, 1979. Pp. 495-508.

Montaner Ferrer, María Eulalia. "*El otoño del patriarca* de Gabriel García Márquez: como mató el patriarca a su hijo". En Marta Cristina Carbonell, ed., *Homenaje al profesor Antonio Vilanova, I & II*. Barcelona: Universidad de Barcelona, 1989. Pp. 433-448.

Navarro, Márcia Hoppe. *O romance do ditador: poder e historia na América Latina*. São Paulo: Icone Editora, 1990.

Neghme Echeverria, Lidia. "Lo verosímil y la intertextualidad en *El otoño del patriarca*". *Hispamérica: Revista de Literatura* 12, 35 (diciembre 1983), 87-99.

Palencia-Roth, Michael. "El círculo hermenéutico en *El otoño del patriarca*". *Revista Iberoamericana* 50, 128-129 (julio-diciembre 1984), 999-1016.

———. "Intertextualities: Three Metamorphoses of Myth in *The Autumn of the Patriarch*". En Julio Ortega y Claudia Elliot, eds., *Gabriel Garcia Marquez and the Powers of Fiction*. Austin, TX: University of Texas Press, 1988. Pp. 34-60.

Proano, Franklin. "El poder y sus paradojas en *El otoño del patriarca* de Gabriel García Márquez". En Felix Menchacatorre, ed., *Ensayos de literatura europea e hispanoamericana*. San Sebastián: Universidad del País Vasco, 1990. Pp. 393-398.

Ramos, Juan Antonio. "El choteo caribeño y la violencia en dos novelas del dictador". *Caribe* 3, 4 (1982), 147-153.

———. *Hacia "El otoño del patriarca": la novela del dictador en hispanoamérica*. San Juan: Instituto de Cultura Puertorriqueña, 1983.

Richards, Timothy A. B., y Luis Arturo Ramos. "El patriarca rabelesiano: la mistificación de la dictadura a través del cuerpo grotesco". *La Palabra y el Hombre: Revista de la Universidad Veracruzana* 67 (julio-septiembre 1988), 111-118.

———. "Grotesque Realism in *El otoño del patriarca*". En Luis T. González del Valle y Catherine Nickel, eds., *Selected Proceedings of the Mid-America Conference on Hispanic Literature*. Lincoln, NE: Society of Spanish and Spanish-American Studies, 1986. Pp. 103-112.

Rocha, María Emília Pereira da. "Aspectos históricos de *El otoño del patriarca*". Tesis, Texas Tech University, 1985, 1986.

Rozo Acuña, Eduardo. *Análisis socio-político de "El otoño del patriarca"*. Bogotá: Universidad Externado de Colombia, 1976.

Segre, Cesare. "El problema de la voz narrativa en *El otoño del patriarca* de García Márquez". *Dispositio: Revista Hispánica de Semiótica Literaria* 9, 24-26 (1984), 139-148.

Serra, Edelweis. "Rasgos textuales de *El otoño del patriarca*". *Discurso Literario: Revista de Temas Hispánicos* 3, 2 (primavera 1986), 447-456.

Smith Grillo, Dana Edward. "*El otoño del patriarca* by Gabriel García Márquez: The Archetype of the Caudillo". Tesis, Texas A & M University, 1979.

Tittler, Jonathan. "Tropos tropicales: paisajes figurados en *María*, *La vorágine* y *El otoño del patriarca*". *Discurso Literario: Revista de Temas Hispánicos* 2, 2 (1985), 507-518.

204 Nelly S. González

Tobin, Patricia. "The Autumn of the Signifier: The Deconstructionist Moment of García Márquez". *Latin American Literary Review* 13, 25 (enero-junio 1985), 65-78.

Ugalde, Sharon Keefe. "Ironía en *El otoño del patriarca*". *Inti: Revista de Literatura Hispánica* 16-17 (otoño-primavera 1982-1983), 11-26.

Williams, Raymond L. "Entrevista con Gabriel García Márquez: *El amor en los tiempos del colera* y *El otoño del patriarca*". *Revista de Estudios Colombianos* 6 (1989), 61-63.

El señor presidente

Alvarez de Scheel, Ruth. *Análisis y estudio de algunos rasgos caracterizadores de "El señor presidente"*. Guatemala: Universidad de San Carlos de Guatemala, Facultad de Humanidades, 1968.

Arango, Miguel Antonio. "El surrealismo, elemento estructural en *Leyendas de Guatemala* y en *El señor presidente* de Miguel Angel Asturias". *Thesaurus: Boletín del Instituto Caro y Cuervo* 45, 2 (mayo-agosto 1990), 472-481.

Bellini, Giuseppe. *De tiranos, héroes, y brujos: estudios sobre la obra de M.A. Asturias*. Rome: Bulzoni, 1982.

———. "Tres momentos quevedescos en la obra de Miguel Angel Asturias". En Jaime Alazraki et al., eds., *Homenaje a Luis Alberto Sánchez*. Madrid: Insula, 1983. Pp. 63-80.

Brown, James W. "A Topology of Dread: Spatial Oppositions in *El señor presidente*". *Romanische Forschungen* 98, 3-4 (1986), 341-352.

Campion, Daniel. "Eye of Glass, Eye of Truth: Surrealism in *El señor presidente*". *Hispanic Journal* 3, 1 (otoño 1981), 123-135.

Cardoza y Aragón, Luis, y Manuel Arce. "La tiranía inefable o el sustento mágico del poder: 'Brujos y soldados de Momostenango lo guardaban'". *Kanina: Revista de Artes y Letras de la Universidad de Costa Rica* 8, 1-2 (1984), 33-38.

Costa, Danuta Teresa Mozejko de. "La circulación de dones en *El señor presidente* de Miguel Angel Asturias". *Acta Semiótica et Lingvistica: International Review of Semiotics and Linguistics* 3 (1979), 135-159.

Francini, Graziella. "Bifurcación de la mirada en *El señor presidente*". En Mariateresa Cattaneo et al., eds., *Studi di letteratura ibero-americana: Offerti a Giuseppe Bellini*. Rome: Bulzoni, 1984. Pp. 259-269.

García-Nieto Onrubia, Luisa. "Organización artística del capítulo 'El viaje' de *El señor presidente*". *Iris* (1992), 9-22.

Gutiérrez Mouat, Ricardo. "La letra y el letrado en *El señor presidente* de Asturias". *Revista Iberoamericana* 53, 140 (julio-septiembre 1987), 643-650.

Himelblau, Jack. "Chronologic Deployment of Fictional Events in M. A. Asturias's *El señor presidente*". *Hispanic Journal* 11, 1 (primavera 1990), 7-28; 12,2 (otoño 1991), 181-209.

————. "Tohil and the President: The Hunters and the Hunted in the *Popol Vuh* and *El señor presidente*". *Romance Quarterly* 31, 4 (1984), 437-450.

Martin, Gerald. "Miguel Angel Asturias: *El señor presidente*". En Phillip Swanson, ed., *Landmarks in Modern Latin American Fiction*. Londres: Routledge, 1990. Pp. 50-73.

Mejía Ruiz, Carmen. "*Tirano Banderas* y *El señor presidente*". *Beitrage zur Romanischen Philologie* 29, 1 (1990), 51-64.

Muller Delgado, Martha Virginia. "Las repeticiones al servicio de la atmósfera en *El señor presidente*". *Kanina: Revista de Artes y Letras de la Universidad de Costa Rica* 4, 1 (enero-junio 1980), 33-40.

Osorio T., Nelson. "Lenguaje narrativo y estructura significativa de *El señor presidente* de Asturias". *Escritura: Revista de Teoría y Crítica Literarias* 3, 5-6 (enero-diciembre 1978), 99-156.

Rodríguez, Teresita. *La problemática de la identidad en "El señor presidente" de Miguel Angel Asturias*. Amsterdam: Rodopi, 1989.

Ruffinelli, Jorge. "Las 'traiciones' textuales de *El señor presidente*". *Escritura: Revista de Teoría y Crítica Literarias* 3, 5-6 (enero-diciembre 1978), 63-77.

Saint-Lu, Jean Marie. "Hacia un estudio lingüístico de la obra de M. A. Asturias: notas al capítulo XII de *El señor presidente*". *Escritura: Revista de Teoría y Crítica Literarias* 3, 5-6 (enero-diciembre 1978), 157-175.

Salmon, Russell O. "The Structure of Personal Power Politics and the Hispanic World". En Gene Bell-Villada et al., eds., *From Dante to García Márquez*. Williamstown: Williams College, 1987. Pp. 297-312.

Silva de Velázquez, Caridad L. "Desarrollo y función del paralelo político-religioso en *El señor presidente*". En Alan M. Gordon y Evelyn Rugg, eds., *Actas del Sexto Congreso Internacional de Hispanistas celebrado en Toronto del 22 al 26 agosto de 1977*. Toronto: Department of Spanish and Portuguese, University of Toronto, 1980.

Urza, Carmelo. "Metáfora y deshumanización" en *El señor presidente*". *Explicación* 14, 1 (1985-1986), 79-83.

22. Africa in the Works of Afro-Hispanic Writers: A Selective Bibliography

Scott Van Jacob

> ". . . yendo a buscar motivos para su obra
> creativa en el corazón del Africa."
>
> José Artel, *Poemas con botas y banderas*

Scope

The black Latin American writers chosen for this work have written in the twentieth century and have a black ancestry. Each selected work must use some significant aspect of Africa within the work. These writers have been selected from the Caribbean, Central American, and Andean regions. The works, written in Spanish, include poetry, short stories, and novels. Essential periodicals, bibliographies, and anthologies dealing with this literature form the first part of this bibliography and are followed by an author and subject index.

Annotations describe the aspects of Africa in each work, with criticism from book reviews, critical works, or interviews included in some. These works are cited.

The elements of African cultural traits identified in the work fall into two categories. The first category is the use or exploration of the writer's African cultural legacy to authenticate his/her own identity. This legacy includes cultural traits such as African race, religion, music, language, history, and dance. The vitality of this legacy is apparent owing to the fact that it has survived over the past three centuries in societies that have had other dominant cultures. The second category is the use of political ideology to authenticate identity. These ideologies, which arose largely in the twentieth century, include Pan-Africanism and Third Worldism. Pan-Africanism addresses the diaspora by uniting all those of African descent around Afrocentricism. Marcus Garvey's "Back to Africa" movement can be placed within this larger movement. Third Worldism is formed along common economic and geographic lines shared among countries of the developing world.

Critical Works of Note

Jackson, Richard L. *Black Literature and Humanism in Latin America.* Athens: University of Georgia Press, 1988.

————. *Black Writers in Latin America.* Albuquerque: University of New Mexico Press, 1979.

Lewis, Marvin. *Treading the Ebony Path: Ideology and Violence in Contemporary Afro-Columbian Prose Fiction.* Columbia, MO: University of Columbia Press, 1987.

Smart, Ian. *Central American Writers of West Indian Origin: A New Hispanic Literature.* Washington, DC: Three Continents Press, 1984.

Periodicals

1. *Afro-Hispanic Review.* Columbia, MO: Department of Romance Languages, University of Missouri, 1982—.

    Deals almost exclusively with Afro-Hispanic literature, although works from the social sciences appear periodically. Not only the major source of Afro-Hispanic literary criticism but also a forum for poetry and short stories by Afro-Hispanic writers.

2. *The Journal of Afro-Latin American Studies and Literatures.* Washington, DC: Department of Modern Languages and Literatures, Howard University, 1993—.

    A new journal that will publish its first issue in late 1993. The scope is broader than the *Afro-Hispanic Review* since it includes works from the humanities and social sciences.

Bibliographies

3. Jackson, Richard L. *The Afro-Spanish American Author: An Annotated Bibliography of Criticism.* New York, NY: Garland, 1980.

    Highly useful work that begins with an essay on trends in Afro-Hispanic literary scholarship. It is followed by useful lists of Afro-Hispanic authors according to their country of origin, the time period they wrote in, a section of general critical studies, and anthologies. The main portion of this book cites the works and criticism of the twenty-five best-known Afro-Hispanic authors.

4.   ———. *The Afro-Spanish American Author II: An Annotated Bibliography of Recent Criticism.* West Cornwall, CT: Locust Hill, 1989.

An update of Jackson's earlier work (see number 3). The same structure is followed as in the above work with the addition of a section titled "Creative Works and Translations Published since 1979." This section also includes works then in progress. The main section on the authors has been updated from the earlier work and adds forty-two additional writers.

5.   Jahn, Janheinz. *A Bibliography of Neo-African Literature from Africa, America and the Caribbean.* New York, NY: Frederick, 1965.

Provides historical background on Afro-Hispanic writers before 1965. Latin America is divided into two regional groups: the Caribbean and Guianas, and Latin America, which includes Brazil. Lists new editions and translations of Afro-Hispanic works.

Anthologies

6.   Watson Miller, Ingrid. *Afro-Hispanic Literature: An Anthology of Hispanic Writers of Hispanic Ancestry.* Miami, FL: Ediciones Universal, 1991.

Goes beyond an anthology as it includes critical essays. The work begins with an essay by Ian Smart that provides a good introduction to the works of these authors. There are three other essays that deal with historical aspects of Afro-Hispanic literature. This is followed by suggested readings and two bibliographies: one, critical literary works on Afro-Hispanic writers and, two, culturally related works.

This anthology includes short stories of eight Afro-Hispanic writers who have each contributed significantly to the body of Afro-Hispanic literature. The acknowledged father of this literature, Nicolás Guillén, is included, as well as the most currently critically acclaimed author of this group, Manuel Zapata Olivella.

Works

7.   Artel, José. *Antología poética.* Medellín, Colombia: Universidad de Antioquia, 1985.

The first of three sections focuses largely on celebrating ethnic identity and ties with Africa. *Mapa de Africa* is told from the point of view of someone looking at a present map of Africa and lamenting the political boundaries imposed by colonial Europe that cut across past ethnocultural boundaries.

8.   Campbell, Shirley. "A Nicolás Guillén." *Afro-Hispanic Review* 12,1 (Spring 1993), 48.

      A eulogy to the famous Afro-Hispanic Cuban poet gives him credit for his vision of celebrating and promoting the surviving African cultural legacy among Afro-Hispanics.

9.   Chiriboga, Luz Argentina. "Vituperio." *Afro-Hispanic Review.* 10, 1 (January 1991), 24.

      In this short poem Chiriboga strikes out in the first person against forces that deny her identity. She states her name as Ecuambé and, at the end of the poem, she posits that the Yoruba god, Obatalá, gave her his code of love and his musical ability.

10.   Cubena. "La abuelita africana." *Afro-Hispanic Review* 2, 2 (May 1983), 27-30. English translation included.

      Cubena, probably the most knowledgeable Afro-Hispanic writer on African culture, describes the efforts of a slave woman to save her daughter from becoming a slave. She accomplishes this task through great personal sacrifice and through prayer to the Yoruba gods of her ancestors. When her freed daughter finally is able to buy her mother's freedom and brings her home, her granddaughter refers to her as "Grandmother Africa." This story illustrates the generational transference of African cultural values.

11.   ———. *Afroexiliados.* Miami, FL: Ediciones Universales, 1989.

      "Cubena continues his pedagogical campaign and his timely portrayal of contemporary and historical black consciousness (Richard L. Jackson, *Black Literature and Humanism in Latin America* [Athens: University of Georgia Press, 1988], p. 77)."

12.   ———. *Chombo.* Miami, FL: Ediciones Universales, 1981.

      Cubena tells the story of the *chombos*, Afro-Hispanics who labored on the Panama Canal. He dramatizes their plight as they struggle against oppression and cruel work conditions. Throughout the work he weaves African themes such as cosmology, folklore, and ritual (Brenda Frazier Clemons, *Afro-Hispanic Review [AHR]* 1, 1 [1982], 33).

13. ———. "Eco ancestral." *Afro-Hispanic Review* 8, 1/2 (May 1989), 23.

In "Eco ancestral" Cubena claims to be the echo of his African heritage. He lists the atrocities committed against his ancestors starting with the taking of Africans to the New World as slaves, the rape of black women by white men, and the incarceration and castration of black men in the new world.

14. ———. *Pensamientos del Negro Cubena.* Los Angeles, CA: N.p., 1977.

"The poem titled 'In Exilium' tells a story of an African living in exile who has to change his name from Ashanti to Carlos, since Ashanti cannot be pronounced in the U.S. This shows the difficulty faced by Africans in maintaining their identities within other cultures. In the second section of this book Cubena decries the oppressive conditions in South Africa and Rhodesia (Richard L. Jackson, *Black Writers in Latin America,* pp. 182-188)."

15. ———. *Los nietos de Felicidad Dolores.* Miami, FL: Ediciones Universal, 1990.

The story of a group of black Cuban Americans traveling to Panama to celebrate the transfer of the Panama Canal from the United States to Panama. Many of the individuals within the group had ancestors who labored on the canal. Each character relates a personal oral history that often includes references to African ancestors, who are remembered as accomplished and vital people. Many African cultural traits, such as praying to African deities, are displayed by these characters.

16. Díaz Sánchez, Ramón. *Cumboto.* Santiago, Chile: Editorial Universitaria, 1967.

Set on Cumboto, a coconut plantation, the novel revolves around the relationship of Federico, son of the white plantation owner and a lover of European classical music, and Natividad, an Afro-Hispanic girl whose family works on the plantation. Federico, enticed by the music and dance of the Afro-Hispanic workers, has a son with Pascua, a young Afro-Hispanic woman, who flees Cumboto when she finds out she is pregnant. The son returns years later and plays the piano for Federico and Natividad. The music is a syncretic mixture of the African influences of his mother with the classical music of his father. Díaz Sánchez uses this story to show that the mulatto can be the culmination of what is good of the two races (Janet Hampton, *AHR* 10, 1 [January 1991], 3-9).

17. Duncan, Quince. *Los cuatro espejos*. San José, Costa Rica: Editorial Costa Rica, 1973.

A learned Afro-Costa Rican returns to his rural roots to discover himself and rid himself of an oppressive feeling of alienation. Through the trip to the home of his youth, he realizes his African heritage and his close relationship to the Afro-Hispanics of Costa Rica (Jackson, *Black Writers in Latin America*, p. 178).

18. ————. *Hombres curtidos*. San José, Costa Rica: Cuadernos de Arte Popular, 1971.

A novel based on the theme of identity faced by a Costa Rican family. The sons of the family, who immigrated from Jamaica, idealize Jamaica as being a much more peaceful place to live. This idealization forces the issue of why they left Jamaica and the need to understand the connection of Afro-Hispanic blacks with their African ancestry. The protagonist is motivated to continue his daily struggles through a chance meeting with a group of followers of Marcus Garvey.

19. ————. *La paz del pueblo*. San José, Costa Rica: Editorial Costa Rica, 1978.

The protagonist of the story, a messiah figure, draws inspiration and strength from ancestral spirits to resist oppression. ". . . builds message through complex structures and using African religious symbolism" (Jackson, *Black Writers in Latin America*, p. 70).

20. ————. *La rebelión pocomia*. San José, Costa Rica: Editorial Costa Rica, 1976.

The final story of this volume of short stories, titled "Los mitos ancestrales," relates the fall of an African village, Kumasi, to colonialism and its return to independence. The story is told by a young artist from the village who travels to Europe for his education and learns about his village's history through the reports of the first explorer and trader with the village. He returns to overthrow the local governor, who is a descendant of that first trader.

21. Guillén, Nicolás. *Motivos de son*. Havana, Cuba: Editorial Letras Cubanas, 1980. 50th anniversary edition.

"El cosmonauta" presents Guillén's story of a new order where blacks are no longer treated like the African slaves of the colonial era (Keith Ellis, *AHR* 7, 1-3 [1988], 19-23).

22. ———. *El son entero*. 5th ed. Buenos Aires: Editorial Losada, 1971.

He uses the choteo, "an African communicative system that satirizes and parodies people often in a riddling form," in the poem "Adivinanzas". In "Son Número 6" he writes of an acceptance of a dual cultural heritage between blacks and whites, but there is a constant refrain in the poem for the Afro-Hispanics: "Soy yoruba. Soy lucumi, mondingo . . ."

23. ———. *Sóngoro cosongo y otras poemas*. Havana, Cuba: La Verónica, 1942.

Guillén addresses political and ethnicity issues in these poems. He compares the oppressive conditions of his enslaved African ancestors with those of blacks in the 1940s (Keith Ellis, *AHR* 7, 1-3 [1988], 19-23).

24. Jiménez, Blas R. *Caribe africano en despertar*. Santo Domingo: Nuevas Rutas, 1984.

Chapter two of this book of poetry is titled "Africano." This group of poems focuses on black ethnic identity through the description of physical characteristics and the unity of the race brought about by the discrimination and oppression suffered by all Afro-Hispanics.

25. ———. *Exigencias de un Cimarrón (en Sueños)*. Santo Domingo, Dominican Republic: Editorial Taller, 1987.

A work of poetry based on Jiménez's dreams and desires for a better future for Afro-Hispanics and other oppressed blacks throughout the world. In chapter five he writes a poem titled "Africa del Sur" that sympathizes with the plight of black South Africans (James J. Davis, *AHR* 7, 1-3 [1988], 63).

26. Joseph, Dolores. *Tres relatos del Caribe costarricense*. San José, Costa Rica: Programa Regional de Desarrollo Cultural, Ministerio de Cultura, Juventud y Deportes, 1984.

A book of short stories containing the work "Nancy Stories," which narrates the telling of tales within an African family by the elders to the children. The moral of the stories is that wit is important for survival.

27. Junco, Tito. *O'Key Charley*. Buenos Aires: Corregidor, 1977.

A collection of short stories set mainly in the United States and Europe. "Todos los hijos del señor" recounts a vacation to South Africa by an Argentine couple where they are disturbed and saddened when encountering apartheid. Later, they are invited to visit a school where both blacks and whites study together. This experience persuades them that apartheid can be overcome.

28. Malony, Gerardo. *Latidos*. Panama: Fundación Cine Video Cultura, 1991.

A number of poems express Malony's love for Brazilian black culture with its inclusion of African Gods such as Changó. Another poem titled "Garvey" describes how blacks failed to unite behind him to found a "patria" in order to escape white oppression.

29. Morejón, Nancy. *Parajes de una época*. Havana: Editorial Letras Cubanas, 1979.

Probably Morejón's best known poem, "Mujer Negra," due to its inclusion in a number of anthologies, establishes the black woman within the context of her ancestral past and her positive role in the present. The first part of the poem deals with the enslavement and transplantation of Africans to the new world.

30. ———. *Octubre imprescindible*. Havana: Unión de Escritores y Artistas de Cuba, 1982.

A collection of poetry in which Morejón supports the independence movement of Guinea in the poem "El camino de Guinea." "Hora de la Verdad" is a history of the colonization of Africa to the Cuban revolution in a land where Changó still is honored.

31. ———. Elogio de la danza. México, D.F.: Universidad Nacional Autónoma de México, 1982.

This book's title poem describes the dance's relation to natural phenomena such as the wind, earth, and the human body. Natural elements, such as the wind, in the African worldview have a life force of their own. "El Tambor" builds a repetitive rhythm through the constant use of the term "mi cuerpo" in brief lines that gives the feeling of drums playing. She continues with the theme of the dance in "Elogio de Nieves Fresneda," a well-known Cuban folk dancer who had died the year before the book was published. This poem describes the African influences in Fresneda's dance.

32. Morera, Carlos Manuel. "Justificación de una tez." Afro-Hispanic Review 12, 1 (Spring 1993), 51.

Morera describes in detail the transport of enslaved Africans to the New World. He states at the end that Afro-Hispanics have not forgotten their past or the accumulative beatings they have taken through the generations.

33. Ortiz, Adalberto. Juyungo. Buenos Aires: Editoriales America, 1943.

The work is filled with supernatural stories, superstition, and religion rooted in Africa. This is one of the classics of Afro-Hispanic literature, with one of its best-known protagonists, Ascensión Lastre (Jackson, Black Writers in Latin America, pp. 41-49).

34. ———. El animal herido: antología poética. Quito, Ecuador: Editorial Casa de La Cultura Ecuatoriana, 1959.

"Casi Color" is told by a mulatto ancestor who sees that his identity lies with his black heritage rather than with his white heritage.

35. ———. Tierra, son y tambor. Guayaquil, Ecuador: Casa de la Cultura Ecuatoriana, 1953.

Chapter one of this volume of poetry includes a number of poems in which Ortiz calls for pride in the African legacy of Afro-Hispanics. In particular, the poem "Contribución" finds Ortiz lamenting on the capture and enslavement of his African ancestors, while "Sinfonía Bárbara" celebrates the African influence on festival drumming in Ecuador.

36. Portalatín, Aida Cartagena. *Del desconsuelo al compromiso.* Santo Domingo, Dominican Republic: Colección Montesinos, 1988.

    A collection of selected poetry from Portalatín's earlier works. Includes the poem "Memorias Negras" which depicts the war and hunger that plagues Africa.

37. Preciado, Antonio. *Jolgorio.* Quito, Ecuador: Editorial Casa de la Cultura Ecuatoriana, 1961.

    A work of poetry that offers vivid descriptions of life in the largely Afro-Hispanic Ecuadorian region of Esmeraldas. Preciado uses many African cultural traditions, such as dance and drums, that are still alive today. The poem "Bom Bom Bom" speaks to the spread of African drumming, from Africa to Cuba and finally to Ecuador.

38. Sánchez-Boudy, José. *Aché, Babalú ayé (retablo Afrocubano).* Miami, FL: Ediciones Universal, 1975.

    The poems describe the daily activities of male Afro-Cubanos, e.g., praying to the divinities of the Afro-Cuban religion such as Ochun, Obatalá, and Changó. These poems celebrate the joy of life and outlook of the Afro-Cuban.

39. ———. *Ekué abanakué ekué.* Miami, FL: Ediciones Universal, 1977.

    As with *Aché, Babalú ayé,* these poems center on the religious divinities and rituals of the Afro-Cubans that are rooted in African religion.

40. ———. *Leyendas de azúcar prieta.* Miami, FL: Ediciones Universal, 1977.

    The author recounts six folktales gathered from various Cuban provinces. Most of the stories are based on African folktales.

41. Santa Cruz, Nicómedes. *Cumanana; décimas de pie forzadas y poemas.* Lima, Peru: J. Mejia Baca, 1964.

    Volume of poems which focuses largely on the question of Afro-Hispanic identity through titles such as "Negra!," "Ritmos Negros de Perú," and "Soy un Negro Sabrosón." "El Café" compares the black diaspora with the expansion of the coffee trade as both have made significant impacts on cultures as they spread throughout the world.

Another poem states that the African Gods, Changó, Ochún, and Ague, shout for freedom from racism and repression throughout the Americas. His poems also address political events in South Africa and the Congo; he also addresses a poem to George Wallace, whom he refers to as "the king of racism." This volume is one of the most politicized and Pan-African of the works in this bibliography.

42. ———. "Canto a Angola." *Casa de las Américas* 99 (1976), 73.

Santa Cruz believes that the leftist faction in the Angolan War promotes Pan-African unity.

43. Smith-Fernández, Alberto. "Panamá la patria nuestra." *Afro-Hispanic Review* 3, 1 (January 1984), 10.

A proud declaration of ancestry and nationality. The author, speaking in the first person, establishes a forceful and loving connection with his African ancestry. He states "Africa yo la amo . . . la quiero aquí conmigo . . . ¡con nosotros!"

44. Sojo, Juan Pablo. *Nochebuena negra.* Caracas, Venezuela: Empresa el Cojo, 1968.

The use of African cultural traditions such as drums and oral story-telling is present throughout this novel (J. Bekunuru Kubayanda, *AHR* 3, 3 [September 1984], 5-10).

45. Truque, Carlos Arturo. "Sonatina para los Tambores." Translated in *Afro-Hispanic Review* 6, 3 (September 1987), 30-32. First published in *El día que terminó el verano y otros cuentos* (Bogotá, Colombia: Instituto Colombiano de Cultura, 1973).

The protagonist, Santiago, is caring for his wife, who is in the final hours of her life due to lung disease. As he mourns and cares for his wife, the city in which they live begins its annual celebration for its patron saint, who is heralded by constant drumming. The drumming raises conflicting feelings in Santiago, as he wants to join his friends in the celebration and is angry for having to care for his wife, but he feels guilty for having these thoughts.

46. Vicioso, Chiqui. *Viaje desde el agua.* Santo Domingo, Dominican Republic: Visuarte, 1981.

    A book of poetry. Vicioso laments in the poem "Bissau" that the African cultural influences in the Dominican Republic are ignored. She asks for a healing of relations between Haiti and the Dominican Republic in the poem "Haiti," by pointing out the common African heritage that the two countries share.

Wilson, Carlos Guillermo. *See* Cubena.

47. Zapata Olivella, Manuel. *Changó. El gran putas.* Bogotá, Colombia: Oveja Negra, 1983.

    As with Gabriel García Márquez's epic *Cien años de soledad,* Zapata Olivella's novel views time as cyclical, constantly repeating itself. The book begins with the descendants of the Yoruba God, Changó, banished to the New World and condemned to slavery and exile. The remainder of the book finds the characters attempting to regain their freedom to return to Africa. Within this narration, notable Afro-Americans (for example, Malcolm X and Harriet Tubman) of the past interact freely with the novel's characters. This work is widely acclaimed to be the best work by an Afro-Hispanic to date (Ian I. Smart, *AHR* 3, 1 [1984], 31).

48. ———. *Tierra mojada.* Bogotá, Colombia: Editorial Espiral, 1947.

    The black rice farmers of rural Colombia fight both nature and their oppressors. Through their trials they come to respect and identify with the natural environment, as many African ethnic groups do. Zapata Olivella also stresses the importance of cultural identity to the farmers. For example, a strong oral tradition within the group promotes this ethnic unity. Also, the dance of the cumbia which evolved through music of the African tambor (drum) and the indigenous gaita (flute) brings these Afro-Hispanics together.

Index of Authors by Nationality

Colombia

Artel, José
Truque, Carlos Arturo
Zapata Olivella, Manuel

Costa Rica

Campbell, Shirley
Duncan, Quince
Joseph, Dolores
Morera, Carlos Manuel

Cuba

Guillén, Nicolás
Junco, Tito
Morejón, Nancy

Dominican Republic

Jiménez, Blas R.
Portalatín, Aída Cartagena
Vicioso, Chiqui

Ecuador

Chiriboga, Luz Argentina
Ortiz, Adalberto
Preciado, Antonio

Panama

Cubena (Wilson, Carlos Guillermo)
Maloney, Gerardo
Smith-Fernández, Alberto

Peru

Santa Cruz, Nicómedes

Venezuela

Díaz Sánchez, Ramón
Sojo, Juan Pablo

Subject Index

23. Pitfalls and Quandaries in Compiling a Reference Book: *Index to Latin American Poetry in Anthologies*

Iliana Sonntag Blay

I have been a reference librarian with a specialization in Latin America for many years. During those years I learned to like reference books. One thing I miss now that I don't work in the library anymore is the opportunity to look up information in one of the encyclopedias or dictionaries. Every chance I have I will buy one, but I can't buy the *Encyclopedia of Medieval Studies,* or the *Encyclopedia of Religion,* or more than a standard dictionary for the most common modern languages. In the English language we probably have all the reference tools that anyone could need for any purpose, both printed and electronic, but that is hardly the case with respect to Latin America, or to Latin American literature. We do have excellent bibliographies, guides, and indexes which I do not mention to avoid leaving any out, but in my work I experienced firsthand the need for more specialized reference tools to assist students and scholars of Latin America.

The need for an index to poetry occurred to me when trying to answer questions about any of the hundreds of poets of Latin America and their works. Most libraries in universities with a strong program in Spanish literature will have the complete works of major Latin American poets. There are hundreds of poets in Latin American countries, however, who are well known and loved, and who should be studied by a Spanish literature major, but whose works are not easy to find. For questions such as: "Who wrote the poem that starts 'Hay cementerios solos . . .' ('Solo la muerte,' Neruda)" or "Where can I find a poem by Alfonsina Storni called 'Hombre pequeñito'?" the answer is to be found either in our memory or by going through as many anthologies as we have at hand.

The index that I am compiling should be of help in ascertaining if a poet has been anthologized and where. I envisioned an index modeled after *Granger's Index to Poetry,* which is found in almost every library, public and academic, and is commonly used to find poems in the English language. These can be searched by author, title, first line, or subject.

I thought I could do it, by myself. I probably could have applied for an NEH grant and gotten it; it was that big a project. But I did not want the bother, nor did I want to be told how to do it. I felt comfortable about doing it partly on my own time, with help from a small grant from San Diego State University (SDSU) which allowed me to assign student assistants to do preliminary searches, and a little later, to start inputting the data.

My first task was to select the anthologies to be used. I perused all the poetry anthologies in the SDSU collection to familiarize myself with the type of material I would be using. Then I consulted Walter Rela's *Guía bibliográfica de la literatura hispanoamericana desde el siglo XIX hasta 1970*, and his *Spanish American Literature: A Selected Bibliography/ Literatura hispanoamericana: bibliografía selecta, 1970-1980*, the *Index to Spanish American Collective Bibliography* edited by Sara de Mundo Lo, and other bibliographies and guides to the literature, and made a tentative list.

Next I searched the literature on appropriate software to do indexing and called several sources listed. Most software was suitable for doing back-of-the-book indexing, as their creators said, but I was told what I was attempting to do was a multiple index of some complexity and was advised to use D-Base. I took the advice and bought this software, only to realize that even the best guides were not going to make me understand how this worked. At this time if was eligible for a sabbatical leave and I decided to ask SDSU for a larger grant to work seriously on what I saw as my contribution to my profession: an important and needed reference book. I got that and I hired a programmer who was able to customize D-Base to my needs and, above all, to make it friendly to me.

During the time of my leave I made a trip to the Southern Cone and visited libraries in Buenos Aires, Montevideo, and Santiago. I searched through their catalogs to see what books they had on their respective major poets and to get an idea of what anthologies they had. Upon my return I bought a computer and a printer (which I have since replaced; that was in 1987) and set to work.

Initially I had thought of covering all the poetry, from pre-Columbian to the contemporary period, but I soon saw the need to limit the project in some way and decided to cover only the twentieth century starting with Modernismo to contemporary times. So far I have indexed 69 anthologies published since 1950 with the majority dating from the 1970s and 1980s. Thirty of these anthologies deal with Latin America in general, 3 of which are of women poets, 3 Afro-Latin American, 3 poetry of protest, 1 erotic poetry, and 1 surrealist; and 41 from individual countries, of which 2 are women poets, 2 are protest. I have tried to include at least one anthology from each country, but publication records vary greatly from one country to another. Thus we have more books published in Chile than in Ecuador or Guatemala, for instance. I believe all major poets are covered, and as many "young poets" as are anthologized. I have excluded Brazilian anthologies. For me this would have presented additional difficulties, and I believe a separate work is required. I call it *Index to Latin American Poetry in Anthologies* rather than *Index to Spanish American Poetry in Anthologies* because Chicano poetry is not included either, and neither is any poetry of Spain. These exclusions are due only to the need to keep the project to a manageable size and do not reflect negatively on the need for other reference materials devoted to these other literatures. An effort was made to include bilingual anthologies, that is, those in which poems by Latin American authors are given in the original Spanish and in their English translation. Books of translated poetry only, however, are not included.

Originally I had thought of not assigning any subjects. I believed it would be presumptuous of me after a hurried reading of a poem to decide what it is about or what the poet had in mind. In poetry, as in painting, the interpretation is up to the reader or viewer who will find in it what his knowledge and experience suggest. For that reason, my subjects cannot be objective; I see social injustice where others might have seen a quaint local scene. On the other hand, I think it simplistic to assign a subject that a first reading would indicate. Innumerable examples come to mind where a poet uses the metaphor of a rose to mean the bloom of youth.

My instinct notwithstanding, when I requested the second grant, a committee who evaluated my proposal strongly recommended I include a subject index. In their opinion, it would make the book much more useful to students. And the truth is, college freshmen sometimes look for a poem "about something," for example, love, war, a place, or a person. That does not seem to be the case with students of Latin American literature, at least in my experience. It seemed to me that what was needed was identification of a poem, or of the works of a given poet. I consulted two faculty members in the Spanish departments at SDSU and the University of Arizona, and they thought the assignment of subjects was superfluous. Nevertheless, I had to please the committee or risk not receiving my grant; so following their advice, I compiled a list of forty-five general themes that attempt to cover most human interests and emotions: "the brevity of life, love, nostalgia, how we ponder our destiny or we interpret our circumstances." In a few cases where I thought the writing was dictated by form, I grouped them by genre (e.g., modernism).

Over the last few years, other events in my life took precedence over this project and, though never abandoned, it was relegated to the back burner. Every time I returned to it, I found questions and problems, or thought of slightly different ways of doing things.

The question of fragments is an example. Anthologists are very fond of including fragments, but many times it is difficult to establish whether the fragment is the beginning of the poem or any other verse. At first I had excluded all of them, but after much thought, I decided to exclude only numbered fragments because those would most probably not include the first line. However, when something is entitled "Poema 3" and is part of a book of poems, it is included. In some cases I was forced to leave out a famous poem such as Huidobro's "Altazor" because none of the anthologists included the first verse.

At times, the same poem appears under somewhat varying titles, or the first line says something slightly different, as in "Fundación mítica de Buenos Aires" and "Fundación mitológica . . ." by Borges, in which case, after much pondering, I entered them under each variation. Neruda's beautiful poems from *Veinte poemas de amor y una canción desesperada* appear individually in different anthologies as "Poema 5," or "Poema Cinco," or "Poema V." As the poem is the same either way, I decided on only one way of writing its title. Along the way, I realized that I had too many poems without titles which I had begun listing as "Untitled." It would have been very time-consuming to go through all in order to find the one I sought, so I substituted as title the first line, or a recognizable part of it.

The problem of the theme or subject of a poem is the most troublesome, though. First, because many poems are about several things: for instance, about someone who died and is mourned; he died in a war; and the poet thinks it was a very unconscionable war fueled if not started by Yanqui imperialism. What subject? Death, War, Imperialism? Unlike a book, a poem cannot have more than one. And second, because through time I have thought of better classification schemes, but changing that part now is unthinkable.

Having the index on a computer is marvelous, but it presents some risks and unexpected problems. Something can go wrong with alphabetizing; I discovered that all lines starting with a question or explanation mark are placed at the end of the list, following *z*. Titles or first lines with commas after the first word lose their place also. "Yo el brujo" and "Yo, el brujo" may be found in different anthologies and may be entered separately twice and be far from each other in the alphabet. That is where I am now, with my programmer, correcting such things and adding and revising endlessly.

About the arrangement, when I said I modeled my index after *Granger's*, I did not mean it would be in any way comparable. Note that *Granger's* is in the tenth edition, the first being in 1904. It indexes 12,500 poems and lists thousands of subjects. The last edition incorporates last lines, in addition to first. The *Index to Latin American Poetry in Anthologies* has indexed 9,800 poems by more than 2,045 poets and is not completed yet; as in *Granger's*, all poems can be accessed by author, title, first line, and subject. There will also be a list of authors with country of origin and dates, and pseudonyms; and a list of anthologies with their acronyms.

There are six indexes: in the Author Index, under each author's name are listed the titles of all the poems found and acronyms for each pertinent anthology.

Another index by author, called All Poems by [name of author] lists under the author's name the title, subject ID, and first line (see sample below). There are two ways of accessing title indexes: one, the Title Index lists under each theme the title and author's last name. Notice that every index gives the author's name. Naturally, the poems are in Spanish, except when translated, but the preface and instructions for use will be in English and Spanish; the lists of themes are in Spanish as well. I believe it will be very comprehensive and easy to use and will be equally useful in book form or in CD-ROM.

SAMPLE AUTHOR INDEX

All Poems by Alfonsina Storni

Title, Subject ID
    First line

Una, 43
    Es alta y es perfecta, de radiadas pupilas
Aching, 50
    I should like on this divine October afternoon
Ancestral weight, 41
    You told me my father never wept
Capricho, 41
    Escrútame los ojos, sorpréndeme la boca
Cara copiada, 28
    Es la cara de un niño transparente, azulosa
Carta lírica a otra mujer, 46
    Vuestro nombre no sé, ni vuestro rostro
Círculos sin centro, 50
    Esponja el cielo
El clamor, 41
    Alguna vez, andando por la vida
Cuadrados y ángulos, 37
    Casas enfiladas, casas enfiladas
El divino amor, 46
    Te ando buscando, amor que nunca llegas
Dolor, 50
    Quisiera esta tarde divina de octubre
El ensayo, 37
    Si el corazón me fuera percutido

She Who Understands, 41
    With her black hair fallen forward
Silencio, 24
    Un día estaré muerta, blanca como la nieve
Small Man, 41
    Small man, small man
Soy, 33
    Soy suave y triste si idolatro, puedo
Tiempo de esterilidad, 55
    A la mujer los números miraron
Tú me quieres blanca, 41
    Tú me quieres alba
Tú, que nunca serás, 41
    Sábado fue y capricho el beso dado
Una vez más, 43
    Es una boca más la que he besado
Voy a dormir, 31
    Dientes de flores, cofia de rocío
Voz, 32
    Te ataré/a los puños
Words for Delmira Agustini, 20
    You are dead and your body, beneath a Uruguayan cloak
Y la cabeza comenzó a arder, 30
    Sobre la pared/negra/ese abria
You Would Have Me Immaculate, 41
    You would have me immaculate

ANTHOLOGIES
(Incomplete)

Abril Rojas, Gilberto, comp. *Poesía joven de Colombia*. México: Siglo Veintiuno, 1975. No bibliographical data. ABRIL

Albareda, Ginés de, ed. *Antología de la poesía hispanoamericana: Colombia*. Madrid: Biblioteca Nueva, 1957. 570p. Preceded by a bibliographical essay. GINCO

————. *Antología de la poesía hispanoamericana: Perú*. By Ginés de Albareda and Francisco Garfias. Madrid: Biblioteca Nueva, 1963. 492p. Introductory essay on Peruvian poetry and on its literary periods. Gives dates for each poet. PERU

————. *Antología de la poesía hispanoamericana: Uruguay*. Coeditor Francisco Garfias. Madrid: Biblioteca Nueva, 1968. 498p. Brief analysis of each literary period, and bibliography of each poet. GINURU

————. *Antología de la poesía hispanoamericana: Chile.* Madrid: Biblioteca Nueva, 1961. 489p. Critical essays of periods with biobibliographies of poets. GINCHI

————. *Antología de la poesía hispanoamericana: Argentina.* Ginés de Albareda and Francisco Garfias. Madrid: Biblioteca Nueva, 1959. 509p. In an introductory essay the editor gives biographies and critical analysis of poets included. GINAR

Aray, Edmundo, ed. *Poesía de Cuba; antología viva.* Caracas: Universidad de Carabobo, 1976. 355p. Critical introduction and biobibliographies of all poets. ARAY

Argueta, Manlio, ed. *Poesía de El Salvador.* San José: EDUCA, 1983. 359p. Critical biobibliographies of each poet. SALVA

Arteche, Miguel, comp. *Poesía chilena contemporánea.* By Miguel Arteche, Juan Antonio Massone, and Roque Esteban Scarpa. Santiago: Editorial Andrés Bello, 1984. 358p. Includes place and date of birth of poets. ARTE

Baciu, Stefan, comp. *Antología de la poesía surrealista latinoamericana.* México: Joaquín Mortiz, 1974. 243p. Approximately half the book is text. Includes a list of the poets' published works. BACIU

Baeza Flores, Alberto, ed. *Antología de la poesía hispanoamericana.* Buenos Aires: Tirso, 1959. 303p. Biobibliographic notes for each poet and an introduction to Latin American poetry. BAEZA

Bedregal, Yolanda, ed. *Antología de la poesía boliviana.* La Paz: Los Amigos del Libro, 1977. 626p. Brief biographical information. BEDRE

Boccanera, Jorge, ed. *La novísima poesía latinoamericana.* 2d ed. México: Editores Mexicanos Unidos, 1980. 309p. Brief data on authors and their main works. BOCCA

————, comp. *Palabra de mujer: poetisas de ayer y hoy en América Latina y España.* México: Editores Mexicanos Unidos, 1982. 278p. Gives birthplace and dates, and lists works. BOCPA

Caillet Bois, Julio, ed. *Antología de la poesía hispanoamericana.* Madrid: Aquilar, 1965. 2072p. Biographical notes and major titles, plus a very detailed periodization. CAILL

Calderón, Alfonso, comp. *Antología de la poesía chilena contemporánea.* Santiago: Editorial Universitaria, 1971. 383p. CALA

Cardenal, Ernesto, comp. *Poesía nueva de Nicaragua.* Buenos Aires: Lohlé, 1974. 418p. CARDE

Carpentier, Hortense, ed. *Doors and Mirrors: Fiction and Poetry from Spanish America, 1920-1970.* New York: Grossman, 1972. 454p. In this book of literary selections, only the poetry has been included, in both Spanish and English. DOORS

Cea, José Roberto, comp. *Antología general de la poesía en El Salvador.* San Salvador: Editorial Universitaria, 1971. 482p. CEA

Cohen, Sandro, comp. *Palabra nueva, dos décadas de poesía en México.* México: Premiá, 1981. 368p. Brief information on authors. COHEN

Debicki, Andrew, comp. *Antología de la poesía mexicana moderna.* London: Támesis, 1977. 305p. DEBI

Donoso Pareja, Miguel, ed. *Poesía rebelde de América.* México: Editorial Extemporáneos, 1974. 397p. Very brief identification of authors. DONOSO

Escalante, Evodio, comp. *Poetas de una generación, 1950-1959.* 152p. México: Premiá, 1988. Biobibliographical notes. GENERA

Escalona Escalona, José Antonio, comp. *Antología actual de la poesía venezolana, 1950-1980.* 2 v. Caracas: Mediterráneo, 1981. ESCA

Fernández Moreno, César, and Horacio Jorge Becco, comps. *Antología lineal de la poesía argentina.* Madrid: Gredos, 1968. 384p. Includes biobibliographies of authors. FERNAN

Fierro, Enrique, comp. *Antología de la poesía rebelde hispanoamericana.* Montevideo: Ediciones de la Banda Oriental, 1967. 139p. Brief data on authors. FIERRO

Flores, Angel, and Kate Flores, comps. *The Defiant Muse: Hispanic Feminist Poemas from the Middle Ages to the Present: A Bilingual Anthology.* New York: The Feminist Press, 1986. 145p. FLORES

Gonzáles Salas, Carlos, ed. *La poesía femenina contemporánea en México.* Ciudad Victoria, Tamaulipas: Instituto Tamaulipeco de Cultura, 1989. 350p. SALAS

González, José Luis, and Mónica Mansour, comps. *Poesía negra de América.* México: ERA, 1976. 474p. MANSOU

Homenaje a El Salvador. Edited with an introduction by Claribel Alegría; prologue by Julio Cortázar. Madrid: Visor, 1981. ALEGRI

Jiménez, José Olivio, ed. *Antología crítica de la poesía modernista hispano-americana.* Madrid: Hiperión, 1985. MODER

————. *Antología de la poesía hispanoamericana contemporánea, 1914-1970.* Madrid: Alianza Editorial, 1979. 511p. Includes bio-bibliographies. JIMEN

Jiménez, Reynaldo, ed. *El libro de unos sonidos: 14 poetas del Perú.* Buenos Aires: Ultimo Reino, 1988. 282p. Brief data about poets and their works. LIBRO

Kofman, Fernando, ed. *Años de ceniza y escombros*. Buenos Aires: Ocruxaves, 1988. 62p. Brief bios. KOFMAN

Lafforgue, Jorge, ed. *Poesía latinoamericana contemporánea*. Edited by Jorge Lafforgue, Daniel Friedemberg, Delfina Muschietti, and others. Buenos Aires: Centro Editor de América Latina, 1988. Pagination is not consecutive. Twelve poets whose selected works are prefaced by substantive criticism by a different editor. Includes biographical notes. CEAL

Lagos, Ramiro, comp. *Mujeres poetas de hispanoamérica*. Bogotá: Tercer Mundo, 1986. Biobibliographical information on poets. LAGOS

Letona, René, ed. *Ocho poetas hispanoamericanos en Madrid*. Madrid: Playor, 1987. 114p. Includes bibliographies of poets. LETONA

Márquez, Robert, comp. *Latin American Revolutionary Poetry/Poesía revolucionaria latinoamericana: A Bilingual Anthology*. New York: Monthly Review Press, 1974. 505p. Brief biobibliographical data on poets. MARQUE

Marzan, Julio, ed. *Inventing a Word: An Anthology of Twentieth-Century Puerto Rican Poetry*. New York: Columbia University Press, 1980. 184p. In Spanish and English; includes biographical notes on poets. MARZAN

Medina, José Ramon, comp. *Antología venezolana*. Madrid: Gredos, 1962. 335p. Biographical notes on poets. MEDINA

Molina, Alfonso, comp. *Poesía revolucionaria del Perú*. 2d ed. Lima: Ediciones América Latina, 1965. 158p. MOLINA

Mondragón, Sergio, comp. *República de poetas*. México: Martín Casillas, 1985. 407p. Includes biographies, lists of works, and brief analysis. MONDRA

Monsivais, Carlos, comp. *La poesía mexicana del siglo XX*. México: Empresas Editoriales, 1966. 838p. MONSI

Morales, José Luis, comp. *Poesía afroantillana y negrista*. Río Piedras: Editorial Universitaria de Puerto Rico, 1976. 269p. Brief notes on authors and a glossary of Afro-Spanish dialect. MORA

La mujer en la poesía chilena de los '80. Gemina Ahumada et al. Santiago de Chile: Inge Corssen Editora, 1987. CORSSEN

Murguía, Alejandro, and Barbara Paschke. *Volcan, Poems from Central America: A Bilingual Anthology*. San Francisco, CA: City Lights Books, 1983. 159p. Brief notes on poets, but no dates or place of birth. VOLCAN

Ortega, Julio, ed. *Antología de la poesía hispanoamericana actual*. México: Siglo XXI, 1987. 505p. Biobibliographical notes. ORTEGA

Paz, Octavio, ed. *Poesía en movimiento: México 1915-1966*. México: Siglo XXI, 1988. 476p. Introduction by Octavio Paz. Biobibliographic notes of the poets. PAZ

Poesía cubana contemporánea: antología. Madrid: Editorial Catoblepas, 1986. CATO

Quezada, Jaime, comp. *Poesía joven de Chile*. México: Siglo XXI, 1973. 133p. Brief biobibliographical notes. QUEZA

Quirós, Juan, ed. *Indice de la poesía boliviana contemporánea*. 2d ed. La Paz: Gisbert, 1983. 534p. For each poet there are dates, brief bibliography, and critical notes. QUIROS

Reyes, Sandra, ed. *One More Stripe to the Tiger*. Fayetteville: University of Arkansas Press, 1989. 311p. A selection of contemporary Chilean poetry and fiction. Edited and translated by Sandra Reyes. In Spanish original and English translations. Prose sections not included. Brief biobibliographies precede each poet's works. REYES

Rodríguez, Armando, comp. *Antología de la poesía latinoamericana*. 5th ed. México: Editores Mexicanos Unidos, 1983. 530p. ROAL

Rodríguez Luis, Julio, comp. *Sensemayá: la poesía negra en el mundo hispanohablante*. Orígenes, 1980. 323p. Very brief biographical notes. SENS

Rodríguez Padrón, Jorge, ed. *Antología de poesía hispanoamericana (1915-1980)*. Madrid: Espasa-Calpe, 1984. 443p. Careful biobibliographical notes, with portraits, and 60 pages of literary criticism. PADRON

Ruano, Manuel, ed. *Y la espiga será por fin espiga*. Lima: Ediciones Consejo de Integración Cultural, 1986. 239p. Brief biographical notes. RUANO

Scarpa, Roque Esteban, comp. *Antología de la poesía chilena contemporánea*. Madrid: Gredos, 1968. 370p. SCARPA

Schulman, Iván A., and Evelyn Picón Garfield, eds. *Poesía modernista hispanoamericana y española: Antología*. Madrid: Taurus, 1986. 520p. Includes brief biobibliographies. SCHUL

Strand, Mark, ed. *New Poetry of Mexico*. Selected with notes by Octavio Paz, Alí Chumacero, José Emilio Pacheco, and Homero Aridjis. New York: Dutton, 1970. 224p. Notes on each poet. Poems are in Spanish and English. STRAND

Tapia Gómez, Alfredo, comp. *1ª Antología de la poesía sexual latinoamericana*. Buenos Aires: Freeland, 1969. 301p. Selection, introduction, and notes by Alfredo Tapia Goméz. Dates and major works by poets. TAPIA

Tarn, Nathaniel, comp. *Con Cuba: An Anthology of Cuban Poetry of the Last 60 Years*. London: Goliard, 1969. TARN

Toro Montalvo, César, comp. *Antología de la poesía peruana del siglo XX*. Lima: Mabu, 1978. TORO

Vallejos, Roque, ed. *Antología crítica de la poesía paraguaya contemporánea*. Asunción: Don Bosco, 1968. 195p. Analytical essays place poets into decades; no birthdates or bibliographies. VALLE

Veiravé, Alfredo, ed. *Los poetas del 40*. Buenos Aires: Capítulo, 1968. 75p. No data on poets other than their generation. VIERA

Villegas, Juan, ed. *Antología de la nueva poesía femenina chilena*. Santiago: Editorial La Noria, 1985. 197p. Biobibliographical data on authors. Bibliography on women's writings. VILLE

Villordo, Oscar Hermes, comp. *50 años de poesía argentina contemporánea, 1930-1950*. Buenos Aires: Revista Cultura, 1985. 180p. VILLOR

White, Steven F., ed. *Poets of Chile: A Bilingual Anthology, 1965-1985*. Greensboro, NC: Unicorn Press, 1986. 283p. WHITE

―――. *Poets of Nicaragua: A Bilingual Anthology, 1918-1979*. Greensboro, NC: Unicorn Press, 1982. Biobibliographies of poets. NICA

Zaid, Gabriel, ed. *Asamblea de poetas jóvenes de México*. México: Siglo XXI, 1980. 290p. Large amount of data on the poets as a group. Also bibliographical information. ZAID

24. The Bookseller as Bibliographer

Howard L. Karno

Booksellers have contributed greatly to the development of Latin American bibliography. Their catalogs and monographs were, and still are, excellent reference sources not only for the detailed bibliographic information they contain but for the historical and biographical data they provide. The better catalogs often reveal previously unknown titles or correct long existing errors. In some cases, they record auction sales of important collections.

The purpose of this essay is to enumerate and to describe some of the more significant catalogs and monographs by bookdealers that apply to the book in the colonial period of Spanish America. (Portuguese and Brazilian dealers and their catalogs have not been covered, nor is there a claim to absolute comprehensiveness in the areas that are discussed.)

Not all bookseller catalogs are equally important to the academic researcher, the acquisitions librarian, the serious collector, and the antiquarian bookdealer; however, the good ones should have the basic bibliographic data such as author, title, edition, place and date of publication, and pagination, as well as the number of plates, maps, and tables, if any, and the book's dimensions. They should also describe the type and condition of the book and binding. The primary purpose of the catalog description is to determine a book's completeness and condition, but the complementary notations are also of considerable value. The great American bibliographer Henry Harrisse, in the introduction to his major work, *Bibliotheca Americana Vetustissima,* says that:

There is no reason why the bibliographer should limit his efforts to a faithful transcription of titles, coupled with minute collations. He may, without trespassing upon the province of Belles-Lettres give the history of the book, enumerate its contents, ascertain its precise place in the chronology of literature, state the references which mark its influence in the preparation of other works, quote the opinions expressed by competent critics, divulge its author or editor when published anonymously, and, if it be devoid of imprint, discover the date at which, and the place where, it was printed, and by which printer. He must, furthermore, describe the typographical peculiarities of the book, the changes they inaugurate, and their bearing upon the history of the art of printing. [1]

As one Spanish author explained, bookseller catalogs are powerful bibliographic instruments, and the older the better, since they preserve for us the record of books no longer in existence, they illustrate the typography, and they give us useful information about the development of commerce. [2]

Apart from the scholarly advantages derived from bookseller catalogs, there is also the pleasure of acquisitiveness. Carlos A. Pueyrredón, an Argentine, wrote:

One of the great pleasures of the book lover is to receive catalogues from famous antiquarian bookdealers of Europe and the United States. When he finds in one of them a title lacking in his collection he is overjoyed, and although agonized by the price, he disregards hunger and thirst and orders the book. [3]

The vast majority of catalogs devoted to Spanish Americana and produced prior to the nineteenth century tended to be simple lists of titles. There were, however, some notable bibliographies by bibliophiles and scholars such as Antonio de León Pinelo, Nicolás Antonio y Bernal, and Juan José Mariano Beristáin de Souza, all of which are discussed later in the text. The small size of the rare book market, and the lack of bibliographic expertise, precluded many bookseller catalogs. By the middle of the nineteenth century, however, a number of European and American booksellers were producing important catalogs and bibliographies in response to an increased demand for Latin Americana as libraries and collectors in North America and in Europe began to build up extensive holdings. This was especially true of Mexican imprints, as reflected by the famous European auction sales of the nineteenth century and their accompanying catalogs. The Mexican section of this essay elaborates this point. [4]

Spanish scholars produced the earliest bibliographies essential to a Latin Americana reference library. The first bibliography that included the Americas as well as Spain was that of Nicolás Antonio y Bernal. Published in 1672 and written in Latin, his *Biblioteca Hispana* referred to many American authors and, in addition to the titles, provided the place and date of imprint as well as the dimensions. [5]

The *Epítome de la biblioteca oriental i occidental náutica i geográfica* by Antonio de León Pinelo is generally considered the first bibliography consisting solely of Americana. First published in Madrid in 1629 by Juan González, it was later augmented by Andrés González de Barcía Carballido y Zúñiga in 1737-1738.

Outstanding Spanish booksellers' catalogs began to appear in the latter half of the nineteenth century. A good example is that of Pedro Salvá y Mallén, who published in Valencia in 1872 a superb two-volume catalog of 4,040 titles belonging to himself and to his father, the noted bookdealer Vicente Salvá y Pérez. José Toribio Medina declared that nothing could be of greater importance for the Americanist than the Salvá work, since, apart from the many volumes of interest to the Americanist, there is a section entirely devoted to books of the Indies that is described with a true luxury of detail. [6]

The true bible for the Latin Americanist (also the work of a bookseller) is the *Manual del librero hispano-americano* by Antonio Paláu y Dulcet. The author began work on the bibliography in 1907, completed the seven-volume first edition in 1927, and commenced almost immediately to work on the second. After seventeen more years of labor, the first volume appeared in 1948. Although the elder Paláu died in 1954, he lived long enough to see volume eight almost completed. His five sons took up the task, and in 1977, finished the twenty-eighth. In total, 381,897 titles are described plus numerous variant editions. To date, several supplemental volumes have been published. The *Manual del librero,* commonly referred to as "Paláu," provides basic bibliographic information, occasional historical data, and prices when available. One critic noted that the work was more commercial than properly bibliographic, but that did not detract from its usefulness, as it was indispensable for both the bookseller and the collector, not to mention the librarian. [7]

Pedro Vindel, along with Antonio Paláu y Dulcet and Vicente Salvá y Pérez, is considered to be one of the greats of the Spanish book trade and the art of bibliography. He was the first to publish, in Spain, magnificently illustrated catalogs containing title page facsimiles. He had been a bookseller since the 1880s, and upon his death in 1921, his library was divided among his sons Pedro, Francisco, and Víctor, all of whom remained in the business and published comprehensive catalogs. One of the elder Pedro Vindel's most famous catalogs was his two-volume *Bibliografía gráfica,* printed in 1910 in Madrid, which described and illustrated 1,224 books with facsimiles of title pages. [8] Pedro's son Francisco utilized the same graphic technique, embodying 2,500 photocopies of title pages of books once belonging to the Casa Vindel, in his monumental *Manual gráfico-descriptivo del bibliófilo Hispano-Americano (1475-1850).* This twelve-volume work, published in Madrid in 1930-1934, illustrated the colophons of 450 Spanish incunabula, approximately 1,800 sixteenth-century title pages, 1,200 of the seventeenth century, and 500 rare eighteenth- and nineteenth-century titles.

Worthy of note are the catalogs and publications of José Porrúa Turanzas and his son, José Porrúa Venero, also located in Madrid. The recent *Catálogo no. 14: Documentos novo-hispanos, siglos XVIII-XIX* describes 131 printed and handwritten documents pertaining to Mexico. Porrúa Venero is also the publisher of the *Colección Chimalistac,* a series of limited and finely printed books relating to the history of New Spain. [9]

The first bookdealers in New Spain itself were also printers. During the sixteenth century, the book trade was surprisingly extensive, despite restrictive regulations on imports. The large number of Mexico City dealers active in 1576 would seem to demonstrate considerable evasion of official restrictions and/or indifference on the part of the Spanish administration. [10] Medina, in his introduction to *La imprenta en México,* remarks that there are few traces of colonial booksellers in Mexico but does mention two men who were bookdealers in the sixteenth century, Bartolomé de Torres and Juan Fajardo, as well as Diego de Ribero in the seventeenth century and Francisco Sedano, a native of Mexico City, who, according to Medina, was the most notable bookseller of the eighteenth century. José Mariano Beristáin de Souza, the bibliographer, knew Sedano and respected his abilities. [11]

Juan José Eguiara y Eguren was the first Mexican to write a bibliography of Mexican books. Only volume I of his *Prólogos a la Biblioteca Mexicana,* letters A-C, was published in 1755; the rest of the manuscript is now at the University of Texas at Austin. Eguiara y Eguren wrote the bibliography to refute the assertions of Manuel Martí, the Dean of Alicante, Spain. Martí attempted to persuade a young student to study in Rome instead of in Mexico, declaring that Mexico was a vast literary desert lacking both teachers and students. Eguiara y Eguren imported a press from Spain to print the work, which was written in Latin with first names in alphabetical order. Prefaced by twenty chapters designated *Anteloquía,* it presented a panorama of Mexican culture up to 1754, the year the manuscript was finished. Unfortunately, the use of Latin and the listing of entries by first names (much less known than the last) makes the bibliography difficult to use. [12]

Aside from lists enumerating names of books for sale, the first catalog printed in Mexico by a bookdealer contained 1,336 titles in sixty-two pages. The catalog was the work of Agustín Dherbe, a Mexico City bookseller during the eighteenth century. Eguiara y Eguren refers to him in the *Anteloquía* and comments that recently Dherbe had returned from Europe with a magnificent collection of books for sale. [13]

The nineteenth century witnessed the rape of Mexican literary treasures by European and American collectors and libraries. Padre Agustín Fischer, the leading culprit of the outflow of Mexicana, was a true calamity for the history and literature of Mexico, according to the collector José María de Agreda. [14] Fischer, born in Germany in 1825, went to Mexico and was ordained a priest after failing as a goldminer in California. He managed to attach himself to the Emperor Maximilian's court and used his influence to traffic in books, selling to Mexico's leading collectors, such as Nicolás León, Joaquín García Icazbalceta, and others. Foreseeing the fall of

Maximilian, he shipped himself and approximately two hundred cartons of books to Europe. Much of the shipment consisted of the José María Andrade collection formed by the Mexican bookseller and editor over a forty-year period. Although no record exists of the sale, it had been acquired by Maximilian as the nucleus of an imperial collection. Thanks to Fischer, in 1869 the Paris bookselling firm of List and Francke issued a sales catalog of the Andrade collection encompassing 4,484 titles, of which 2,335 items were Mexicana. This was the first of the large European sales of Mexican materials. The introduction to the Mexican part of the catalog emphasized the richness and rarity of the titles; six of them were published between 1543 and 1547. A number of prominent booksellers attended the sale, including Joseph Sabin of New York and J. Whitaker of London, who represented Hubert H. Bancroft, the American bookdealer, writer, and editor. Bancroft purchased some 3,000 volumes which later formed the basis of the Bancroft collection at the University of California, Berkeley. [15]

Fischer fell ill soon after his arrival in Europe and, lacking funds, sent his own books to auction in London, where the bookselling firm of Puttick & Simpson published an impressive sales catalog in 1869. The catalog, *Biblioteca Mejicana,* described an extraordinary collection of books and manuscripts, almost all relating to the history and literature of North and South America, particularly Mexico. As in the Andrade sale, Bancroft bought a number of valuable titles. [16]

A subsequent noteworthy Mexicana sales catalog was also the work of Puttick & Simpson. In 1880 it conducted the auction of the José Fernández Ramírez collection. Ramírez, a lawyer, politician, and book collector, served as President of Maximilian's first cabinet and as his Minister of Foreign Relations. With the Empire's collapse, he moved to Europe after having already shipped there his famous collection of rare Mexicana, which included codexes and manuscripts. He finally settled in Bonn, where he died in 1871. The Mexican historian Alfredo Chavero bought the collection from the heirs and brought it back to Mexico. Later, he sold it to Manuel Fernández del Castillo on the express condition that it never leave the country. Unfortunately, Padre Fischer convinced Chavero to send the collection to auction at Puttick & Simpson, which issued a superb sales catalog. [17] Bancroft was again represented at the auction, this time by Henry Stevens, another prominent London dealer of Americana. Stevens was the second highest purchaser at the sale, buying some 306 lots and spending more than a thousand pounds sterling for his American client. The leading purchaser at the sale was Bernard Quaritch, perhaps the most important Americana dealer in England in the latter half of the nineteenth century. At the sale in 1880, he purchased 275 of the rarest and most valuable lots. [18] Shortly afterward, Quaritch published an excellent catalog listing 524 of the titles he had acquired. The Quaritch firm is still a formidable Americana dealer, especially in travel literature; a most useful catalog is his no. 554: *Americana Incunabula* (London, 1938).

In 1883 the Paris bookselling firm Viuda de Adolphe Labitte produced an important catalog for the sale of the Alphonse Louis Pinart and Charles Etienne Brasseur de Bourbourg collections consisting primarily of Mexicana.[19] Later in 1891 the French bookdealer Eugéne Boban authored the last major Mexicana catalog of the nineteenth century. In this case, the books were not for sale but were donated to the Bibliothèque Nationale of Paris by their owner, M. E. Eugène Goupil. The lavish two-volume catalog, plus atlas, consisted of Joseph Marius Alexis Aubin's collection of codexes and manuscripts bought from him by Goupil.[20]

Before World War I, J. H. Stargardt of Berlin cataloged and sold several important Americana collections. The first, the Baron Kaska sale, occurred in 1911. Kaska, an Austrian chemist, had accompanied Maximilian to Mexico City and remained there until 1907. This collection contained 632 choice Mexican titles.[21] Stargardt's next major catalog, no. 229, issued in 1912, contained 1,346 mostly Mexicana titles that had previously belonged to Dr. Antonio Peñafiel, the renowned historian and expert on Mexican geography and antiquities.[22]

The Mexican sales catalogs by European bookdealers in the latter half of the nineteenth century and the early twentieth century reflect the loss to Mexico of many of her greatest treasures. They are also representative of the bookseller's bibliographic skills and are still of great reference value to collectors, librarians, and bookdealers.

Dealers in Mexico also were active in selling, via catalogs, to collectors in Mexico and abroad. Among the most successful was Wilson Wilberforce Blake. The great bibliographer Nicolás León counted him as one of the three most important booksellers in Mexico at the time.[23] Blake issued a series of extensive catalogs, consisting primarily of Mexicana, from 1892 to 1910; perhaps the most important was published in 1909. The catalog listed a great quantity of inquisition documents as well as manuscript and documentary materials relating to the Viceroys, Agustín de Iturbide et al.[24]

Pedro Robredo and Manuel Porrúa were the other two Mexican dealers of importance, according to León. They both had come to Mexico from Spain early in the 1900s and opened bookshops in Mexico City. Robredo began to publish *Boletines bibliográficos* in 1908. His first catalog appeared in 1918. This and subsequent issues were of high quality and valued accordingly.[25] A fine example is catalog no. 22, containing most of the José María Agreda y Sánchez collection, from which Henry R. Wagner acquired thirty sixteenth-century Mexican imprints, which are now in the Huntington Library. [26]

Manuel Porrúa, who arrived in Mexico prior to Robredo, was joined by his brothers, and the bookshop in 1910 became Librería Porrúa Hermanos. It, too, published a *Boletín bibliográfico,* and the firm continues to do so at this time. Porrúa's first catalog containing primarily Mexican material appeared in 1913, but the catalog of 1915, edited by Nicolás León, comprising 1,627 titles including various incunabula, established his reputation. [27] Perhaps the most-cited Porrúa Hermanos catalog is the 1949 *Bibliografía Americana no. 5: Catálogos de libros Mexicanos o que tratan de América y de algunos otros en España.* This work, limited to 440 copies, describes 9,088 titles in 879 pages. It is invaluable for linguistics, Maximiliana, and the like.

Apart from Quaritch and Stargardt, there were, in the nineteenth century, a number of other European dealers cataloging colonial Americana. The London bookseller Obadiah Rich, active from 1828 to 1850, published *Bibliotheca Americana Nova* between the years 1835 and 1846, listing hundreds of titles printed between 1700 and 1844. José Toribio Medina thought quite highly of his catalogs. [28]

Henry Stevens, another London dealer, also produced catalogs of Americana and, as mentioned previously, attended the important book auctions. His 1861 catalog, *Historical Nuggets,* listing and describing colonial Latin American rarities, earned Medina's praise. For the British Museum, Stevens prepared a *Catalogue of the American Books in the Library of the British Museum at Christmas MDCCCLVI* (London, 1866). The fourth and last part lists Mexican and Spanish American titles. Quite impressive is his *Bibliotheca histórica,* a catalog describing 5,000 titles, issued in 1870 after Stevens's death. [29]

There are several other English booksellers who have produced significant Americana catalogs. First and foremost is Maggs Brothers which, throughout the 1920s, issued the eight-part *Bibliotheca Americana et Philippina* series. The first catalog, 429, published in 1922, lists and describes 1,686 titles. Part II, catalog 432, also issued in 1922, describes thirty-three letters from Father Kino to the Duchess d'Aveiro of Lisbon. Part III, catalog 442, issued in 1923; part IV, catalog 465, issued in 1925; part V, catalog 479, issued in 1926; part VI, catalog 496, issued in 1927; and part VII, catalog 502, issued in 1928, describe several thousand rare American titles and, along with part VIII, *Bibliotheca Brasiliensis,* issued in 1930, provide an enormous amount of bibliographical and historical data. Another catalog issued in 1927, catalog 495, *Books Printed in Spain and Spanish Books Printed in Other Countries* (1,358 works described), is also a mainstay of most Americanist reference libraries. Maggs still continues to publish fine catalogs of travel literature as well as more general fare.

A London bookseller of recent vintage, Richard von Hünersdorff, has produced an exemplary catalog number 10: *America. Books, Manuscripts and Historical Documents Relating Mostly to the Geography and History of Latin America. Voyages and Travels of Discovery and Exploration. Precolumbian Civilizations, Indian Linguistics and Ethnography. The Struggles for National Independence* (London, n.d.). It contains 420 titles plus subject index. Another European, the Leipzig dealer Karl W. Hiersemann, sold large quantities of both old and new books to North and South America in the late nineteenth and early twentieth centuries. [30]

Still useful is a three-part catalog published in the year 1872 by the Dutch bookseller Frederik Muller: *Catalogue of Books, Maps, Plates on America, and a Remarkable Collection of Early Voyages, Offered by Sale at Frederick Muller at Amsterdam, Literary Agent of the Smithsonian Institution Washington. Including a Large Number of Books in all Languages with Bibliographical and Historical Notes and Presenting an Essay towards a Dutch-American Bibliography.* The catalog describes 2,288 titles.

A famous and much cited French bookseller's catalog is *Bibliotheca Americana. Histoire, Géographie, Voyages, Archéologie et Linguistique des Deux Amériques et des Iles Philippines,* in three parts (Paris: Maisonneuve, 1878-1887) by Ch. Leclerc, which describes 3,260 titles. In Medina's view, it was the best of all Americana sales catalogs in number of titles described, minutiae of detail, and biographical information. [31]

With the exception of Mexico, there is little evidence of Latin American booksellers' catalogs during the colonial period, apart from simple lists, even though there was a thriving book trade in Peru and in the La Plata region. [32] The historian Rubén Vargas Ugarte's *Biblioteca Peruana* (Buenos Aires: Baiello, 1935-1957, 12 volumes) provides considerable bibliographical data on Peruvian colonial imprints. In addition, a bookseller, the German-born Federico Schwab, who moved to Lima in 1930, wrote a number of bibliographic articles for the University of San Marcos's *Boletín bibliográfico* in the late 1930s and early 1940s. Schwab, the owner of E. Iturriaga y Cía., also published as director of Peru's Foreign Ministry's archives several catalogs of the archive's colonial period documents and manuscripts until his death in December, 1986. [33]

Carlos Casavalle, who in 1862 established a printing press and the Librería de Mayo in Buenos Aires, probably published the first booksellers' catalog in that city. He also began publication of a *Boletín bibliográfico sudamericano* in 1870; the first volume contained twenty-two issues listing 800 titles. [34]

Other Buenos Aires booksellers at the time were Angel Estrada, Félix Lajouane, and the Igon brothers, but it was not until the early twentieth century that rare Americana catalogs frequently appeared. Among the better ones were those of Gustavo Mendesky, owner of the Librería Rivadavia, who issued his first in 1910. [35]

Julio Suárez, who founded Librería "Cervantes" in 1914, produced excellent catalogs in the period 1933-1935. A famous Suárez catalog is *Catálogo de libros americanos de Librería "Cervantes,"* describing 6,000 titles in two thick volumes. Later, useful catalogs were to be regularly issued by the Librería L'Amateur and Gerardo Fernández Zanotti of the Librería Fernández Blanco.

A number of bookdealers established themselves in Montevideo, Uruguay, in the first half of the nineteenth century, perhaps the earliest being José Fernández Cutiellos. [36] In Valparaíso, Chile, Santos Tornero founded the Librería Española in 1840. Shortly afterward, Pedro Yuste established a bookshop in Santiago; however, there appears to be no record of their catalogs. Another Chilean, José Toribio Medina, issued a catalog of duplicate books from his own collection that he wished to sell: *Catálogo de una pequeña colección de libros antiguos sobre la América Española* (Santiago, 1888).

As in Europe, Mexico, and Latin America, booksellers in the United States, through sales catalogs and scholarly bibliographies, have contributed significantly to the knowledge of the book in the Americas. Joseph Sabin is, of course, the most cited authority, but a number of U.S. dealers are also well represented in many reference libraries. The English-born auctioneer and bookseller Joseph Sabin came to the United States in 1848. At various times, he owned bookshops in Philadelphia and in New York City. In 1856, he began to write what he hoped would be a bibliography of all the written works pertaining to the Americas; by 1879, he was devoting all of his time and efforts to his monumental *Bibliotheca Americana: A Dictionary of Books Relating to America, from Its Discovery to the Present Time.* The first part appeared in 1867, and a total of twelve volumes were published by Sabin's death in 1881. For a short period, his sons continued the immense task until Wilberforce Eames, a Brooklyn bookseller, and later R. W. G. Vail concluded it in 1935. In total there are twenty-nine volumes which describe 106,413 titles, plus numerous variant editions. Although heavily weighted toward North America, the bibliography is quite useful, especially in reference to North American imprints dealing with Latin America. [37]

Three catalogs by the New York City firm of Lathrop C. Harper Co. deserve special mention: *Cat. 12, Texas, Mexico, and the Southwest. The Republic of Texas. The Mexican War* (New York, n.d.), which covers the period 1813-1850, listing 423 titles; *Cat. 14, Americana Ibérica. Books, Pamphlets and Broadsides Printed in Mexico, Central and South America, 1556-1866* (New York, 1962), describing more than 800 colonial period imprints, 300 to 400 for the first time (see the foreword to the catalog by Francisco Guerra); and *Cat. 16, Americana Printed in Europe 1492-1889, Being a Collection of Books and Pamphlets Relating to the Discovery, Settlement and Development of the Western Hemisphere* (New York, n.d.), which describes 850 titles. All three catalogs have subject and name indexes and have been reprinted by Lathrop Harper in a single volume.

Eberstadt & Sons, also of New York City, issued a number of valuable catalogs in the years 1936-1956. Numbers 103-138 were reprinted and bound together in four volumes in 1965. In addition, an excellent Texas catalog was produced in 1963: *Cat. 162, Texas, Being a Collection of Rare and Important Works & Manuscripts Relating to the Lone Star State*, with an introduction by Archibald Hanna.

More or less contemporary with Eberstadt was the New York City firm of H. P. Kraus which, beginning in the 1930s, issued many catalogs containing rare Latin Americana. Kraus is world famous for the rarity of his books, maps, and manuscripts, and the high quality of his book descriptions.

Warren Howell of John Howell Books in San Francisco recently produced two outstanding catalogs: *Cat. 50, California. The Library of Jennie Crocker Henderson with Additions* (San Francisco, 1979-1980), published in five parts (part I applies to the Spanish Exploration period and the years up to statehood); and *Cat. 52, Americana. A Selection of Printed and Manuscript Materials Relating to the Western Hemisphere, Hawaii, and the Philippine Islands* (San Francisco, 1980). Howell, who had been president of the firm since his father's death in 1950, died in 1984, and the bookstore's stock was auctioned in a series of sales in 1985.

Kenneth Nebenzahl, the Chicago bookdealer, has also produced some fine Americana catalogs that apply to Latin America. His *Cat. 4, Latin Americana. Rare Books and Manuscripts Pertaining to Mexico, Central America and Southwest and The West Indies* (n.d.), is an example. Most recently, he has written and published a superb atlas of maps from the discovery of the Americas period, *Atlas of Columbus and the Great Discoveries* (Chicago, New York, San Francisco: Rand McNally, 1990). The Los Angeles firm of Bennett & Marshall, no longer in business, produced a notable catalog prepared by Richard Marshall before his death in 1967: *Cat. 4, Books of the Western Hemisphere Printed prior to 1801* (301 titles are described in detail).

Perhaps the most prolific of the more recent U.S. dealers has been the recently deceased John H. Jenkins of Dallas, Texas. Besides issuing almost 200 catalogs consisting primarily of Americana, he authored and published

242 HOWARD L. KARNO

several important bibliographic monographs and documentary compilations. Examples are *Papers of the Texas Revolution, 1835-1836*, 10 vols. (Dallas: Presdial Press, 1973); *Printer in Three Republics. A Bibliography of Samuel Bangs. First Printer in Texas, and First Printer West of the Louisiana Purchase* (Austin: Jenkins Publishing Co., William Reese Co., Frontier America Corporation, 1981); and *Basic Texas Books. An Annotated Bibliography of Selected Works for a Research Library* (Austin: Jenkins Publishing Co., 1983). This bibliography describes in detail 224 books that Jenkins considered essential, discusses another 1,017 titles, and provides an annotated guide to 217 Texas bibliographies. Examples of his many good catalogs are *Cat. 127, Texas History: One Thousand Rare Books. With Additional Sections on Texas Maps, Photographs, and Manuscripts and a Selection on the Mexican War* (2,686 titles) (Austin, n.d.); and catalogs 185 and 196, which contain more than 4,000 titles, mainly Latin Americana. All the above catalogs have been published since 1980.

Also in recent years, William Reese of New Haven, Connecticut, has produced an extensive series of Americana catalogs, including numerous Latin American colonial period materials. A good example is *Cat. 46, Latin Americana and the Caribbean* (374 titles).

Dorothy Sloan of Austin, Texas, is an excellent cataloger. She worked in that capacity for Warren Howell and John Jenkins in the 1970s and early 1980s. Now, independently, she has produced several fine catalogs, among them *Cat. 2, Americana*, with 442 titles, including many from the colonial period. In New York City, Richard C. Ramer frequently publishes catalogs of rare Portuguese materials, which incorporate rare Latin Americana, particularly Braziliana.

David Szewczyk of Philadelphia Rare Books and Manuscripts Co. deals almost exclusively in colonial materials. He is well known for his knowledge of indigenous languages and arcane paleography. His catalogs and lists, written while he was with the William Allen Co. in Philadelphia, and later independently, are quite useful.

Another bookseller distinguished by his scholarship is Professor Maury A. Bromsen, a leading authority on the life and works of José Toribio Medina. In 1960 he edited *José Toribio Medina, Humanist of the Americas: An Appraisal* (Washington, DC: Pan American Union). He is currently writing a biography of Medina's life. Finally, recognition should be given to George F. Elmendorf, the founder of the Latin American Bibliographic Foundation and recipient of the 1988 José Toribio Medina award, for his monumental three-volume *Nicaraguan National Bibliography, 1800-1978*.

In summation, booksellers' catalogs beginning in the past century have enriched our knowledge of the book in Latin America. Moreover, their bibliographic contributions are an ongoing process; additions and corrections are constantly being made to the two "giants"—it is not at all unusual to note catalog entries marked "not in Medina" or "not in Paláu." Attesting to the bookseller's expertise and the esteem in which it is held are the large number of their catalogs in library reference sections. It would seem evident, in view of their many contributions, that bookdealers are an integral component in the field of Latin American bibliographic scholarship.

NOTES

1. Henry Harrisse, *Bibliotheca Americana Vetustissima: A Description of Works Relating to America Published between the Years 1492 and 1551* (Madrid: Librería General Victoriano Suárez, 1958), p. viii.

2. Antonio Rodríguez-Moñino, *Catálogos de libreros españoles (1661-1840)* (Madrid: n.p., 1945), p. 9.

3. Carlos A. Pueyrredón, *Bibliófilos y libreros anticuarios. Publicado en "La nación" del domingo 15 de diciembre de 1957* (Buenos Aires: n.p., 1958), p. 7. "Uno de los grandes placeres del bibliófilo es recibir catálogos de famosos libreros anticuarios de Europa y de los Estados Unidos. Cuando figura en ellos algún ejemplar que falta en su colección, se alegra, se aflije por el precio, pero ahorra sobre el hambre y la sed, para pedirlo."

4. See José Toribio Medina, *Biblioteca Hispanoamericana (1493-1810)*, Facsimile edition (Santiago de Chile: Fondo Histórico y Bibliográfico José Toribio Medina, 1958-1962), vol. VI, prologue, part III for a short history of Latin American bibliography. Also useful is Josefa E. Sabor, *Manual de fuentes de información*, 3d ed. (Buenos Aires: Edic. Marymar, 1979), pp. 130-147.

5. See Medina, *Biblioteca Hispanoamericana*, pp. cxi-cxii.

6. Ibid., p. cxxii. The complete title of the Salvá catalog is *Catálogo de la Biblioteca Salvá, escrito y enriquecido con la descripción de otras muchas obras, de sus ediciones, etc.*, 2 vols. (Valencia: Imp. de Ferrer de Orga, 1872) (reprinted in Barcelona in 1962).

7. Sabor, *Fuentes de información*, p. 171. For Antonio Paláu y Dulcet's comments on the book trade in Spain and the decision to write the *Manual*, see his prologue to the first edition of Paláu reprinted in the second, vol. I, pp. v-xi. His autobiography, *Memorias de un librero catalán, 1867-1935* (Barcelona: Lib. Catalonia, 1935), is an excellent history of the Spanish book trade's golden decade, the twenty years before the Spanish Civil War.

8. The complete title is *Bibliografía gráfica. Reproducción en facsímiles de portadas, retratos, colofones y otras curiosidades útiles a los bibliófilos, que se hallan en obras únicas y libros preciosos o raros*, 2 vols. (Madrid: Imprentas de A. Marzo y de la Sucesora de M. Minuesa de los Ríos, 1910).

9. Most impressive is the *Chimalistac* series of *Californiana* edited by Dr. W. Michael Mathes.

10. Irving A. Leonard, *The Books of the Brave, Being an Account of Books and Men in the Spanish Conquest and Settlement of the Sixteenth-Century New World* (Cambridge, MA: Harvard University Press, 1949), p. 199, and p. 247 for the book trade in Mexico City in 1600. For documentation on the sixteenth-century book trade in Mexico, see Francisco Fernández del Castillo, *Libros y libreros en el siglo XVI. Publicaciones del Archivo General de la Nación, VI* (Mexico: Tip. Guerrero Hnos., 1941). For a good overview of early Latin American book trade, see José Torre Revello, *El libro, la imprenta y el periodismo en América durante la dominación española* (Buenos Aires: Universidad Nacional de Buenos Aires, 1940).

11. José Toribio Medina, *La imprenta en México, 1539-1821* (Santiago de Chile: Impreso en Casa del Autor, 1907-1912), Vol. I, pp. ccxix-ccxx.

12. Joaquín García Icazbalceta, *Obras,* tomo II, Opúsculos Varios 11 (New York: Burt Franklin, 1968), pp. 124-130, reprint of 1896 edition. For Spanish translation and analysis, see Juan José Eguiara y Eguren, *Prólogos a la Biblioteca Mexicana. Nota preliminar por Federico Gómez de Orozco. Versión Española anotada, con un estudio biográfico y la bibliografía del autor por Agustín Millares Carlo* (Mexico: Fondo de Cultura Económica, 1944).

13. Eguiara y Eguren, *Prólogos,* p. 123; and Genaro Estrada, *200 notas de bibliografía mexicana,* Monografías Bibliográficas Mexicana, no. 31 (Mexico: Imp. Secretaría de Relaciones Exteriores, 1935), n. 57.

14. Agustín Millares Carlo and José Ignacio Mantecón, *Ensayo de una bibliografía de bibliografías mexicanas (La imprenta, el libro, las bibliotecas, etc.)* (Mexico: Biblioteca de la II Feria del Libro y Exposición Nacional de Periodismo, 1943), no. 1427.

15. Estrada, *200 notas,* n. 155; and Joaquín Fernández Córdoba, *Tesoros bibliográficos de México en los Estados Unidos* (Mexico: Editorial Cultura, T.G.S.A., 1959), p. 9. For reduced facsimile of catalog's title page, see Felipe Teixidor, *Ex libris y bibliotecas de México,* Monografías Bibliográficas Mexicanas, núm. 20 (Mexico: Imp. Secretaría de Relaciones Exteriores, 1925), p. 350.

16. See Fernández Córdoba, *Tesoros bibliográficos,* p. 19. For a reduced facsimile of the title page, see Teixidor, *Ex libris,* p. 359. The sale also included the library of Dr. Carl Herman Berendt, a specialist in Mexican native languages.

17. Fernández Córdoba, *Tesoros bibliográficos,* p. 13.

18. See Teixidor, *Ex libris,* p. 458, for reduced title page of Puttick & Simpson catalog, and p. 460 for dealer names, number of lots they bought, and amount of money they spent. Estrada, *200 notas,* n. 109, relates the prices paid for some of the individual titles.

19. For details see Fernández Córdoba, *Tesoros bibliográficos,* pp. 7-8, and Estrada, *200 notas,* n. 165.

20. See Fernández Córdoba, *Tesoros bibliográficos,* p. 6, and, for the complete title of Boban's work, p. 125, n. 4.

21. Millares Carlo, *Ensayo de una bibliografía,* no. 1431; Teixidor, *Ex libris,* p. 447, n. 1; and Estrada, *200 notas,* n. 170.

22. Fernández Córdoba, *Tesoros bibliográficos,* p. 21; Estrada, *200 notas,* n. 169.

23. Nicolás León, *Bibliografía bibliográfica mexicana, compilado por el Dr. . . . , profesor decano del Museo Nacional de México,* Primera parte (Mexico: Talleres Gráficos del Museo Nacional de Arqueología, Historia y Etnografía, 1923), prólogo (cited in Millares Carlo, *Ensayo de una bibliografía,* no. 446).

24. Fernández Córdoba, *Tesoros bibliográficos,* pp. 149-151.

25. Millares Carlo, *Ensayo de una bibliografía,* nos. 1454 and 1459; Estrada, *200 notas,* n. 85.

26. Fernández Córdoba, *Tesoros bibliográficos,* pp. 25-26. In 1935 Robredo sold out to José Porrúa e Hijos. See Paláu y Dulcet, *Memorias de un librero catalán, 1867-1935,* p. 504.

27. Millares Carlo, *Ensayo de una bibliografía,* no. 1474, lists the incunabula.

28. Medina, *Biblioteca Hispanoamericana,* VI, cxxiii. See Millares Carlo, *Ensayo de una bibliografía,* nos. 388 to 392 for list of Rich's principal catalogs.

29. Medina, *Biblioteca Hispanoamericana,* VI, cxxiii; Millares Carlo, *Ensayo de una bibliografía,* no. 397.

30. Millares Carlo, *Ensayo de una bibliografía,* nos. 356-372, lists a number of the more important ones. For more on Hiersemann, see Pablo Pedro Figueroa, *La librería en Chile. Estudio histórico y bibliográfico del canje de obras nacionales establecido y propagado en Europa y América por el editor y librero Don Roberto Miranda, 1884-1894,* 2d ed. (Paris: Librería de Garnier Hermanos, 1896), pp. 90-91.

31. Medina, *Biblioteca Hispanoamericana,* VI, cxxiii.

32. For Peruvian book trade, see José Toribio Medina, *La imprenta en Lima (1584-1824)* (Santiago: Casa del Autor, 1904-1907), I, lxxx-lxxxi. For La Plata, see Torre Revello, *El libro en América* and Domingo Buoncore, *Librero, editores e impresores de Buenos Aires* (Buenos Aires: Librería Editorial "El Ateneo," 1944); also Guillermo Furlong, *Historia y bibliografía de las primeras imprentas rioplatenses, 1700-1850* (Buenos Aires: Editorial Guaranía, 1953-1959), III, 247.

33. Examples are *Catálogo de la Sección Colonial del Archivo Histórico* (Lima: Imp. Torres Aguirre,1944); and *El índice del Archivo del Tribunal del Consulado de Lima. Ministerio de Hacienda y Comercio, Archivo Histórico, Sección Colonial* (Lima: n.p., 1948).

34. Buoncore, *Librero de Buenos Aires,* pp. 40-45.

35. Ibid., pp. 97-98.

36. Arbelio Ramírez, *Una librería de la época colonial* (Montevideo: n.p., 1952), pp. 2-12.

37. For a brief history of the project, see "Sabin's Dictionary," by Robert W. G. Vail, pp. 1-9 in the *Papers of the Bibliographical Society of America* 31, part 1 (1937). Also see William S. Reese, "Joseph Sabin," *American Book Collector* n.s. 5, 1 (January/February 1984), pp. 3-24.

BIBLIOGRAPHY

Antonio y Bernal, Nicolás. *Bibliotheca Hispana sive Hispanorvm, qvi vsqvam vnqvamve sive Latina sive populari sive alia quavis lingua scripto . . . .* Romae es officina Nicolai Angeli Tinassi, MDCLXXII, 2 vols.

Bromsen, Maury A. *José Toribio Medina, Humanist of the Americas: An Appraisal.* Washington, DC: Pan American Union, 1960.

Buoncore, Domingo. *Librero, editores e impresores de Buenos Aires.* Buenos Aires: Librería Editorial "El Ateneo," 1944.

Eberstadt & Sons. *Catalogue 162, Texas, Being a Collection of Rare and Important Works and Manuscripts Relating to the Lone Star State, with an Introduction by Archibald Hanna.* New York: n.p., n.d.

Eguiara y Eguren, Juan José. *Prólogos a la Biblioteca Mexicana. Nota preliminar por Federico Gómez de Orozco. Versión Española anotada, con un estudio biográfico y la bibliografía del autor por Agustín Millares Carlo.* Mexico: Fondo de Cultura Económica, 1944.

Elmendorf, George F., ed. *Nicaraguan National Bibliography, 1800-1978. Bibliografía nacional nicaraguense, 1800-1978.* 3 vols. Redlands,

CA: Latin American Bibliographic Foundation; Managua, D.N.,
Nicaragua: Biblioteca Nacional Rubén Darío, 1986-1987.

Estrada, Genaro. *200 notas de bibliografía mexicana.* Monografías
bibliográficas mexicana, no. 31. Mexico: Imp. Secretaría de
Relaciones Exteriores, 1935.

Fernández del Castillo, Francisco. *Libros y libreros en el siglo XVI.*
Publicaciones del Archivo General de la Nación, VI. Mexico: Tip.
Guerrero Hnos., 1941.

Fernández Córdoba, Joaquín. *Tesoros bibliográficos de México en los
Estados Unidos.* Mexico: Editorial Cultura, T.G.S.A., 1959.

Figueroa, Pablo Pedro. *La librería en Chile. Estudio histórico y
bibliográfico del canje de obras nacionales establecido y propagado
en Europa y América por el editor y librero Don Roberto Miranda,
1884-1894.* 2d ed. Paris: Librería de Garnier Hermanos, 1896.

Furlong, Guillermo. *Historia y bibliografía de las primeras imprentas
rioplatensess, 1700-1850.* 4 vols. Buenos Aires: Editorial Guaranía,
1953-1959.

García Icazbalceta, Joaquín. *Obras.* 10 vols. New York: Burt Franklin,
1968.

Harper, Lathrop C. *Cat. 12, Texas, Mexico, and the Southwest. The
Republic of Texas. The Mexican War.* New York: n.p., n.d.

———. *Cat. 14, Americana Ibérica. Books, Pamphlets and Broadsides
Printed in Mexico, Central and South America, 1556-1866.*
New York: n.p., n.d.

———. *Cat. 16, Americana Printed in Europe 1492-1889, Being a
Collection of Books and Pamphlets Relating to the Discovery,
Settlement and Development of the Western Hemisphere.* New York:
n.p., n.d.

Harrisse, Henry. *Bibliotheca Americana Vetustissima. A Description of
Works Relating to America Published between the Years 1492 and
1551.* Madrid: Librería General Victoriano Suárez, 1958.

Howell, Warren. *Cat. 50, California. The Library of Jennie Crocker
Henderson with Additions.* 5 vols. San Francisco: n.p., 1979-1980.

———. *Cat. 52, Americana. A Selection of Printed and Manuscript
Materials Relating to the Western Hemisphere, Hawaii, and the
Philippine Islands.* San Francisco: n.p., 1980.

Hünersdorf, Richard von. *America. Books, Manuscripts and Historical
Documents Relating Mostly to the Geography and History of Latin
America. Voyages and Travels of Discovery and Exploration.*

Precolumbian Civilizations, Indian Linguistics and Ethnography. The Struggles for National Independence. London: n.p., n.d.

Jenkins, John H. *Basic Texas Books. An Annotated Bibliography of Selected Works for a Research Library.* Austin: Jenkins Publishing Co., 1983.

———. *Cat. 127, Texas History: One Thousand Rare Books. With Additional Sections on Texas Maps, Photographs, and Manuscripts and a Selection on the Mexican War.* Austin: n.p., n.d.

———. *Papers of the Texas Revolution, 1835-1836.* Dallas: Presdial Press, 1973, 10 vols.

———. *Printer in Three Republics. A Bibliography of Samuel Bangs. First Printer in Texas, and First Printer West of the Louisiana Purchase.* Austin: Jenkins Publishing Co., William Reese Co., Frontier America Corp., 1981.

Leclerc, Ch. *Bibliotheca Americana. Histoire, Géographie, Voyages, Archéologie et Linguistique des Deux Amériques et des Iles Philippines.* In three parts. Paris: Maisonneuve, 1878-1887.

León Pinelo, Antonio de. *Epítome de la biblioteca oriental i occidental, náutica i geográfica.* Madrid: Juan González, 1629.

Leonard, Irving A. *The Books of the Brave, Being an Account of Books and Men in the Spanish Conquest and Settlement of the Sixteenth-Century New World.* Cambridge, MA.: Harvard University Press, 1949.

Maggs Brothers. *Bibliotheca Americana et Philippina.* London: n.p., 1922-1928.

———. *Cat. 546, Bibliotheca Brasiliensis.* London: n.p., 1930.

———. *Cat. 495, Books Printed in Spain and Spanish Books Printed in Other Countries.* London: n.p., 1927.

Marshall, Richard. *Cat. 4, Books of the Western Hemisphere Printed Prior to 1801.* Los Angeles: n.p., n.d.

Medina, José Toribio. *Biblioteca Hispanoamericana (1493-1810).* Facsimile edition. Santiago de Chile: Fondo Histórico y Bibliográfico José Toribio Medina, 1958-1962, 7 vols.

———. *Catálogo de una pequeña colección de libros antiguos sobre la América Española.* Santiago de Chile: Imprenta del Autor, 1888.

———. *La imprenta en Lima (1584-1824).* Santiago de Chile: Impreso y Grabado en Casa del Autor, 1904-1907, 4 vols.

———. *La imprenta en México, 1539-1821.* Santiago de Chile: Impreso en Casa del Autor, 1907-1912, 8 vols.

Millares Carlo, Agustín, and José Ignacio Mantecón. *Ensayo de una bibliografía de bibliografías mexicanas (La imprenta, el libro, las bibliotecas, etc.).* Mexico: Biblioteca de la II Fería del Libro y Exposición Nacional de Periodismo, 1943.

Muller, Frederick. *Catalogue of Books, Maps, Plates on America, and a Remarkable Collection of Early Voyages, Offered by Sale at Frederick Muller at Amsterdam, Literary Agent of the Smithsonian Institution Washington. Including a Large Number of Books in All Languages with Bibliographical and Historical Notes and Presenting an Essay towards a Dutch-American Bibliography.* Amsterdam: n.p., 1872.

Nebenzahl, Kenneth. *Atlas of Columbus and the Great Discoveries.* Chicago, New York, San Francisco: Rand McNally, 1990.

————. *Cat. 4, Latin Americana. Rare Books and Manuscripts Pertaining to Mexico, Central America and Southwest and the West Indies.* Chicago: n.p., n.d.

Paláu y Dulcet, Antonio. *Manual del librero Hispano-Americano. Inventario bibliográfico de la producción científica y literaria de España y de la América Latina, desde la invención de la imprenta hasta nuestros días, descritos, por . . .* Barcelona: Librería Anticuaria. San Pablo, 41, Imprenta de Octavia Viader, de San Feliu de Guixols, 1923-1927, 7 vols.

————. *Manual del librero Hispano-Americano. Bibliografía general Española e Hispanoamericana desde la invención de la imprenta hasta nuestros tiempos con el valor comercial de los impresos descritos, por . . . segunda edición, corregida y aumentada por el autor.* 28 vols. Barcelona: n.p., 1948-1977.

————. *Memorias de un librero catalán, 1867-1935.* Barcelona: Librería Catalonia, 1935.

Porrúa Hermanos. *Bibliografía Americana no. 5. Catálogo de libros Mexicanos o que tratan de América y de algunos otros en España.* Mexico: n.p., 1949.

Porrúa Venero, José. *Catálogo no. 14: Documentos novo-hispanos, siglos XVIII-XIX.* Barcelona: n.p., n.d.

Pueyrredón, Carlos A. *Bibliófilos y libreros anticuarios. Publicado en "La nación" del domingo 15 de diciembre de 1957.* Buenos Aires: n.p., 1958.

Quaritch, Bernard. *Catalog no. 554: Americana incunabula.* London: n.p., 1938.

Ramírez, Arbelio. *Una librería de la época colonial.* Montevideo: n.p., 1952.

Reese, William S. *Catalog 46: Latin Americana and the Caribbean.* New Haven: n.p., n.d.

———. "Joseph Sabin." *American Book Collector* n.s. 5, 1 (January/February 1984).

Rodríguez-Moñino, Antonio. *Catálogos de libreros españoles (1661-1840).* Madrid: n.p., 1945.

Sabin, Joseph. *Bibliotheca Americana. A Dictionary of Books Relating to America, from Its Discovery to the Present Time.* 29 vols. New York: n.p., 1867-1935.

Sabor, Josefa E. *Manual de fuentes de información.* 3d ed. Buenos Aires: Edic. Marymar, 1979.

Salvá y Mallén, Pedro. *Catálogo de la Biblioteca Salvá, escrito y enriquecido con la descripción de otras muchas obras, de sus ediciones, etc.* 2 vols. Valencia: Imp. de Ferrer de Orga, 1872.

Schwab, Federico. *Catálogo de la Sección Colonial del Archivo Histórico.* Lima: Imp. Torres Aguirre, 1944.

———. *El índice del Archivo del Tribunal del Consulado de Lima. Ministerio de Hacienda y Comercio, Archivo Histórico, Sección Colonial.* Lima: n.p., 1948.

Sloan, Dorothy. *Catalog 2: Americana.* Austin: n.p., n.d.

Torre Revello, José. *El libro, la imprenta y el periodismo en América durante la dominación española.* Buenos Aires: Universidad Nacional de Buenos Aires, 1940.

Teixidor, Felipe. *Ex libris y bibliotecas de México.* Monografías bibliográficos Mexicanas, no. 20. Mexico: Imp. Secretaría de Relaciones Exteriores, 1925.

Vail, Robert W.G. "Sabin's Dictionary." *Papers of the Bibliographical Society of America* 31, part 1 (1937).

Vargas Ugarte, Rubén. *Biblioteca Peruana.* Buenos Aires: Baiello, 1935-1957, 12 vols.

Vindel, Francisco. *Manual gráfico-descriptivo del bibliófilo hispano-americano (1475-1850).* 12 vols. Madrid: Imp. Góngora, 1930-1934.

Vindel, Pedro. *Bibliografía gráfica. Reproducción en facsímiles de portadas, retratos, colofones y otras curiosidades útiles a los bibliófilos, que se hallan en obras únicas y libros preciosos o raros.* 2 vols. Madrid: Imprentas de A. Marzo y de la Sucesora de M. Minuesa de los Ríos, 1910.

III
Regional Views of Latin American Collections

United States of America

25. The Manuscripts Collection of the Latin American Library, Tulane University

Guillermo Náñez Falcón

During the SALALM conference at the University of Texas in 1992, a reception was given by the Benson Latin American Collection wherein one of the staff presented a history of the founding of the Collection. She focused on the Genaro García collection, which formed the nucleus around which the Benson Collection came to be built. I could not help but note the similarities in the history of the Benson Collection and that of the Latin American Library at Tulane University. Thus, I welcomed the invitation extended to me by Esperanza de Varona to participate in a panel with her and my colleague from the University of Texas, Jane Garner, and to speak about the Latin American Library's manuscripts collection.

Both the Texas and Tulane collections were established in the early 1920s, and both began with the acquisition of the personal collection of a Mexican bibliophile. The Benson Collection dates its history to the purchase of the Genaro García collection by the Board of Regents of the University of Texas. The Tulane collection started with the purchase of the William Gates collection by the University to form the nucleus of a research facility for the newly established Department of Middle American Research (DMAR), whose focus of investigation was to be Mexico and Central America.

In 1924, William Gates, an inveterate collector of Mexicana, decided to sell his collection of books and manuscripts at auction through the American Art Association in New York. Before the public sale, Samuel Zemurray, President of the Cuyamel Fruit Company, purchased the entire collection for Tulane. Genaro García's death had been the cause for his family's sale of his library. Gates promoted himself as part of the purchase agreement and came to Tulane as the first director of the Department of Middle American Research.

Immediately, problems arose. First, some of the items listed in the auction catalog were not originals but photostats of manuscripts in other depositories. Although the copies were clearly identified as such in the catalog, ill will developed between Gates and Tulane. Other items in the catalog did not reach Tulane, and it was rumored that Gates had sold some things separately to other institutions, which indeed he had. Also, Gates's plans for the development of the DMAR as a center for tropical biology did not fit in with Tulane's ideas. His personality, moreover, was perhaps too chimerical for the Tulane Board of Administrators, who viewed him as high-handed and grandiose. Within a year the Board had dismissed him.

The value of the Gates collection to the incipient library cannot be underestimated, photostats and prior sales notwithstanding. Gates's collection contained several thousand books, including dozens of Mexican incunables and other rare colonial imprints; hundreds of late-nineteenth-century government publications that he had acquired from other collectors, such as Antonio Peñafiel (including laws, statistics, documentary compilations); volumes relating to the Maximilian period and to the Porfiriato; and contemporary works and ephemera of the Mexican Revolution. There were also several thousand manuscripts that complemented the collection of books. Over time, the DMAR cataloged most of the volumes for the stacks collection, but rare items were cataloged, following the Dewey classification system, for a cage area, which eventually became the rare books collection.

The manuscripts were selectively culled, according to physical format and according to their potential interest to faculty. Those manuscripts large enough to stand on a shelf, or bound in some manner, were cataloged as part of the cage collection, and interfiled with the books. (Rare books and manuscripts cataloged in the 1920s and 1930s still bear the notation "Cage" on the catalog card.) Among the items cataloged in this manner were the Codex Chalco, a finely executed nineteenth-century copy of a lost sixteenth-century pictorial manuscript; Fray Andrés de Olmos's 288-leaf manuscript "Arte de la Lengua Mexicana" from 1547; two seventeenth-century choral books; several grammars and catechisms in Mexican Indian languages; and many others.

Loose manuscripts from the Gates purchase, those that did not readily respond to Dewey treatment, were simply wrapped in brown paper, tied with a string, and placed on shelves in random fashion without identification. If some researcher knew about the existence of the manuscripts, staff attempted to make the material available; otherwise, the majority of the manuscripts were forgotten. The manuscripts fell into several distinct groups. Among these were Gates's extensive collection of colonial Mexican manuscripts; his file of several hundred letters from the military commandants of Yucatán (late-eighteenth to early-nineteenth century); the papers of the U.S.-born journalist-diplomat Ephraim George Squier; correspondence of the Iturbide court; the Moctezuma Family Papers; and hundreds of pieces of printed ephemera of the Mexican Revolution, including several dozen original Posada engravings.

The DMAR acquired other manuscripts as well, but development of its archival collections in the first decade reflected a lack of direction and focus. Two purchases that were made in the early 1920s demonstrate this. The Rudolf Schuller papers were the notebooks, field notes, vocabulary lists, manuscripts, and photographs of an Austrian-born linguist and ethnographer who worked primarily in the Huasteca region of Mexico. This collection fit in the Mesoamerican focus of the DMAR. The papers of U.S. ethnologist and archaeologist George Hubbard Pepper, relating largely to his work with Southwest Indians and in the Chaco Canyon, did not. By the 1930s, however, the DMAR restricted manuscript acquisitions to the areas of faculty research, that is, Mayan Mexico and Central America.

Other manuscripts acquired in the 1920s and early 1930s were more germane to the research orientation of the DMAR, which by then was sending regular archaeological expeditions to Yucatán and to the other Mayan areas of Mexico and Central America. Often, the expedition directors had the opportunity to purchase ancient documents that today would be prohibited from leaving the country. Among these were several manuscript dossiers of land disputes, the Crónica de Maní, the Crónica de Yaxcukul, and the Crónica de Chicxulub. These contain documents from the sixteenth to the eighteenth century, and the Maní is said to be the oldest example of writing of the Mayan language in Spanish characters. From the Mixtec region of Oaxaca came the so-called Codex Tulane, an Indian pictorial manuscript from the mid-sixteenth century that is painted on a 12-foot strip of deer skin. In 1933, the DMAR acquired Fray Pedro de Oroz's priceless 1585 manuscript history of the Franciscan order in New Spain.

In addition to individual manuscripts, the DMAR purchased collections of documents. From Porrúa, in 1932 it acquired a collection of about 3,000 miscellaneous, but historically valuable, dossiers dating from the mid-sixteenth century to early Independence, from all parts of Mexico and covering a gamut of subjects. Porrúa also provided, in 1934, a collection of 44 volumes of administrative records from New Spain, including a 400-leaf volume of minutes of the Royal Audiencia from 1575 to 1602. In 1933 also, the DMAR purchased from the daughter-in-law of Captain Callender Irvine Fayssoux, aide-de-camp to William Walker, records of Walker's armies and of the invasions of Nicaragua in 1855, 1857, and 1860.

Clearly, the acquisition of Latin American manuscripts such as those above (except the Fayssoux-Walker papers) would be difficult today, as they could not easily leave the country of origin. I personally feel a certain uneasiness when scholars from abroad question why the manuscripts are at Tulane, and I have discussed the matter with colleagues. Most agree that preservation and availability to an international scholarly community justify our having these treasures. In many cases, the manuscripts were literally "rescued" by the persons who brought them to this country, as the physical condition of the manuscripts and the personal narratives of the collectors themselves attest.

For five or six decades, the Latin American manuscript collections enjoyed a mixture of sporadic attention and thorough neglect. In the 1930s, the WPA undertook projects throughout Louisiana to prepare catalogs or transcriptions of important manuscript collections in the state. One unit came to work in the DMAR. From their work resulted published calendars of the Fayssoux-Walker papers and the Gates Yucatán letters, collections that were easily arranged and individual pieces described. In 1948, the Middle American Research Institute (or MARI as the DMAR had come to be known) published an inventory of the Mexican Administrative Papers which the Institute Librarian had prepared.

Work on the Porrúa Mexican documents, which eventually came to be called the Viceregal and Ecclesiastical Mexican Collection, proceeded irregularly from the late 1930s through the 1950s. Little progress was made, however. The manuscripts presented great problems, which I believe illustrate a number of important issues in dealing with Latin American archival collections. Persons who wrote descriptions of the documents were Spanish speakers, U.S.-born graduate students in Spanish, or simply individuals who had "studied" Spanish. In general, training in Spanish paleography, subject background, familiarity with abbreviations, knowledge of colonial civil and ecclesiastical institutions and administrative structure, and other skills were not criteria for selecting catalogers. Additionally, whatever work was done on the archival collections was selective—most collections were ignored altogether. Compounding the adverse situation further was the absence of an overall plan or goal for the archive, and a lack of coordination of efforts with guidelines and criteria for the arrangement of materials and the creation of finding aids. Consequently, most of the collection was unprocessed and virtually unusable by researchers.

In 1979, the Latin American Library (LAL, as the MARI's library had come to be known in 1968) received a two-year grant from the National Endowment for the Humanities (NEH) to catalog its manuscript collections. The Manuscripts department of the main library lent my services. I became the project supervisor, and Mrs. Ruth Olivera of the Latin American Library served as my assistant. I saw the assignment not only as a return to the area of my academic training but also as an opportunity to set up the archive from the beginning, with all the files, provenance records, finding aids, and archival housing that one ideally seeks to have.

The project was a voyage of discovery for me and for Mrs. Olivera. At the beginning, we were aware of some twenty identified collections. With the assistance of several graduate students from the Latin American program, we sorted through scores of unidentified packages wrapped in brown paper, which had been sitting about for some fifty years. We discovered numerous collections that people had forgotten that the University had acquired, including several sixteenth-century painted manuscripts from Mexico, the George Pepper papers, the E. G. Squier photographs from Honduras (1850s) and Peru (1863). We had to examine crumbling files in the LAL and in the MARI to reconstruct provenance records, and we found correspondence of the Gates tenure as director of the DMAR and of the Matilde Giddings Gray expeditions to Mexico and Central America. By the end of the project in 1981, we had identified and established bibliographic control over sixty-five collections. Subsequently, new discoveries and recent acquisitions have brought the number of collections to more than one hundred and more than ten series. Realization of the size and importance of the archive led the Tulane Library to create a half-time position of Manuscripts Curator for LAL.

The NEH project finally made available to a scholarly public thousands of previously unknown manuscripts. We established systems for public use and for the maintenance of repository records. Each collection was described on a unit card, which formed the basis also for an in-house manuscripts shelf list. Accession sheets and files contained all the documentation that we could uncover about the history of the collection. The depth of cataloging depended on content, size, and complexity. For the Viceregal and the Central American Printed Ephemera Collections, which consisted of several thousand unrelated items, we prepared shelf lists. In certain cases a guide with a diagram of the arrangement of a collection and a description of the various sections was sufficient. We prepared extensive guides to thirty-two of the collections and have subsequently completed several dozen more. For some collections, such as the William Gates and the Nicolás León, there was not sufficient time to complete an inventory. Here, we organized the manuscripts in chronological order and made a general description, which established rudimentary bibliographic control until an inventory could be completed at a later date. In certain instances, where we had a substantial number of separately acquired documents that were somehow related by area, subject, or format, we created artificial series, such as the Yucatán Collection, the Chiapas Collection, the Indian Language Document Series, and the Central American Printed Ephemera Collection.

Public finding aids consisted of the aforementioned collection guides as well as a separate chronological file and a 32-drawer dictionary card catalog of personal names, place names, and subjects. For subject entries, we used then-current Library of Congress headings as often as possible, but we were often forced to adapt these, or devise headings, to fit a diverse body of subjects. To maintain control of subject entries used, we established an in-house authority file. We tried to check personal names and places as carefully as possible in available printed sources, and we regularized the spelling when necessary.

The manuscripts collection continues to grow through gifts and occasional purchases. A number of scholars have left their collections to LAL, including Lewis Hanke, Fernando Horcasitas, José Díaz Bolio, and Seymour Liebman. Other donors have given letterbooks of President Joaquín Zavala Solís of Nicaragua, a collection of autograph documents of Independence leaders of the Andean republics, and papers relating to Bolivian Communist parties and the death of Che Guevara.

Occasionally, there is the opportunity (and money) to buy a collection that someone has for sale. Here, we follow guidelines that the collection fit within the area of repository strength, that is, relating to Mexico or Central America. We do not buy single pieces, such as autographs of famous individuals, although these are the items most frequently offered. We do not have the funds to purchase the sort of manuscript items or collections that well-known dealers have in their catalogs, even when these dovetail closely with existing holdings. The pace of acquisition has so far permitted us to avoid having a large backlog of uncataloged materials.

In addition to the manuscripts collections, the Library has a photographic archive of some 25,000 images from Latin America. These consist of about seventy-five collections that date from the 1850s (Squier's original photographs of an interoceanic survey in Honduras) and the early 1860s (Squier's stereoscopic views of Peru and Bolivia) to the present. The principal areas of the collection are Mexico, Central America, and Peru. There are photographs of archaeological sites and colonial monuments, as well as ethnographic and contemporary images.

Collections of historic photographs of Mexico and Central America include those of Juan Yas, Fritz Henle, and Ernest Crandall, and copy prints of Eadweard Muybridge photographs. Contemporary images are in collections of Judith Sandoval and Mitchell Denburg. Peru is represented by five outstanding collections: the aforementioned Squier photographs, which number about 350 images; Emilio Harth-Terré images of colonial architecture (more than 4,300); Abraham Guillén (about 900); Martín Chambi (about 100); and recent photographs by Fernando La Rosa (about 200). The Library has prepared several traveling exhibits from these Peruvian collections. Another unusual collection is that of Richard Ahlborn: 2,000 images of Hispanic architecture and art in the Philippine Islands.

Also I must mention our other unique collection, the Merle Greene Robertson rubbings of Mayan relief sculpture. This collection consists of more than 2,000 rubbings made in situ in the jungles of Mexico and Central America. The stone monuments documented by the rubbings are not easily accessible to researchers, and some pieces have even been plundered from the sites since the rubbings were made. Photographs of the rubbings enable scholars to study the images without having to unroll the fragile, full-scale pieces. Mrs. Robertson has also prepared scanned copies of the photographs on optical disk.

I would like to close with some thoughts about responsibility for the administration of a manuscript collection, such as that of the Latin American Library. In the age of electronic access, the question of accessibility vs. conservation becomes more pressing. Does the archivist adapt different criteria for usage and copying of documents that are 200, 300, or 400 years old, than for more recent ones? Nineteenth- and early twentieth-century documents, which make up the largest part of the Central American holdings, present special problems, given the fragile, and often deteriorated, condition of the paper. Should we advertise more widely that we own certain documents, or is it enough to expect that scholars know that the material is at Tulane and will come to see it? Although the colonial documents are, for the most part, written on cloth paper and in a good state of preservation, will increased use deteriorate them? Will requests for research and photocopying exceed the ability of a limited staff to cope with requests? Certainly, at Tulane I must face the reality that the Latin American archive is not a priority for staffing compared to the circulating stack collection and public information needs. Further, can a repository responsibly impose a limit on copying, and should not repositories with similar collections work together to develop uniform policies? I hope that in the future there will be a collegial discussion of these and other related issues at SALALM.

26. Cuban and Cuban-American Bilingual Archives in the University of Miami Library

Esperanza B. de Varona

Introduction

The University of Miami, located in Coral Gables, part of the Greater Miami Metropolitan Area, enjoys a cooperative relationship with its neighbors in the Americas and the Caribbean which dates back to its charter. The University opened its doors in 1926. The motto in the early days was "North American culture for the Latin Americans and Latin American culture for the North Americans." That motto exemplifies the relationship the University of Miami would sustain in the coming years with its neighbors in the Caribbean and, more specifically, with its neighbors in Cuba.

The Dade County census of 1990 depicts a true tri-ethnic community consisting of 49 percent Hispanics, 30 percent non-Hispanic whites, and 21 percent blacks. Cubans make up almost 80 percent of these Hispanics. Once dominant only in the Little Havana area of central Dade, today Cubans are a majority in more than half of the county's residential areas.[1]

The University of Miami has been closely associated with Cuba and its people since its foundation and continues to be historically associated today with the Cuban-Americans. As early as 1926, faculty from the University of Havana came to teach at the University of Miami. The first Hispanic-American student to register at the University of Miami was a Cuban-born woman from Santiago de Cuba. The University of Miami football team played the University of Havana for the first time on Thanksgiving Day 1926.

When the Communist regime of Fidel Castro seized power in Cuba in 1959, Cubans began to leave Cuba for political reasons, not for economic reasons, with the hope of returning in the near future. Miami's geographical location made it the logical point of entry into the United States for most Cubans at that time.

The University of Miami opened its doors to the Cuban community and established a series of programs to assist the newly arrived refugees from 1961 to the early 1980s. The programs helped recently arrived Cuban exile physicians, lawyers, economists, teachers, and others assimilate to life in the United States. Beginning in 1930, in the University of Miami Library, materials on Latin America and the Caribbean grew to provide support for the numerous courses taught at the University. The University library expanded to keep pace with the rest of the University, and, in 1962, the Otto G. Richter Library was dedicated. During the 1960s, with the addition of several exiled Cuban librarians to the Richter Library staff, the Cuban Collection expanded to include an increasing number of materials.

The University of Miami Library has been collecting Cuban materials since its opening. Today, the Otto G. Richter Library holds one of the largest Cuban collections outside Cuba and contains books, periodical publications, and archival materials.

The Cuban books and periodicals provide secondary sources of information for researchers and are complemented by our Cuban archival collection, an excellent primary source of information. The Library's Cuban book collection includes approximately 45,000 volumes, both rare and contemporary. The Cuban periodical publications include newspapers, magazines, journals, and newsletters, which are divided into four categories:

Older publications dating from the colonial period to the twentieth century

Periodicals published in Cuba from circa 1910 to 1958

Periodicals published in Cuba from 1959 to the present

Cuban periodicals published in exile from 1959 to the present

The Cuban exile periodicals collection is one of the most important collections. It is a unique collection; no other like collection exists anywhere else in the world. Its size is approximately 1,086.0 lin. ft.

The Cuban Archives

The Cuban Archives include materials produced in Cuba which deal specifically with Cuba up to the Castro regime and do not contain exile materials. The Archives also include materials produced by Cuban exiles and Cuban-Americans from 1959 to the present. Therefore, the Cuban Archives could be divided into four historical periods:

Colonial period, 1492-1901

Republican period, 1902-1958

Communist period, 1959-present

Cuban exile period, 1959-present

The Cuban exile period began with the exodus of the Cuban people in 1959, mainly to the United States. At that time, their status was Cuban refugees. Various factors and events in the years following their arrival in 1959 caused a change in their status, thirty-four years later. First, many Cuban refugees became American citizens and integrated themselves into the communities in which they lived. Second, a new generation emerged of those born in the United States and other countries. Currently, we have materials produced by Cuban-Americans as well as materials produced by those who have recently arrived.

The Cuban Exile Collection bears great importance for various reasons. Through these primary sources, researchers and historians can analyze the changes that have taken place in the Cuban community since its exile in 1959. In addition, further studies can be made on the socioeconomic and historical impact that the Cuban exiles have had on many areas of the United States, the state of Florida, and particularly the Greater Miami area.

The Cuban Exile Collection is a documentation of the hopes and aspirations of the Cuban people in exile, of the struggle to maintain a unity of purpose, and of the need to preserve, add to, and transmit a cultural heritage. It also depicts the very nature of the exile soul striving to be once again, someday, in a free Cuba. Our Cuban collections have been recognized by many authors, journalists, students, and other researchers from around the world as the best source of information about Cuba and Cuban exiles. The size of the Cuban Archives is approximately of 1,586 lin. ft. and includes:

Audio and videotapes
Broadsides
Clippings
Collections of personal and corporate papers
Ephemera
Historical and literary manuscripts
Maps
Phonograph records
Photographs and negatives
Postcards
Posters

Some of the more important material found in the Cuban Archives are described below.

The Colonial Period, 1492-1901
Historical and Literary Manuscripts

1. A Journal of the Siege of Havana by the English Navy in 1762. Expedition under the command of the Earl of Albermarle and Sir George Pocock against Cuba by an English squadron and troops, March-August, 1762.

2. The manuscript of the novel *Leonela* by Nicolás Heredia, who was born in Santo Domingo and lived in Cuba since he was ten years old. Therefore he is considered a Cuban author. This novel was written in Havana in 1886 and printed in 1893. In this novel the author

describes the Cuban life and customs of the last twenty years of the nineteenth century.

3. Autographed letter signed by José Martí and General Máximo Gómez to the officials of the Jiguaní region. Cuartel General en Campaña del Ejército Libertador, 12 de mayo de 1895. José Martí was the Cuban patriot, poet, and journalist, and General Máximo Gómez was the commander in chief of the Cuban Liberation Army in the War of Independence against Spain, 1895-1899.

Ephemera

4. Carnet of a Gala Ball honoring Major General Máximo Gómez, commander in chief of the Cuban Liberation Army. It took place in Havana at the end of the Independence War, February 11, 1899.

Maps

5. *L'Isle de Cuba,* by R. Bonne. Paris, 1780. Black & white; 20.6 x 31.3 cm.

6. *A View General of the City de Havana of Amerique.* Paris, ca. 1800. Hand colored engraving; 26 x 36 cm. Engraving depicting ships in the harbor at Havana and a portion of the city.

7. *A Plan of the Siege of the Havana,* drawn by an officer on the spot, 1762. London, ca. 1775. Black & white; 16.5 x 24.5 cm. Extract from *Universal Magazine.* Informative plan showing the fleets, fortifications, and roads.

Photographs

8. "Mambises a la carga." Cuban Liberation Army during the War of Independence 1895-1899, against Spain.

9. "José Martí" portrait by Mercier, 1895. Copper engraved. José Martí was the Cuban patriot and Apostle of the Independence War of 1895. This portrait was sent to the University of Miami by the Cuban government on the occasion of a homage to Cuba on the Pan-American Day of 1934.

Illustrations

10. *Raza Negra—Negros de Guinea en Cuba* (Black Race—Blacks of Guinea in Cuba), by M. Pujadas. Barcelona: Montaner & Simon, 1820. Color; 34 x 24 cm.

11. *Alameda de Paula,* by Pierre Toussaint Frederic Mialhe. In *La Isla de Cuba Pintoresca.* [Havana, 1838.] Colored lithograph; 26 x 33.5 cm. The artist was a French lithographer who went to Cuba in 1830. He traveled through the island of Cuba and remained there for six years. He is known for his Cuban lithographs.

The Republican Period, 1902-1959
Historical and Literary Manuscripts

12.   Autographed letter signed by Tomás Estrada Palma to Alberta Gavín.
       Havana, Dec. 28, 1904. Tomás Estrada Palma was the first president
       of the Republic of Cuba in 1902. Alberta Gavín was the woman
       who gave to Major General Máximo Gómez two silken Cuban flags
       during the War of Independence. In this letter Estrada Palma showed
       his appreciation to her for her love and sympathy for Cuba.

13.   Autographed letter signed by Fidel Castro to Luis Conte Aguero. Isla
       de Pinos, July 6, 1954. A letter to his close friend, Luis Conte
       Aguero, prominent poet and political leader in Cuba at that time.
       Conte Aguero left Cuba as an exile in 1960.

Collection of Personal and Corporate Papers

14.   *The Lyceum and Lawn Tennis Club Collection.* This collection
       contains correspondence, official records, photographs, and
       publications of one of the most important women's clubs in Cuba,
       founded in 1929 to promote cultural understanding from all
       viewpoints, social consciousness, and social service. On March 16,
       1968, the Lyceum was closed by the Castro government. Many of
       its members, including the last president, left Cuba and went to the
       United States and other countries as exiles. Size: 3.0 lin. ft.

15-16. *Gerardo Machado Collection.* This collection contains correspond-
       ence, speeches, financial papers, conferences, and photographs from
       1925 to 1939. Gerardo Machado was the youngest general of the
       War of Independence and the fifth president of Cuba, from 1925 to
       1933. When Machado was reelected president for a second period,
       opposition against him began to grow, and finally he was over-
       thrown from his dictatorial presidency in 1933. After having taken
       refuge in different countries, he came to Miami Beach, where he
       died in 1939. Size: 10.5 lin. ft.

17.   *Lydia Cabrera Personal Papers.* In this collection one finds
       excellent documentation in the field of Afro-Cuban folklore, Cuban
       history, and literature, from 1930 to 1991. Lydia Cabrera was an
       internationally renowned Cuban scholar and chronicler of Afro-
       Cuban culture and religion. It was she who first recognized and
       made public the richness of Cuban culture. Lydia made valuable
       contributions in the area of literature, anthropology, and ethnology,
       depicting the rich folkloric tradition of Cuban blacks with a proper
       narrative style. Lydia left Cuba as an exile in 1960, settling in

Miami. One of the most important manuscripts in this collection is the unpublished book "Arere Marekén," written by Lydia in Paris in 1930 and illustrated by Alexandra Exter, the famous Russian painter exiled in Paris after the Bolshevik Revolution.

18. *Ramón S. Sabat Collection.* This collection contains the LP records and audiotapes of Cuban music of the Cuban Plastics and Record Corporation of Havana, Cuba, known as the Panart records, as well as the Panart records of its affiliated company, the Panart Recording Company of New York. Ramón Sabat was the founder and owner of the Panart records established in Cuba in 1943. He left Cuba in 1964 when his company was taken over by the Communist regime. Size: 4.0 lin. ft.

Maps

19. *Cuba.* Chicago, IL: George F. Cram, 1930. This map shows the six provinces of Cuba which had been established in the colonial period.

Ephemera

20. One peso, the official bill used in Cuba from the beginning of the Republic through 1959.

Postcards

21. *San Rafael Street.* Havana: Edición Jordi, 1920.

22. *Capitol Building.* Havana: Casa Morris, 1950.

In the postcard collection we have approximately 800 items from 1900 to 1950 of buildings, street scenes, beaches, churches, historical events, and the like.

Photographs

23. *Havana.* Aerial view, 1958.

The bulk of the collection is comprised of photographs of buildings from 1902 to 1958.

The Communist Period, 1959 to the Present
Historical and Literary Manuscripts

24. Collection of cables received at the Cuban Embassy in Spain from the Castro government, dated 1961 to 1964.

Collection of Personal and Corporate Papers

25. *Tad Szulc Research Papers.* In this collection we find the transcripts of Tad Szulc's interviews with Fidel Castro and with eighteen of Castro's close associates in the Cuban Communist government, and other documents for Szulc's book *Fidel, a Critical Portrait,* published

in 1986. These interviews were taped in Cuba during 1984-1985. Tad Szulc is an American journalist. Size: 1.25 lin. ft.

Maps

26. *El Comunismo quitó El Cobre del mapa* . . . 1975. Color; 28 x 43 cm. This map shows the new provinces and municipalities of Cuba established by the Castro government. Cuba is now divided into thirteen provinces plus the capital district of the City of Havana.

Ephemera

27. A three-peso bill with the portrait of Ernesto "Che" Guevara. Havana, 1969.

28. "Los diez días que estremecieron al mundo." A cultural homage to commemorate the sixtieth anniversary of the Russian Revolution of 1917. Havana: Ministerio de Cultura, 1977.

Posters

29. *World Day of Solidarity with Cuba, July 26th,* by Eduardo Muñoz Bachs. Havana: OSPAAL, 1968. Color; 59 x 29 cm. This revolutionary poster has as its aim universal education and the power of mass mobilization for warfare. This poster belongs to the golden age of Cuban posters.

30. *Sonia Calero en Rumba,* by Antonio Fernández Reboiro. Havana, 1973. Silkscreen, color; 76 x 51 cm. The author was a designer in the publicity department of the International Film Distribution Center and now lives in Europe as an exile.

31. *Contra la Política Agresiva y Aventurera del Imperialismo Yanqui en el Caribe,* by Modesto Braulio Florez. Havana: OCLAE, 1982. Color; 69 x 51 cm. Through this political poster the author calls for collective participation against the United States.

A movement of political and cultural posters emerged in Castro's Cuba. They represent a new expression of Cuban painting since 1959 in revolutionary Cuba owing to the fact that the revolution had an urgent need to spread Communist doctrine among the people. During the '60s these posters gained international transcendency; in the '70s this transcendency declined; in the '80s the transcendency was minimal; and in the '90s the transcendency is in crisis.

The Cuban Exile Period, 1959 to the Present
Collection of Personal and Corporate Papers

Very important among the materials within the Cuban Exile Archives is the collection of personal papers from distinguished Cubans in exile. The major portion of this collection has been donated. At present, we have 78 Cuban exile personal papers collections. Size: circa 1,200 lin. ft.

32. *The Truth about Cuba Committee, Inc. Records.* This collection includes more than 390,000 pages of testimony, pamphlets, photographs, clippings, correspondence, and audiotapes from 1961 to 1975. This Committee represented all sectors of the Cuban exile community. It was the first and the most important group formed in exile. It was established to uncover the truth about what was happening on the island. Size: 68.5 lin. ft.

33. *David Masnata Collection.* This collection contains substantial material on genealogy and heraldry, compiled by Cuban exile attorney, David Masnata y de Quesada, Marquis of Santa Ana and Santa María, grandson of Gonzalo de Quesada, a distinguished Cuban political leader of the late nineteenth century, known as José Martí's protégé and preferred disciple. Masnata founded in Cuba the Institute of Cuban Genealogy and was a member of genealogical institutions throughout Europe and the Americas. He was exiled in New York from 1961 until his death in 1988.

34. *Pedro Pan Project Collection.* This collection contains correspondence, photographs, and ephemera from 1960 to 1964. The bulk of the collection consists of letters from Cuban children to Sara Yaballí, the nurse at Matecumbe Camp in Florida, and photographs and ephemera of children at the Matecumbe, Opa-Locka, and Boyshome camps in Florida. The Pedro Pan Project was established in 1960 between the United States and Cuba. The first children to leave Cuba under this project were received in Miami by Monsignor Bryan O. Walsh, Executive Director of Catholic Community Services. This project was established to save Cuban children from Communist indoctrination. In Cuba, hundreds of volunteers under the leadership of Polita Grau and Ramón Grau Alsina built a network that reached from one end of the island to the other. This was all done in secrecy. As a result, many of the volunteers in Cuba paid with their freedom. Size: 3.0 lin. ft.

Photographs

35. "Municipios de Cuba en el Exilio." Miami, 1970. Meeting of the Cuban Municipalities in exile.

36. "Three Kings Parade." Miami, 1987. This annual parade commemorates the Epiphany marching along Calle Ocho, Little Havana, Miami. Color print; 8.5 x 13.5 cm.

37.   "Gloria Estefan." Miami, 1993. Internationally renowned Cuban
      exiled lead singer of Miami Sound Machine, a band formed in the
      late 1970s by Cuban exiled musicians.

Postcards

38.   Cuban flag and a poem to the Cuban flag by Agustín Acosta, the
      Cuban national poet. Miami, FL: Language Research Press, 1971.

Posters

39.   *Para romper las cadenas que atan a Cuba . . .* [Miami, FL,] 1990.
      Poster showing the Human Chain of Democracy. Cuban exiles linked
      together from Miami to Key West, February 24, 1990.

40.   *Para Cuba que sufre.* Limited ed. [Miami, FL, 1989.]

41.   *Carnaval,* by Renato. Miami, FL: Kiwanis Club, 1993. Autographed.
      Annual fiesta organized by Cuban exiles since 1978.

Ephemera

42.   "Academia Cubana de Ballet. Dade County Auditorium, Miami,
      domingo 26 de marzo de 1972." Program of the Cuban Ballet
      School in exile. The directors were members of the Ballet Alicia
      Alonso in Havana, Cuba, now in exile.

43.   "Patronato Ramón Guiteras Memorial Library, XI Ciclo de
      Conferencias. Los presidentes de Cuba, 1933-1959." Program.

44-45. "La Esquina de Tejas Restaurant." Menu of a Cuban restaurant in
      Little Havana, Miami. Autographed by Ronald Reagan, when he
      came to Miami in 1983.

NOTE

1.   "South Florida's Evolving Diversity," *The Miami Herald, Viewpoint,* March 7, 1990.

Canada

27. Hispanic Studies and Collections at the University of Alberta

Wanda Quoika-Stanka

The University of Alberta has been collecting in the fields of Spanish language and literature since the University first opened its doors in 1908. Naturally, the collection originally supported courses at the undergraduate level only. Over the decades, research interests and the curricula expanded to include Latin American topics in faculties and departments as diverse as educational foundations, agricultural economics, and arts, in particular departments such as anthropology, history, political science, and romance languages and literatures.

The expansion and consolidation of the collection, however, really date from the early 1960s when academic programs were extended to the graduate level and considerable resources were made available to develop a comprehensive collection. During this time, attention was given to the acquisition of materials both from the Iberian peninsula and Latin America. In addition to maintaining a purchasing program of current imprints, opportunity purchases on the secondhand book market allowed retrospective purchases to be made and many of the gaps in the collection to be filled.

The 1960s and 1970s were decades of relative wealth, and purchases of entire collections and personal libraries or sections of bookstores were not uncommon. Selection of library materials was "largely the prerogative of faculty. Librarians and/or bibliographers were seen as expediters who received and processed faculty orders. Their role was distinctly secondary. The rationale for this arrangement was that the faculty were best qualified, by training, experience, and academic responsibility, to determine the needs of the collection." [1] Librarians also selected library resources on behalf of their liaison areas with monies allotted to the libraries. Needless to say, there were certain disadvantages to this method, such as duplication of orders, lack of orders being generated by faculty who were already over-committed, poor communication within teaching departments, or wholesale purchases of entire collections or materials in poor condition. A great deal, therefore, depended on the level of communication between professors and librarians.

In the late 1970s, formal collection policies were drafted by liaison librarians in conjunction with faculty for the areas of Hispanic studies as well as all faculties and departments campuswide. These policies were not intended to be engraved in stone, and continue to be reviewed on an ongoing basis.

Finally, in the 1980s, the Humanities and Social Sciences Library, which was the only exception on campus, gained control of the faculty discretionary accounts. This change has been instrumental in solidifying the ties and links between librarians and faculty. Several activities are conducted in consultation with faculty. They are:

1. Identifying new areas for collection development
2. Constructing desiderata files
3. Evaluating the collections in relation to the curriculum
4. Participating in faculty meetings
5. Identifying and securing faculty requests.

Additional activities undertaken by liaison librarians are:

1. Advising faculty and graduate students of new publications of interest to them
2. Weeding materials from area collections
3. Following comprehensive bibliographies and dealers' catalogs
4. Discovering new materials in pertinent fields through systematic perusal of bibliographies, publishers' catalogs, and reviews in journals
5. Attending national professional library association meetings
6. Performing advanced reference services. [2]

Furthermore, there is a strong Latin American interest group on the campus composed of faculty, librarians, and students who meet either formally or informally over lunch to arrange events such as guest lecturers. The interest has shifted to Latin American topics and away from Spain and Spanish issues or subjects since the 1970s. In addition, the city of Edmonton has a rapidly increasing Latin American community which has been instrumental in raising the awareness of Latin American culture by sponsoring film festivals, poetry readings, and the like.

At present, however, the University of Alberta still does not possess an official Hispanic or Latin American area studies program. Efforts are being made to achieve this objective, as the Dean's Advisory Committee on Interdisciplinary Studies in the Faculty of Arts requested that faculty submit plans for the development of an enhanced area program. This will allow for better financial control of Spanish and Spanish-American materials and make it easier to obtain relevant statistics as well as to obtain extra grants or endowments. However, owing to financial restraints, that did not occur. Currently, the library budget is divided into departmental allocations rather than into area studies programs. In practical terms, it means that several librarians can be selecting for Hispanic materials. Therefore, good communication among librarians has become absolutely essential.

The Latin American or Hispanic collections of the University of Alberta must be seen within the context of the 6,901,492 items that make up the entire collection. They include 3,216,685 microforms and 18,000 subscriptions in the systemwide holdings. In addition to the volumes in readily identifiable call number ranges, Latin American topics are covered in depth in thousands of volumes that have general classifications: history, political science, sociology, education, languages, and literatures. For example, works on South American Indian antiquities are grouped with more general ones on indigenous peoples of the Americas. The abundant writings of the South American scholar and political activist Paulo Freire class generally in educational philosophy. Seventeen thousand books are classified in history and twenty thousand in Hispanic languages and literatures. Recently unclassified is a major Latin American acquisition. In 1989 we received the gift of the largest private anthropology collection in Canada (30,000 volumes appraised at $400,000.00 Cdn.), the principal focus of which is Central and South America. In addition, there exist extensive holdings of microform collections, including items such as CIA Research Reports, Latin American Special Studies, and the entire Human Relations Area Files. The Government Publications branch of the Humanities and Social Sciences Library is a full depository for materials issued by the United Nations Economic Commission for Latin America and the Caribbean and, as well, for UNESCO documents.

Expenditure on monographs that are specifically Hispanic in content has been difficult to assess, but amounts to at least $30,000.00 Cdn. annually. The commitment to journal subscriptions is $8,000.00 Cdn. and microforms on subscription are approximately $4,500.00 Cdn. annually.

There are several departments throughout the university campus which have long maintained strong research interests in Hispanic studies. As the Hispanic collection is not housed in a separate building or facility, I summarize the areas of collecting strength by individual departments.

(a) *Anthropology*—The collection policy for this department has always emphasized Central and South America, in particular topics such as: indigenous peoples, mythology, religion, folklore, archaeological excavations, alternative medicine, and gender-related issues such as sex roles. The greater portion of the collection in this field is in Spanish, the rest being in English, French, and German. There are also significant holdings on microform for this department. In 1992 the University of Alberta also successfully completed a grant application to the Social Sciences and Humanities Research Council of Canada for $30,000.00 to purchase materials on indigenous peoples in North, Central, and South America.

(b) *History*—Collecting has been focused on colonial and twentieth-century material. Areas of strength are Mexico, Colombia, Peru, and Bolivia. Materials are collected primarily in English and Spanish, followed by French.

(c) *Political Science*—Here the emphasis is on Central America and the Caribbean, especially Nicaragua, El Salvador, and Cuba. Twentieth-century politics and revolutionary changes of the twentieth century are areas of strength. The next most important area is international relations between Latin American nations and the rest of the world. There are significant holdings on microform for this department, especially in the Government Publications collection.

(d) *Romance Languages and Literatures*—The collection policy for this department emphasizes primary materials. Collecting is done in Spanish with little or no purchases in Portuguese as there are no courses taught on Portuguese language or literatures. Additional materials may be bought in English or French. The Spanish American literature collection includes comprehensive coverage of all the republics, although Bolivia and Ecuador and some of the Central American states are not strongly represented, and coverage of the nineteenth century is understandably lacking in general depth. The strength of holdings for Spanish America is in materials for the twentieth century, which is the period most frequently touched on by staff and students in teaching and research. All major authors are represented in holdings that include both their writings and the critical literature. The strongest areas, undoubtedly a reflection of the strength of the publishing industries in these countries, are Argentina, Chile, Cuba, and Mexico. Moreover, consolidation of the collection continues through acquisition of texts identified through the development of particular research projects. In the near future, for example, requests will be made to the Library for purchase of Argentine and Uruguayan materials arising from a research project currently in progress during which holdings in twentieth-century fiction will be reviewed.

Finally, it should also be noted that particular holdings for Spanish American literature are complemented by those in other fields to which students and researchers in the area have frequent recourse. The Library's holdings in literary theory and critical methodologies (comparative literature) are especially impressive and, of all fields that might be included under the rubric of Latin American studies, history, especially of the colonial period, is particularly well represented. The last five years have witnessed increasing interest in literature of the Caribbean and Central America as well as women authors and children's literature. The addition of a women's studies program in the 1990s has strengthened interest in women authors and women's issues.

The Herbert T. Coutts Education Library supports the research and teaching of the Department of Educational Foundations which has a particular concentration on the following Latin American topics:

Sociology of development and education
Social stratification and social change
History of education
Anthropology of development
Intercultural education
Third World education

As graduate programs have evolved at the University of Alberta, courses have developed over and beyond the "general assortment of more-or-less standard courses on Latin American literature, politics, geography, history, and so on."[3] The changes in research interests or arrival of new faculty has resulted in an increased topical or thematic specialization. This causes new "gaps" or lacunae to appear as collecting was not attempted in these areas previously. Some of these "new" subjects of interest at the University of Alberta are children's literature, women authors, women's issues, Latin American popular culture, and ethnomusicology. The agonizing question librarians must contend with here is whether or not to continue to support older, more established topics or to concentrate wholeheartedly on the more recent research interests.

Since the early 1970s, librarians have offered a course in the Department of Romance Languages and Literatures called Romance Literature 500—Bibliography and Thesis Style. The objective of this course has always been to make the students independent library users as well as to train them to write proper footnotes and bibliographies. The course, which began as a noncredit course and is now given for credit, is open to graduate students only and covers all secondary sources for Latin American language and literature, an introduction to the Library facilities, instruction in the use of the Library catalogs, assignments and exercises, and the production of a final assignment, usually a bibliography on a topic of interest to the student. All graduate students in the department must take this course, which has been taught by different instructors over the decades and, at times, was even team taught.

The collection of Hispanic studies at the University of Alberta is not housed in a separate building or reading room, but is instead dispersed throughout the library system. Access to the collections is available through the OPAC. Presently, all faculty can have access to our OPAC from their offices if they have a computer and a modem. They simply have to obtain an MTS account and an ID and they can access our catalog from anywhere on campus. Access for off-campus users is more restricted as only a finite number of IDs are allotted to individuals in the city as well as to post-secondary institutions throughout the province. Because the new chief librarian is a strong supporter of resource sharing of collections, it is now possible to access our DRA system called the GATE. University of Alberta Library records can, of course, be seen via the Internet.

In summary, the University of Alberta libraries do not contain the oldest nor the most unique collection of materials in the field of Hispanic studies, in particular Hispanic literature. However, the growing interest in this area both on and off campus, as well as Canada's entry into the Organization of American States and the signing of the North American Free Trade Agreement (NAFTA), has necessitated increased support for this discipline. It is hoped that the future will allow us to continue to provide support at the same or even at a superior level.

NOTES

1. William D. Ilgen, "Collection Development within the Institution: The Role of Latin American Bibliographer and the Role of the Faculty," in B. G. Valk, ed., *Collection Development Cooperation at the Local and National Levels*, Papers of SALALM XXIX, Chapel Hill, North Carolina, June 3-7, 1984 (Madison, WI: SALALM, 1987), p. 17.

2. Robert D. Steuart, *The Area Specialist Bibliographer: An Inquiry into His Role* (Metuchen, NJ: Scarecrow Press, 1972), p. 106.

3. W. Glade, "Librarians and Readers: The Coming Showdown in Area Studies," in *The Multi-Faceted Role of the Latin American Subject Specialist*, Papers of SALALM XXII, Gainesville, Florida, June 12-17, 1977 (Austin, TX: SALALM, 1979), p. 155.

28. Development through Adversity: The Latin American Collection at the University of Calgary

Nora D. S. Robins

I would like to begin by "setting the scene" and making a few observations about the development of Latin American studies at the University of Calgary. A description of the library collection follows.

The University

Calgary, Alberta, a city of approximately 800,000, is situated in the foothills of the Rocky Mountains. Its economic base is oil and gas, ranching, tourism, and some diversification. Calgary is the home of the Calgary Flames hockey team, Calgary Stampeders football team, the Calgary Stampede and Rodeo, and the University of Calgary. The University of Calgary is a medium-sized, regional institution. It began its academic life as a satellite campus of a more established university when, in 1945, the Calgary Normal School became a branch of the Education Faculty of the University of Alberta in Edmonton, the capital of the province, situated 300 kilometers north of Calgary. The University of Calgary gained full autonomy as a degree-granting institution in 1966, with the goal of focusing on the population in the southern part of the province.

Today, the University of Calgary is a research and teaching university with sixteen faculties and more than sixty academic departments and major program areas (including law and medicine). In 1993/94, the University enrolled 18,000 full-time students, 4,311 part-time students, and 9,791 spring/summer students for a full-time equivalent of 21,672 students. Of these, 3,740 are graduate students. [1] The University offers a number of area studies and other highly specialized programs, including Latin American studies.

Dr. W. Armstrong, the first president of the University, placed a high priority on foreign area studies. He saw Latin American studies as one way to establish an area of program excellence at a new and expanding university. He was able to persuade the well-known Mesoamericanist

AUTHOR'S NOTE: In the preparation of this paper, I would like to acknowledge the assistance of my colleague Sharon Neary, formerly Archaeology Librarian, now DATA Librarian, University of Calgary Library System.

Dr. Scottie MacNeish, then a researcher at the National Museum of Canada, to come to Calgary and establish a department of archaeology. As a result of Dr. MacNeish's influence, the University created the first and only Department of Archaeology completely independent from a department of anthropology. (In many North American universities, anthropology was traditionally the site of archaeological studies.) Dr. MacNeish was also influential in the establishment of a post-graduate program in archaeology, including a doctorate. This was the only doctoral program in the Social Sciences taught at the University of Calgary at the time. Following this promising start in archaeology, the Latin American program was expanded through the hiring of specialists (many of them Americans) in other areas of Latin American studies: anthropology, economics, geography, history, political science, sociology, language, and literature.

With the coming of the budgetary restraints of the late 1970s, the expansion of the area studies programs slowed, although the Latin American program was able to maintain its early level of excellence through the maturation of Latin American studies scholars. The boom times of the early half of the 1980s enabled the University to further promote the program and brought the University, through the Alberta Heritage Fund, substantial library collections. By the late 1980s, however, times were tough, with revenues from the oil and gas industry suffering a decrease from 76 percent to 26 percent of provincial revenues. It is not difficult to envisage the sort of impact this had on the University.

Today, courses on Latin America are taught in anthropology, archaeology, economics, history, geography, law, language, literature, medicine, political science, and sociology at the undergraduate and graduate levels. Latin American scholarship at the University has received national and international recognition, owing in part to major awards won by our scholars in North America and Latin America. More than ninety theses on Latin America have been completed by our students. [2]

The Faculty of General Studies offers a minor in Latin American studies. The faculty is currently proposing that the status of the program be modified to include an undergraduate major.

There has been a steady increase in the number of students taking courses in Latin American studies through the Faculty of General Studies (figure 1). We have witnessed also a steady increase in the number of students enrolled in Spanish language courses (figure 2).

In related developments over the past twenty-seven years, the University has moved on several broad fronts. In 1967, the Department of Archaeology held its first Chacmool Conference. This conference has since become an annual event of international significance. In 1979, the University instituted the Latin American Summer School Programme, at

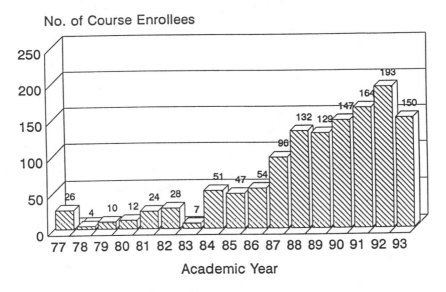

Figure 1. Enrollment in University of Calgary Latin American
Studies courses, 1977-1993

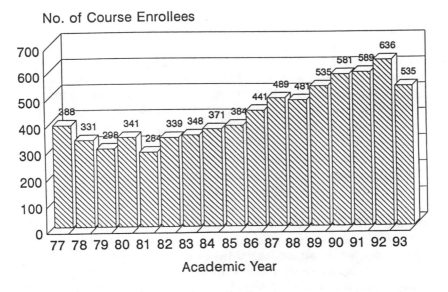

Figure 1. Enrollment in University of Calgary Spanish courses, 1977-1993

first biennial, now annual. There have been fifteen summer schools held primarily at different sites in Mexico but also in Central America and the Caribbean. In 1991, the Mexicanists at the University of Calgary founded the *Canadian Mexicanist Network Newsletter*. In 1993, FOCAL-WEST was established at the International Centre of the University of Calgary as the Western branch of the Ottawa-based Canadian Foundation for the Americas because of a perceived need to represent more effectively the particular needs of the western region and in recognition of the remarkable range of expertise on Latin America that exists in academic and business communities in western Canada. The purpose of FOCAL is to promote academic, business, cultural, and political cooperation with Latin America and the Caribbean. In 1993, the University entered into a trilateral consortium with El Colegio de la Frontera Norte in Tijuana and San Diego State University in California. This will lead to faculty and student exchanges. We look forward to the founding of the Canadian Association of Mexican Studies, thanks in no small part to the initiatives of the University's very active Latin American Studies Group.

By now you will have noticed the emphasis on Mexico. There is no other university in Canada that brings together such a broad range of scholars and researchers and a library collection of such depth. The Latin American and Mexican studies expertise of Calgary's faculty is considered to be the strongest in Western Canada, and with regard to faculty oriented to Mexico, possibly the strongest in Canada.

The Library

The University of Calgary Library System consists of one main library and four branches. In the past twenty-eight years we have acquired a collection comprising 1,633,276 volumes; 10,950 current periodical subscriptions; 95,044 pamphlets; 178,750 maps; 3,240,141 items of microform; 873,577 air photos; 311,608 government documents; 318,266 plans and posters; and 98,314 audio visuals.[3] The base budget for acquisitions was $3,349,535 in 1993/94. It is expected to remain unchanged for 1994/95.

I must preface my comments about the Latin American portion of our collection with some cautionary remarks concerning the criteria for major status as a Latin American collection outlined in the articles of Carl Deal.[4] I believe I can state with some certainty that no Canadian library has a collection of 150,000-200,000 volumes on Latin America or library budgets of $100,000 devoted to the acquisition of Latin American materials. Calgary certainly does not. If we are judged by Deal's latest survey, we fall into Group III.[5] It is, therefore, rather difficult to give volume counts for anything other than specific sections of the collection such as national histories and literatures. That portion of the collection shelved in F 1403 through 3799 contains more than 14,000 volumes, of which approximately 4,000 are on Mexico. Latin American literature comprises another 4,000 volumes, of which approximately 2,000 volumes relate to Mexican literature. We have more than 1,100 items of microform, of which 700 pertain to Mexico, and 1,800 maps, of which 600 relate to Mexico. We subscribe to 65 current periodicals relating to Latin America.

The interdisciplinary nature of Latin American studies at the University of Calgary is reflected in the fact that bibliographers in virtually all humanities and social science disciplines select at least some material on Mexico and Latin America. We have a Latin American Area Studies Fund that supports the acquisition of material in the social sciences (including history). In 1993/94, the fund was $12,600, unchanged for the last five years. Approximately 40 percent of the fund supports periodical subscriptions. About $4,000 is spent per year on Mesoamerican archaeology and $6,000 for Latin American literature. Other funds such as fine arts, drama, and geography spend portions of their acquisition budgets on Latin American materials. (We have not yet canceled periodical titles, but I expect this will change.)

Material is acquired through approval plan, exchange, and gifts. The History Librarian is currently responsible for coordinating the acquisition of material funded by Latin American area studies monies and for the provision of library instruction and faculty liaison to students and faculty in the social sciences and in general studies. The acquisition of material in Hispanic literature is the responsibility of another librarian, fine arts by a third librarian, and so forth.

Given the small acquisitions budget, the library is dependent upon gifts and grants. In 1965 the Library was fortunate to acquire the personal collection of Samuel Lothrop, the Mayanist. This collection formed the basis of our archaeological collection.

In the 1980s, through the prudent use of Alberta Heritage funding, the Library expanded its holdings of primary materials by purchasing Mexican documents on microform and in reprint series. In the past few years, thanks to the efforts of several of our librarians, the Library has been the recipient of several grants from the Social Sciences and Humanities Research Council of Canada. Consequently, we have been able to buy retrospective material in Mesoamerican archaeology and Mexican history.

I have titled this paper "Development through Adversity" because, living as we do in a province with an economy subject to boom and bust, we have experienced several periods of adversity over the last twenty-seven years. Nothing, however, prepared us for what we are facing today.

With a provincial deficit exceeding $4 billion, the government of Alberta has mandated a 21 percent cut in provincial grants to secondary education over the next three years: 11 percent in 1994/95 ($18 million); 7 percent in 1995/96; and 3 percent in 1996/97. Further funding cuts of $18 million are expected. The effects are already being felt: 10 percent of our faculty are retiring; position abolishment is in force; faculty and staff salaries and benefits have been cut; tuition fees are on the rise. The Library's base budget for the acquisition of materials has been frozen since 1992/93. We are purchasing fewer books and, of course, canceling periodicals. I would point out that in Canada we are heavily dependent on foreign publishing and must often cope with the sharp decline of the Canadian dollar against foreign currencies. We also pay taxes on books.

Where are we going from here? Economic pressures and the realization that we cannot nor should we be all things to all people are forcing us to focus on the rationalization of resources and resource sharing. Latin American studies is and will continue to be an established strength both in our academic programs and in the university library.

NOTES

1. University of Calgary, Office of Institutional Analysis, *University of Calgary Facts, 1993-94.*

2. *University of Calgary Thesis: A Bibliography* (Calgary: University of Calgary, 1985–).

3. University of Calgary, *Library Statistics 1993/94.*

4. Carl W. Deal, "Latin American Collection: Criteria for Major Status," in Paula Ann Covington, ed., *Latin American Frontiers, Borders, and Hinterlands: Research Needs and Resources,* Papers of SALALM XXXIII, Berkeley, California, June 5-10, 1988 (Albuquerque, NM: SALALM, 1990), pp. 62-71.

5. Carl W. Deal, "A Survey of Latin American Collections," in Deborah L. Jakubs, ed., *Latin American Studies into the Twenty-First Century: New Focus, New Formats, New Challenges,* Papers of SALALM XXXVI, San Diego, California, June 1-6, 1991 (Albuquerque, NM: SALALM, 1993), pp. 315-324.

29. A Librarian-Faculty Partnership: Challenges and Opportunities

Nicole Michaud-Oystryk

Objectives

This paper is in two parts. The first part is a description of the Latin American collection at the University of Manitoba; the second part discusses the partnership that librarians strive to establish with the faculty to strengthen the collection development and management process.

Description of the Collection

To put the Latin American collection in its institutional context: the University of Manitoba, founded in 1877, is the first university to be established in western Canada. With its liberal arts and sciences programs and its professional schools, it remains one of the largest universities in Canada. It supports 12 libraries with collections totaling approximately 1.6 million books and bound periodicals, and employs a full-time equivalent staff of 195, including 56 librarians. The libraries serve a community of approximately 28,000 full-time and part-time students, faculty, and citizen borrowers.

One of the 12 libraries, the Elizabeth Dafoe Library, which serves the faculties of arts, human ecology, nursing, and social work, is the main repository of materials related to Spanish language and literature and Latin American studies. Although there is evidence of minimal collecting activity in Latin American studies in earlier years, the collection flourished in the 1970s. This intense collecting activity, of course, corresponded to the establishment of a Latin American studies program at the university. Today, the collection remains a modest one, with a total of approximately 12,000 monographs and some 50 journals and newspapers. It provides adequate support for the minor in Latin American studies, which offers a cross-disciplinary choice of courses in anthropology, economics, geography, history, and literature, and meets the basic research needs of faculty and graduate students specializing in Latin American anthropology and history.

In the social sciences, students focus on different regions or periods through survey or special topics courses. The current emphasis is on Mexican, Meso-American, and Andean topics, Latin American civilizations including the pre-Columbian, ethnogeography, ethnohistory, and general history. The majority of the materials selected are in English. However, basic texts, major reference works, and publications specifically requested by faculty are ordered in the original language.

In the humanities, the collection supports teaching and research to the advanced bachelor's degree level in the areas of language study, literature and literary history, and criticism for all literary periods. In the area of Latin American literature, which focuses primarily on novels and short stories with some coverage of poetry and theater, the countries that are well represented are Argentina, Chile, Colombia, Cuba, Mexico, Peru, Uruguay, Venezuela, and the West Indies. While primary works are purchased almost solely in the original language, many secondary works are ordered in English, with only a small selection in French and German. Materials that fall outside the sphere of language and literature but are related to civilization and culture are selectively purchased to round out the collection. As well, every attempt is made to maintain a good reference collection which will serve the basic research needs of faculty and students.

The library holds a representative number of core journals in Latin American literature, history, and anthropology, as well as periodicals of an interdisciplinary nature for the geographical areas covered. It maintains subscriptions to 3 newspapers: *La Nación, El País,* and *Uno Más Uno.* Of the estimated 50 serials, approximately half are in Spanish. This is in stark contrast to the 16 newspapers and approximately 90 journals and annuals which were held in the 1970s and early 1980s, but were cut gradually as budgets diminished. It goes without saying that few new serial subscriptions have been established in recent years despite the expressed need for additional journals.

In the 1970s, the collection grew significantly, owing in large part to the existence of blanket orders. Monographs published by major publishers were automatically received. In the early 1980s, these also became victims of budget cuts; blanket orders were eliminated in favor of highly selective firm ordering. However, the growing interest in Latin American studies and the flourishing publishing industry in Latin America provided the impetus for the library to respond to the need for a stronger, more comprehensive collection of Latin American literature. In the mid-1980s, Latin American literary works that were not held by the library were identified and regular budget and gift funds were used to fill these gaps. During this period, two substantial gift collections also enriched our holdings.

Approval plans have come back into favor in the past few years, not because budgets have improved but rather to gain better vendor discounts, to speed up delivery, to improve interdisciplinary coverage, and to help subject librarians cope with an increased work load. Although Latin

American studies has not yet been included in the approval plan profiles, we intend to establish a literary author plan in the near future.

The selection of Latin American materials offers a unique challenge to subject librarians. In addition to the ubiquitous difficulties in acquiring materials owing to the political, economic, and cultural characteristics of many Latin American nations which have an impact on the publishing industry, bibliographers at the University of Manitoba must work within the limitations inherent to an institution that does not collect vast amounts of material in this area. Selection is not systematic, selection tools are often inadequate, and language barriers must be overcome in an effort to build a good and well-balanced collection.

In terms of ordering, it has been difficult to establish a solid, long-term business relationship with appropriate bookdealers. Currently, our acquisition department is well served by Puvill Libros and the Latin American Book Co. At times, the supply of serials, primarily newspapers, has also been less than satisfactory because of unacceptable delays in delivery and nonreceipt of issues. Despite these acquisition problems and budget limitations, the collection is growing at a slow but steady pace.

Librarian-Faculty Partnership: Opportunities and Challenges

Collection development and management provides an ideal opportunity for creating a strong and effective partnership between librarians and faculty. At the University of Manitoba, an organizational structure is in place, formalizing the interaction between the faculty and the library and fostering an effective working relationship for the benefit of the university community.

One of the most basic opportunities for cooperation at our institution is the selection of materials. Although the library has control over the acquisitions budget allocation and collection management functions, and public service librarians, in their dual role as bibliographers, are responsible for the development and management of collections in specific disciplines, faculty have a vested interest and a responsibility to participate in collection management processes. As a subject librarian, I welcome faculty recommendations for purchase and rely on their involvement in building a balanced, coherent, and dynamic Latin American collection that will meet the needs of all our users.

As budgets decline and libraries become more dependent on donations of materials, faculty also play a vital role both in the acquisition and the evaluation of gift collections. First, their contacts in the community often lead to the identification of private collections which will supplement the resources of the library. In fact, such a contact resulted in the acquisition of the personal collection of a former consul to Mexico. The collection consisted primarily of Mexican literary and historical works. Second, their input in the evaluation of gift materials suitable for the collection is often extremely valuable.

Special projects offer an additional opportunity for librarian-faculty liaison. Experience has shown that librarians and faculty members can collaborate quite successfully in obtaining financial and human resources for special projects. For the past several years, librarians have worked closely with faculty members to submit grant proposals for the purchase of expensive research sets, retrospective materials, and CD-ROM subscriptions.

A formal channel for faculty involvement is the user library committees which are composed of representatives from the academic departments. The library representatives in committee maintain liaison between the faculty and the library, make recommendations on general policy, and provide input into the allocation of the acquisitions budget, including addressing issues such as access vs. ownership. Individually, they are an excellent source of information related to new course emphases and trends, new research interests, and thesis topics. Their assistance is also critical when the serials collection is being reviewed whether for the cancellation of journals or for the establishment of new serial subscriptions.

Another opportunity for strengthening the librarian-faculty partnership is offered by two University Senate committees which have responsibility for all matters relating to the submission of new undergraduate and graduate courses and curriculum and program changes. These proposals have traditionally contained a statement from the library as to its ability to support a new program or emphasis and to cope with any effects the proposal may have on the availability of library resources. The library statements must indicate that the necessary resources are available or that the requisite budget priorities have been adjusted to provide them. In the past few years, the library has become much more stringent in its evaluations and has been more realistic when assessing library resource requirements. As might be expected, this has created a degree of frustration and indignation among some of the faculty, who view the library's new approach as interference and question the subject librarians' competence in evaluating resources in their field of expertise.

However, the committees dealing with these matters have been supportive of the library's position. A report recently submitted to the University Senate recommended that a stronger partnership be developed in the planning and delivery of courses and programs. On the one hand, departments and faculty should consult the library on the availability of resources when first considering the introduction of new courses or programs or the modification of existing ones. On the other hand, subject librarians should consult with departments and other appropriate groups to discuss the necessity of and the methodology used in assessing the library resources required to support new and existing courses and programs. It recognizes the fact that library resources needed for new courses and programs cannot be divorced from those required to service already existing ones. Therefore, it is essential that in making program and course proposals, academic units should explicitly identify the relative priority to be accorded new initiatives in light of the resources available to service all of their offerings. These are strong recommendations which stress the importance of having librarians and faculty working together.

To strengthen the librarians' position when they prepare statements on the level of library support, the revision of collection policy statements dating from 1975-76 was undertaken at the beginning of 1993 as part of a complete collection assessment project. From the beginning of the process, subject librarians were advised to consult closely with their respective faculty when completing the narrative statements. They were encouraged to discuss with them the process and the goal of producing policy statements along with a completed conspectus for all relevant subject areas. This is an attempt to produce narrative statements that reflect a consensus of library and faculty views as to what needs to be collected to support teaching and research needs. Working cooperatively with the faculty in identifying the level and scope of library resource requirements is recognized as essential, since their input will guide collection development for the future.

The second phase of this process will be the analysis of the collection using an adaptation of the WLN (Western Library Services) Conspectus, which is a specialized database management program designed to facilitate collection assessment. The goal of the conspectus assessment is to describe the scope, depth, and quality of the collection in a systematic, standardized way in order that this may be evaluated in the context of the universe of knowledge and other comparable collections. Information that can be used in assessing the collection (identifying what is and is not collected, the currency of the material, and the foreign language characteristics) is gathered through the examination of shelflist data, direct examination of the collection, list checking (the method most often used), and citation analysis to determine three elements: the current collection level, the acquisitions commitment, and the collection goal. Language coverage codes are also assigned to provide further depth to the analysis.

This phase will also demand the involvement of faculty. It is desirable to agree on the techniques that will be used to assess the collection, that is, in the case of list checking, it is important to select a list or bibliography mutually agreeable to both parties if the results are to be accepted, and to consult with them as experts. Their experience in using the collection will offer another valuable dimension to the analysis.

The completion of this two-phase project will culminate with the signing of the document by all the key players in the process: the subject librarian, the library unit head, the faculty library representative, the faculty department head, the faculty dean, and the director of libraries. The project promises to facilitate the collection evaluations which are required regularly as part of the faculty proposals for new or modified courses and programs.

While many opportunities obviously exist to build a stronger partnership between faculty and librarians, often the opportunities are not seized through lack of knowledge or understanding. A survey [1] which I conducted with two colleagues in 1985 explored faculty perceptions of academic librarians at the University of Manitoba. Many faculty openly declared that they did not know enough about the educational background and training of librarians. Survey respondents often questioned or showed a misunderstanding of the role of librarians in the academic environment. In fact, the survey showed that faculty members who had interacted with librarians had a better understanding of their functions and the value of their expertise.

Encouragingly, though, the results revealed the importance that faculty place on collection development. When asked how useful it may be for librarians to acquire a subject specialization through a graduate degree in their area of responsibility, faculty responded that subject specialization was most important in the area of collection development. Comments expressed at the end of the questionnaire also stressed their concern for collection development. Many lamented the lack of funds to develop collections and questioned the allocation of funds for other activities which were not seen as benefiting the collections. Some advocated a more active role for faculty in collection development.

The challenge for librarians rests in ensuring that faculty are more adequately informed of the librarians' expertise, the services they offer, the issues with which they are struggling, and their dual responsibility of responding to the immediate information needs of users and of fulfilling the long-term goals of the institution. They must foster a closer working relationship with faculty in collection development and management. More contact between the two groups through consultation, committee work, joint projects, and so on, will promote a deeper understanding of what librarians and faculty can achieve together and will create an alliance that will be mutually beneficial and will better serve the institution as a whole.

NOTE

1. Gaby Divay, Ada Ducas, and Nicole Michaud-Oystryk, "Faculty Perceptions of Librarians at the University of Manitoba," *College and Research Libraries* 48 (January 1987), pp. 27-35.

Latin America

30. The Mellon Program at the Mortenson Center for International Library Programs

Susan Schnuer

This paper is a brief overview of the Mortenson Center program and our newest grant from the Mellon Foundation. Thanks to two generous gifts to the University of Illinois Library from C. Walter and Gerda B. Mortenson, the Mortenson Distinguished Professorship for International Library Programs and the Mortenson Center for International Programs were established in 1989 and 1991 respectively. The purpose of the Center is to strengthen international ties among libraries and librarians.

We strive to fulfill this mission in various ways, such as facilitating the involvement of librarians in international exchange programs, hosting short-term group visits (for example, shortly a USIA-organized group of seventeen librarians from all over the world), cosponsoring conferences and exhibits, promoting international exchanges of library materials, and enhancing access to resources for scholarly research and teaching. By providing the means to further international exchanges of knowledge and people, the Mortenson Center intends to accomplish the goal of its benefactors—promoting tolerance and peace by enabling people everywhere to have access to knowledge.

The Mortenson Center is based in the Library of the University of Illinois at Urbana-Champaign. There is a real commitment to international librarianship at the University of Illinois Library. The University Librarian, Robert Wedgeworth, has long been active in international library activities. Mr. Wedgeworth, who is the current president of the International Federation of Library Associations (IFLA), is very enthusiastic about the Mortenson Center, in general, and the exchange program, in particular, and meets with the visitors during their stays as his schedule permits. Of course, Nelly González and Carl Deal have been extremely supportive of our current grant, and we have been grateful for their assistance and the great resources of our Latin American collection. The director of the Center, Marianna Tax Choldin, has been involved in international librarianship for many years.

The Mortenson Center has unique experience in designing and implementing an exchange program that facilitates both the visits of our library faculty to other countries and the continuing education and training program at our library for librarians from outside North America. In the past three years, more than eighty librarians from around the world have come to the University of Illinois through the Mortenson Center and several librarians from the University Library have had the opportunity to visit libraries in Germany, Great Britain, India, Australia, Ecuador, Russia, South Africa, and Uganda. The chief criteria of selection of candidates for the program are a strong command of English, the quality and usefulness of the applicant's stated goals, the suitability of the goals to the time frame, and demonstrated institutional support for the visit. We have been very pleased and impressed with the personal and professional development we have witnessed in the librarians who participated in the exchange program, and we are gratified by the links formed between our library and libraries in these countries.

The continuing education and training program for librarians from outside the United States provides the visitors—known as Mortenson Associates—with broad knowledge of, and exposure to, the theory and practice of librarianship in America. The format of extended visits, usually four to six months, is particularly crucial because it allows visitors to gain a deep understanding of the connection between the stated goals of the profession and the actual provision of services to an extent that is simply not possible through book learning alone.

An important issue, of course, is the financing of visits to the University of Illinois Library. Until recently the Mortenson Center gifts supported all the costs of the exchanges; however, increased demand has made it necessary for us to seek additional funding sources. The cost of these visits, including international airfare, housing, living expenses, health insurance, local travel, a modest stipend for necessary supplies, and taxes comes to roughly $9,000 for a four-month stay, and nearly $13,000 for a six-month stay. We have written several successful applications over the past year, but I would like to focus on our Mellon Foundation grant.

We submitted a proposal to the Mellon Foundation. Our goal was to undertake a program of leadership and institutional development in academic and research libraries in four Central American countries: Costa Rica, El Salvador, Guatemala, and Nicaragua. We proposed to train ten librarians in the University of Illinois libraries over the next two years, who would then return to their countries to serve as trainers for their colleagues. In addition to training, the program will also contribute to facilitating the exchange of information within and among the partner countries and between these countries and the rest of the world. We were very pleased when we were awarded the grant. We have already had one competition for the candidates, and in addition to our three conference speakers, two other Associates will be arriving at the University in August.

The training program at the Mortenson Center has several components. The first objective is skills development with automated library tools:

1. Our Associates are given e-mail accounts and intensive individual training in the use of electronic mail. They will have access to national and international bulletin boards and list-servers, and are able to dial to databases available through the Internet. They will all be taught how to use MOSAIC. They also receive training on how to search OCLC and other databases that may be critical to their libraries.

2. To enable them to make best use of the Library's resources, Associates receive individualized instruction on how to use the automated online catalog, CD-ROM products, locally mounted databases, and commercial online databases. With this group, we plan to dedicate one afternoon a week to learning how to use a specific automated tool.

3. A critical aspect of the automation training program for Associates is the opportunity to observe automated systems at a variety of libraries in order to understand fully the choices in the field. We plan many local tours to observe several systems in different types of libraries: public, special, school, and the like.

The Associates are also able to audit classes offered in the University of Illinois Graduate School of Library and Information Science (GSLIS). The courses available through GSLIS cover a wide variety of topics in general librarianship as well as resources and services for specialized communities.

A recent feature of the Mortenson Center program is the development of a series of library-based seminars addressing topics such as library administration, fund-raising, and automation. Our Associates have found these seminars to be instructive and very practical.

Another aspect of the training program is consultation with library faculty: The Mortenson Center staff arranges meetings with faculty in various library departments. These may take the form of tours of the departments, one-time one-on-one meetings, or ongoing discussions involving substantive professional questions. When appropriate and feasible, we will also try to arrange a short internship for our Associates.

We were very pleased that our three Associates were able to arrive in time for this SALALM conference. All of our Mellon-Mortenson Center Associates will attend a national conference, and we plan other visits. With our current group, we have begun discussions with the Commission on Preservation and Access to determine appropriate site visits.

Finally, we look for opportunities to allow our colleagues to share information about their libraries and the status of librarianship in their countries with American librarians. This panel is a good example of that effort. Before their departure our Associates will give a talk to librarians at the University of Illinois. We also hire a free-lance writer to interview and write a profile for each librarian. We promote those profiles by submitting them to appropriate journals.

A second objective of the Mellon grant is to link libraries through electronic mail and network connections. We will provide each participating institution with a basic setup to enable connection to electronic mail: a microcomputer with monitor, modem, and printer. If the library already has an e-mail connection, they will still receive the equipment; we hope this will improve access. Where necessary, we will also provide additional infrastructure, such as the installation of telephone lines or payment of telephone charges for the computer connections. Each of the four countries has a different level of technological infrastructure, and we are just beginning discussion with our colleagues about what is needed.

The final objective of the Mellon grant is to provide additional training and consultation on site. To insure that the equipment we provide is used to the best advantage, we will send a technical advisor to each institution to provide troubleshooting, advice, and on-site supplemental training of both staff and trainers. We also plan to promote the exchange of ideas and experience among the participants and to enhance the emphasis on regional cooperation, by having the Mellon-Mortenson Associates and the Mortenson Center staff meet in Central America in the year following the program's conclusion. In particular, the most important issues to be discussed at the conference will be the problems of returning to the home institutions, the role of libraries in the future of the region, and new advances in the region's libraries.

31. A Library Fellow in Honduras: Automatización de la Colección Hondureña

Laura D. Shedenhelm

Library Fellows Program
History of the Program

The Library Fellows Program in Honduras is funded under the authority of the Fulbright-Hayes Act by the United States Information Agency and administered by the American Library Association. Designed to increase international understanding through personal and professional interaction and the accomplishment of mutual goals, to promote international sharing of resources and to increase access to U.S. materials in the host country, and finally, to enable U.S. librarians to enhance and enrich their careers through an experience of overseas service, the Program began in 1986.[1] The 1993-94 Fellows constituted the seventh "class" of the Program to send U.S. librarians to institutions throughout the world. Having read many of the previous and current Fellows's vitae, I feel honored to have been chosen for the Fellowship at the Universidad Nacional Autónoma de Honduras, and to be included among such a diverse and accomplished group of librarians and information specialists in representing our profession to our colleagues outside of the United States.

Host Institution

Originally established in 1845 by Padre José Trinidad Reyes, named Bishop of Honduras, as the Academia Literaria de Tegucigalpa, in 1847 it became the Universidad de Honduras by act of Juan Lindo, then president of the country. The major areas of study at that time were Latin, philosophy, and civil and canon law. The 1880s saw contemporary science, legal and social sciences, and medical sciences added to the curriculum. During the first half of the twentieth century, the University began to offer degrees in engineering, chemical sciences, pharmacy, economic sciences, and odontology. Autonomous status was granted in 1957.[2]

The Universidad Nacional Autónoma de Honduras (UNAH) is now the largest public university in Honduras. The current total student population is about 39,500, with approximately 8,000 teaching and administrative personnel. The main campus is located in the Ciudad Universitaria near Suyapa, part of the Tegucigalpa metropolitan area. Also in Tegucigalpa, but separate from the main campus, is the Medical School. There are two branch campuses located in San Pedro Sula (Centro Universitario Regional del Norte, CURN) and La Ceiba (Centro Universitario Regional Litoral Atlántica, CURLA). The University Library System maintains facilities in all of these locations.

The Central Library on the main campus houses various collections including General Circulation, Reference, Reserve, Periodicals, Centro de Recursos de Aprendizaje (an extensive audiovisual facility with tele-conferencing capabilities), and the Colección Hondureña (CH). Most departments are open for service eighty hours each week, including weekends. While the service audience is the University community, the libraries are open to the public during special hours (for example, the Honduran Collection is open to anyone on Wednesdays). In general, bibliographic access to the collections is still maintained by card catalogs and printed indexes. At this time, there are no public access terminals due to the costs of equipment and the level of building security. All of the collections are closed stacks and utilize a paging system in an attempt to reduce loss through theft. The Central Library shares its building with the University Administration, which lacks a permanent home. This circumstance results in overcrowding for both administrative units and disrupts the flow of movement for both university personnel and library patrons.

Also located in the Central Library building are separate departments for Acquisitions and Technical Processes which centrally order, receive, and process almost all materials for the System. The Honduran Collection is an exception in that it catalogs and physically processes all of its own materials and the Honduran materials for the branches. Total staffing for the Library System includes 95 members among the Central and Medical Libraries and 27 members divided evenly between the two branch campus libraries. All department heads, as well as the director and branch library heads, have master's degrees in Library Science, thus making the UNAH Library System the only professionalized library in the country. This is quite remarkable when one considers that Honduras lacks any type of organized library training, much less a library school.

There is no legal mandate for any agency in the country to collect or preserve Honduran-related materials. The Colección Hondureña (CH) was founded in 1974 in an effort to preserve the heritage of Honduras in the form of a national bibliography. Specifically, CH is trying to collect all materials published within Honduras on all topics by any author, materials written by Hondurans but published outside of Honduras, or any materials published about Honduras. The collection is separated into the following sections: monographs, theses of UNAH, periodicals, government and corporate documents (e.g., annual reports), nonconventional materials (a combination clip-service and pamphlet collection for Honduran topics), a few microform materials, and a rare book collection. At each of the branch campus libraries, there are also Honduran Collections which generally duplicate titles held at the main campus but which reflect the curriculum emphasis of the branch.

Goals of the Project

The general description in the ALA proposal form stated that the project proposed to be accomplished by the Library Fellow would provide assistance to the Central Library as well as to the libraries in the regional centers. This could include any combination of the following components: training, automation, management, and/or collection analysis.

The project which has occupied the bulk of my time concentrates on automating the bibliographic records of the monographs collection in the Colección Hondureña located at the Central Library of the Library System. After consulting with Orfylia Pinel, Library Director, Gloria Núñez Flores, Acting Head of CH, Cecilia García, Head of Technical Processes, and Magda Sánchez of CH, we decided that my specific work during the year should be focused on this collection. We proposed to recatalog all of the monographs to AACR2r standards (slightly modified for local application), to reclassify them with Dewey 20 using 3 Cutter numbers instead of 2, to apply subject terms from appropriate thesauri, and to enter the new records into MicroISIS (a bibliographic program provided by UNESCO). We are creating new card catalogs for CH and the corresponding regional libraries utilizing the program CATALOGA. While the Library System would like to have the various automated catalogs connected by a LAN eventually, realistically, card catalogs will be used for many years to come. In order to ensure a high-quality database for the planned network of all the libraries in the UNAH system, there are various quality-control revision points throughout the process.

Changes in the Project

We knew from the outset that this proposal was a major undertaking, the entirety of which probably would not be completed during my year in Honduras. The collection consists of about 5,000 monographic titles (approximately 15,000 volumes). Originally we thought that one of the regional librarians with extensive knowledge of Honduran literature would be aiding in the recataloging of the 800s. However, there was much confusion among the branch ownership records which has resulted in the abandonment of this approach. This would have brought the title count for the project down to approximately 3,040, or about 18 titles per day, based on the approximately 169 days available to the project after subtracting national holidays, vacation periods, university holidays, and so on. Normal full-time cataloging production in a 40-hour-per-week work environment is 80-120 titles per month, or 4-6 titles per day per cataloger. The UNAH work day is only 6.5 hours. The Honduran full-time equivalent hours for permanent cataloging staff in CH is approximately .75 (3/4) of one employee. After reviewing these data, it was clear that we could not expect any number close to U.S. production standards. Therefore, we knew we needed contingency plans in terms of training and documentation. Given that we have had to recatalog in all subject areas, it is fortuitous that we planned ahead.

The two major contingency plans are (1) various types of training for the members of the CH staff and (2) compilation of a departmental manual. A weekly series of one-hour training sessions began in the spring of 1994. They cover a variety of topics ranging from very elementary (e.g., basic work skills and habits, how to alphabetize catalog cards, and how to shelve books properly) to more esoteric (e.g., the history of the unit, where to locate governmental statistics, and professional rights and responsibilities). These sessions have been supplemented by both individual training and small group classes. For much of its history, the Colección Hondureña has functioned without any specific direction other than the ideal of filling the void of a lack of a national bibliography. Even this ideal is not well documented. (I was only able to locate two short documents which described the collection: first, a two-page outline of the collection services and personnel and organization chart, and second, a four-page project description entitled *Proyecto: Base de datos sobre bibliografía nacional*, 1986, sponsored by the UNAH Library System.) Exacerbating the lack of specific goals is the fact that the unit has often been without appropriate leadership. From time to time, the head position has been filled with "political" appointees (who may or may not have had a professional library background) or has been vacant (the situation during 1993/94). Also, when I arrived, the functions and processes within the unit were retained only within the institutional memory; little was in writing. Compilation of a departmental manual which will contain a description of the goals of the unit, a basic collection development policy, and written instructions for all job positions and procedures has become a priority.

From the start, it was clear that in order for the project to achieve the goal of a completely automated catalog, the staff of CH would have to support the project on an emotional as well as a working basis. Benefits of the various aspects of the project were not self-evident to many of these library employees. I received questions like: Why do we need catalog cards if the data are in the computer? The answer, of course, is: What happens when there is no electricity (an increasing problem in Honduras) to run the computer? Even when there is electricity, only one person at a time can use the machine; many people can use the card catalog simultaneously. For some of the staff, the knowledge that CH had a purpose (to preserve their cultural heritage) was news, but also stimulated their interest. We have tried to include as many of the CH staff as possible in the project, thereby offering them the opportunity to see the project as the product of their efforts, not just the work of some outsider. Also, we have made every effort to fit the recataloging processes within the preestablished workflow and therefore diminish the shock of "change." The combination of these techniques has been having a positive effect on the unit, especially in the last few weeks. We are beginning to see the product of our efforts: a new reference section in the department which is fully recataloged, a new card catalog, a new shelflist, and a 50 percent increase in the size of the database while simultaneously imposing quality control and clean-up measures on previously input records.

One of the changes in the original intent of the project occurred due to the vacancy of the department head position. While Ms. Núñez Flores is still Acting Head, she also has her own department to run, which leaves her little time for the daily administration of CH. Through Ms. Pinel's encouragement and empowerment, I have been the head of the department during most of this year. While the problem solving, scheduling of personnel, and planning stack shifts and inventories have been wonderful administrative experiences for me, they have consumed much of the time I would otherwise have used cataloging and devoting to the primary project, thus placing the main project behind schedule. On the positive side, we have been able to streamline the workflow, create much needed space, incorporate a new automation project, and discover caches of unprocessed materials which will enrich the collection.

The structure of the project has created benefits beyond automating the collection. An extremely important by-product is an inventory of the monographs collection. Theft and loss of materials have been devastating to the library. The inventory is yielding a list of replacement titles for collection development. A second area of collection development centers on the reference collection in CH. As titles are recataloged, we are relocating to the reference section bibliographies, almanacs, dictionaries, and other quick reference tools that we find in the general stacks.

Contribution to the Institution

The Library System is working to automate its various departments and regional libraries. Concurrently, they are investigating equipment and program needs in order to create a network for the System. They plan to begin with a local area network for the Central Library, then expand to bring the other campuses on line. The automation of the bibliographic records of the Colección Hondureña meshes well with this plan. The materials in the collection have been problematic for the Library personnel to catalog as the items often lack basic bibliographic data such as publishing information. Also, they are often photocopies of out-of-print materials or parts of larger works (analytics or articles), unusual circumstances that often pose their own cataloging problems. The work during the last year has laid a foundation in Anglo-American cataloging practices and procedures which will enable the CH staff to continue the automation project, thus adding significantly to the future network.

As a result of having the ALA/USIS project for automation, the Library System has recently been chosen by the Instituto Interamericano de Ciencias Agrícolas (IICA) in Costa Rica to coordinate a database project on basic grains. The UNAH Library System was awarded the country-level responsibility for the project, Programa Regional de Reforzamiento a la Investigación Agronómica sobre los Granos en Centroamérica (PRIAG), to identify bibliographic materials about basic grains. The Instituto cited the automation already completed and expertise already attained as the basis for choosing UNAH for the project. As part of this project, members of the Honduran Collection will be searching international and local agricultural databases for citations relevant to Honduras and entering them into the automated catalog. Members of the Library System are receiving training and the Library has received equipment that will eventually be connected through a network to the other project stations in Guatemala, Nicaragua, and Panama.

Ancillary Experiences

As an extension of the individual training of personnel in the Honduran Collection, Dr. Cecilia García, Head of the Technical Processing Department, and I coordinated a seminar on the changes to AACR2 brought about by the 1988 revisions. The course ran for six days, two hours each day, and was filmed by Centro de Recursos de Aprendizaje (CRA) in order to use it as a training tool. The format of the class was lecture, in-class work assignments, and group problem solving. To accompany the tapes, we have created a guide that describes each lecture and includes copies of the handouts and assignments. It also includes a series of questions and requests for clarification which were posed by the first group to view the tapes for training. Dr. García and I met with this group to respond to these problems, and we have included these data in the guide. At this time, copies are being made for the Honduran Ministry of Culture and the USIS regional librarian for training purposes in the Central American area.

Orfylia Pinel, Dr. García, and I also team-taught a three-day seminar sponsored by the Honduran Ministry of Natural Resources and the MADELENA project about general library practices and forestry-specific information sources. The topics I taught, in particular, covered creation and use of automated records, theory and use of controlled vocabulary, and application of specific thesauri for agriculture and forestry.

I also had the opportunity to observe the initial phase of financial negotiations among various Central American university libraries, the Consejo Superior Universitario Centroamericano (CSUCA), and funding agents at the Central Bank to create a university-based online network for Central America. This was a fascinating experience which certainly would not be available to me in the normal course of events in my job category in the United States.

Experience of Living in Another Country
Living Conditions

The Tegucigalpa metropolitan area is made up of Tegucigalpa itself, its twin city Comayagüela, the airport district, and other outlying "colonias" or neighborhoods. We live on the south side of the city, near the airport, while the University is on the east side near the colonial town of Suyapa. While there are numerous buses, direct- and collective-taxis, commuting sometimes proves to be a real challenge. Road construction and/or repair often combines with "wildlife" (cows, burrows, horses, pigs, chickens, and, of course, dogs) to stop or slow traffic on major metropolitan thoroughfares.

Housing in Tegucigalpa is surprisingly expensive. However, we have had the good fortune to find living quarters with a Honduran family. On weekends, we often visit our host family's *finca* (small ranch) in Valle de Angeles outside of Tegucigalpa. The children can ride horses, swim, and generally run free without fear of crime or danger. (Personal security is a problem throughout this city of approximately 1 million inhabitants.) Until 1990, the lempira (the local currency) by law was exchanged at the rate of 2 lps. to the U.S. dollar.[3] Now that it is on the international exchange, the rate is about 8.5 lps. to the U.S. dollar. During our stay in the country, beans (a staple in the Honduran diet) became scarce during certain times, and sugar tripled in price. The precarious economic condition of the country means that it is not surprising that most of the library employees live with their extended families.

Comments on the Fellowship
Reflections on Living and Working in Another Country

Before leaving the United States, the Library Fellows all had the opportunity to view a set of videos about the psychological and emotional highs and lows of overseas assignments. While I have traveled and lived outside of the United States at various times, reviewing the classic cycle of euphoria (new setting, new challenges), depression (nothing works, the "challenges" are overwhelming), and equilibrium (everything in stride, all problems are manageable if not completely solvable) was useful. I experienced all of these stages at some point or other during my stay. There still is the stage to face of returning to the "former life" and reintegrating with family, friends, and work environment which have not undergone a form of "outer body experience" before I can complete the cycle.

In terms of working in Honduras in particular, I have observed a similar mixture of positive and negative. As a whole, the professionally trained librarians in the university system demonstrate a competence and ethical commitment to their work which is uncommon in Honduras. To say that the country maintains an approach to work that is different from Canada, Europe, or the United States is a severe understatement. Honduras utilizes a traditional patronage system throughout much of the government and in many of the private companies in the country. The system effectively rewards only personal or political support. Productivity which stems from timeliness and activity is, in most areas, of just secondary interest, and may actually work against an employee whose zeal may inadvertently make a powerful colleague look bad. This undermining of standard work principles is one of the major adverse conditions affecting the country and condemns Honduras to remain in the Third World.

Perhaps the greatest single lesson I have learned while on this project is to accept existing situations. If there is a problem, avoiding it or going around it is often more effective than confronting it. The years taken to create a problem will not be countered through direct action in the short run. More can be accomplished through finding a way around a problem or setting it to one side than through beating one's head against the "adobe" wall.

Ongoing Personal Benefits of Projects after the Fellowship

Several publishing opportunities have been presented as a direct result of my experience in Honduras. I am currently working on an annotated bibliography of Honduran literature from 1956. As an extension of my investigations on Honduran literature, among other topics, I have noted a need for creation of appropriate reference tools currently lacking for various subjects relating to Honduras. Also, I have noted that Honduran publishing is more extensive than I had previously believed, but that it is not well known outside of the region. I believe that this is an area ripe for investigation which, hopefully, would result in expanded markets for Honduran publications.

NOTES

1. Information taken from the pamphlets *The Library Fellows Program* and *U.S. Information Ambassadors: The 1991-92 Library Fellows* available from Library Fellows Program, American Library Association.

2. Harvey K. Meyer, *Historical Dictionary of Honduras*, Latin American Historical Dictionaries Series, no. 13 (Metuchen, NJ: Scarecrow Press, 1976), pp. 210, 300, 362-363.

3. United States Information Service, *Welcome Kit: Honduras* (Tegucigalpa: The Service, 1993), p. 3.

RECOMMENDED READING

In keeping with the theme of SALALM XXXIX, I have noted a few titles which I would recommend for anyone interested in knowing more about Honduras from a foreigner's point of view. All of the titles are in English and none are written by Hondurans.

Paul Theroux, *The Mosquito Coast* (New York, NY: Penguin Books, 1982). I read the book because I liked the movie. However, Harrison Ford was much more appealing than the Allie Fox in the story.

Shelly Tabar, *Pateplumas: A Short Story Collection on Honduras* (Tegucigalpa: Scandinavian Press, 1992). Pateplumas, or featherfeet, is the nickname of the residents of the Department of Santa Barbara. The stories are descriptive of small-town life in Colinas, Santa Barbara, where the author was a Peace Corps volunteer. I found that I "recognized" the people in the stories, and so believe that they are indicative of the Honduran *campo* and culture.

Guillermo Yuscarán, *Points of Light: Honduran Short Stories,* English ed. (Tegucigalpa: "Nuevo Sol" Publications, 1990). Yuscarán is the pen name of William Lewis, who wrote these stories (Puntos luminosos) during his first visit to Honduras in 1972-73. These stories of the underdogs in Honduras, the street urchins, the crippled, etc., are a vivid contrast to Tabar's stories.

Harvey K. Meyer, *Historical Dictionary of Honduras,* Latin American Historical Dictionaries, no. 13 (Metuchen, NJ: Scarecrow Press, 1976). While this is not "literature," Meyer's writing style is very entertaining. The data are *very* dated. For example, the beautiful line drawing of the Cuartel tower of San Pedro Sula is the only remembrance you'll have of this landmark. The building no longer exists. I understand that a new edition of this title is due to be published soon. I hope that it retains the "flavor" of the first edition.

32. Análisis de la situación actual de la biblioteca central de la Universidad Centroamericana, Managua, Nicaragua

Conny Méndez Rojas

Introducción

En este trabajo se presenta una descripción general de los servicios bibliotecarios de la Universidad Centroamericana (UCA), vistos a partir de octubre de 1988. Se mencionan brevemente los cambios que éstos han tenido en esta etapa, los proyectos y problemas actuales, así como las perspectivas de desarrollo que estos servicios tienen dentro del esquema de trabajo de la UCA.

Antecedentes

La biblioteca central de la UCA fue fundada el 22 de mayo de 1967, con una colección de 10,000 volúmenes, que en su mayoría habían sido donados por embajadas acreditadas en el país. El edificio de la biblioteca fue destruido por el terremoto de 1972, y desde entonces ocupa el edificio actual, hecho de manera provisional, y supuesto a albergar la biblioteca por un período no mayor de dos años. Este edificio tiene un área de 616 metros cuadrados, que se dividen en cinco secciones: administrativa, estantería, atención al público, sala de referencia y lectura. La sección de la hemeroteca ocupa un espacio adicional de unos 190 metros cuadrados.

Finalidad de la biblioteca central

La biblioteca central tiene la finalidad de atender las demandas de información de los usuarios que están relacionadas de manera directa con el desarrollo de los programas académicos de la comunidad universitaria; desarrollar una colección que cumpla con esas demandas de información; y preservar esa colección en las condiciones adecuadas de forma que pueda garantizar su permanencia y durabilidad en un estado aceptable de utilización.

Colección bibliográfica de la biblioteca central

Casi durante una década (a partir de 1983) dada las restricciones de presupuesto que sufrió la universidad, la biblioteca fue sensiblemente afectada al no contar con ninguna asignación presupuestaria para la compra de libros y suscripciones de revistas. Esta falta de recursos originó otros fenómenos, pudiendo mencionarse especialmente el hecho de que a partir de entonces las nuevas adquisiciones y otros materiales dependían de las donaciones del exterior, que aunque no respondían a los programas académicos de la época, eran los únicos recursos disponibles para trabajar. Como ejemplo de esto, las revisiones de la colección realizadas en los últimos cuatro años señalan que cerca de un 62% de la bibliografía está desactualizada y no cubre las necesidades mínimas de información que corresponden a los programas académicos actuales.

Esta deficiencia aceleró el decaimiento de los servicios bibliotecarios, ya que mientras considerablemente crecía la población estudiantil, aumentaba la demanda y necesidad de estos servicios. El fenómeno más relevante, y que tiene una relación directa con la situación anterior, fue que por la falta de recursos bibliográficos en la biblioteca central de la universidad, las escuelas y departamentos de las distintas facultades salieron en busca de sus propios recursos. Y fue así que nacieron los centros de documentación, que son en realidad bibliotecas especializadas, habiendo hasta el momento un total de ocho.

La creación de estos centros generó otro problema. Estos fueron fundamentalmente creados por las escuelas e independientemente de la biblioteca central, cada uno cuenta con un sistema de organización distinto al ya establecido en ésta, y en su mayoría, la información no ha sido debidamente organizada. Además, en muchos casos esos centros de documentación no están dirigidos por personal con preparación en bibliotecología.

A partir de 1993 la universidad asignó a la biblioteca central un presupuesto para la compra de libros. Esta asignación presupuestaria fue de unos 15,000 dólares y se consideró un verdadero triunfo para la biblioteca si tomamos en cuenta la caótica situación en que se encuentran las universidades nicaragüenses en cuanto a recursos económicos se refiere.

Para el año 1994, la universidad mantiene el mismo presupuesto para la compra de libros, y además se cuenta con un fondo de un proyecto danés (DANIDA, Agencia Danesa para el Desarrollo Internacional) consistente en una partida de U.S. $10.000 para este año, y una cantidad igual para 1995. Las cantidades en dinero son mínimas comparadas con la necesidad de bibliografía que tiene la biblioteca para cumplir con las demandas de profesores y estudiantes. Sin embargo, es esta la actividad que está fortaleciendo el servicio bibliotecario de la universidad, y aunque a pasos lentos, la bibliografía se va renovando.

Como procedimiento para la compra de materiales se utiliza el mecanismo de solicitar a los decanos de las facultades y a los jefes de departamentos, el envío de sus necesidades bibliográficas a la biblioteca central, sin importar que la facultad o departamento que está solicitando materiales bibliográficos cuente con un centro de documentación. La compra de libros está canalizada a través de la biblioteca central. Cuando los materiales llegan, la biblioteca los procesa y los envía a la facultad o departamento que los solicitó. Los materiales son remitidos bajo la condición de préstamo. En este sentido, la biblioteca funciona como un centro catalográfico para toda la universidad. Esta situación tiene una explicación práctica que será detallada en otro aspecto de este trabajo.

Personal

El personal de la biblioteca central está constituido por una directora, una subdirectora, dos jefes de departamento (estos son procesos técnicos y servicios al público), un técnico en encuadernación, tres encargados de las secciones de hemeroteca, referencia y circulación, tres técnicos en clasificación y catalogación, y diez asistentes de circulación. De este personal, hay seis profesionales (cuatro en bibliotecología, uno en biología y uno en trabajo social). Tres estudian la carrera de bibliotecología, y el resto son estudiantes de otras áreas.

A nivel general, se considera que el personal cumple básicamente con las funciones asignadas, aunque siempre se presentan dificultades por falta de manejo de técnicas, o por carencia de formas adecuadas de supervisión del trabajo. La principal debilidad en el personal, particularmente con los profesionales, se da en la falta de actualización en el campo, que en algunos casos se da también por falta de interés y estímulo económico.

A finales de 1988 el problema de personal capacitado en la biblioteca central era crucial. Para resolver esto, se inició un programa de capacitación a partir de 1989, y desde entonces se ejecutan por lo menos dos cursos cada año. Estos cursos se programan de acuerdo a las áreas que se contemplen como más débiles en los recursos humanos disponibles, y ha incluido todas las áreas de bibliotecología. Este trabajo se ha hecho con recursos humanos nacionales, pero también se ha logrado traer a reconocidos especialistas en el campo de las ciencias de la información, principalmente de Centro América, los Estados Unidos y Canadá.

Ultimamente se le ha dado mayor énfasis a la capacitación en el uso de computadoras y programas para el manejo de bases de datos. En estos cursos participan tanto los profesionales como los técnicos. Sin embargo, dentro del país nunca ha habido capacitación bibliotecaria a nivel de posgrado, y la dificultad general para salir a estudiar al exterior es la falta de manejo de un idioma extranjero. En resumen, se han hecho muchos esfuerzos para elevar los niveles técnicos del personal bibliotecario de la UCA, y de otros centros bibliotecarios del país, pero lo ideal sería montar cursos de capacitación que superen los niveles actuales de los profesionales.

Servicios que ofrece la biblioteca

La biblioteca tiene sus puertas abiertas al público 13 horas diarias (73 horas a la semana). Los servicios al público más importantes son: circulación y préstamo, referencia, hemeroteca, elaboración de bibliografías, alertas y boletines de adquisiciones. Un detalle interesante sobre los servicios y que hay que mencionar es que a pesar de lo pobre que es la biblioteca en cuanto a bibliografía se refiere, los servicios de circulación y préstamos atienden entre 300 y 500 usuarios cada día, en un espacio donde sólo caben más o menos 110 personas.

Este problema se agudiza con la demanda de los estudiantes de otras universidades creadas recientemente (hay por lo menos tres), que tienen servicios bibliotecarios exiguos. Las otras universidades existentes tienen una situación similar a la de la UCA, en lo que a carencia de bibliografía actualizada se refiere.

El problema de falta de servicios bibliotecarios en las otras universidades incide directamente en la biblioteca de la UCA en el sentido que nuestra biblioteca recibe a una enorme cantidad de estudiantes foráneos en busca de bibliografía para consultar. Además, entre los solicitantes hay estudiantes de secundaria que visitan la biblioteca para utilizar las obras de referencia. En los momentos críticos, cuando la biblioteca está tan llena, no hay espacio para circular en las áreas de los servicios al público.

Por esta razón hemos determinado no atender a usuarios externos para poder asegurar un espacio mínimo a los estudiantes de la UCA. Esta determinación también provoca una situación difícil para los trabajadores de la biblioteca. Aunque esta no es la mejor solución porque estamos negando un servicio, es lo más práctico que se puede hacer en esta situación, ante la falta de espacio y material adecuado para atender a los usuarios de la UCA, que son el objetivo de atención primordial de la biblioteca.

Edificio

Es necesario mencionar brevemente la situación del edificio de la biblioteca central, dado que este tiene una conexión directa con los servicios que ésta ofrece. Tal como se señaló en los antecedentes, el edificio que ocupa la biblioteca fue construido improvisadamente para proteger los materiales y equipos que pudieron salvarse del terremoto en el año 1972, y mantener el servicio bibliotecario. Se consideraba que iba a permanecer en este espacio por un período máximo de dos años (esto se refiere a los años 1973 y 1974).

En aquella época la universidad tenía 2,000 estudiantes. Actualmente hay 5,000 estudiantes matriculados, y la biblioteca sigue ubicada en el mismo espacio donde sólo cabe un total de 103 sillas. De acuerdo a los libros sobre construcción de edificios de bibliotecas, deberíamos tener 255 sillas y/o cubículos para los usuarios, para atender a un 5.10% del total de la población estudiantil. En otras palabras, el problema del edificio es tan delicado como la falta de bibliografía en la biblioteca central de la UCA.

Hasta la fecha se han presentado por lo menos tres proyectos de ampliación y/o construcción de un edificio nuevo para la biblioteca. Sin embargo, esto aún no tiene una solución definida. La universidad se encuentra actualmente gestionando la ampliación del edificio de la biblioteca con el financiamiento de un organismo alemán. La situación de este proyecto en estos momentos está en la revisión de terrenos y del actual edificio. La esperanza es que esto sea aprobado a más tardar en julio de este año.

Proyectos de desarrollo

Dentro del plan de trabajo hay tres proyectos fundamentales para el desarrollo de los servicios bibliotecarios de la UCA. Estos proyectos ya en ejecución son:

1. El diseño de una base de datos de las monografías (o tesis) de los graduados en la UCA. Este proyecto se inició el año pasado, teniendo como paso inicial la capacitación del personal en el manejo del programa MicroIsis. La jefe de procesos técnicos se está especializando en el uso de este programa y es la persona que lo dirigirá, asistida por la subdirectora de la biblioteca.

La automatización de las monografías es el objetivo principal de la biblioteca porque son consideradas parte del patrimonio de la universidad. Prácticamente todo el personal técnico de la biblioteca está siendo capacitado en el manejo de la base de datos para que así la mayoría participe en el ingreso de los datos correspondientes a dicha base. Hasta la fecha ya se han ingresado los datos de unas 450 monografías. Este trabajo se ha realizado de manera lenta por las dificultades técnicas que presenta el manejo del programa MicroIsis. En el país hay varias personas que son especialistas en el manejo de dicho programa, pero la biblioteca no tiene los recursos económicos necesarios para pagar honorarios por asesorías en este campo. Por eso, la preocupación principal es que haya una persona especialista dentro del personal de la biblioteca, y que todos los trabajadores podamos contar con los conocimientos básicos para administrar nuestra base de datos.

El paso siguiente dentro del proyecto de creación de bases de datos es el registro en la computadora de todas las obras nuevas que están ingresando a la colección, y a continuación, el material que se selecciona después de un exhaustivo programa de descarte de la colección existente en la biblioteca.

2. La capacitación continua del personal. Se hace hincapié en los aspectos relacionados con automatización, pero también es de gran importancia el manejo de los servicios al público, y el uso de técnicas de clasificación y catalogación. Igualmente, los conocimientos básicos sobre conservación y preservación de materiales. El proyecto de la capacitación se seguirá realizando con recursos internos, y a través de la cooperación de organismos e instituciones externas que apoyan este tipo de actividad.

3. Proyecto de actualización de la colección. Este proyecto también en ejecución, es el más difícil porque no se puede descartar el material existente si no tenemos los recursos suficientes para reemplazar las colecciones con materiales actualizados y de acuerdo a los requerimientos de los programas académicos de la universidad.

Se supone que dentro del proyecto de ampliación del edificio de la biblioteca habrá también una pequeña partida para la compra de libros y suscripciones de revistas. Igualmente, a través de la rectoría se han presentado solicitudes de donaciones de libros a organismos internacionales y embajadas.

Entre los organismos que respondieron positivamente se encuentra Asociación Sueca para el Desarrollo Internacional (ASDI), que en enero de 1993 donó a la biblioteca 90 títulos con 500 ejemplares. Esta donación fue hecha a través de un proyecto presentado por todas las universidades a fines de 1989. Los libros donados fueron seleccionados previamente por los directores de las bibliotecas universitarias que participaron en el proyecto.

Balance y perspectivas de desarrollo de la biblioteca central
Problemática

El principal problema para la biblioteca central de la UCA, al igual que las otras bibliotecas universitarias del país, es la falta de recursos económicos básicos para operar y para la compra de equipo. Por ejemplo, la única computadora que existe fue conseguida con un fondo especial que la biblioteca recibe del alquiler de un local para librería ubicado dentro del recinto de la universidad. Con ese mismo fondo se han comprado materiales indispensables para el trabajo diario, y se espera que a través de éste, se pueda conseguir otra computadora para agilizar el plan de trabajo de automatización bibliográfica, antes de que finalice este año.

Otro aspecto considerado como un problema de la biblioteca es la falta de integración de ésta con los centros de documentación. Hasta ahora se ha podido lograr que aquellos centros que están clasificando y catalogando sus materiales utilicen, a la par de su propio sistema, el sistema de clasificación de Dewey, que es el sistema que oficialmente utiliza la biblioteca (y es el más utilizado en el país). Esto se hace para contar con un elemento común al momento de integrar todas las colecciones, ya sea físicamente, o a través de un sistema automatizado. Además, se había mencionado antes, los materiales bibliográficos que actualmente la biblioteca adquiere para las facultades y departamentos, se registran y procesan con la intención de integrarlos y recuperarlos más tarde por estos mismos medios.

Como se mencionó anteriormente, el problema más agobiante y complicado continúa siendo la planta física de la biblioteca. Se ha esperado por varios años que este problema se resuelva a través de financiamiento externo, pero hasta ahora esta ha sido una tarea que sigue pendiente. Prácticamente en todos los informes anuales de la biblioteca se comenta esta deficiencia de la universidad, y se ha planteado cómo esto afecta particularmente la calidad y cantidad del trabajo y el desarrollo de los servicios. Aunque este problema es reconocido en todos los niveles, la solución no se da internamente debido a que la universidad no cuenta con presupuesto para la construcción o mejoras de sus edificios.

Estrategias y actividades de desarrollo

Un elemento importante para el desarrollo bibliotecario es contar con personal debidamente capacitado. Esto ha sido una de las principales debilidades de la biblioteca. A fines del 1988 sólo habían dos personas profesionales, la directora y la subdirectora. En este aspecto se ha mejorado porque actualmente se ha podido contratar personal profesional con mayor nivel de calificación.

Sin embargo, dentro de este personal se encuentran algunas dificultades en el manejo de técnicas bibliotecarias. Muy pocas personas se manejan al día con el desarrollo del campo bibliotecológico a nivel nacional e internacional. Una de las razones es por falta de recursos para adquirir personalmente bibliografía del campo, o las pocas oportunidades para participar en actividades profesionales. Los bajos salarios que a nivel general tienen las universidades nicaragüenses no permiten el desarrollo y actualización profesional.

Se pueden mencionar también algunas actividades que permanentemente se ejecutan en pro del desarrollo de la biblioteca. Entre las más relevantes se encuentran: la divulgación de las actividades bibliotecarias en páginas educativas y culturales; sesiones de trabajo con docentes, directores y representantes estudiantiles para dar a conocer los servicios y beneficios que generamos; foros sobre sistemas de información para docentes, bibliotecólogos y personal que labora en el manejo de información.

Conclusión

Hay que señalar que a pesar de las limitaciones que se presentan, y que son elementos indispensables para el desarrollo de cualquier biblioteca, hemos podido contar con mucha solidaridad de amigos bibliotecarios e instituciones que apoyan servicios bibliotecarios universitarios.

Por ejemplo, la OEA financió la capacitación en uso de disco compacto a la subdirectora de la biblioteca, y donó además una máquina lectora de disco compacto (donde caben seis discos), y la colección de discos de CD MARC Bibliographic de la Library of Congress y un ejemplar de EBSCO Academic Abstracts (también en disco compacto).

Finalmente, la demanda de servicio de tantos usuarios ha sido el mejor estímulo para continuar atendiendo con tantas limitaciones de espacio y bibliografía. No obstante, es evidente que mientras no tengamos un edificio que cuente con las condiciones mínimas, el trabajo que se realiza será siempre difícil y con alguna carga de frustraciones, reconociendo que los servicios bibliotecarios en una universidad son esenciales para el cumplimiento del plan de estudiois y el desarrollo global de esa institución, y que las debilidades mencionadas rompen continuamente el equilibrio mínimo deseado para el desarrollo de nuestra biblioteca universitaria.

Sin embargo, la conciencia de que nuestros servicios bibliotecarios son indispensables se manifiesta cada día en nuestros usuarios. Y esta es la razón primoridal por la que estamos siempre en búsqueda de los medios necesarios para superarnos profesionalmente, y de los recursos básicos que nos permitan seguir brindando un servicio sencillo pero eficiente.

33. El Sistema Nacional de Información Científica y Tecnológica en Costa Rica

Jeannette Alfaro Ugalde

Costa Rica ha venido desarrollando múltiples esfuerzos para coordinar el Sistema Nacional de Información Científica y Tecnológica (SINICYT). Dentro de las actividades que se han planteado para organizar, administrar y brindar mayor acceso a los usuarios de información, cabe destacar la labor que realiza el Consejo Nacional de Investigaciones Científicas y Tecnológicas (CONICIT), institución que promociona y financia la investigación científica y tecnológica del país y que a través de su Dirección de Información, coordina las acciones y proyectos de información, en forma conjunta con otras instituciones gubernamentales de los diferentes sectores del desarrollo, como lo son el sector público, el sector académico y el sector privado.

Dentro del Programa Nacional de Ciencia y Tecnología que se ha venido desarrollando desde hace tres años, dentro del campo de información mediante el Préstamo BID/CONICIT/CONARE, Costa Rica ha tenido la oportunidad de plantear la creación del Sistema Nacional de Información Científica y Tecnológica. El objetivo principal es fortalecer y desarrollar la capacidad de los recursos humanos y la dotación de equipo para la transferencia de información cualitativa, que brinde y asista con sus servicios a los sectores productivos del país. De esta manera se pretende crear una conciencia general de la importancia de la información como materia prima, para el sector productivo, que tiene la necesidad de mejorar sus productos para contribuir a que Costa Rica pueda figurar dentro de la apertura comercial internacional, con mayor competitividad. Al inicio de este proyecto se consideró la necesidad de aprovechar la infraestructura existente, o sea, involucrar a siete centros especializados de información, que pertenecen al sector público y que se dedican a la prestación de servicios de información, según su área de competencia como ser: industria, agricultura, salud, exportaciones, energía, tecnología y ciencia y tecnología.

Mediante el financiamiento del Banco Interamericano de Desarrollo (BID), estos centros de información se han dotado de equipo y material bibliográfico. Asimismo, se ha incentivado la necesidad de promover el uso de las nuevas tecnologías de información con la capacitación que el Programa permite, para entrenar a los bibliotecarios que tienen a cargo dichas funciones. Cabe mencionar que el proyecto ha sido un éxito, gracias al papel que han desempeñado los centros mediante su cooperación, lo cual ha permitido el trabajo conjunto para constituir la primera red local de servicios de información interconectados y que en este momento tienen la posibilidad de ampliar sus servicios por medio de Internet.

Los centros especializados participantes en la red son:

1. Centro Nacional de Información Agropecuaria (CENIA): coordinador de la información agropecuaria del país.
2. Centro de Información en Energía (CIE): brinda los servicios de información sobre este tópico.
3. Centro de Información Industrial (CII): mantiene el sistema de información industrial y brinda sus servicios a este sector.
4. Centro de Información Tecnológica (CIT): ofrece los servicios a las empresas del sector productivo.
5. Biblioteca Nacional de Salud y Seguridad Social (BINASSS): cubre los servicios de información de la comunidad médica del país.
6. Centro de Información en Exportaciones (CICEX): presta sus servicios de información especializados a exportadores, inversionistas, importadores y productores del país.
7. Centro de Información Científica y Tecnológica (CICYT): recupera y pone al servicio de sus usuarios toda la información concerniente sobre los recursos científicos y tecnológicos con que cuenta el país, investigadores, unidades de investigación, áreas de investigación, y los proyectos de investigación en curso. Además tiene como función primordial la coordinación de adquisición de material bibliográfico para los centros integrantes de la red.

BIBLIOGRAFIA

Cerdas Lopéz, Max. "El Sistema Nacional de Ciencia y Tecnología". *Boletín SIERN* (1991), 20-21.

González M., Javier. Centro de Documentación Energética CIE. San José: CIERN, 1992.

Seminario Nacional de Política de Información. San José, 1989.

34. La biblioteca de la Universidad Centroamericana "José Simeón Cañas"

Josefina Castro de Roque

La biblioteca de la Universidad Centroamericana José Simeón Cañas (UCA) fue fundada en 1966, al año siguiente de ser fundada la universidad. Se inició con un fondo bibliográfico de 8.000 volúmenes y funcionaba en un salón del Instituto Don Rúa. En 1973 se trasladó a un nuevo edificio, construido especialmente para ella, con una superficie de 3.225 metros cuadrados distribuidos en cuatro plantas con capacidad para 600 lectores. En 1994, el fondo bibliográfico asciende a más de 100.000 volúmenes que incluyen libros, folletos, tesis, etc., y 1.300 títulos de revistas. Además de las colecciones básicas para el apoyo docente, existe una rica colección centroamericana (con énfasis en El Salvador) y un seguimiento de artículos de revista que tratan sobre el país.

Los servicios que presta la biblioteca incluyen préstamo de materiales a domicilio y en sala, servicio de fotocopias, elaboración de bibliografías y referencia. Atiende un promedio anual de 371.000 usuarios. El personal está constituido por 30 empleados que cubren las áreas de servicios al público, procesos técnicos, automatización y administración y servicios.

La biblioteca de la UCA es una de las bibliotecas mejor organizadas del país. Sus procesos técnicos se realizan en base a normativas internacionales tales como las Reglas de Catalogación Angloamericanas 2. ed., Código de Clasificación de la Biblioteca del Congreso, Listado de Encabezamientos de Materia del Instituto Colombiano de Fomento a la Educación (ICFES) y de la Biblioteca del Congreso (LCSH), formato MARC, Normas del Instituto Interamericano de Ciencias Agrícolas (IICA) para la redacción de referencias bibliográficas, etc.

A nivel internacional la biblioteca pertenece a asociaciones tales como American Library Association (ALA) e International Federation of Library Associations and Institutions (IFLA), y a nivel nacional, Sistema de Información Bibliográfica de El Salvador (SIBES), Red de Bibliotecas Universitarias del SIBES, Red Nacional de Información en Salud y Club de Usuarios de MicroIsis.

Automatización

Utilizando el software MINISIS versión G, desarrollado por el International Development Research Centre (IDRC) de Canadá, y el formato MARC en combinación con un equipo Hewlett-Packard 3000, la biblioteca ha desarrollado su sistema integrado de administración de bibliotecas, del cual al momento se encuentran funcionando los siguientes módulos: catalogación, catálogo en línea y préstamo de materiales. Los módulos de publicaciones periódicas y selección-adquisición se encuentran parcialmente desarrollados.

Hasta la fecha se han ingresado y puesto a disposición del público un total de 5.000 registros que contienen información de libros y tesis adquiridos por la biblioteca desde enero de 1992. Simultáneamente con el ingreso de nuevas adquisiciones se trabaja en la retroconversión de 40.000 registros manuales de los materiales ingresados hasta 1991. Además, se cuenta con otra base de datos de artículos de revista, que incluye todas las revistas publicadas por la UCA y artículos publicados en revistas extranjeras (recibidas en la biblioteca) que se refieren a El Salvador. Los primeros 4.000 registros de esta base de datos ya han sido incluidos en el CD-ROM de Bancos Latinoamericanos II producido por la Universidad de Colima de México.

Cabe observar en este aspecto que la adaptación del personal y los usuarios a la nueva tecnología ha sido buena, y en general ha mostrado un balance positivo. El personal ha aprendido mucho y con muy buena actitud. Los estudiantes en su mayoría están fascinados con el uso de terminales y han hecho incluso propuestas de mejoras que se están tomando en cuenta.

Proyecciones

A corto plazo la biblioteca proyecta conectar el equipo de computadoras personales a través de una red Novell y a mediano plazo conectarse con una amplia red internacional como Internet, que nos permita optimizar nuestro servicio de referencia, poniendo a disposición de nuestros usuarios, además de nuestras propias bases de datos otras bases de datos internacionales. Otros proyectos que se están considerando a corto plazo son preservación de materiales, desarrollo de colecciones y materiales audiovisuales.

Conclusiones

Todo el desarrollo alcanzado hasta el momento ha sido posible en primer lugar gracias al efectivo apoyo que brindan las autoridades de la UCA a todos los planes y proyectos de la biblioteca en combinación con el excelente trabajo en equipo que ha realizado el personal; y en segundo lugar, pero no menos importante, gracias a diferentes personas e instituciones que nos han brindado su apoyo moral y económico, entre ellas: AMCOSUCAS, Mellon Foundation y actualmente el Mortenson Center de la Universidad de Illinois, Urbana-Champaign.

El prestigio alcanzado por la biblioteca de la UCA y sus proyectos la sitúa en una posición de liderazgo en el campo de la bibliotecología en El Salvador, por lo que constantemente se reciben solicitudes de consultoría de diferentes instituciones, tanto a nivel nacional como centroamericano.

Dicha posición de liderazgo constituye un serio compromiso que nos obliga a mantenernos en continua actualización y aprendizaje a fin de poder apoyar efectivamente uno de los principales objetivos de la Universidad, como es el de enfocar su quehacer universitario hacia el pueblo salvadoreño.

La oportunidad que brinda el Mortenson Center en este momento, al traer bibliotecarios de Centro América y en mi caso de El Salvador, es doblemente valiosa, ya que en primer lugar nos permite dos cosas muy importantes: aprendizaje y actualización tan necesarios para continuar adelante con nuestros proyectos y la no menos valiosa oportunidad de conocer a otros profesionales con los cuales poder establecer contactos y mantener comunicación. En segundo lugar, es un excelente apoyo al gremio bibliotecario salvadoreño en general, ya que dada la orientación social de la UCA, toda esta experiencia será compartida con otras instituciones y especialmente con bibliotecarios a nivel nacional.

BIBLIOGRAFIA

Rivera-Aguilera, Alma B. "El Salvador". En *World Encyclopedia of Library and Information Services*. Chicago, IL: American Library Association, 1993. Pp. 280-281.

Universidad Centroamericana "José Simeón Cañas". Biblioteca. *Informe anual de labores, 1989-1993*. San Salvador, El Salvador: La Biblioteca, 1989-1993.

————. *Reporte de las actividades realizadas durante el primer semestre 1992 en el proyecto de automatización y referencia*. San Salvador, El Salvador: La Biblioteca, 1992.

35. Bibliotecas particulares de intelectuais brasileiros: Descrição da situação na Universidade Estadual de Campinas e na Catholic Unversity of America

Vera Cristina Neumann

Aproprio-me de uma frase da colega nicaragüense Conny Méndez Rojas em seu trabalho "Algunas reflexiones sobre lo que SALALM podría ofrecer a los bibliotecarios nicaragüenses", publicado no SALALM XXXVI, e início também minha apresentação assim: "Es necesario iniciar esta presentación haciendo la consideración de que para la mayoría de los bibliotecarios nicaragüenses (e, aqui, também os brasileiros) la sigla SALALM es totalmente desconocida".

O que vou relatar não tem diretamente ligação com a citação acima, apesar de julgá-la extremamente apropriada e digna de reflexão e debate. Por que efetivamente SALALM não é uma sigla conhecida na Nicarágua, Brasil e provavelmente em vários outros países das Américas?

Essa constatação é apenas um parênteses dentro do trabalho que pretendo apresentar nesta edição do SALALM. Ocupar-me-ei em descrever o trabalho realizado na Diretoria de Coleções Especiais da Biblioteca Central da Universidade Estadual de Campinas (UNICAMP), no tocante à recepção, processamento técnico, serviço de referência e manutenção de bibliotecas particulares, tentando depois traçar um paralelo com as atividades desenvolvidas na Oliveira Lima Library, na Catholic University of America, onde estagiei por seis meses (de novembro de 1993 a abril de 1994).

Universidade Estadual de Campinas (UNICAMP)

Criada em 1966 pelo médico Zeferino Vaz, a UNICAMP forma juntamente com a Universidade de São Paulo (USP) e a Universidade Estadual Paulista (UNESP) o trio das universidades públicas do estado de São Paulo, responsável por mais de 50% de toda a pesquisa científica realizada no Brasil, qualquer que seja a área do conhecimento.

NOTA DO AUTOR: Agradeço as sugestões oferecidas por Peter Johnson (Princeton University), Laurence Hallewell (Columbia University), Claire-Lise Benaud (University of New Mexico) e Sonia Silva (UNICAMP). Este trabalho é dedicado à memória do bibliotecário e amigo brasileiro Paulo Tarcísio Mayrink, professor do Departamento de Biblioteconomia e Documentação da UNESP, campus de Marília.

A UNICAMP conta com aproximadamente 12 mil alunos, 3 mil professores e 10 mil funcionários (sendo que destes mais de 4 mil trabalham no setor hospitalar). Desde sua criação a Universidade vem se destacando como centro de excelência em pesquisa e extensão, dando-se ênfase ao ensino de pós-graduação (mestrado e doutorado).

As três últimas gestões dos reitores da UNICAMP vem privilegiando o Sistema de Bibliotecas, dirigido pela Diretora da Biblioteca Central, que coordenada a parte técnico-operacional de 22 bibliotecas secionais.

Diretoria de coleções especiais da Biblioteca Central da UNICAMP

Desde 1983 o assunto bibliotecas particulares é mencionado com grande freqüência na universidade onde trabalho, a UNICAMP, localizada no estado de São Paulo, Brasil. A partir dessa época, o tema também vendo sendo tratado com maior assiduidade nos veículos de comunicação, principalmente nos jornais. Em contrapartida praticamente quase nada foi escrito ou discutido sobre bibliotecas particulares pela classe bibliotecária. Pode-se então concluir que o assunto interessa a jornalistas e pouco incomoda os bibliotecários brasileiros? Triste e perigoso fim para tesouros que passam das mãos dos proprietários para a mão dos vendedores, sem que o bibliotecário sequer tenha sabido da sua existência.

Há algumas décadas atrás, vivendo realidade, o escritor, o historiador, o pesquisador podia alimentar-se intelectualmente de papel, já que outros veículos ainda estavam sendo inventados. O dinheiro mais farto, as casas maiores e a generosidade dos amigos, aumentavam o tamanho das bibliotecas.

Hoje o prazer/necessidade de ter livros foi substituído por veículos de informação mais ágeis e sedutores. (Será?) O tamanho das residências diminuiu, passando de amplas casas para apertados apartamentos. O preço do livro no Brasil também pode ser considerado alto, e isso pelo fato das tiragens serem tão pequenas. Ou seja um ciclo que diminuiu o tamanho e a quantidade de bibliotecas particulares.

Desde meados da década de 70 ouve-se falar de transações que envolvem vendas de bibliotecas e milhares de dólares. A grande maioria dessas coleções foi vendida para donos de alfarrábios ou particulares. Poucas vezes instituições públicas o privadas tiveram orçamento suficiente para encarar uma dessas vendas.

A aquisição pela UNICAMP em 1982, da biblioteca particular do historiador Sérgio Buarque de Holanda (1902-1982), acredito eu, foi a primeira a realmente motivar debates na imprensa escrita brasileira. Qual seria o melhor destino para a biblioteca?

1. Para a Universidade de São Paulo (USP), onde Sérgio havia sido professor e aposentado-se compulsoriamente em 1968 em solidariedade aos colegas cassados pelo Ato Institucional n.5 (AI-5)?

2. Para alguma universidade americana que talvez pudesse oferecer melhores condições de armazenamento, tornando-a acessível a um número maior de pessoas?

Bem, ela acabou indo parar na UNICAMP, então uma jovem universidade (tinha 16 anos na época), graças a intervenção de alguns professores amigos da família do historiador.

Foi a partir daí que o assunto "bibliotecas pessoais" começou a vir mais a baila, fazendo com que outras importantes bibliotecas conseguissem ser mantidas intactas após o falecimento dos titulares. Ou seja, livros, periódicos e documentos puderam escapar da venda desenfreada. À época e desde então, sempre que bibliotecas particulares são compradas e mantidas intactas surgem comentários e questionamentos sobre a validade dessa manutenção integral. À revelia do espírito desintegrador de alguns críticos que teimam em usar argumentos de custos elevados e duplicidade de informações, a UNICAMP optou pelo caminho oposto, qual seja o de privilegiar a integridade de acervos de "vultos importantes" da historiografia brasileira, tornando-os acessíveis, justamente na sua integridade.

Para justificar este tipo de atitude, utilizo palavras do professor Antonio Candido, em discurso feito quando da inauguração das novas instalações da Biblioteca Central da UNICAMP:

. . . relativo ao interesse que pode ter o estudo das coleções formadas por compra ou doação de bibliotecas pessoais, que chegam íntegras, com a sua fisionomia própria, sendo mantidas assim em vez se dissolverem no todo . . . porque o estudo de tais coleções vem a ser um instrumento útil para investigar a formação das mentalidades num dado momento histórico. A evolução da cultura de um homem se evidencia nos livros que leu. Através desta cultura é possível esclarecer a história intelectual de um período, pois a formação de uma biblioteca equivale geralmente à superposição progressiva de camadas de interesse, que refletem a época através da pessoa . . . .[1]

Instituições privadas, bancos, universidades, prefeituras abriram os olhos para a grande importância desses acervos particulares, resultado de décadas de estudo e de pesquisa, passando que adquirí-las e geralmente tornando-as acessíveis. Coleções como as de Gilberto Freyre, Pedro Nava, Orígenes Lessa, José Guilherme Merquior, José Olympio, Carlos Lacerda entre outras, hoje podem ser conhecidas e consultadas.

Com a aquisição da biblioteca particular de Sérgio Buarque, foi criada na Biblioteca Central da UNICAMP, a Diretoria de Coleções Especiais que desde 1984 vem sendo dirigida por Sonia Dias Gonçalves da Silva. Atualmente a Diretoria conta com cinco bibliotecários que são responsáveis pelo serviço de referência e processamento técnico de mais de 40 mil volumes. A catalogação/classificação do acervo de Sérgio Buarque demorou aproximadamente cinco anos para ser completada. Entre 1983 e 1987, os 10 mil volumes da coleção, sendo 8 mil os livros, foram processados manualmente, utilizando-se o Código de Catalogação Anglo-Americano 1 e a Classificação Decimal de Dewey. Em cada jogo de ficha matriz que era duplicado, utilizando-se um arcaico mimeógrafo a tinta, eram identificados não só os elementos comuns de toda catalogação, mas também as possíveis anotações de Sérgio, as dedicatórias que havia em aproximadamente 20% do acervo, as intervenções dele nos livros: autoria de capítulos, de prefácios, de orelhas, etc. Com isso obteve-se um retrato bastante completo e inusitado da coleção, uma vez que nas fichas de autor, de título ou de assunto todas essas informações podem ser encontradas. No começo do processamento técnico optou-se pelo não carimbamento e não utilização de etiquetas colantes nas lombadas, visando preservar a coleção. Porém a situação mudou muito em dez anos e ante a possibilidade de roubo, o inevitável foi carimbar os livros e usar etiquetas.

Paralelo ao processamento técnico vem sendo também feito um levantamento bibliográfico da produção científica de Sérgio Buarque de Holanda. Em quase 60 anos ele escreveu vários livros e mais de 400 artigos que foram publicados em jornais, periódicos, catálogos, etc. Tenta-se trazer para sua biblioteca tudo esse material, de preferência no original, porém quando não é possível, ao menos cópias xerográficas. Ou seja após mais de uma década de trabalho, a Diretoria de Coleções Especiais possui não só a biblioteca de Sérgio, mas também 95% de tudo o que ele escreveu e cerca de 85% de tudo o que foi escrito sobre ele.

Em 1988, a viúva do historiador, Maria Amélia Buarque de Holanda, doou à UNICAMP o arquivo de seu marido, constituído de fotos, originais, recortes, documentos, cadernos de anotações e alguma correspondência. Esse material foi encaminhado para o Sistema de Arquivos (SIARQ) da universidade que está trabalhando no seu inventário visando futura publicação.

Em junho de 1989 a Biblioteca Central mudou para novas instalações. Num prédio de 12 mil metros quadrados, divididos em cinco pisos, a Diretoria de Coleções Especiais, doravante chamada DCE, ocupa todo um lado do último piso.

Junto com o prédio novo chegava também uma coleção nova: livros, móveis (dois armários e uma escrivaninha) e alguns objetos que formavam a Coleção Aristides Candido de Mello e Souza (1985-1942). Doada pelo professor da USP e crítico literário Antonio Candido de Mello e Souza, levou o nome de seu pai, eminente médico reumatologista. O acervo é formado de aproximadamente 3500 volumes (sendo 3200 os livros), basicamente nas áreas de literatura portuguesa, francesa e brasileira. Destes, metade são remanescentes da biblioteca particular do médico Aristides, que havia sido muitos anos antes doada por sua viúva à Faculdade de Medicina da Universidade de São Paulo de Ribeirão Preto. A outra metade já é um pedaço da biblioteca do próprio Antonio Candido. Constituída de livros de literatura brasileira moderna, esta parte da coleção é rica em dedicatórias.

Esse acervo assim como os demais não pode ser emprestado. As consultas são feitos no local e apenas é permitido cópias xerográficas se o exemplar não for raro e se estiver em boas condições.

O processo de recuperação bibliográfica em relação a coleção Aristides Candido é um pouco mais longo, porque envolve o levantamento da produção científica de/sobre três pessoas: o próprio Aristides que escreveu artigos em periódicos especializados de medicina; o professor Antonio Candido que em mais de 40 anos de vida científica, sempre ligada ao ensino acadêmico escreveu centenas de trabalhos; e sua esposa Gilda de Mello e Souza, também professora da Universidade de São Paulo e autora de vários livros e artigos.

A intenção de DCE é, digamos, "fechar o cerco": fazer com que cada uma das coleções que vão sendo incorporadas tornem-se um centro referencial sobre a vida e a obra do proprietário da biblioteca, evitando com isso que outros pesquisadores precisem correr o país (lembrando sempre das dimensões continentais do Brasil) à procura de informações sobre os titulares dessas bibliotecas.

A respeito do ítem: manter ou não unido todo o acervo de uma pessoa, é muito apropriado ler o artigo "The Martin Luther King Library and Archives at the Crossroads",[2] onde numa determinada altura discute-se sobre manter ou não num mesmo local e sob um mesmo comando toda a documentação de/sobre o líder Martin Luther King. Esta documentação está hoje dividida entre o Martin Luther King Center for Nonviolent Social Change, em Atlanta, e a Boston University.

Os argumentos utilizados pelos não-favoráveis a essa união, também são merecedores de reflexão. Para Taylor Branch, autor do elogiado *Parting the Waters,* a decisão do júri de continuar como está, ou seja dividido, foi uma vitória. Segundo ele: "I'm hardly alone in waiting to sound a warning about the abuse of control that the King Family already has. If they gained control of all papers, there's every reason to believe the monopoly would get worse".[3]

Sem entrar no mérito dessa polêmica específica, o argumento poderia também ser utilizado em relação a DCE/UNICAMP que busca reunir todo o material sobre os intelectuais brasileiros aqui já citados.

Neste caso porém, o que a Diretoria de Coleções Especiais objetiva é efetivamente facilitar a pesquisa e o acesso a documentação, colocando-a toda junta.

Em setembro de 1989 aportou na DCE a biblioteca do historiador norte-americano Peter Eisenberg (1942-1988). Professor da UNICAMP desde 1975, autor de alguns livros e vários artigos, Peter era proprietário de uma biblioteca de 5 mil volumes, sendo 3500 os livros. Acervo extremamente especializado, principalmente em história e ciências sociais das Américas, com concentração para os estudos sobre cana-de-açúcar no Caribe e no Brasil. Quando da venda da coleção, o arquivo que servia como base às pesquisas do historiador também foi adquirido, passando a fazer parte do acervo do Arquivo Edgar Leuenroth, do Instituto de Filosofia e Ciências Humanas (IFCH) da UNICAMP.

No início de 1990, a DCE recebia outra coleção. Desta vez era a biblioteca pessoal do professor da UNICAMP, ensaísta e ex-adido cultural do Brasil na Itália, Alexandre Eulalio Pimenta da Cunha (1932-1988). Sua biblioteca foi comprada pela Universidade e durante um ano esteve instalada no Instituto de Estudos da Linguagem (IEL), onde ele lecionava. Por falta de espaço adequado os 14 mil volumes (11 mil livros) foram transferidos para a Biblioteca Central onde passaram a integrar o acervo das Coleções Especiais.

É importante salientar que mesmo com o crescimento do acervo, cada uma das bibliotecas manteve sua integridade física, seguindo os padrões previamente estabelecidos. Não houve união das coleções, embora elas ocupem o mesmo espaço físico.

Alexandre Eulalio foi um intelectual reconhecido no Brasil por sua cultura erudita. Teve uma produção científica que caracterizou-se pela falta de linearidade; escreveu muito, porém pouco foi reunido em livro enquanto ele era vivo. Atualmente existe um grupo de professores, colegas de trabalho do mesmo departamento, que estão resgatando sua obra, conseguindo com que boa parte de seus artigos (em jornais e periódicos) seja editada, tornando-a mais acessível à consulta. Ele era, segundo seus alunos, prolixo na sala de aula, nunca terminando no mesmo assunto por onde havia começado. Ou, como dizemos no Brasil, ele "viajava". O mesmo, Antonio Candido dizia sobre Sérgio Buarque de Holanda. O conhecimento acumulado desses intelectuais era de tal forma abrangente, que suas aulas eram verdadeiras viagens no tempo e no espaço previstas pela história e pela literatura.

O arquivo de Alexandre Eulalio, formado de uma hemeroteca bastante completa em literatura (mais de 100 mil recortes), fotos e originais, encontra-se no Centro de Documentação Alexandre Eulalio (CEDAE) no IEL, onde também está sendo preparado um inventário desse material.

Em 1992, a Reitoria da UNICAMP recebeu a oferta da doação de um biblioteca particular de aproximadamente 10 mil volumes. A doação estava sendo feita pelos filhos do Professor José Albertino Rodrigues (1923-1991), falecido ao lado da esposa, a lingüísta Ada Natal Rodrigues, num trágico acidente de carro. O sociólogo José Albertino era professor da Universidade Federal de São Carlos (USFCar) e, com a esposa, proprietário de uma biblioteca bastante eclética. Junto aos livros de estudo e de pesquisa de ambos, podiam ser encontrados centenas de romances, que iam da literatura brasileira aos clássicos franceses, passando pela mais instigante literatura policial. Dada a característica dessa biblioteca em especial, e tendo em vista que a finalidade das coleções adquiridas pela UNICAMP não é o lazer, mas sim a pesquisa, a Coleção José Albertino Rodrigues foi a primeira e única, até agora, a ser desmembrada.

Foram separados os romances que, juntos somavam mais de 2 mil volumes, sendo posteriormente incorporados à Coleção de Lazer mantida pela Biblioteca Central, que mantém regras próprias de empréstimo. Os livros de lingüística, predominantemente francesa, de propriedade de Ada (também professora da UFSCar) foram listados e oferecidos à biblioteca do Instituto de Estudos da Linguagem (IEL) que possui um Departamento de Lingüística com cursos de mestrado e doutorado. Depois dessa separação, a DCE manteve em seu acervo o que chamou de núcleo da coleção José Albertino Rodrigues, qual seja, livros e periódicos sobre ciências sociais (especialmente sociologia e política) e história. No total há por volta de 3 mil volumes (2500 livros). Desse material também foi feita uma listagem.

Albertino Rodrigues foi um grande ativista em torno da pesquisa científica no Brasil tendo pertencido aos quadros da Sociedade Brasileira para o Progresso a Ciência (SBPC) durante muitos anos. Sua produção científica girou em torno das questões relativas à sociologia do trabalho, importância dos sindicatos e alguns estudos de teoria sociológica, tendo orientado teses e participado de dezenas de bancas de mestrado e doutoramento dentro e fora de sua universidade. Seu arquivo de trabalho, composto de fichas de leitura, tabelas estatísticas e entrevistas de pesquisas de campo ficou de propriedade da Universidade de São Carlos. Parte entretanto de sua documentação pessoal está nas Coleções Especiais da UNICAMP.

É interessante salientar aqui que cada uma dessas coleções apesar de pertencerem a intelectuais brasileiros tem em seu acervo metade dos livros e periódicos em outros idiomas, que não o português. Sérgio Buarque por exemplo era um perfeito poliglota. Em sua biblioteca encontramos lidos e anotados livros em francês, inglês, italiano, espanhol e alemão. Efetivamente, Sérgio viveu dois anos na Alemanha (1929-1930) e dois anos na Itália (1953-1954) e ofereceu cursos e conferências várias vezes nos Estados

Unidos. Todos seus livros com grifos e anotações, assim como aqueles que tem dedicatórias, estão devidamente identificados no fichário.

Antonio Candido tem o francês como segunda língua e boa parte de seu acervo e dos livros que foram de seu pai está em língua francesa. Ele também esteve nos Estados Unidos lecionando.

Alexandre Eulalio tem quase metade dos livros de sua biblioteca em outros idiomas. Viveu por quase oito anos na Itália, nas décadas de 60 e 70, onde fez muitos amigos e incrementou sua coleção. Lia e falava também francês, inglês e espanhol, embora a predominância seja em língua italiana.

Peter Eisenberg pelo fato de ser americano possuía em seu acervo mais de 50% do material em inglês, o que com certeza facilitava-lhe as pesquisas.

Já Albertino Rodrigues fez seus estudos de doutoramento na Universidade de Sorbonne, portanto seu acervo é recheado de obras em francês, apesar de ter também centenas em inglês e espanhol. Característica em comum a esses intelectuais é a leitura das obras clássicas na sua língua original. Poucas traduções são encontradas nesses acervos.

Descrição das etapas de trabalho
Recepção

Quando alguém tem interesse em vender ou doar uma biblioteca particular para a Universidade Estadual de Campinas, a pessoa (geralmente a viúva ou os filhos do ex-proprietário) entra em contato com a Reitoria, falando do interesse na venda ou na doação, e pedindo que a universidade providencie algum tipo de visita para avaliar o acervo. Na maioria dos casos quando trata-se de venda, a família já tem um valor em mente, que nem sempre corresponde à realidade.

O reitor encaminha a solicitação para a Coordenadora Geral do Sistema de Bibliotecas da UNICAMP que discute e analisa o assunto com a Diretora de Coleções Especiais. Posteriormente, uma bibliotecária dessa diretoria é designada para conhecer a coleção e fazer avaliação do acervo, ou seja, determinar tamanho (quantidade de volumes), tipo e condições gerais, detectar raridades e analisar o nível de duplicidade dessa biblioteca com o acervo já existente na universidade. Em momento algum a bibliotecário determina valores para a biblioteca. Se aprovada a aquisição, o assunto preço é discutido em outros instâncias dentro da universidade.

O fato de um intelectual ser famoso e ter vasta produção científica necessariamente não o qualifica para ter sua biblioteca particular entre as coleções especiais da UNICAMP. Para que isso ocorra a biblioteca tem que possuir uma certa uniformidade de acervo em que sejam encontrados livros e periódicos compatíveis com as políticas de aquisição prescritas pela DCE. Nos últimos tem havido muitas ofertas de bibliotecas, muitas delas com acervo bastante significativo, porém esse mesmo acervo repete-se nas coleções já existentes na DCE, inviabilizando sua aquisição.

Essa grande oferta deve-se ao fato das coleções estarem se tornando conhecidas no meio acadêmico, dada a forma como elas são tratadas, o que sensibiliza as famílias interessadas na venda ou doação.

Quando da mudança da coleção para a Biblioteca Central pode-se fazer necessário que o bibliotecário que fez a primeira visita converse com o encarregado da companhia transportadora para alertá-lo sobre alguns detalhes em relação, por exemplo, a fragilidade do material a ser transportado. Em algumas vezes, acompanhando os livros podem vir também móveis: estantes, mesas, etc., o que denota cuidados especiais. É interessante para a DCE receber também móveis e objetos, já que o ambiente de trabalho do intelectual pode ser recriado com maior fidelidade, assim como, com isso podem ser evitados em vários casos a compra de mobiliário para as recém-adquiridas coleções. Assim que os livros chegam, eles passam por um processo geral de limpeza (não está suposto neste caso tratamento químico do material), dependendo do estado em que se encontram. Depois de limpos, os livros são encaminhados para a Diretoria de Coleções Especiais.

O primeiro passo é retirar livro por livro das caixas, aproveitando para procurar papéis deixados entre as páginas. Quando isso ocorre, o papel, qualquer que seja ele, uma folha com anotações, um cartão postal, um recorte de jornal, uma carta, etc. e retirado e imediatamente identificado. Ou seja, numa ficha a parte é escrito o autor, título do livro e o dia em que foi encontrado o documento. Posteriormente eles serão tratados como material de arquivo. Muitas vezes são encontradas folhas em branco, propaganda de outros livros, marcadores de página, folhas de árvore, calendários, embalagens de bombons, que não tendo importância arquivística são jogados fora. É nessa altura também que são separados "a grosso modo" os periódicos dos livros das obras de referência para posterior classificação.

Inventário

Depois de processada a limpeza e a primeira olhada no acervo, com os livros já postos nas respectivas estantes, procede-se o inventário que é feito utilizando-se um microcomputador e um programa desenvolvido pelo Centro de Computação da UNICAMP, chamado SISLIS (Sistema de Listagem). O SISLIS é bastante simples no seu manuseio. Pede que sejam preenchidos os campos de autor, título, editora e ano do livro, assim como definir se o material é brochura ou encadernado. O mesmo programa pode ser utilizado também para os periódicos, porém na DCE os dados dos periódicos são transcritos diretamente para fichas do tipo kardex que são arquivadas nos respectivos fichários, sendo as coleções identificadas através de siglas. Esse sistema mostrou-se mais prático que a listagem dos periódicos por computador. Cada livro recebe um número que é escrito a lápis na folha de rosto. O programa SISLIS numera automaticamente os livros, o que impede que o mesmo número seja usado duas vezes na mesma coleção.

Isto significa que uma coleção como a de Alexandre Eulalio, que tem 11.112 livros (incluindo os folhetos, teses, obras iconográficas e obras de referência), possui o registro número 1 que corresponde ao primeiro livro da primeira prateleira da primeira estante e também possui o registro número 11.112 que significa o último livro da coleção posto na última prateleira.

É óbvio que no inventário não há classificação por assunto, assim sendo exemplares iguais podem ser encontrados em lugares diferentes. Isso porém não oferece problemas quando da pesquisa, porque o SISLIS fornece listagens de autor e de título. Portanto se houver uma consulta sobre obras de Machado de Assis, basta buscar na listagem de autores, fazer uma relação dos números encontrados e retirar os livros nas estantes. O sistema tem se mostrado de uma grande eficácia; enquanto os livros não são classificados por assunto.

Cada livro recebe um carimbo na folha de rosto e na última página (no local onde viria o bolso dos cartões de empréstimo, que no caso da DCE, não existe). Recebe então uma papeleta (pedaço de papel colocado no meio do livro) com o seu número. Com esse sistema não é necessário se preocupar com erros nas entradas de autor, porque a qualquer momento pode-se corrigir esses erros e imprimir novamente a listagem. Tomando ainda como exemplo a coleção Alexandre Eulalio, a listagem definitiva foi revisada várias vezes e ainda assim aparecem erros nas suas quase 300 folhas.

Com exceção da coleção Sérgio Buarque, que chegou na fase pré-automação, todas as outras coleções tem seu inventário e suas listagens por autor e título, e estas vem sendo utilizadas há vários anos como sucesso.

Processamento técnico

Em relação ao processamento técnico, encontramos diferentes estágios, uma vez que as bibliotecas chegaram em épocas diferentes e em cada uma dessas épocas havia um padrão para catalogação/classificação. Por exemplo, a biblioteca Sérgio Buarque de Holanda foi, como já disse anteriormente, processada de 1983 a 1987, quando a UNICAMP ainda não integrava a rede de catalogação cooperativa BIBLIODATA/CALCO. Sendo assim, a coleção foi catalogada pelo Código de Catalogação Anglo-Americano 1, manualmente, gerando jogos de fichas; no já comentado mimeógrafo a tinta; de autor, título, assunto, para um catálogo, na época, sistemático. O sistema de classificação utilizado foi e continua sendo a Classificação Decimal de Dewey (CDD).

Com a coleção Aristides Candido ocorreu o mesmo, uma vez que também comecou a ser processada no período em que a UNICAMP dava seus primeiros passos dentro do sistema em rede e quando ainda não havia uma definição sobre o que fazer com as coleções especiais, já que as informações contidas dentro do tópico "notas" eram por demais minuciosas para serem inseridas num sistema em rede. Portanto por volta de 40% da biblioteca Aristides Candido está ainda no antigo sistema manual e o restante será catalogado já dentro do CALCO.

Antes porém de falar sobre a situação das outras coleções, é importante situar o CALCO e dizer o que ele significou em termos de avanço do sistema de catalogação cooperativa dentro do Brasil. E, para falar mais sobre o sistema, uso trechos de trabalhos de Zanaga[4] e de Mercadante e Zanaga,[5] profissionais que estão ligadas diretamente ao projeto de inserção da UNICAMP na Rede CALCO.

"CALCO (Catalogação Legível por Computador) é um formato desenvolvido e apresentado em 1972, por Alice Principe Barbosa, em sua dissertação de mestrado, denominada 'Projeto CALCO', baseado no formato MARC II, utilizado na Library of Congress".[6]

De 1972 até o final da década, o sistema passou por várias revisões. Nos primeiros dez anos de funcionamento, a Rede BIBLIODATA/CALCO cresceu lentamente, mesmo com o esforço da própria Fundação Getúlio Vargas, da Biblioteca Nacional e das bibliotecas pioneiras que a ela se integraram. Como não possuía grande número de participantes, não contava com grande número de registros e essa situação não atraía novos membros. Em 1987, com as ações do PNBU (Plano Nacional de Bibliotecas Universitárias) recomendando e apoiando a entrada das bibliotecas universitárias, é que a base inicia um período de maior expansão.[7]

Em setembro de 1989, a UNICAMP através de seu Sistema de Bibliotecas, vinculou-se à Fundação Getúlio Vargas (FGV) para utilização dos serviços oferecidos pela Rede BIBLIODATA/CALCO, visando a inclusão de monografias de seu acervo corrente.

Atualmente a rede conta com cerca de 60 bibliotecas cooperantes e as obras nela cadastradas podem ser consultadas on-line, através de RENPAC e via microfichas de cadastro".[8]

Contando com mais de 20 pessoas (entre bibliotecários e auxiliares) envolvidas no processo de pesquisa de autoridade de autor, de descrição e atribuição de cabeçalhos de assunto, de digitação e separação de materiais, a Biblioteca Central da UNICAMP vem obtendo destaque dentro da Rede.

Após discussões com os bibliotecários das Coleções Especiais verificou-se que o melhor seria também inserir esses acervos dentro da Rede, fazendo com que essas obras, muitas vezes de difícil acesso pudessem ser utilizadas, mesmo que fosse apenas no local. O mais importante era tornar esses acervos especiais conhecidos.

Aproveito para esclarecer que cada uma das já citadas coleções possui seu próprio fichário, e que o jogo de fichas (autor, título e assunto) está reproduzido no Catálogo Coletivo da UNICAMP, localizado nas dependências da Biblioteca Central.

A partir daí, iniciou-se o processamento da Coleção Peter Eisenberg, que tem o acervo de idade mais recente, isto é, Peter não era um bibliófilo, não tinha obras raras em sua biblioteca. Sua coleção era estritamente para uso de suas pesquisas, de seu trabalho, o que fazia-a repleta de bibliografia básica, tornando-a atraente para a Rede e possibilitando em muito a "cooperação", ou seja, encontrar o mesmo registro já dentro da base.

Ainda de acordo com Zanaga, "o pré-requisito para processamento de material em CALCO é o tombamento do mesmo na Biblioteca Central. Deve-se esclarecer que somente o acervo corrente esta sendo trabalhado". (No caso aí, incluídas as Coleções Peter Eisenberg, Alexandre Eulalio e José Albertino Rodrigues.)

Em relação ao acervo retrospectivo (Coleções Sérgio Buarque e Antonio Candido), estão apenas entrando no CALCO, obras destas coleções quando um mesmo exemplar é encontrado em outra biblioteca da UNICAMP, havendo assim também "cooperação".

Após o tombamento, faz-se a pesquisa nas microfichas de cadastro. (Essas pesquisas agora já podem ser feitas on-line.) A pesquisa também inclui verificação no catálogo de fichas matrizes do Sistema de Bibliotecas da UNICAMP. Se a entrada para autores pessoais e coletivos não constar das microfichas de autoridade, ela é confeccionada. Em seguida, o livro é planilhado, passando-se a determinação do cabeçalho de assunto. Se ele não figurar na lista da FGV, utiliza-se a lista da Library of Congress, fazendo-se a tradução apropriada do termo. Completada a planilha, ela segue para a digitação, de onde os disquetes são encaminhados para a Fundação Getúlio Vargas uma vez por semana. Aguarda-se daí o retorno dos produtos: etiquetas e jogos de fichas. [9]

Referência

Dada a natureza dessas coleções e tendo em vista que bibliotecas particulares nada mais são do que o reflexo de um indivíduo, em relação a seus interesses profissionais e pessoais, os acervos da UNICAMP geram uma consulta diferenciada assim como diferenciados também são seus usuários e as questões que eles trazem.

Como cada uma das citadas coleções tem um acervo fixo, ou seja, não cresce em tamanho, a não ser quando se trata de incorporar edições, traduções, livros e periódicos sobre o titular da biblioteca, é mais fácil para o bibliotecário conhecer profundamente o acervo.

Levando-se então em conta a especificidade do acervo, também os usuários que dele se utilizam são pessoas bastante especializadas em seus campos de estudo, notadamente nas ciências sociais, história e literatura. Conseqüentemente o tratamento requerido e dispensado a esses usuários torna-se mais prolongado e minucioso.

O usuário que efetivamente consulta as coleções especiais é no mínimo estudante de pós-graduação, quer de mestrado ou de doutorado e muitas vezes é professor universitário. Na maioria dos casos vem em busca de informações que julga ter certeza encontrar nos acervos, ou por que conheceu a biblioteca particular ainda na casa do proprietário, ou porque soube através de outras pessoas da "qualidade" dos acervos.

O acompanhamento do bibliotecário em relação à pesquisa é constante, não encerrando-se no momento em que o usuário deixa a biblioteca. Isso aumenta ainda mais o nível de confiança entre ambas as partes, porque a partir daí o bibliotecário torna-se realmente um auxiliar de pesquisa. É função do bibliotecário das Coleções Especiais instruir o usuário no tocante à técnicas e instrumentos de pesquisa, facilitando-lhe o acesso ao acervo.

Aos usuários da DCE é inicialmente mostrado o funcionamento das coleções e a fase de processamento técnico em que cada uma delas se encontra; após isso o consulente é posto em contato com a coleção com que pretende trabalhar, e sempre que possível, ele trabalha sozinho. Cada usuário é treinado para ser independente no trato com o acervo, porém recorrendo ao bibliotecário sempre que tiver dúvida.

Nas coleções especiais são freqüentes os casos de usuários que estão consultando os acervos há mais de três ou quatro anos. O resultado dessas pesquisas são geralmente dissertações e teses, ensaios e livros.

Os usuários, que pelos motivos já expostos, não são muitos em termos numéricos, dispõem de salas de leitura individuais, onde podem deixar seu material de pesquisa durante o tempo que estiverem trabalhando nos acervos.

Se observarmos os padrões de referência utilizados nas coleções especiais da UNICAMP veremos que, sob uma certa ótica, podem ser considerados elitistas. É bem possível que o sejam. A proposta é oferecer o máximo de comodidade e profissionalismo, para que esses elementos colaborem com o nível da pesquisa que está sendo desenvolvida.

Manutenção

Mesmo não havendo empréstimo do acervo, constantemente são realizadas verificações, para observar o estado físico do material, assim como perceber se existe algum problema em relação a "sumiço" de livros (infelizmente um problema bastante atual e corriqueiro nas bibliotecas brasileiras). Periodicamente também são efetuadas limpezas buscando-se identificar a existência de elementos nocivos: umidade, fungos, traças, etc.

Oliveira Lima Library, Catholic University of America

Em novembro de 1993 recebi uma bolsa da Fundação VITAE de São Paulo para auxiliar no trabalho que vinha sendo desenvolvido na Oliveira Lima Library (OLL), localizada fisicamente na Catholic University of America (CUA) na cidade de Washington, D.C., nos Estados Unidos.

Apoiada por um afastamento concedido pela UNICAMP, o intuito do projeto aprovado pelas três instituições era colaborar com o trabalho na Lima Library, doravante chamada OLL, e participar do maior número possível de situações profissionais nos Estados Unidos, de forma a alargar o conhecimento técnico podendo eu, além de ser útil à Coleção Oliveira Lima, trazer "bagagem profissional" que viesse a ser importante para o desempenho de minhas funções na Universidade Estadual de Campinas. Para isso contei desde o início com o apoio do professor Thomas Cohen, curador da Oliveira Lima Library.

Manoel de Oliveira Lima (1867-1928), nascido no estado de Pernambuco, Brasil, foi um historiador, diplomata e jornalista que coletou livros, manuscritos e objetos de arte. Educado em Portugal, ele entrou para o serviço diplomático brasileiro em 1890, tendo servido em Lisboa, Berlin, Washington, Londres, Tóquio, Caracas e Bruxelas. Autor de inúmeros livros e artigos de cunho histórico, ofereceu palestras na Sorbonne (1911), em Stanford (1912) e em Harvard (1915). Membro fundador da Academia Brasileira de Letras, contribuiu para diversos jornais e periódicos estrangeiros.

Já em 1912, Oliveira Lima considerava a possibilidade de doar sua biblioteca para a Catholic University of America, o que ele acabou fazendo realmente em 1916. Por causa de I Guerra Mundial, a remoção de milhares de seus livros, vindos de Londres, Lisboa e Bruxelas, foi adiada. Em 5 de fevereiro de 1924 a biblioteca foi formalmente aberta ao público. De acordo com Luke Williams,

the collection, rich in material for political, economic, military, and social aspects of Portuguese and Brazilian history, originated in 1916 as a gift of the personal library of Manoel de Oliveira Lima and since his death the university has continued to expand the collection so that it now contains approximately 50,000 books, manuscripts, and other historical items relating to this particular area of research. [10]

Embora o referido artigo seja datado de 1967, ou seja quase 30 anos atrás, ele mantém sua atualidade. O autor Luke Williams, em poucas páginas, consegue oferecer um retrato histórico bastante completo da biblioteca Oliveira Lima.

De 1928 até 1940, a viúva do diplomata, Flora de Oliveira Lima, filha da rica aristocracia pernambucana, foi a responsável pela biblioteca. Quando do seu falecimento, a direção da Oliveira Lima Library (OLL) passou para as mãos do historiador português Manoel Cardoso que esteve à frente da biblioteca por 45 anos, até sua morte, em 1985.

Até 1990 a biblioteca não teve uma direção efetiva, o que acabou fazendo com que o pó e os problemas se acumulassem. Em 1991, o professor Thomas Cohen, do Departamento de História da Catholic University of America, torna-se o curador de Coleção. Ele vem tentando desde então tornar a Biblioteca Oliveira Lima organizada tecnicamente e acessível aos pesquisadores, quer aqui nos Estados Unidos, quer no Brasil.

A OLL tem como ponto forte sua coleção de obras raras, editadas dentro e fora do Brasil, dos séculos XVI a XIX, notadamente a seção que trata dos viajantes. Também possui uma coleção muito importante de folhetos (por volta de uns 4 mil). Parte considerável do acervo da OLL foi adquirido durante a gestão de Manoel Cardoso, através de compra ou de doação. Enquanto o historiador português esteve à frente da OLL houve sempre algum bibliotecário trabalhando. Mesmo que hoje não seja tão fácil recuperar seus nomes, pode-se ver na biblioteca o que foi feito em termos de organização.

Oliveira Lima era como Mario de Andrade, um "correspondente contumaz". Sua correspondência passiva está devidamente separada por ano. Em 1938, Godrey F. Ferris organizou suas cartas, num trabalho intitulado "Names of the Correspondents with Dr. Manoel de Oliveira Lima, 1884-1928". Em sua monografia, bastante rudimentar e sem normalização bibliográfica, tomando-se os padrões atuais, ele ordenou a correspondência na ordem cronológica e dentro dela, em ordem alfabética de sobrenome de correspondente.

O professor da USP, Antonio Dimas, esteve visitando e trabalhando na OLL, em 1977 e sobre a correspondência acima citada disse:

... vi pela frente 20 gavetas de aço contendo a correspondência do historiador e diplomata pernambucano ... organizadas segundo um critério cronológico e alfabético, essas gavetas armazenam um material espistolográfico de valor inestimável e cobrem um período bastante importante de nossa evolução: 1884 a 1927, aproximadamente.[11]

Há na biblioteca também um fichário bastante extenso, que acredito deve ter sido muito completo numa determinada época, de anotações de leitura, provavelmente feitas por Manoel Cardoso e outras ainda do tempo do próprio Oliveira Lima.

Em relação a outros materiais, tidos como sendo de arquivo já não pode-se dizer o mesmo. Há pouca ou nenhuma organização. Há fotos, mapas, centenas de cartões de visita, telegramas, documentos pessoais,

"scrapbooks" começados pela esposa de Oliveira Lima no final do
século XIX, que estão simplesmente a mercê do tempo e da boa vontade de
alguém.

Especificamente em relação aos livros, podemos encontrá-los divididos
em várias fases: alguns já devidamente catalogados e classificados de
acordo com a Library of Congress e outros (a grande maioria) sem
processamento técnico algum. Há um fichário, onde encontramos fichas
catalográficas de milhares de volumes, muitas sem sequer número de
chamada. Algumas estão manuscritas, outras datilografadas.

Visando minimizar os efeitos desse "caos bibliográfico", a bibliotecário
da coleção, assessorada por Cecilia Sercan, de Cornell University, entendeu
por bem realizar um inventário do acervo. As estantes foram devidamente
identificadas, assim como cada uma de seus corpos e cada uma de suas
prateleiras. É importante acrescentar que o espaço físico atualmente ocupado
pela Oliveira Lima Library é inapropriado, principalmente se levarmos em
consideração as raridades e os valores do acervo e das obras de arte
(pinturas, principalmente) da coleção. Ainda em relação ao espaço físico,
essa situação é temporária uma vez que está prevista a mudança da coleção
para novas instalações, qual sejam, as da antiga Faculdade de Direito da
Catholic University, que está ganhando um prédio novo. A mudança deve
ocorrer ainda durante o ano de 1994.

Identificadas então estantes e prateleiras, procedeu-se ao inventário,
cada um dos livros recebendo um número. Exemplificando: na estante 12A
(isso significa um conjunto de cinco ou seis corpos de estantes), existe
o corpo dois e a prateleira C e aí o livro número 1, número 2, número 3,
e assim por diante. A apresentação desses dados na ficha proposta,
assemelha-se à posição do número de chamada: no topo, à esquerda.
Portanto cada início de prateleira tem o livro número 1.

Enquanto isso vem sendo feito, paralelamente as fichas vem sendo
pesquisadas no "Authority File". Quando este não é encontrado, procede-se
à pesquisa no OCLC. Quando o título é encontrado na base do OCLC e o
registro pertence a Library of Congress, copia-se o número do OCLC e
acrescenta-se um "label" vermelho à ficha, o que facilitará o processo de
catalogação propriamente dito. Se o livro é encontrado no OCLC porém não
foi processado pela LC, apenas copia-se o número do OCLC, o que
significa que aquele registro será conferido posteriormente, quando se
instalar efetivamente a fase do processamento técnico da coleção. Caso o
título não se encontre no OCLC, então é feita uma busca na própria Library
of Congress, onde dada a extensão de seu acervo relativo a assuntos luso-
brasileiros, muitas vezes o título pode ser encontrado ainda na fase
PREMMARC. Posto isso as fichas manuais são alfabetadas e podem servir
como catálogo provisório caso haja alguma pesquisa. Como a coleção não é

de livro acesso, as consultas precisam ser feitas mediante entendimentos anteriores.

Conclusão

Gostaria de acrescentar que entre as inúmeras diferenças que observei, em relação à postura profissional existentes entre bibliotecários brasileiros e norte-americanos, uma me chama a atenção toda vez que ponho meus dedos no teclado de um computador. Infelizmente no Brasil, no mundo dos livros e das bibliotecas, ainda vive-se a fase do "medo da máquina". Enquanto aqui nos Estados Unidos, logo nos primeiros dias em que cheguei, deram-me acesso a uma conta e a um "user name", mostraram-me como acessar Telnet, Internet e Gopher, ensinaram-me os comandos de entrada no OCLC e no WordPerfect, no Brasil a situação é bastante mais tímida e acomodada.

Ainda existe no Brasil muita mistificação do que seja trabalhar com automação em bibliotecas. Os bibliotecários que tem o privilégio de lidar com computadores tem também o medo o a insegurança profissional de que aquele "conhecimento" lhe fuja das mãos a partir do momento em que seja compartilhado com outros colegas de profissão. No meio bibliotecário brasileiro, de uma forma geral, automação está intimamente ligada à manutenção de poder dentro das instituições. Há poucas tentativas de socialização do conhecimento, o que é uma forma muito arcaica de pensar a vida profissional, ainda mais num setor como automação em que a cada dia, literalmente, surgem tópicos novos.

Dentre as inúmeras atividades de que participei nesses quase dez meses que passei nos Estados Unidos, vários exemplos são possíveis de uso e adaptação na UNICAMP. Pelo que pude observar empiricamente nessa temporada, há que se levantar e difundir principalmente, a forma como a "informação" é tratada aqui, ou seja quanta importância lhe é atribuída e como ela é acessível a todos que necessitam dela.

Para finalizar, diria que nesses quase 80 anos da Coleção, ela passou pelas mais diversas e diferentes fases, porém somente a decisão política de "colocar a mão na massa" é que pode tornar esse precioso acervo, acessível a pesquisa, e, pelo que percebi é exatamente isso que o professor Thomas Cohen vem tentando fazer à frente da Oliveira Lima Library.

NOTAS

1. Antonio Candido de Mello e Souza, "Livros, ou a história mental de uma época", *Jornal da UNICAMP* 34:2 (agosto 1989), 2.

2. Ron Chepesiuk e Gloria Kelley-Palmer, "The Martin Luther King Library and Archives at the Crossroads", *American Libraries* 25:2 (fevereiro 1994), 148-151.

3. Ibid., p. 150.

4. Mariangela Zanaga, "O sistema de bibliotecas da UNICAMP na rede BIBLIO-DATA/CALCO", trabalho apresentado à disciplina Metodologia para Desenvolvimento de Sistemas, na Pontifícia Universidade Católica de Campinas (Campinas, 1990).

5. Leila Mercadante e Mariangela Zanaga, "Catalogação cooperativa e produtividade", trabalho apresentado no VII Seminário de Bibliotecas Universitárias, Rio de Janeiro, 1991.

6. Zanaga, "O sistema de bibliotecas".

7. Mercadante e Zanaga, "Catalogação cooperativa".

8. Zanaga, "O sistema de bibliotecas".

9. Ibid.

10. R. J. Luke Williams, "The Oliveira Lima Library", *The Library Quarterly* 37:3 (julho 1967), 279-283.

11. Antonio Dimas, "Uma visita a Oliveira Lima Library: Cartas de Jackson de Figueiredo (11), Nestor Vitor (1), Machado de Assis (6) e Aluisio de Azevedo (1)", *Revista Língua e Literatura* 6 (1977), 339-368.

IV

Evaluation of Latin American
Literary Collections

36. Chilean Literature: Models for Collection Evaluation

Karen Lindvall-Larson

Historically, the reasons most often cited for evaluating collections have been to determine whether the collection is meeting its objectives, that is, if users' needs are being met, to locate deficiencies, and to determine areas to strengthen. More recently, the systematic evaluation of collections has become crucial to the conspectus-based approach to cooperative collection development. In their recent article, "The Conspectus Approach to Collection Evaluation: Panacea or False Prophet?," Blake and Tjoumas find that the collection analysis required is critical to the success of the conspectus. The facts that no guidelines are provided for this analysis and that individual librarians approach their collections in a subjective manner based on their experience and knowledge of the discipline have a direct impact on the value of these data for cooperative collection development.

With cooperative collection development as a major goal, the evaluation should take into account not only the needs of local users but also the expectations of a broader audience. Collection evaluation should be conducted against a well-defined and standardized body of literature to allow for the cooperative agreements between libraries that lead to less duplication and greater breadth. An added benefit of such systematic evaluation would be the in-depth information on the collection that would be available to scholars using the collections.

This paper explores models for evaluating collections of Chilean literature written since 1956 which could lead to greater consistency in collection evaluation, providing information that could be used by librarians to consider cooperative collection development and by researchers to determine whether collections have strengths pertinent to their research needs. I have focused on three specific projects: (1) a general bibliographic check of Chilean literature from 1956 to the present; (2) a project focused on the Generation of 1950; and (3) a project focused on writers gaining prominence after 1973.

While this project will focus on models that could be used at any library, I would like to begin with a description of the Latin American collections and Chilean programs at the University of California, San Diego (UCSD). UCSD was established thirty years ago, and the focused development of the Latin American collections began approximately twenty years ago. Chile today is our second most important geographical area of interest. Faculty members whose primary area of research is Chile include Jaime Concha, a prominent Chilean literary critic who joined the literature department in 1981. From 1987 to 1993 we had a virtually unrestricted blanket order for all genres of Chilean literature. Because of budgetary considerations and changing campus interests, we canceled this blanket order in 1993 and severely restricted our acquisition of secondary authors of fiction, poetry, and drama. Our current focus is on major twentieth-century poets and novelists, with a particular interest in fiction since 1973, including the new feminist literature.

For the first project, I wanted the most broadly defined bibliography of Chilean literature for the period covered. Through the Melvyl system, the University of California's online union catalog, we have access to OCLC's Firstsearch and RLIN's Eureka. While these are excellent sources of critical works on Chilean literature or particular authors, the lack of a subject approach to individual authors' works severely limits their use to develop a list of authors. A useful source is Gaston Somoshegyi-Szokol's "Contemporary Chilean Literature in the University Library at Berkeley," but it was published in 1975. To bring the collection check as close as possible to the present, I decided to use the *Handbook of Latin American Studies,* with its most recent humanities volume published in 1992. In reviewing the sections on Chilean prose from volumes covering the period from 1956 to the present, I found that until volume 23 (1961) all Latin American nineteenth- and twentieth-century prose works, both primary and critical, were combined, with the exceptions of Brazilian and Haitian works. In volume 24 (1962), Chile is combined with Argentina and Uruguay, often with no indication of the nationality of the author, making collection checking against this bibliography haphazard at best. Volume 25 (1963) has a separate section on Chilean prose literature, a section that continues to this day. I checked nine randomly selected volumes and found that UCSD holdings went from a low of 11 percent of titles listed in 1963 to a high of 86 percent of the volumes listed in 1992. In between were such puzzlers as our having 76 percent of the titles listed in 1972 and 21 percent of the titles listed in 1976. I found that the dates of the titles listed varied widely from the dates of publication of the *Handbook*, with some titles published up to ten years earlier. Of greater concern were notes such as "mediocre novel" or "noteworthy only as a literary curiosity." Many of the titles listed that I would not have selected and others that are part of the collection have not circulated since they were acquired.

My second project was to focus on a literary movement, the Chilean "Generación del 50," and to measure the strength of our collection. I chose five prominent authors from this group and checked their writings against our holdings. I found that we had 39 percent of Guillermo Blanco's works, 93 percent of José Donoso's works, 86 percent of Jorge Edwards's works, 40 percent of María Elena Gertner's works, and 62 percent of Enrique Lafourcade's works. To complete a summary of our holdings for this period, I would compile a list of critical works about these authors from the Melvyl system, Firstsearch, and Eureka, and check that list against our collections.

My third project most closely ties in with the interests of on-campus users. I again selected a literary "generation" and chose five representative authors, referred to as the "Generación del 70" or the "post-golpe" writers. I was looking for authors who might have written in the sixties but who rose to prominence after the military coup in 1973. This group reflects the splintering of the cultural community in Chile, with many writers forced into exile. Another major issue is the emergence of a feminist literature for Chile. While Chile has a large body of literature written by women (as reflected in Cortina's excellent bibliography), only three had received international recognition before the 1970s (Luisa Bombal, Marta Brunet, and Gabriela Mistral). While I have chosen Isabel Allende to represent the "post-golpe" group, books and articles written about the new writers list many women writers who are making major contributions to Chilean literature. My collection checks revealed that we had 100 percent of Isabel Allende's literary works, 67 percent of Poli Delano's works, 80 percent of Ariel Dorfman's works, 79 percent of Antonio Skarmeta's works, and 66 percent of Raúl Zurita's works. While virtually all of the works of the "Generación del 50" were published in Chile or Spain, the works of the "Generación del 70" are published all over the globe. Again, to complete the picture of holdings, I would like to review critical works on these authors listed under their names as subjects and verify the percentages we own.

In reviewing the three projects detailed above, I find the *Handbook of Latin American Studies* the least useful for collection analysis because of the unevenness of the items selected for review and the combination of primary and critical works. Only libraries wanting a conspectus-level 5 or completely comprehensive collection on Chilean literature would need all the items listed. It also required that each individual title be checked to see if it was in the collection; it was a very time-consuming process.

Developing the list of authors to be checked in the second and third projects was a useful exercise, allowing me to strengthen my awareness of Chilean literature. The "Generación del 50" list was easy to assemble because the group of authors is defined by having begun to publish in the 1950s, although several continue to publish. The "Generación del 70" is

342 KAREN LINDVALL-LARSON

continuing to develop, and the return of democracy will have a continuing impact on both writers who remained in Chile and those who are returning from exile. Because of the nature of these two projects, checking against the Melvyl system, Firstsearch, or Eureka was straightforward.

Based on these projects, I would propose a model for collection evaluation, specifically for Latin American literature. Within a group or consortium, the University of California system, for example, individual bibliographers would be assigned specific countries. Each bibliographer would prepare a core list of authors for that country, identifying important movements or genres and listing important reference resources. Authors and specific subjects could be checked against online catalogs, indicating date checked and percentage of items held. Evaluative comments could be attached to the conspectus in scope notes with specific strengths, inclusion in collection of secondary authors, focus on a particular movement, and so on. The lists could easily be updated with new authors, movements, or genres.

There are benefits for both researchers and bibliographers in this approach to collection evaluation. Researchers are provided with a clear indication of a collection's strength that goes beyond a formulaic description that does not distinguish among poetry, fiction, drama, movements, and, most certainly, gender. For me, this project offered an exciting opportunity to expand my awareness of Chilean literature, campus interests and programs, and the strengths and weaknesses of our collections beyond a repetitive checking of bibliographies. The models can easily be reconfigured for other countries and can be shared with other bibliographers, allowing for a systematic comparison of collections which provides for effective cooperative collection development.

BIBLIOGRAPHY

American Library Association. Subcommittee on Guidelines for Collection Development. *Guide to the Evaluation of Library Collections.* Chicago, IL: American Library Association, 1989.

Blake, Virgil L. P., and Renée Tjoumas. "The Conspectus Approach to Collection Evaluation: Panacea or False Prophet?" *Collection Management* 18:3/4 (1994), 1-31.

Cortina, Lynn Ellen. *Spanish-American Women Writers: A Bibliographical Research Checklist.* New York: Garland, 1983.

Godoy, Eduardo. *La generación del 50 en Chile.* Chile: Editorial La Noria, 1991.

Jara, René. "Chile." In *Handbook of Latin American Literature,* David William Foster, ed. New York: Garland, 1992. Pp. 123-178.

Promis, José. "Balance de la novela en Chile: 1973-1990." *Hispamérica* 19:55 (April 1990), 15-26.

Somoshegyi-Szokol, Gaston. *Contemporary Chilean Literature in the University Library at Berkeley: A Bibliography.* Berkeley: Center for Latin American Studies, University of California, Berkeley, 1975.

37. Analysis of Brazilian Literature Holdings in the University of New Mexico Library

Russ Davidson

My analysis of the Brazilian literature holdings in the University of New Mexico (UNM) Library is very much in the traditional vein. It breaks no new ground conceptually or methodologically nor offers any new insights into the established process. On the contrary, the analysis relies upon techniques with which we are all more or less familiar, that is, the checking of a series of general and specialized lists and bibliographies against the Library's catalog, to accomplish three things: (*a*) determine the number and percentage of titles and authors held; (*b*) reach certain conclusions about the current state of the collection and its ability to support in-depth study and research; and (*c*) chart some possible lines for its future development. I first lay out the boundaries of the study. Chronologically (and in keeping with the conference theme), the primary emphasis is put on the contemporary period, or on Brazilian literature of the last thirty to forty years. Geographically, there are no limits; all of Brazil is covered. However, no bibliographies devoted to any particular genre, topic, or author have been searched, and certain genres—such as children's literature—have been excluded, and the main emphasis is on books and periodicals in printed form.

As a point of departure for this analysis, I decided to use William V. Jackson's *Library Guide for Brazilian Studies*, published in 1964, since it would impart some sense of the relative size and strength of UNM's holdings in both Brazilian studies and Brazilian literature, respectively. Jackson's *Guide*, an outgrowth in part of the 1963 SALALM Conference, provides a broad-scale description by subject area and format, replete with tables and statistics of scholarly resources for Brazilian studies in U.S. government, academic, and special libraries, as such resources were reported to him in 1963 and early 1964. Jackson's findings are instructive. He divides the libraries surveyed into four groups. In the top group, which numbers seven libraries, collections on Brazil must be comprehensive in scope and contain a minimum of 7,000 volumes. The second group consists of those libraries, nine in number, "possessing strong but not outstanding collections." [1] The 4,500 titles of Braziliana contained in the University of New Mexico Library comprise mainly literature and history, placing it near the top of this second group. Although Jackson has little to say of a descriptive nature about New Mexico's Brazilian literature collection, he does place it—in terms of sheer volume count—among the four or five largest within the several dozen academic and research libraries he surveyed. Additional evidence of the size of the UNM collection in this field and of the continuing emphasis being put on Brazilian acquisitions by the UNM Library was provided in a second publication, titled *Catalog of Luso-Brazilian Material in the University of New Mexico Libraries*, published by Scarecrow Press in 1970. This catalog lists some 12,000 volumes of Luso-Brazilian material which had been processed by the Library through May 1968, approximately half of which was Brazilian either in origin or in subject matter, and half of which, or around 3,000 volumes, also pertained specifically to Brazilian literature.

In sum, these two publications—the Jackson guide and the Scarecrow Press catalog of UNM Luso-Brazilian holdings—offer some perspective on the relative size and standing of the UNM Brazilian literature collection twenty-five to thirty years ago. For the purposes of this analysis, they are useful as broad quantitative measures. With these benchmarks in place, what I next attempted to do, within the limits spelled out above, was to answer two questions: first, how successful has the UNM Library been since 1970 in maintaining the growth of its Brazilian literature holdings? and second, what are the apparent strengths and weaknesses of this collection? The approach I used to answer these questions was very straightforward and focused on selecting and checking against our holdings several core lists of monographs, journals, and reference works. These were supplemented by a series of author lists. The composite picture that emerged, though necessarily superficial given the narrow range of sources checked, yielded some interesting answers.

Taking the book collection first, I decided—as a means of gauging our coverage of the broad monographic literature—to check the sections on Brazilian literature, inclusively, in the *Handbook of Latin American Studies (HLAS)* over a twenty-year period from 1972 through 1992.[2] The *Handbook*'s coverage, while highly selective, is also representative of the full range of literary production. It encompasses books, pamphlets, chapters in anthologies, journal articles and issues, as well as collections and reeditions, issued by trade, university, small press, and assorted government publishers throughout Brazil. All major genres are covered, including prose fiction in novels and short stories, poetry, drama, cronicas, and literary history and criticism. Moreover, the sampling, numerically, is perhaps not quite as small as one might fear. Over the full twenty-year span, a total of 2,683 entries were checked. Of this total, 1,593, or a composite 60 percent, were found in the UNM catalog. The percentages, however, are not evenly distributed, as they range from a low of 33 percent (90 of 273 entries) for the 1974 *HLAS* volume to a high of 70 percent (218 of 314 entries) for the 1986 volume. Also, a clear division exists between the early period of this sampling—the first three volumes encompassing 1972 through 1976—when the library's coverage averaged only 43 percent, and the later, longer period of 1978 through 1992, when the coverage averaged 66 percent. This discrepancy suggests that the acquisition of Brazilian literature by the UNM Library languished during the early 1970s and then recovered after that. This recovery notwithstanding, the overall 66 percent of monographic titles found during the approximately fifteen-year period between 1978 and 1992 is somewhat disappointing. My assumption would be that the "strong collection," into which category Jackson had placed the University of New Mexico, would be a collection somewhere in the 75 percent range. In any event, the *HLAS* analysis proved very useful in highlighting a pronounced weakness within an otherwise strong part of the collection.

My next strategy, still within the arena of the book collection, was to search three Brazilian author lists. These were, first, a portion of the author index in Massaud Moisés's *Pequeno dicionário de literatura brasileira;* second, all of the entries in the *Dictionary of Contemporary Brazilian Authors*, edited by David William Foster and Roberto Reis; and third, those authors from the reference work *Brazilian Literature: A Research Bibliography,* also edited by Foster with the assistance of Walter Rela, not already included in the just-cited *Dictionary.* The results were as follows: Nearly a third, or 114 of the more than 350 individual authors found in the Moisés work, were randomly searched, solely as authors, in the UNM catalog, and 97, or 85 percent, were found. Moisés's *Dicionário*, it should be noted, covers all of Brazil for all periods of its history. On the basis of this relatively large sample, one could extrapolate that the UNM collection probably holds 80 percent or more of the 350+ Brazilian authors cited in the Moisés dictionary. Nevertheless, the limitations of this approach are obvious. First, one would have to analyze the results carefully both by historical era and by geographic region to document any variant patterns. (In fact, my preliminary observation was that most of the authors not found in this sampling were from the eighteenth century.) Second, when taken no further, an author search of this type says nothing either about particular editions or printings held or about the completeness of holdings for authors of more than one book. Little, in other words, can be said about the opportunities for specialized, in-depth research on an individual author or school of authors. The value of the Moisés *Dicionário* author search, as with the two additional author searches described below, is therefore in the possibilities they open up for more extended analysis.

The *Dictionary of Contemporary Brazilian Authors*, characterized by Laurence Hallewell as ". . . indispensable for information on the contemporary scene,"[3] lists a total of 193 authors, of whom 190 (98.5 percent) are found as authors in the UNM collection. Foster and Reis's emphasis is on younger Brazilian writers, both those well known to the public and those less well known, as of the 1970 publication date of their work. Authors from throughout Brazil, of prose, poetry, drama, and cronicas, have been included, as have a handful of literary critics and historians. In an effort to augment the number of recent Brazilian authors covered, I also searched all of the authors listed in Foster and Rela's 1990 reference work, *Brazilian Literature: A Research Bibliography*, who had not been included in the *Dictionary*. Of the 101 authors falling into this category (of 150 overall), a total of 95 (94 percent) were found in the UNM catalog. Unlike the *Dictionary*, however, this bibliography incorporates Brazilian authors from earlier periods, especially from the nineteenth century. The limitations cited above with reference to the Moisés *Dicionário* apply with equal force to these works. The results they yield suggest that the UNM collection is very strong for representative and better-known Brazilian authors of the nineteenth and twentieth centuries. Also, to the extent that this line of analysis is productive, one could undertake a truly exhaustive author search, if time permits, by checking, for example, each of the 3,800 authors listed in Raimundo de Menezes's 1978 work, *Dicionário literário brasileiro* ("often the best place to look first for information about a specific author,"[4] according to Hallewell).

Before turning to a different category of material, I want to mention one final source of data on the UNM monographic collection in Brazilian literature. This is what might be called "the mother of all quantitative indicators," namely, the *National Shelflist Count (NSC)*. To make more effective use of the *NSC* (the edition I used is the latest available: 1989), I placed UNM within a special peer group of thirteen academic libraries having major or superior Latin American collections. There are two *NSC* call number sequences pertinent to this analysis, PQ9500–PQ9696, "Portuguese literature of Brazil, to 1800," and PQ9697–PQ9699, "Portuguese literature of Brazil, since 1800." Unfortunately, no more specific breakdowns are made in the *NSC* tables. The figures reported are interesting, and bear out Jackson's findings from the early 1960s. In the category "Portuguese literature of Brazil, to 1800," UNM ranks fourth of thirteen, with 827 titles classified, and for "Portuguese literature of Brazil, since 1800," the UNM collection ranks third of thirteen, with 7,590 titles classified. Of course, there are inherent flaws in this technique, the two most glaring being that cataloging backlogs are not taken into account and that several libraries with prominent Latin American collections (especially in Brazilian literature) did not participate in the survey. Allowing for these factors, the *NSC* is useful as a gross quantitative indicator.

More or less matching the strength of the general monographic collection was the representation in UNM's holdings of reference sources in and for Brazilian literature. As a means both of identifying specialized bibliographies to search and of evaluating this category of material in itself, I checked parts of three listings of Brazilian literature reference works. These were, first, the "Bibliography" section, compiled by Laurence Hallewell, of the chapter on Brazilian literature in the Covington guide, *Latin America and the Caribbean: A Critical Guide to Research Sources;* second, the MLA publication, edited by Bobby J. Chamberlain, titled *Portuguese Language and Luso-Brazilian Literature: An Annotated Guide to Selected Reference Works;* and third, the chapter on "Literature" in Ann Hartness's book, *Brazil in Reference Books, 1965-1989: An Annotated Bibliography.*

In all three of these, partly for the sake of consistency and partly for lack of time, I omitted from the analysis entries for regional literature, union lists of library catalogs, children's literature, and such topics as stylistics and linguistics. Moreover, there was some, but not much, overlap among them. The results were as follows: In 95 sources checked of Hallewell's bibliography, the UNM Library holds 84 (88 percent); in 110 titles of the Chamberlain guide searched, the collection holds 94 (85 percent). For Hartness's book, the results were more mixed: 52 titles were checked, of which the Library holds 30 (58 percent). Now, as with its counterpart for the book collection, this analysis, made of holdings of reference sources for Brazilian literature, has obvious drawbacks. First and foremost, the number and nature of sources checked are too limited to yield any but a superficial picture. Clearly, one would have to widen the list considerably to be able to make any solid assessment of whether the reference collection supports advanced research into specialized topics and themes in Brazilian literature, whether by period, regional division, or some other mode of analysis. Within the acknowledged limits, however, this was a useful exercise, primarily because it identified a handful of important sources apparently missing from the collection. These include the recently published *Enciclopédia de literatura brasileira,* edited by Afrânio Coutinho and José Galante de Sousa, [5] and five of the seven volumes of the massive work by Wilson Martins, *História da inteligência brasileira,* the latter characterized by Hallewell as "an essential, if not the essential, tool for reference work on Brazilian literature." [6]

The final category of material included in this analysis is journals. Here, the results of my checking were more problematic and call into question, depending upon the criteria employed, the definition of the UNM

Brazilian literature holdings as "strong." As valid as this may be for the book collection, it does not appear to hold for the journal collection. The analysis of the journals also involved a limited group of "core" lists, in this case three in number, of periodicals published both in and outside of Brazil during both the nineteenth and twentieth centuries with the emphasis falling heavily on titles appearing within the last thirty years.

The first list searched was developed from scrutinizing pertinent citations, over approximately a ten-year period (1982-1992), in the *Hispanic American Periodicals Index (HAPI)*. The citations thus identified, distributed under some 36 different subject headings, in turn produced a list of 59 journals and cultural magazines containing material of substance (i.e., more than the occasional review) on Brazilian literature. The UNM Library holds all 59 of these titles, either in complete or virtually complete runs. Furthermore, all are either currently subscribed to or are received via exchange. For the purposes of this analysis, however, to hold 100 percent of the *HAPI* periodicals is hardly cause for celebration, since very few either originate in Brazil or, if published elsewhere, devote themselves exclusively to Brazilian literature. Rather, they are the titles which any collection that purports to serve Latin American literature generally must have.

The two remaining periodical lists searched were, first, *A Preliminary Listing of Foreign Periodical Holdings in the United States and Canada which Give Coverage to Portuguese and Brazilian Language and Literature,* compiled by Oscar Fernández at the University of Iowa in 1968, and, second, the chapter on journals in *Brazil: A Working Bibliography in Literature, Linguistics, Humanities and the Social Sciences,* a reference work edited by Ronald Harmon and Bobby Chamberlain and published in 1975 by the Arizona State University Center for Latin American Studies. In the case of the Fernández bibliography which covers both the nineteenth and twentieth centuries, I searched only the strictly Brazilian titles. These numbered 114. Unfortunately, when writing up the results of the analysis, I could not locate the table summarizing my findings from the Fernández listing. I clearly remember, however, that the UNM Library holds fewer than 50 percent of the 114, and that the older, more specialized literary periodicals make a particularly poor showing in our collection. (Fernández's bibliography, incidentally, is one of the eleven reference sources out of the 95 searched from Hallewell's list, which is not found in our holdings. It was borrowed on interlibrary loan from the University of Iowa.) Moreover, a significant percentage of the 50 or so titles owned by New Mexico are held in very incomplete runs. Essentially the same result was obtained for the list of periodicals found in the chapter on "Literature" in the Harmon and Chamberlain bibliography. A total of 48 titles were checked, of which 24 (exactly 50 percent) were found in the UNM collection. Again, those not held by the Library were the older (1930s-1960s), specialized literary journals and magazines published in Brazil, whereas the non-Brazilian titles were almost all held in full runs.

These results, albeit obtained from a rather restricted sample, indicate to me that the UNM journal collection in Brazilian literature is, at best, mediocre. On the positive side, however, the collection does turn up, as I know occurs at other libraries, a number of specialized and regionally based literary periodicals either too obscure, or too recent, or both, to be found in published lists and bibliographies.

In this context, I should mention the collection at New Mexico of Brazilian small press publications, since it contains nearly 200 recent and current literary periodicals and little magazines from throughout Brazil, in addition to some 3,000 monographs. A portion, but not a large one, of this collection is duplicated in a handful of other libraries. Also worthy of mention, although falling outside the general framework of this analysis, would be our collection of *Literatura de cordel,* or popular poetry pamphlets, which contains approximately 3,500 titles, all of which— primarily thanks to federal funding (but also to Gayle Williams's dedication before she left New Mexico)—have been individually cataloged on OCLC, deacidified, and housed in the Special Collections Department.

I would like to sum up by drawing a few simple and probably self-evident conclusions. First, the analysis of a broad area of the collection, such as Brazilian literature, is not something to be done in one shot. Rather, it is a multitiered process or project. The first task is to lay the foundation by defining the boundaries, identifying the appropriate core lists, and seeing how the collection measures up in a general quantitative sense. The next task is to go below the surface and analyze particular segments of the collection. In the case of Brazilian or any other national literature, this would entail checking by period, genre, format, region, and literary movements (such as Modernism or Vanguardism), and finally, by individual author. It would also be helpful to bring in validation studies or any other conspectus-based tools that exist.

NOTES

1. William Vernon Jackson, *Library Guide for Brazilian Studies* (Pittsburgh, PA: University of Pittsburgh Book Centers, 1964), p. 80.

2. Kathy Gienge, a member of the UNM General Library Ibero Team, provided valuable assistance in searching the *Handbook of Latin American Studies.*

3. See entry No. 4068, p. 526, in Hallewell's bibliography, found in the chapter on Brazilian literature in Paula Hattox Covington, ed., *Latin America and the Caribbean: A Critical Guide to Research Sources.*

4. Afrânio Coutinho and José Galante de Sousa, *Enciclopédia de literatura brasileira*, 2 vols. (Rio de Janeiro: Ministério da Educação, Fundação de Assistência ao Estudante, 1990, c1985).

5. From entry No. 4111, p. 530, in the same piece by Hallewell in Covington, ed., *Latin America and the Caribbean*.

BIBLIOGRAPHY

Antelo, Raúl. *Literatura em revista*. São Paulo: Editora Atica, 1984.

Bernd, Zilá. "Bibliografia específica sobre literatura negra no Brasil." *Revista de Antropologia* 29 (1986), 175-183.

Bruesch, Mary, and Russ Davidson, eds. *UNM General Library Holdings in Selected Latin American and Iberian Subject Areas: A Quantitative Study Based on the National Shelflist Count*. Albuquerque: University of New Mexico General Library, 1991.

Chamberlain, Bobby J. *Portuguese Language and Luso-Brazilian Literature: An Annotated Guide to Selected Reference Works*. Selected Bibliographies in Language and Literature, 6. New York: The Modern Language Association of America, 1989.

Coutinho, Afrânio, and José Galante de Sousa. *Enciclopédia de literatura brasileira*. 2 vols. Rio de Janeiro: Ministério da Educação, Fundação de Assistência ao Estudante, 1990.

Covington, Paula Hattox, ed. *Indexed Journals: A Guide to Latin American Serials*. SALALM Bibliography Series, 8. Madison, WI: SALALM Secretariat, 1983.

———. *Latin America and the Caribbean: A Critical Guide to Research Sources*. Bibliographies and Indexes in Latin American and Caribbean Studies, no. 2. New York: Greenwood Press, 1992.

Doyle, Plinio. *História de revistas e jornais literários*, vol. 1. Coleção de estudos bibliográficos, 1. Rio de Janeiro: Centro de Pesquisas, Fundação Casa de Rui Barbosa, 1976.

Fernández, Oscar. *A Preliminary Listing of Foreign Periodical Holdings in the United States and Canada which Give Coverage to Portuguese and Brazilian Language and Literature*. Iowa City: University of Iowa, 1968.

Foster, David William, and Roberto Reis. *A Dictionary of Contemporary Brazilian Authors*. Tempe: Center for Latin American Studies, Arizona State University, 1981.

Foster, David William, and Walter Rela. *Brazilian Literature: A Research Bibliography*. Garland Reference Library of the Humanities, vol. 1162. New York: Garland Publishing, Inc., 1990.

Guide to the Evaluation of Library Collections. Collection Management and Development Guides, no. 2. Chicago, IL: American Library Association, 1989.

Hallewell, Laurence. "Bibliography." In Paula Hattox Covington, ed., *Latin America and the Caribbean: A Critical Guide to Research Sources.* Bibliographies and Indexes in Latin American and Caribbean Studies, no. 2. New York: Greenwood Press, 1992. Pp. 511-538.

————. *Literature with Language, Art and Music.* Latin American Serials, vol. 3. London: The Committee on Latin America, 1977.

Harmon, Ronald M., and Bobby J. Chamberlain. *Brazil: A Working Bibliography in Literature, Linguistics, Humanities and the Social Sciences.* Special Study, no. 14. Tempe: Center for Latin American Studies, Arizona State University, 1975.

Hartness, Ann. *Brazil in Reference Books, 1965-1989: An Annotated Bibliography.* Metuchen, NJ: Scarecrow Press, 1991.

Igel, Regina. "Imigrantes na ficção brasileira contemporânea." *Revista Interamericana de Bibliografia* 41:1 (1992), 83-101.

Jackson, William Vernon. *Library Guide for Brazilian Studies.* Pittsburgh, PA: University of Pittsburgh Book Centers, 1964.

Lara, Cecilia de. "Da transfiguração do regionalismo." *Caravelle* 57 (1991), 83-97.

Martins, Wilson. *História da inteligência brasileira.* 7 vols. São Paulo: Editora Cultrix, 1976-1978.

Menezes, Raimundo de. *Dicionário literário brasileiro.* Pref. Antonio Candido. 2d ed. Rio de Janeiro: Livros Técnicos e Científicos Editora, 1978.

Moisés, Massaud. *Pequeno dicionário de literatura brasileira.* 2d rev. ed. São Paulo: Editora Cultrix, 1980.

Moyano Martin, Dolores, ed. *Handbook of Latin American Studies: Humanities.* Austin: University of Texas, 1935–.

National Shelflist Count: Titles Classified by the Library of Congress and National Library of Medicine Classifications, 1989. Chicago, IL: American Library Association, 1990.

Nunes, María Luisa. "Resources for the Study of Brazilian Literature." *Neohelicon* 1-2 (1976), 225-238.

Placer, Xavier. *Modernismo brasileiro: Bibliografia (1981-1971).* Rio de Janeiro: Biblioteca Nacional, 1972.

Valk, Barbara G., ed. *Hispanic American Periodicals Index (HAPI)*. Los Angeles: UCLA Latin American Center, University of California, 1977–.

Zilberman, Regina. "Brasil: Cultura e literatura nos anos oitenta." *Hispania* 74:3 (September 1991), 577-583.

Zubatsky, David. "A Bibliography of Cumulative Indexes to Luso-Brazilian Journals of the Nineteenth and Twentieth Centuries: Humanities and Social Sciences." *Luso-Brazilian Review* 8:2 (1971), 71-81.

Part Three

New Trends and Challenges
in Acquisition, Cataloging,
Microfilming, and Publishing
of Latin American
Library Materials

I

Issues in Acquisition, Cataloging, and Microfilming of Latin American Library Materials

38. Access versus Ownership: Issues for Small and Medium-Sized Libraries

Molly Molloy

It is important for librarians and bibliographers to know that even though they see themselves as members of a cooperative venture in their institutions, their primary job duties determine their perspective on the access versus ownership issue.

David Tyckoson has written that while "patrons tend to view the library as information providers, we [librarians and especially bibliographers] tend to view ourselves as information collectors." He goes on to state that "public services librarians are the members of the library community who have most embraced the paradigm of access. This shift in thinking among those who interact with the public is probably not in response to some great forward-thinking vision inherent in public services, but is a result of a survival tactic created in response to patron demands." [1]

The Access Paradigm or "Guerrilla Reference"

We often use what I like to call "guerrilla tactics" to obtain access to an item of information to meet a user's specific need which cannot be met by the materials owned by the library. The survival tactics that we use on the front lines of public service often mean that we will resort to "any means necessary" to find out if and where some piece of information exists (i.e., an article, a book). We will also often bypass the time delay of interlibrary loan and employ personal networks to obtain the piece of information for a patron. This might mean telephoning or e-mailing a colleague at another library for a fax of an article, asking that citations from an electronic database be sent over e-mail, or even requesting the full text of an article be downloaded from a commercial database and sent over e-mail.

The Ownership Paradigm and the Shift

Tyckoson reports:

Recent ARL statistics demonstrate the magnitude of the commitment to the paradigm of ownership. Out of an average acquisitions budget of $3,083,287 for ARL libraries in 1986, 97 percent was allocated for the direct purchase of materials for the library collection. Only 3 percent of the average budget was spent on other materials, including access to online vendors and bibliographic utilities. [2]

Among some libraries in more recent years, however, there is evidence of a shift in this still-dominant paradigm. At a recent meeting of the International Association of Technological University Libraries (Kansas City, May 1994), directors of ARL and other libraries with strong technological programs reported that the access budgets of many of their institutions were doubling each year. At some schools, the access budget is up to 15 percent of the annual materials budget. [3] As a representative of a smaller, less financially endowed institution, I can say that it is likely that the growth of the *access* budget, at the expense of the acquisitions or *ownership* budget, is likely to continue.

Rationale for the Access Paradigm—Tiny, Shrinking Budgets

The entire New Mexico State University (NMSU) library budget for 1992-93 was about $4.2 million. The materials (acquisitions) part of this budget was about $1.7 million, of which more than 64 percent went to maintaining serials subscriptions, most of these journals in engineering and the sciences. Expenditures on Latin America-related monographs in 1992-93 were approximately $25,000. Many of these items are acquired through a basic academic approval plan for English-language materials and through standing orders with university presses. This total also includes materials relating to the U.S.-Mexican border region which are published in the United States. The library currently has only one foreign approval plan, with Mexico Norte, to acquire materials from the state of Chihuahua. The amount of the approval plan is $1,000, but including firm orders, NMSU spent more than $3,000 last year for northern Mexico materials. The Center for Latin American Studies provides the library with about $5,000 yearly from its Title VI funding to maintain the Chihuahua approval plan and to purchase other materials on an item-by-item basis. The library also provides about $1,000 in special program funds for Latin American materials. The rest of the $25,000 estimate are materials bought with other departmental funds but which have a Latin American subject focus.

The *access* budget is more difficult to determine, contingent on how access is defined. However, by picking and choosing some budget line figures, it is possible to estimate roughly how much the NMSU library spends on access for all information, not just for Latin American information. The CD-ROM subscriptions (nearly all the library's CD-ROMs provide bibliographic references, thus, they are used to gain access to the universe of information in a subject area, not just materials the library owns) and document delivery consume about $57,000 of the acquisition budget. Other access spending is spread among the Systems budget (online catalog which includes a periodical abstracts database, OCLC, and the library's access to the Internet) and the Information Services budget (online searching, OCLC Firstsearch). It would be difficult to quantify which portion of these budget amounts actually went toward providing access to materials not owned by the library, but a high estimate would be about $125,000. This figure plus the $57,000 in the materials budget totals $182,000; thus about 10.7 percent of the total acquisitions budget could be termed access, not ownership.

How can a library with a small collection and a limited budget meet the information needs of a growing Latin American studies program? This collection development dilemma can be addressed on several fronts that represent some interplay between access and ownership.

Core Materials

The first step is to insure a core collection of major scholarly works on Latin America through standing orders and approval plans with university presses and trade publishers. It is also necessary to identify the major journals that will meet the program's teaching and research needs. Determining a core collection is not easy. The materials needed to support undergraduate classes may be primary, but they will not be enough to support graduate and faculty research. In general, core materials are the minimum materials needed to support undergraduate and graduate programs at an institution, and they will be acquired and owned by the library. Most of these core needs can be met by mainstream academic approval plans.

However, for access to materials for Latin American research, the answer is much more complicated. Most books and journals from the region must be obtained from vendors there. Mainstream approval plan vendors in the United States do not provide access to these materials. For a library not accustomed to foreign approval plans, the whole concept of regional vendors, individual country or regional approval plans must be sold to both library administrators and area studies faculty. If a library has no history of involvement with SALALM, a lot of groundwork must be done.

Defining the core journals for university programs can be more difficult. Public services librarians and bibliographers must work closely with faculty to identify those that support the teaching and research needs of the institution.

Materials described as *secondary* may be used less often and will be approached with a mixture of ownership and access. Document delivery may be a viable, less-expensive option for certain journals that are used only occasionally. At the third level, very rarely used research materials will not be acquired by the library. The existence of these items may be determined by searching through the usual bibliographic tools, including bibliographic utilities (OCLC and RLIN), specialized databases (online or on CD-ROM), print indexes and bibliographies, and online catalogs of other libraries accessible via the Internet. Once an item is known to exist, the user may resort to commercial document delivery (NOT subsidized by the library); interlibrary loan (subsidized but very slow); or in the case of rare or nonloanable materials, the researcher may decide that a trip to the library that does own the materials is the only possible access.

For specialized Latin American research, travel has been and may continue to be a necessary part of research. Many of the larger research libraries still collect comprehensively in selected areas of Latin Americana. It is now possible to search the catalogs of the Library of Congress, the University of California System, the University of Texas, the University of New Mexico, and other large collections via the Internet. If a researcher is considering research travel, it may be possible to optimize research time by identifying sources locally through the networks.

Building a Specialized Research Collection

A second part of the strategy involves identifying an area of specialization on which to build a research level collection. The research collecting focus should build on library and program strengths on the campus and should be established cooperatively between the library and the Latin American studies center. Specialist vendors in the region who can provide materials to meet the collecting profile should be identified. Other collection strengths in the local area should be complemented and cooperative agreements for sharing resources established.

A library might decide to specialize based on past strengths and research interests of faculty. Problems arise when faculty members retire and new ones with other research interests are hired. A research level collection on the history of the Mexican revolution will not be very useful to an economist studying popular organizations in Peru, or a political scientist studying civil-military relations in Central America.

In the case of NMSU, because of its location and some traditional strengths, it was decided to focus research collecting on the U.S.-Mexican border region, especially on the northern Mexican states of Chihuahua and Durango. The library also tries to cover materials in agriculture and technology areas since NMSU is the land grant university, the primary engineering school, and the only agriculture school in the state.

The University of New Mexico (UNM) collects comprehensively in many other Latin American areas. With its small budget, NMSU is trying to cover the Mexican state of Chihuahua fully and to obtain major works from other northern Mexican states. At the same time, to meet the needs of teaching and research that increasingly emphasize Latin America, and especially U.S.-Mexican relations, we try to obtain important works from other major publishers in Mexico City through firm orders from dealer lists. Ideally, a second, small approval plan should be established to get the major new works published in Mexico City—especially those that deal with the border, business, trade, and agriculture—major subjects of interest to NMSU faculty and students. However, when only a small amount of money is available, it is difficult to hand over $500 or $1,000 chunks of it to vendors. It leaves nothing for individual orders, special requests for materials from faculty, or other items that might become available during the year that do not fall into any other subject-selector's profile.

We are fortunate to be close to the University of New Mexico, and our users are able to use the UNM collections via interlibrary loan and in person. Through our library system we can search the catalog of the UNM libraries and students can get a "passport" to check books out from UNM. We are also reasonably close (by southwestern standards) to other strong collections, especially the University of Texas at Austin, the University of Arizona, and Arizona State University. The University of Texas at El Paso also has a strong collection in border materials. We search these library catalogs via the Internet, and the researcher can usually determine whether a trip to a neighboring university would be worthwhile.

Real Access?

To carry out the third part of the strategy, we must emphasize access over ownership where necessary and provide the reference and information services that will make access a viable concept. Some examples:

- earmark a portion of collection funds to provide online and CD-ROM access to fee-based Latin American bibliographic and full-text information;
- provide access to materials not in the collection through document delivery services and interlibrary loan;
- develop expertise with network resources that expand access to public domain information such as library catalogs, academic e-mail conferences, Internet-accessible archives, newsgroups, and government databases.

One way of looking at the access/ownership issue is to see it as a conjuncture where the so-called "new research library paradigm" takes shape. We usually view access as a service—it impacts most heavily on public service librarians and also on the systems experts who are often involved in making access a reality. The systems people do the following:

- maintain the hardware and software required to communicate through national and international electronic networks;
- set up and maintain local area networks that can provide access to a wide range of databases on CD-ROM and in other formats;

- may load and maintain large bibliographic databases on library OPACS;
- maintain the hardware and software needed to set up electronic text and facsimile document delivery; and perhaps most importantly,
- implement administrative decisions to get information out of the library to users by providing access to the library's collections and to other information sources through campus networks.

Reference librarians then take on other considerable tasks:
- learn about the access possibilities in a very complicated information marketplace—CD-ROM databases [networked or stand-alone], flat-fee online databases, commercial full-text services, document delivery services, unit cost online searching, public domain information via the internet, etc;
- train themselves to navigate through the huge mazes of information to find items needed by library users;
- teach users to know what systems are available and how to search various systems to find information that meets both general and specific disciplinary information needs;
- determine how to spend limited funds to provide the best service.

Library administrators (often influenced by the public services perspective) have expressed the idea that user expectations are driving the change to electronic resources. Users want the information, as quickly as possible, and they do not care from where or how the library acquires the article or book.[4] Information consumers in the 1990s have a much wider range of choices. Those with the financial resources can buy access to commercial networks such as Lexis/Nexis, Dow Jones News Retrieval, and Compuserve, which provide the full text of many newspapers, magazines, journals, government publications, and more. Libraries also strive to provide this kind of access, while at the same time developing print collections.

Many university library users also have some knowledge of these databases and may have their own subscriptions. One attitude is that the library should have all of these services, or that these services make the library obsolete. Many novice information consumers believe that a commercial service, or even a seemingly "free" information source such as the Internet, can provide unlimited access to everything. Librarians need to educate their constituents to the sad fact that this is not the case.

Access requires more user instruction. Most basic library users can find some information that they seek by browsing in certain areas of the shelves, or by perusing the tables of contents of a few key journals in a subject area. As reference librarians, we kid ourselves if we think that the majority of our library users use sophisticated indexes and databases to find information in the library. A great deal of "research" happens through browsing and serendipity. *If* library users must *identify* materials that the library does not own, in order to try to get the items via interlibrary loan or document delivery, then all users must really *know how* to use reference tools (indexes, bibliographies, databases, remote library catalogs).

Many users must also be introduced to the idea of access over ownership, and they must be convinced that access can be a viable alternative to ownership. Many library users do not have a clear idea of how large the universe of information actually is. They believe every library should have everything. Or they believe that every CD-ROM or full-text online system has everything. (Try to convince a new and enamored user of Lexis/Nexis that the database does not contain all the information in the world!) They may just assume that any large university library has everything they will need. They may even become angry if they use an index (print, CD-ROM, or online) in the library and find citations to articles and books that are not owned. As a reference librarian, I have often heard the complaint: "I don't know why you have these databases if you don't have the journals."

Another important issue to consider when attempting to substitute access for ownership is equity for all library users. If the cost of document delivery is subsidized for faculty, these materials should also be available to graduate students and undergraduates.

When Is Access Better than Ownership?

In the area of Latin American information, access may sometimes be better than ownership. If a major need is for current news, an electronic source like the Latin America Data Base (LADB) may be better than maintaining numerous newspaper and magazine subscriptions from Latin America. LADB newsletters provide weekly updates on Latin American news and economic affairs. LADB newsletters can be delivered directly to the electronic mailboxes of faculty and students. The library can offer instruction in searching and downloading information from the database. Because the database is full text, the user will not be frustrated by finding citations to information that cannot be located in the library. Expert searchers can provide packets of information from the database in response to reference questions from faculty and students; the library does not need to catalog, preserve, and store the information.

The Internet is expanding the interchange of information between north and south in the hemisphere. When databases (such as the *Handbook of Latin American Studies* or the USAID Latin American & Caribbean Economic & Social Data) are made available over the Internet (currently via the UT-LANIC gopher), the information is accessible to researchers without regard to location. More and more scholars in Latin America are gaining access to the Internet, and so can take advantage of the information in it and can also contribute to it. While the great majority of network users still live in North America and Europe, many developing countries are promoting network access as a way to raise education and technology levels. [5]

The Institute for Global Communications (IGC) provides relatively inexpensive gateways to the Internet in many less developed countries. The IGC has networks in Mexico, Uruguay, Brazil, Ecuador, Nicaragua, and other Latin American countries. The electronic conferences on the IGC networks provide news from Latin America not available from the mainstream wire services. In addition, many grassroots organizations in Latin America are now using networks to disseminate information. As a reference librarian, I have searched IGC conferences and databases to get information on popular organizations in Peru, on the Chiapas rebellion, on human rights abuses against indigenous groups in Brazil, and on many other topics. Much of this information would be very difficult to obtain in a timely fashion through printed sources. Often, these groups speak for people who do not have much of a voice even in the mainstream publications in their own countries. [6]

How Might Emphasis on Access Enhance Latin American Collections?

In some cases, the library may find that access to expensive journals via commercial document delivery may meet the needs of many users. Commercial full-text services may also provide some alternatives to maintaining expensive subscriptions. The systems that come to mind here are Lexis/Nexis or Westlaw for legal and news information. Library users want this kind of knowledge; these systems can be used to answer questions and provide value-added information. They *do not,* however, add to any store of unique data for local users or add to any cooperative collecting effort. The information provided via these systems is mainstream and commercial and provides few perspectives outside of the mainstream. For any library that desires to present other points of view, especially views from different regions of the world (in our case, Latin America), these systems will never be all that is needed.

We might ask, however, if these systems could be used to provide access to some of the mainstream information now acquired, thus making acquisition funds available to buy materials outside of the mainstream, for example, Latin American materials. This could be a way to use the access *over* ownership issue to our (Latin Americanists) advantage. We could promote access over ownership for many "mainstream" materials that are now accessible either on full-text systems such as Lexis/Nexis or via document delivery. If money could be saved by offering access on demand to particular articles from mainstream magazines and journals, then we could make a case for putting acquisition money saved into buying "out-of-the-mainstream" materials from Latin America and elsewhere that will not in any foreseeable future be available via any electronic system.

NOTES

1. David Tyckoson, "Access vs. Ownership: Changing Roles for Librarians," *The Reference Librarian* 34 (1991), 37-45.

2. Ibid., p. 39.

3. Charles Townley, Dean of the NMSU library, personal communication via electronic mail, May 1994.

4. Joseph A. Rosenthal, "Crumbling Walls: The Impact of the Electronic Age on Libraries and Their Clienteles," *Journal of Library Administration* 14:1 (1991), 9-17.

5. Daniel Pimienta, *La comunicación mediante computador: Una esperanza para el sector académico y de investigación del tercer mundo*, GNET Archive, May 1993, p. 3. [FTP document; to access: FTP <dhvx20.csudh.edu> directory <global_net> Filename <cmc_acad_investig.txt>.

6. Association for Progressive Communications, *Global Communications for Environment, Human Rights, Development and Peace*, GNET Archive, 1993. [FTP document; to access: FTP <dhvx20.csudh.edu> Directory <global_net> Filename <apc_brochure.txt>. See also Graham Lane, *Communications for Progress: A Guide to International E-Mail* (London: Catholic Institute for International Relations, 1990).

39. Maintaining Balance between Archival and Access Models for the Future

Terry Charles Peet

No explicit statement by the Library of Congress exists regarding the controversy over collecting for access or for archival purposes. The Library's position, however, may be discerned by its role and mission, and this discernment can lead to several suppositions on which a national policy could be formulated and proposed.

First, the role and mission of the Library or, more appropriately, how the Library of Congress sees itself. The Library is the Library for the U.S. Congress; this is its raison d'être. At its founding in 1800 the Library was projected as a parliamentary library with limited interests. But during the War of 1812, when the Library, then housed in the U.S. Capitol, was destroyed by the British (1814), Congress pondered the offer of former president Thomas Jefferson to sell his private 6,487-volume library to form the core of the Library of Congress. In the ensuing discussions and congressional debate over the purchase of his library, Thomas Jefferson observed: "I do not know that it contains any branch of science which Congress would wish to exclude from their collections; there is, in fact, no subject to which a Member of Congress may not have occasion to refer." When Jefferson's offer was finally accepted, Congress for all time outlined a different future for the congressional library, as its basic character was transformed from a specialized to a general library.

In time the Library of Congress collections grew to such an extent that by the end of World War II, the nation and Congress recognized the Library for what it was, a national library further reinforced by strong commitment to programs not only for increased acquisitions worldwide but for cataloging and making bibliographic data available.

The Library of Congress, whether from self-centeredness or from praise and/or pressure from the outside to assume a wider and more proactive role, is commonly perceived and considers itself to be not only the Congress's own library and the de facto national library, but also the "court of last resort," that is, the library to which other libraries nationwide can turn for assistance, almost always in accessing materials held nowhere else, through traditional interlibrary loan and more recently through electronic technology.

These three roles are alluded to in the codification of the Library's corpus of Collection Policy Statements which acknowledges the Library's responsibilities to serve (1) the Congress and the United States government as a whole, (2) the scholarly community, and (3) the general public. The Library has consciously confined itself to acquiring materials that are of the utmost importance to the American record and world culture. Simultaneously, the Library has deferred to local and state repositories the collecting of purely local and special collections while encouraging research institutions and libraries, which have developed very strong collections in particular subject areas, to expand and consolidate their strengths.

This triple role may be envisioned along with the roles of public libraries, specialized libraries, and academic and professional libraries, small and large, as a set of concentric circles with the smallest and innermost of the circles representing the system of public libraries. These libraries contain and replicate thousandfold core materials of interest to the general public. Larger circles beyond the innermost ones represent deeper collections that today would rank as conspectus level 2 and 3 collections capable of sustaining most research expected at the baccalaureate level and, to a certain degree, the graduate level. Finally, the outermost circle is representative of those libraries whose collections, either generally or specifically, are comprehensive enough to meet the requirements of conspectus levels 4 and 5 capable of supporting serious doctoral research. These libraries are the courts of last resort. Because of its extensive worldwide collecting efforts, the distribution of its cataloging data, and its interlibrary loan program, the Library of Congress has become the archival archetype par excellence, and for these reasons alone the circle depicting the Library of Congress may be in many instances beyond all others.

The access versus archival controversy is largely an outgrowth of shrinking budgets and, to a lesser degree, increased availability of more sophisticated electronic technology. Indeed, only last year the Library was forced because of budgetary issues to suspend its international interlibrary loan program. It is not just who, but how many, should collect what, and how to make materials accessible without placing undue burden on the relatively few courts of last resort. Balance must be struck and maintained. A splendid example of such balance, borne out of the ashes of libraries destroyed during World War II, is the system devised by libraries in Germany to restore what was lost. Aware of not being able to replace all that was lost, the country rebuilt its library system to provide universal public library access and to establish a network of concentrated and comprehensive specialized collections for extensive research. Can such a plan be devised and implemented in the United States of America? I doubt that America has the political will for such an undertaking. Our situation is not dire enough and we are too accustomed to our ways—individualism, parochialism, chauvinism, separatism—to relinquish our respective turfs. As in politics, the way to national level interlibrary cooperation toward maintaining a balance is through our pocketbooks—something Americans, individually and institutionally, understand the best. We must devise ways to "work smarter," as is said in current yuppie administrative parlance, while getting more bang for our proverbial buck.

Some cost-saving techniques are on the horizon and will play an important role in preserving a proper archival/access balance. The techniques being actively considered are the following:

1. The Law Library of Congress has a project to scan full-text the national official gazettes of Mexico and Brazil on a daily basis. The scanned text is then sent electronically via the Internet directly into LC mainframe computers, where it is available for researchers. Ideally, the cost of scanning should be shared (at least among three or more subscribers); the scanning should be done in situ in order to funnel the savings of postage into the scanning process itself; the scanned text is sent regularly to a designated central mainframe whence it could be distributed to the other subscribers. The Law Library is now looking at the feasibility of doing it worldwide. There are nevertheless some negative aspects that must be resolved before abandoning microfilming as the preservation technique par excellence *on a permanent basis*. Electronic scanning equipment costs more than microfilm equipment; standards for digitized images in storage are not yet fully developed; and most important, it will be possible to transfer microfilm materials to digital media as soon as the issue of standards is resolved.

2. The application of selective full-text scanning could benefit certain newspapers. Typically 80 to 85 percent of a newspaper subscription cost is postage, depending on the form and frequency of shipment. If two or three, better yet four or more, institutions agreed to share the cost of scanning, for example, the very sizable *El Mercurio* from Santiago de Chile, the savings derived from four or five institutional subscriptions could easily cover the cost of scanning at a fraction, per institution, of the ink-print subscription. The database could be periodically downloaded onto CD-ROM if desired. Additionally, concerns about space to house growing mounds of newspapers and, among a growing number of librarians, concerns about microfilming or obtaining microfilm would nearly vanish. I allude to those among us who question the longevity of CD-ROM products. There is already a network of U.S. libraries that cooperate in microfilming newspapers. Cannot such a network undertake cooperative scanning operations?

3. Regarding newspapers that consume so much of our budgets and space, LC is currently reviewing its worldwide newspaper subscriptions, both purchase and exchange. In the Hispanic area, we are attempting to

differentiate between those newspapers with time-sensitive content, such as *El Financiero*—the *Wall Street Journal* of Mexico—and those used mainly for historical research. In addition, we have written to the editors of all newspapers currently received, whether by purchase or nonpurchase means, to query them about the preservation of their newspapers, whether they microfilm their own newspaper or subcontract such filming to a commercial firm, and if such microfilm is produced, how frequently is it filmed and is it available for sale? We are currently reviewing the feasibility of purchasing positive microfilm, where regularly available, instead of ink-print copies of those newspapers used primarily for historical research.

4. Also with respect to newspapers, there is some discussion in LC about exploring with the Foreign Broadcasting Information Service (FBIS), which subscribes to dozens of newspapers worldwide, the possibility of sharing ink-print subscription costs. The newspapers received from FBIS are generally not damaged and could be transferred with five or six months delay to LC. We are also aware that the FBIS actually receives a few of its subscriptions via scanning and the Internet.

5. For part of the Hispanic area, that is, monographs acquired from Latin America and the Caribbean, savings have resulted from creating online or in-process acquisition records (preliminary cataloging) at the point of arrival, allowing the Library to identify and, in the case of purchased monographs, to return unwanted and duplicate titles to the dealer. This program commenced April 8, 1993, and in the first six months realized no less than $6,000 in savings.

6. LC is currently working with two vendors who own three dealerships (Puvill Libros, Literatura de Vientos Tropicales, and Mexico Norte) toward the creation of records in acceptable USMARC format. Since dealers must create some form of bibliographic record for their businesses, why not in USMARC format which, after twenty-five years, is widely used nationally and internationally. The records of dealer selections as well as those of items selected by LC will be sent either electronically via the Internet to LC's mainframe or on diskettes for downloading to the mainframe. Either way, the creation of in-process acquisitions records will be enormously expedited, as little must be done to alter the record (the automatic assignment by the computer of the LC Card Number and the addition of the 050 field). This will allow us to accomplish as much if not more with less staff, which describes our situation at the moment. There is a program available to dealers that allows them, with a keystroke, to convert selectively any record from USMARC format to list, card, or other format as needed for any customer, thereby avoiding any rekeying of bibliographic data. As of this date, Puvill Libros of Barcelona, after several months of work, study, and consultation with the Library's Network Development and

MARC Standards Office, and several test diskettes, is poised to send its first batch of records to LC via the Internet. Literatura de Vientos Tropicales (LVT), a firm marketing Central American materials, is embarking on the same process. And since LVT has bought out the highly successful Mexico Norte, materials from northern Mexico should soon be available in USMARC format. Slight increases in book costs notwithstanding, the savings in this area will be critical in order for LC to continue acquiring and collecting at the present rate in the face of dwindling budget and staff.

7. There has been concern expressed about diverting book acquisition funds to the purchase of CD-ROM and database products. Because the Library produces some of its own bibliographic products in CD-ROM format, we have been able to negotiate exchanges of costly CD-ROM products from Latin America for ours. We believe this activity will expand and will enable us to avoid an erosion of our book budget. LC is in the enviable position of having its own CD-ROM products to exchange.

8. Finally, postage expenses are being sharply reduced by using the Internet to send thousands of exchange lists to hundreds of exchange partners yearly. The savings for the Library, which operates an extensive exchange program with more than 13,000 institutions worldwide, is significant.

Perhaps some or all of the above cost-saving techniques could be applied individually or collectively by Latin American collections across the continent. In any case, if we are to maintain the collecting strength of our libraries and the balance among archival libraries without undue burden on them for accessing by other libraries, it is imperative that we adapt to the new economic and budgetary realities by reinventing at least in part the manner by which we acquire materials.

40. Ownership and Access: A Bookdealer's View of Mexico

George F. Elmendorf

The first thing to be noted about the topic ownership and access is that we are dealing with a slogan or a shorthand expression of some concepts that have practical applications. So we must first ask what the slogan means. For purposes of this paper, it is presumed that we are interested in what the slogan means in terms of libraries and, more specifically, in terms of research libraries at some level. We are also going to presume, for purposes of simplification, that we are dealing with books and other printed material, as opposed to manuscripts or other formats that are often collected by libraries.

The word ownership in this case seems straightforward: it means a library has physical proprietary possession of a book. Access is a more difficult word with many meanings to librarians. For purposes of this paper we take it unless otherwise stated to mean methods by which a library can get physical possession, either temporary or permanent, without buying an original copy for ownership.

I think it can be safely presumed that the primary reason this question should arise is money. That is to say, can money be saved by having access to any given book without taking money from the budget to buy it?

The problem I see with the notion of "Access versus Ownership" (the title of the panel at which this paper was presented) is that it has little relationship to acquiring Latin American materials. Furthermore, the subtitle of the panel proclaims "the New Library Paradigm" to which we must all learn to relate. It sounds like a class in truth whose rules we must all learn as soon as possible or fail.

I contend that the propounder(s) of this paradigm do not understand the acquisition of Latin American library materials and that SALALM members as a group are likely to shoot themselves and their libraries in the foot if they fall into line. Perhaps the librarian who suggested at the last SALALM that access versus ownership was a screen for buying databases, that there is no budget crunch but just a diversion of funds, may be right. This suggestion may be overstated, but there may also be enough truth in it to alert SALALM members.

Six years ago Mexico Norte began to examine the proposition that there is enough regional publishing in Mexico to make a significant difference in the overall bibliography of the country. During that six years Mexico Norte has published 48 lists containing approximately 15,000 titles. The monograph/serial mix is about 75 percent monographs and 25 percent serials. Nineteen states are covered and the dates of publication are 1980-1994. Close to complete coverage has been achieved from 1988 to 1994. I would say the proposition has been proven.

The Distrito Federal accounts for well over 50 percent of all material published in Mexico, but when we exclude textbooks, comics, and popular how-to books, the Library of Congress's rule of thumb that no more than 15 percent of the material published is suitable for research libraries in the United States is true.

Conversely, almost all the material published in the United States is suitable for collection by research libraries. Furthermore, 70 percent or more of all the material published in Mexico which is suitable for research libraries and which concerns the 31 states of Mexico is published in those states. It should be mentioned here that 12 states are covered by the company Mexico Sur in the same methodical fashion as the 19 states are covered by Mexico Norte.

It should be noted that virtually no attempt is made by any state or any publishing entity within those states to market their material in the United States, or, for that matter, in the Distrito Federal. The only way to acquire the material is to physically go to each state. And to avoid material going out of print, a visit every six to eight months is required.

Print runs for literature and nonfiction monographs are almost never more than 1,000 copies, and many publications have smaller print runs. The annual publication *Simposio de historia y antropología de Sonora* is now in its eighteenth year. It is one of the best publications of its kind in Mexico; it is, in fact, regional in focus, and appears in two thick volumes with a printing of 500 copies. Six solid academic publications on literature and linguistics of the frontier were published by the humanities faculty of the Universidad de Sonora in 1994 with a printing of 300 copies. Worst of all are the government documents that are never for sale and are often produced on demand in-house.

The problem of redundancy which may occur with publications from the United States simply does not happen with state publications from Mexico. When theft, mutilation, loss, and heavy use are taken into account, it becomes apparent that lack of redundancy is the more common problem. A best seller from the lists of Mexico Norte is ten copies for the entire United States. In very rare cases fifteen copies will sell. Most titles sell from five to ten copies, and often enough, only one or two orders are placed.

Appendix I shows the ranking of the twenty-seven institutions that purchase $1,000 or more annually from Mexico Norte. The 1992 rankings are included for purposes of comparison. It should be noted that Tulane University, which has dropped from the 1993 rankings, is still a collecting research library but is now regional with Mexico Sur material only.

Any institution not listed in Appendix I is not collecting at a research level of any kind in Mexico. Furthermore, $1,000 per state per year constitutes a level 3 of collecting. So we can state that there is one level 5 institution, one level 4 institution, and seven institutions between levels 3 and 4. It should be noted that some regional collectors are collecting at levels 3 to 5 in the regions of their interest. Appendix II lists five groups whose member institutions are no more than one day apart by ground transportation. The thinking behind these groupings is that scholars can access the collections of the institutions in their group via Internet/Telnet or OCLC or RLIN or by a shared database such as Melvyl at the University of California campuses.

I believe that interlibrary loan will become an increasingly less desirable way to secure materials as the *access* mode of library collecting is implemented. Insofar as there are fewer copies or only one copy of an item in the United States, the cost as well as the reluctance to willingly participate are bound to increase. At this time, copyright laws prohibit the electronic copying and transfer of complete texts of most material. Electronic abstracts may run into the same copyright problem depending on the length of the abstract and legal determinations. From a scholar's standpoint, abstracts are only useful as an annotated bibliographic reference.

The United States has been fighting hard to protect intellectual property and the copyright laws during recent international negotiations such as GATT. It is unlikely that the United States will change its position soon. It is also unlikely that Mexican authors and publishers would be willing to allow electronic duplication of their material without serious cost considerations coming into play.

If we take the most reductionist possibility and say that only one copy of any title need be purchased and physically located in the United States, how would any institution in the United States know of the existence of the titles, since all bookdealers would go out of business? Would we be back to the proposed Library of Congress Mexico City office times some number like 100? The Congress of the United States declined to finance that scheme. I suggest that there would be a higher cost per unit and a tragic loss of bibliographic control.

Return to Appendix II and use the District of Columbia group as a base of 100. That is to say, the amount of money spent per year on Mexico Norte material shall be considered 100 percent. The Southwest group would then be at 93 percent; the New England group would be at 80 percent; the Northern California group would be at 50 percent; and the Southern California group at 20 percent.

These groupings require some interpretation to be more readily understandable. Note that the 1993 rank numbers from Appendix I have been placed beside each institution. All the groups except Southern California are headed by a top-ranked institution that is fully collecting in all states and all subjects. The Southwest group has an added strength in its collections of Southwest U.S. material which are collectively the best in the country. If the New England group has any weakness, it is in serials and government documents. On the other hand, it has Princeton Theological Seminary with the best collection of religious material in the country. The Northern California group is stronger than it looks by the percentage. There are only two institutions in it, but both are full collectors and their government document collection is among the strongest in the country. The Southern California group is quite weak as there is no institution fully collecting all the states. Its collection is a level 3 border collection. The inclusion of the Los Angeles County Law Library adds a very strong all-state legal collection.

The usefulness of these groupings would be enhanced by a more sophisticated subject search capability and as many access points for searching as possible. A further aid to the scholar would be inexpensive dormitory housing and school food privileges. In some cases this already exists.

The final part of this paper is a brief consideration of two cooperative collecting consortiums for which Mexico Norte is a provider. I have included the actual approval agreements in Appendixes III and IV.

The first cooperative collecting approval plan will be called the Ephemera Group (Appendix III). Harvard, Yale, Princeton, and Princeton Theological Seminary are the participants. This plan has worked well in some topics and not so well in others. The most successful area has been religious material. Mexico Norte has both a general approval plan and an ephemera approval plan with Princeton Theological Seminary. This has meant there is no necessity to distinguish between what is ephemera and what is not. In addition, it is so broad in its profile that it amounts to "get it all." I have been led to new sources while searching for this material, and the result has been an important increase in the Mexican bibliography. Human rights and ecology are two other areas that have been successful and have led to new sources and an addition to the bibliography. An example of complete failure in locating material is the topic homosexual (gay, lesbian) and bisexual. Mexico Norte was unable to locate any sources. This is a part of a larger problem where the sources for ephemera are completely different from the sources for nonephemeral material. Mexico Norte feels confident, after meeting with the Ephemera Group, that more sources can be developed in the coming year and that the amount of material located can be increased. It is my understanding that the material will be microfilmed and made available to other libraries and that this project is a positive effort in the development of the Mexican bibliography.

The second cooperative collecting agreement includes certain University of California campuses in Southern California and pertains to border materials only (Appendix IV). The agreement, a difficult one to negotiate, was the creation of Ludwig Lauerhass. It was designed to overcome the severe budget deficiencies suffered by those UC campuses that have a history of collecting this material and did not wish to see it terminated. Several schools declined to participate as they had little collecting interest in the area. This meant that two schools had to take responsibility for two states each. Two other universities agreed to collaborate, but declined to put their participation in the form of an approval plan and to order hard copy for the states of their responsibility. I regret to say that one school is in almost complete noncompliance and, thus, has left a large deficiency of materials from one of the border states. It must be said that the three librarians active on the consortium have successfully located extra money during the first fiscal year of the project which allowed their schools to be more active than required by their contractual obligation. Mexico Norte is meeting with the consortium at SALALM and we are attempting to strengthen the collecting effort.

I would like to conclude on a positive note by reporting that a good number of the institutions that rank highest in Appendix I have assured me that their institutions have come down firmly on the ownership side and will continue to collect as vigorously as they can. One librarian told me that his institution did not consider any other option than ownership as they had no desire to degrade their collection. I would hope that Latin American librarians would not willingly participate in schemes that would result (intentionally or unintentionally) in the degradation of the collection at their institutions.

APPENDIX I

Institutional Libraries That Purchase Materials from Mexico Norte

1992

Rank [1]   Library

1   Library of Congress
2   Yale University
3   Harvard University
4   Bancroft Library, University of California, Berkeley
5   University of Texas at Austin
6   University of Arizona
7   University of Virginia
8   Princeton University
9   Stanford University
10   Los Angeles County Law Library
11   Tulane University
12   Indiana University
13   University of Colorado
14   San Diego State University
15   University of California, San Diego
16   University of Pittsburgh
17   New York Public Library
18   Southern Methodist University
19   Princeton Theological Seminary
20   University of Florida
21   La Trobe University
22   University of California, Los Angeles (UCLA)

1993

Rank [1]   Library

1   Library of Congress (F) [2]
2   University of Texas (F)
3   Harvard University (F)
4   Stanford University (F)
5   Bancroft Library, University of California, Berkeley (F); No
      literature
6   University of Arizona (F/R) [3]
7   Yale University (F)
8   New York Public Library (F)

9	University of New Mexico (R)
10	Princeton University (F); No literature
11	Princeton Theological Seminary (F); Religious only
12	University of Virginia (F)
13	University of Texas at El Paso (R)
14	New Mexico State University (R)
15	University of California, San Diego (R)
16	Los Angeles County Law Library (F); Law only
17	University of Florida (R)
18	San Diego State University (R)
19	University of California, Los Angeles (UCLA), (R)
20	University of Colorado, Boulder (F); Limited
21	University of California, Riverside (R)
22	Southern Methodist University (R)
23	University of Pittsburgh (F); Limited
24	Kansas State University (F); Limited
25	Cornell University (F); Limited
26	Indiana University (F); Limited
27	British Library (F); Limited

1. Rank number denotes institutions that purchased $1,000 or more annually from Mexico Norte.
2. F (Full): Institution buys some material from each state.
3. R (Regional): Institution buys from only one state in border region.

APPENDIX II

Regional Groupings of Institutional Libraries
That Purchase Materials from Mexico Norte

Group and Member Institutions

District of Columbia (100%)

1	Library of Congress
8	New York Public Library
12	University of Virginia

Southwest

2	University of Texas at Austin
6	University of Arizona
9	University of New Mexico
13	University of Texas at El Paso
14	New Mexico State University

New England

3	Harvard University
7	Yale University
10	Princeton University
11	Princeton Theological Seminary

Northern California

4	Stanford University
5	Bancroft Library, University of California, Berkeley

Southern California

15	University of California, San Diego
16	Los Angeles County Law Library
18	San Diego State University
19	University of California, Los Angeles (UCLA)
21	University of California, Riverside
28	University of California, Santa Barbara

APPENDIX III

Cooperative Collecting Agreement: Ephemera Group

Princeton University   Libraries
One Washington Road
Princeton, New Jersey 08544-2098

Mrs. Nira Clark   June 15, 1992
Mr. George Elmendorf
Mexico Norte
PO Box 1682
Redlands, CA 92373

Dear Nira and George,

At SALALM, Harvard, Yale, Princeton and Princeton Theological Seminary divided the topical areas of coverage for materials generally considered of ephemeral nature. Enclosed is a list of that subdivision. Given Harvard's particular circumstances, at the moment, they will work out with us financial arrangements covering their portion of coverage. Yale and Princeton will prepare microfilms of the materials and supply positive reels to Harvard.

The materials in this blanket order with you will cover the geographic area of Mexico you specialize in for scholarly works and serials. For the blanket-order materials emphasis should be placed on primary sources rather than studies about these topics. The latter we consider secondary sources and would obtain from your regular lists. Occasionally, working papers may appear from a research think-tank that in your judgment qualitatively is important and at least for Princeton, that type of imprint can be supplied.

Serials coming on the blanket order may or may not receive formal subscriptions. In cases where we do not believe more than a sample or two is worth retaining we will notify you of the fact. Otherwise, it would be appropriate to continue sending the serial as we recognize that many will be irregularly issued and no doubt of a short life span.

For Princeton, please be highly selective with posters, sending only those that have textual content not appearing in other format or that provide important graphic depictions useful for understanding the topic. Ignore those posters which are purely esthetic and repetitive of printed sources. The same observation applies to handbills: supply only those that have information not incorporated elsewhere. A sample of what is distributed should be adequate to gain a sense of the moment and materials for popular sector consumption.

Education and communication (media) as covered by Princeton should include literacy campaigns, and the use of technology in the communication industry particularly as it affects the popular sectors.

Blanket order materials should appear on a single invoice labeled "Blanket Order" and not be mixed with firm orders. Pack blanket order materials separately, ship the cheapest way possible, and the outside label should state blanket order. Credit these purchases against the deposit account.

We will review the materials carefully upon receipt and provide commentary as necessary on the appropriateness of items supplied. Thank you for your interest in obtaining these materials for us.

Sincerely, yours,

Peter T. Johnson
Bibliographer for Latin America,
Spain & Portugal

cc: D. Hazen, C. Rodríguez and D. Vorp

9341/ptj/c

APPENDIX III (Continued)

Distribution of Topical Areas of Coverage

Agrarian reform	Yale University
Children and youth	Princeton University
Education and communication (media)	Princeton University
Environment and ecology	Yale University
Ethnic groups (blacks, Indians, other)	Yale University
Homosexual (gay, lesbian) and bisexual	Princeton University
Human and civil rights (includes refugee groups)	Yale University
Labor and laboring classes (includes unions)	Yale University
Political parties, movements, alliances	Princeton University
Religious organizations, ecumenical groups and movements	Princeton Theological Seminary
Urbanization and squatter settlements	Princeton University
Women and feminists	Princeton University

APPENDIX IV

Cooperative Collecting Agreement:

Plan for the Collaborative Acquisitions
of North Mexican State Materials
among the Southern Campus Libraries of the
University of California
February 22, 1993

In recognition of the growing importance of and interest in the US/Mexico Borderland region, in order to build more effectively our library resources from the North Mexican states, and in order to assure the greatest economy in this effort, we agree to share our responsibility for the acquisition of such material by division along state lines. This collaborative approach will allow our libraries to build more extensive collections, more systematically, and at lower costs to each library than would be possible to do individually. The agreement is based on the following points:

1. The territorial responsibilities for each library are: Baja California and Tamaulipas—UCLA, Chihuahua—UCSD, Coahuila (tentative) and Sonora—UCR, and Nuevo Leon—UCSB.

2. Each library will commit up to $1,000 per year for the purchase of recent materials—either through blanket order or individual selection— from its geographic area of responsibility. Initially the blanket orders and the bulk of the selection from lists will be in collaboration with the firm Mexico Norte. The blankets will be in accord with the attached profile as adjusted to the local needs of the participating campuses. This service will be reviewed by the Southern Campus Latin American selectors on an annual basis and renewed if judged satisfactory.

3. Materials will be sent to and processed by the individual campus libraries in line with their geographic responsibilities by state.

4. Materials will be processed with reasonable haste and entered into the individual campus and Melvyl systems.

5. These materials will be made readily available on Interlibrary Loan.

6. Ultimately, in keeping with the review cycles established in each library, this material may be relocated in SRLF.

7. This agreement will not preclude further purchase or duplication of materials judged to be needed by any of our collections.

8. Each library will also endeavor to maintain serials subscriptions for the pertinent publications issued within the states for which we are responsible.

9. This agreement will go into effect as of March 1, 1993 and will be reviewed in two years by the participating Latin American Studies bibliographers.

Blanket Order Profile

I. Country of Publication: The Mexican States of Baja California and Tamaulipas (UCLA)
    Chihuahua (UCSD)
    Nuevo Leon (UCSB)
    Sonora and Coahuila (tentative) (UCR)

II. Level of Publication: University Research

III. Types of Publication: Commercial, institutions, and government

IV. Exclusions: a) Titles over $50.00 (do not send, but notify), b) Textbooks, c) Translations, d) Reprints (but do not send facsimile and new editions), e) Children's books, f) Flat maps (but do not send national atlases, commercial city plans, and road maps).

V. Periodical and Serial Publications: Send only one sample issue of new periodicals and new institutional monographic series. Separate subscription orders will be placed for those titles wanted on a continuing basis.

VI. Subjects (Relating to Latin America or expressing a Latin American point of view):

    1. Agriculture, only when of social, historical, or economic significance

    2. Anthropology and Archaeology

    3. Art and Architecture, only monographic works and catalogs, not prints or folio texts

4. Bibliography and Reference

5. Biological and Natural Science, <u>only</u> when of social, historical, or economic significance

6. Economics, <u>not</u> business administration

7. Education

8. Geography, Travel, and City Planning

9. History

10. Languages and Linguistics—Spanish and American Indian languages

11. Law, <u>only</u> constitutional

12. Literature—criticism, novels, poetry

13. Medicine, <u>only</u> when of social or historical significance

14. Music and Dance, <u>no</u> musical scores

15. Philosophy and Religion, <u>not</u> religious texts or tracts

16. Political Science and Politics, including political party pamphlets

17. Psychology, <u>only</u> social psychology

18. Sociology

19. Theater, Plays, and Film

41. Wait! I'm Wearing a White Hat! Adventures of a Librarian Turned Publisher

Sharon A. Moynahan

Much has been written about access versus ownership. A cursory review of the library literature identifies a number of articles which seem to point to the access to rather than the ownership of less used titles as a cure for runaway library acquisitions budgets. There is no question that libraries are facing financial crises as book and serial prices seem to ratchet out of control while budgets grow at a snail's pace if at all, barely keeping up with inflation. University administrations have put enormous pressure on libraries to contain their budgets and to cease being "black holes" into which enormous amounts of money are poured. Often, the only response librarians give is an urgent request for even more funds. Many of my colleagues feel that the publishing industry has taken them for a ride, and perhaps certain publishers have. However, librarians must share some of the blame for this situation, since there is, after all, a free market economy out there. I have often wondered at the librarians' preoccupation with "complete runs" of serials and have wondered how libraries thought they could keep adding serial titles without canceling any of the old ones (and breaking the complete run). Perhaps that is because I am in the social sciences and not in the physical sciences, where titles reproduce faster than the proverbial rabbits.

Many reasons for this situation have been advanced and, I am sure, many factors are involved. Often cited is the pressure to publish or perish and to publish research results, or perhaps libraries got too much (?) additional money in the early seventies and didn't have to learn how to live within budgets. The globalization of the economy and politics has led to a diversity of interests on campuses requiring a wider range of materials for scholars. While faculties have placed greater demands on library collections, there is no doubt that prices for these materials have risen faster than inflation. Wayne R. Perryman cites the Book Industry Study Group, which expected serials budgets to rise over 13.5 percent every year for a five-year period while the actual dollars for acquisition would decline by 1/3 to 1/4.[1] Finally, faced with the fact that the money available for acquisitions has reached its limits, librarians have decided that something has to be done.

One of the more popular solutions is to buy fewer books and borrow from other libraries those titles not acquired. Another is to cancel those titles whose prices have risen dramatically or simply have risen past the budget realities of that institution. These make good sense and, perhaps, should have been done a long time ago. Providing access to all titles, most from outside a particular library's collection, presents a solution that should reduce library budget pressures while assuring that scholars have access (although not always convenient access) to all that is available. For example, Margaret Ann Johnson points to the utilization of electronic information and places emphasis on the delivery of information as needed, [2] while Irene Hoadley stresses access as well as ownership and calls for cooperative resource sharing. [3] Solutions that seem at first to make sense may have consequences that will ultimately have surprising effects on those same libraries' budgets.

Taken to the limit, access over ownership would produce large cooperatives in which most libraries would have core collections of heavily used books and serial titles while a few regional libraries would acquire the resources for most upper division courses and research. A very few research libraries would acquire the rarer and rarely used titles, with responsibility for different areas carefully coordinated so that some titles would exist in perhaps only one or two libraries in the United States. In a best case scenario, many libraries could cancel 50 percent or more of their serials titles and stop acquiring numerous monographs. The dollars freed up would be used to provide access to the shared resources (online and paper indexes, CD-ROMS, electronic access, interlibrary loan, electronic transfer of text, and so on). It is certainly a rosy picture for libraries and seems to present a workable solution. Such details as copyright infringement and the inconvenience of spending a considerable portion of research time filling out interlibrary loan forms could be worked out. Publishers and users should understand and help us, since we assist the public. Surely those regional and large research libraries could stand the cost of being everyone else's resource, and, surely, that "resource" won't have to be "my" library, since we have to cut costs. Did someone out there build a collection on Rwanda? Can we borrow it?

As Executive Secretary of the Seminar on the Acquisition of Latin American Library Materials (SALALM), I suddenly found myself on the opposite side of the debate. SALALM publishes bibliographies, finding aids, information series, and papers of its annual conference. As a publisher, I felt as if I had suddenly become the problem and found the solutions offered by the librarians, the "good guys" in this debate, to threaten the organization's publishing program. I began to look at the situation from the other side of the looking glass, as it were.

Since 1990, sales seemed to be falling, and I wondered what we would charge if we could only sell fifteen copies of the annual papers. If something was shared many times by one library but not borrowed over much to any one library, should we look at filing copyright infringement charges? Why were libraries taking out their budget frustrations on small academic publishers when they seemed to have been at least partly responsible for their dilemma by not being fiscally reasonable (as opposed to responsible) earlier? Should they have stood up to the insatiable demands of the teaching faculty early on? Should they have started canceling titles which rose 15 to 50 percent a year right away? Why did they think those price increases would be just temporary? Where was the incentive for publishers to cut costs or to hold down abusive price increases when libraries always managed to come up with the money, no matter how outrageous the increases? How could I, as a librarian turned publisher, not be part of the problem?

Happily, there is a free market out there and a share of common sense to know (although it took a while) when enough is enough, and it has started to work. Libraries are again purchasing monographs! Libraries are canceling titles (sadly, SALALM has felt this trend), and, I bet, most publishers are, like us, examining their operations and managing to hold down expenses. Also, few if any libraries have taken the access solution to its limits, and most librarians have apparently been cautious about abandoning the tradition of ownership until all the ramifications have been thoroughly examined. However, this trend to access rather than acquisition will probably have some effects which may, in the end, only add to the problem, and which may call for some different solutions down the line. With this in mind, I'd like to advance some predictions.

Higher Prices for Smaller Runs

As libraries buy fewer titles and share these titles more, publishers will have to resort to smaller runs. SALALM has resorted to smaller and smaller runs and has flirted with the idea of "just in time" publishing. But publishers who sell only 500 subscriptions or less than 250 monographs per title must either raise prices or go out of business. Start-up costs, editing, cover design, print set-ups, and other costs are fixed regardless of the number of copies produced. Lynne Rienner has faced this problem and has yet to come up with a workable solution. She says:

Simply stated, there are too many books. . . . As a result of this excess, fewer copies are sold of each title—and our sales figures confirm [this]. . . . Unfortunately, though we are selling fewer copies we still have the same overhead to cover. So what do we do? We raise the prices of the books. Then [libraries] with their fixed budgets, buy fewer copies. Then we raise the prices of the books further. This goes on and on and on. [4]

Niche Publishing

SALALM has a niche, as I suspect many small publishers do. We are known for a certain type of publication with a certain level of scholarship and quality, and we serve a very specific sector of the library market. As the cancellations continue, it seems that we are now serving the "hard core" Latin American collections and cannot, at this point, envision a substantially larger market without changing the focus of our publishing. It is therefore necessary to "cut our coat to fit the cloth" in terms of both the physical appearance of books (do we staple it or Permabind it) and their content (we do better with nuts and bolts How To Do It or How to Find It titles). Within the confines of our market niche we are fairly safe and can generally, but not always, make sane, safe decisions and minimize the risks. However, we are not immune to the library acquisitions fracas, and, during this last library budget crisis, we couldn't sell even our usually hot titles. As Graham Gordon points out:

Academics ... should not forget that publishing is a risky business. When publishers look shifty they are actually just nervous. They lie awake at night wondering how it is possible to lose money on each book published or on each journal launched and still make a little money when all are put together. [5]

Nonprofits May Be the Ideal Niche Publishers

Nonprofit organizations may be the ones to produce those titles which are of interest to a limited scholarly audience. Titles that are of substantial interest to a small segment of the book-buying market may not generate enough income to support a commercial publisher. Nonprofit associations that publish benefit from several financial windfalls. For example, SALALM, in addition to its nonprofit motive, does not pay sales tax on its purchases of goods (it does on services, such as the attorney's advice), nor does it have to charge tax and keep those records. There are no fees for checking accounts, and the fees for Visa/Mastercard service are as low as possible. Additionally, many nonprofit associations are at least partly subsidized by libraries or universities. SALALM receives free office space and utilities, free phone lines, and reduced long distance charges, as well as temporary use of office furniture and a computer and a half-time salary for the Executive Secretary. Such subsidies are not unusual but are getting scarcer and scarcer as budget realities force libraries to concentrate more and more on just getting by. Many associations pay no royalties to authors, often members, who submit material for publication for the sake of scholarship rather than for personal gain. Such associations may be the last resort of published titles catering to a limited and specialized audience.

Shakeouts

Some predict that the publishing industry will collapse into the hands of a few powerful companies, while others predict the proliferation of small niche publishers. Regardless of which trend prevails, access over ownership will lead to some kind of shakeout of publishers. As weaker publishers (or those who happened to publish what didn't sell for one or two years) fail, the survivors (who are not subsidized niche publishers) might be bigger, publishing fewer titles on a wider variety of subjects. [6] Perhaps publishers will be larger or smaller, with few in the middle range. If the shakeout is successful, there may actually be less published, thus sparing libraries' budgets. There are others who suggest that publish or perish needs of university faculties will exert the opposite influence. [7] It will be interesting to see which trend wins out and what libraries and publishers will do.

NOTES

1. Wayne R. Perryman, "The Changing Landscape of Information Access: The Impact of Technological Advances upon the Acquisition, Ownership and Dissemination of Information Resources within the Research Library Community," *Journal of Library Administration* 15:1/2 (1991), 74.

2. Margaret Ann Johnson, "When Pigs Fly: Or, When Access Equals Ownership," *Technicalities* 12 (February 1992), 4-6.

3. Irene Braden Hoadley, "Access vs. Ownership: Myth or Reality," *Library Acquisitions* 17 (Summer 1993), 192.

4. Lynne Rienner, "Is the Sky Falling? Scholarly Publishing in the 1990s," in Deborah L. Jakubs, ed., *Latin American Studies into the Twenty-First Century: New Focus, New Formats, New Challenges,* Papers of SALALM XXXVI, San Diego, California, June 1-6, 1991 (Albuquerque, NM: SALALM, 1993), p. 159.

5. Gordon Graham, "The Relationship between Publishers and Academics," *Scholarly Publishing* 24:1 (October 1992), 23.

6. Ibid, p. 22.

7. Dennis P. Carrigan, "Publish or Perish: The Troubled State of Scholarly Communication," *Scholarly Publishing* 22:3 (April 1991), 139.

BIBLIOGRAPHY

Carrigan, Dennis P. "Publish or Perish: The Troubled State of Scholarly Communication." *Scholarly Publishing* 22:3 (April 1991), [131]-142.

Graham, Gordon. "The Relationship between Publishers and Academics." *Scholarly Publishing* 24:1 (October 1992), [13]-23.

Hoadley, Irene Braden. "Access vs. Ownership: Myth or Reality." *Library Acquisitions* 17 (Summer 1993), 191-195.

Johnson, Margaret Ann. "When Pigs Fly: Or, When Access Equals Ownership." *Technicalities* 12 (February 1992), 4-7.

Morris, James McGrath. "Is This Book Making Money? How to Determine the Profitability of a Title." *Small Press* 10 (Spring 1992), 26-29.

Perryman, Wayne R. "The Changing Landscape of Information Access: The Impact of Technological Advances upon the Acquisition, Ownership and Dissemination of Information Resources within the Research Library Community." *Journal of Library Administration* 15:1/2 (1991), 73-93.

Rienner, Lynne. "Is the Sky Falling? Scholarly Publishing in the 1990s." In Deborah L. Jakubs, ed., *Latin American Studies into the Twenty-First Century: New Focus, New Formats, New Challenges.* Papers of SALALM XXXVI, San Diego, California, June 1-6, 1991. Albuquerque, NM: SALALM, 1993. Pp. 159-164.

Tyckoson, David. "Access vs. Ownership: Changing Roles for Librarians." *The Reference Librarian* 34 (1991), 37-45.

42. Latin American Different Editions: The "Dup"-ing of the Academic Library

John B. Wright

I would like to share with you two memories I have of previous SALALM conferences. My intention for doing so, with regard to this panel's theme—the cataloging of Latin American literature—lies in the hope that the past might be able to offer instruction for our present situation as well as to help chart possibilities for the future.

The first memory comes from SALALM in San Diego three years ago in a session with Lynne Rienner, who described a "crisis" in the publishing world. She called it a crisis because she could not think of a better word. We came to understand that the crisis she lamented is the fact that there are just too many books.[1]

My second memory happened two years ago when I gave a report of our successful elimination of the 16,000+ backlog of Spanish and Portuguese materials at Brigham Young University (BYU). At the time, we were very excited to have completed the processing of the backlog and we were confident, perhaps somewhat overly so, in our ability to keep up with the incoming materials. The intervening years have witnessed the opening of the floodgates. Latin American materials keep pouring in at a faster rate than our library is able to process them. I have to agree with Lynne: There are just too many books. I also have to agree with her that perhaps the problem is that there are just too many unnecessary books.

As librarians, we often consider backlogs as dragons to be fought. There are a few twisted members of our profession who euphemistically call these ubiquitous fire-breathers by the simple, and more positive, title "job security." But for me, backlogs are a constant source of irritation. I found, however, through our 2½-year experience of working with BYU's backlog, that there exists at least one value of having a backlog—seeing the current collection in monolithic proportions.

As I worked through the thousands of books added to our collection from 1984 to 1989, I stumbled across something truly interesting. I think I have discovered one source of unnecessary books, whose existence—or should I say preponderance—Lynne Rienner and I lament. These are the Latin American different editions—or "difeds" as we commonly call them.

I found that some difeds were not difeds at all but actually duplicates. Now, I realize that all difeds and duplicates are, practically speaking, alike. But there is something new here; there is something a little bit different. These difeds represent items with varying degrees of problems that result in the duplication of items in the library. These will be encountered by an array of library employees and friends. For example, first is Vendor A who sends us a book published in Country A because the subject matter exactly matches the profile we have established with that vendor. At the same time, Vendor B unknowingly sends us a different edition of the same work published in country B because it too exactly matches the established profile. Next is the subject selector who accepts both approval items. Then comes the acquisitions searcher/bibliographic controller who checks new titles against the library's current catalog. The item finally arrives at the cataloger's desk. Unfortunately, the item is usually cataloged and added to the stacks. Throughout this entire process, various individuals are working with the best professional intentions, and yet, the difed still makes its way into the library. Occasionally, however, they are discovered. The individual making the discovery may often vary, but certainly the difed must be identified and steps should be taken to avoid this duplication of items.

I have brought several examples of Latin American difeds to demonstrate the abundance of unnecessary publications which hamper our ability to handle the influx of Latin American materials. I have artificially classified them into five types of difeds, which will allow me to discuss certain common features of each. Although I lack Laurence Hallewell's potentially omniscient understanding of Latin American publishing, my purpose today is to discuss each type of difed, propose possible reasons for its occurrence, and give suggestions as to how we might deal with these types of difeds while cataloging.

Type 1. Same book published in different places at the same time or at different times

Example—The book entitled *Mi General Torrijos* by José de Jesús Martínez was published during the years 1987-1988. In 1987, Editorial Legado secured the rights to produce this item in Costa Rica. In 1988, the publishing firm of Presencia Latinoamericana, S.A. produced the book in Mexico. These two books represent the most common difed occurrences that most of us will encounter.

Possible reason for its existence—One of the unique anomalies in Latin American publishing is the existence of so many individual countries sharing a common language. Sally A. Taylor, in a series of articles

appearing in the May 17, 1993, issue of *Publisher's Weekly,* discusses the
reviving market of Latin American publishing. In interviews with several
individuals, Taylor uncovers a possible reason why this type of difed
occurs: Each member of the Latin American publishing market fights to
gain exclusive rights to publish a given manuscript. In an interview with
Taylor, Trinidad Vergara of Argentina's Javier Vergara Editor indicates that
their company tries "hard to get all Spanish-language rights, but one
problem is that the agents want to split rights. When an author is too
expensive, we will split between Latin America and Spain."[2] One reason
this type of difed occurs, then, is that obtaining the rights to publish and
market a certain author's work in all the Spanish world is too costly for a
single publisher. The rights are divided between two or more publishers,
each possessing the rights to publish and market that work in a particular
area of the world.

   Cataloging suggestion—Just keep one. There is no need to collect all
the different editions. It is a waste of time to do anything other than return
the duplicate book.

Type 2. Same book published in different places with slightly different title because of place of publication

   Example—In 1986, Laura Restrepo, a Colombian journalist, produced
an exciting work which documents her intermediary experiences in the
discussion held in 1984 between two Colombian guerrilla groups, the
Movimiento 19 de Abril and the Ejército de Liberación Popular. She titled
her manuscript *Historia de una Traición.* It was published by Plaza & Janés
editores in their Colombian office. It was also published the same year in
Madrid, Spain, as a joint venture by IEPALA and Editorial Fundamentos.
They produced the work under the title *Colombia, Historia de una Traición.*

   Possible reason for its existence—This variance in title is obvious: the
Spanish publisher wants to tell the potential purchaser that this work is
about Colombia.

   Cataloging suggestion—I just keep one, but supply a note indicating
that this book is being simultaneously published in [country] under a variant
title. Attaching an author/title added-entry would also help to tie these two
titles together. For example:

> 500::laThis work simultaneously published in Madrid, Spain,
> under the title: Colombia, historia de una traición.
>
> 700:10:laRestrepo, Laura.ltColombia, historia de una traición.

Type 3. Collection of articles published first as a volume in a serial, reprinted in monographic form

Example—All these difeds are not unique to Spanish language materials. Here is an example from Brazil. The serial *Tempo brasileiro* 112 (Jan.-Mar. 1993) contains a collection of articles describing the philosophy of civilization and human existence grouped together under the title "Transcendência e mundo, na virada do século." In 1993, these articles were also published and distributed in book form by Topbooks Editora e Distribuidora de Livros Ltda. under the same title: *Transcendência e mundo na virada do século.*

Possible reason for its existence—This type is fairly self-explanatory. The collection of articles, because monographic in subject, lent itself nicely to a monographic publication.

Cataloging suggestion—Acquiring both of these, although theoretically unnecessary, may be a good idea if the institution is cataloging *Tempo brasileiro* as a serial. Because of each issue's monographic-like emphasis on a particular topic, it may be to an institution's advantage to catalog these separate issues as monographs, treating the serial title as a series title. For example:

> 440: 0:laTempo brasileiro ;lvno. 112

Or, as in our library's case, the decision was made to treat *Tempo brasileiro* as a serial. There is one bibliographic record covering all issues of this serial. When the monographic edition of this work is cataloged, a note indicating that its contents existed previously in the serial issue should be included in the bibliographic record for the book. A title tracing should also be made to tie this to the name of the serial. For example:

> 500: :laThese collected articles appeared as no. 112 in Tempo brasileiro.
>
> 730:01:Tempo brasileiro.

Type 4. A revised edition (published under the same or different title, by same or different publisher)

Example—I have two editions written by Paco Ignacio Taibo II and Rogelio Vizcaíno A., and both deal with the Escuderista movement. The first edition, copublished in 1983 by the Mexican publishers Editorial Extemporáneos and Información Obrera, appeared under the title *El Socialismo en un solo puerto: Acapulco 1919-1923.* The revised edition, published in 1990, once again by a Mexican publisher, Editorial Joaquín Mortiz, S.A. de C.V., was entitled *Las dos muertes de Juan R. Escudero: la comuna de Acapulco, 1918-1923.* What is unique about this difed is that in the revised edition we are told about the existence of the earlier edition. The note to the reader, although buried in a preface statement, reads as follows: "Se advierte a los lectores que la presente es versión corregida y aumentada del libro publicado en 1983 bajo el título *El socialismo en un solo puerto.*"[3] That the information is mentioned is good, but it would be clearer if it were printed in a more conspicuous place. Its absence in all the customary places—the title page, the verso, the colophon—leaves the cataloger without a clear understanding as to the relationship of this edition to the other title.

Possible reason for its existence—Like the preceding type, this difed is somewhat self-explanatory. A publisher received the rights to issue a revised edition of an earlier publication. It is strange that a different publisher was chosen and that the title was so drastically different. One can only speculate as to the reasons why these decisions were made.

Cataloging suggestion—In the revised edition a note and author/title added-entries need to be added to the bibliographic record to indicate its relationship with the former edition. For example:

> 500: :laRev. ed. of the authors' El socialismo en un solo puerto, which appeared in 1983.

or,

> 500: :la "La presente es versión corregida y aumentada del libro publicado en 1983 bajo el título El socialismo en un solo puerto."—p. 8.

and,

> 240:10:laSocialismo en un solo puerto

or,

> 700:10:laTaibo, Paco Ignacio,ld1949- ltSocialismo en un solo puerto.
>
> 700:20:laVizcaíno A., Rogelio.ltSocialismo en un solo puerto.

It would be helpful to add a note and author/title added-entries to the former edition as well. For example:

> 500: :laRev. ed. published in 1990 as: Las dos muertes de Juan R. Escudero.
>
> 700:10:laTaibo, Paco Ignacio,ld1949- ltDos muertes de Juan R. Escudero.
>
> 700:20:laVizcaíno A., Rogelio.ltDos muertes de Juan R. Escudero.

Type 5. Tricks of the trade

I have classified this difed type as "Tricks of the trade" simply because I cannot find a common characteristic among the examples I have, except that they seem to be a combination of elements mentioned in the other difed types. They may have the same or different publishing date. They are published in different areas, and the titles are markedly different for no apparent reason. This may be just a catch-all difed. Of the five types of difeds, however, this is the most problematic because I cannot identify a system, other than serendipity, to track it down in our existing databases, nor can I pinpoint a fail-safe way to catch this difed as it comes across our cataloging desks. Fortunately, these titles were drawn to my attention because of the previously mentioned benefit associated with cataloging a backlog. These difeds also give me the impression that I'm being cheated. They appear to be blatant attempts to increase sales, give the author(s) additional scholarly credit, and intentionally dupe the academic library community. This type of difed tends to consist of books that have as their subject content current news-related topics, even as cover stories of the pseudo-journalistic programming on television. Indeed, the titles of these books sound hyped and sensationalized, and the packaging and their cover art seem based entirely on their ability to sell.

Example—The first example covers the capture as well as the recounting of certain aspects of the life of Klaus Barbie. The three items in this example are all authored by Gustavo Sánchez S. and Elisabeth Reimann and appeared during 1987. (The Cuban edition was published in 1988.) I have two of the three editions of this book. The first example includes an edition published in Buenos Aires by Editorial Legasa entitled *Barbie, criminal hasta el fin* and an edition published in Bolivia by the Federación de Trabajadores de la Prensa de Bolivia entitled *Barbie en Bolivia: criminal hasta el fin*. The other title found in the national databases is *Klaus Barbie en Bolivia: criminal hasta el fin* and was published in Cuba by Editorial Ciencias Sociales. Another edition under the same title was published in Barcelona by Ediciones B. The contents of these editions are exactly the same. They really are not difeds at all. Between the covers of each, there is no mention whatsoever of the other editions.

The second example, again, involves a "hot issue" topic—the contras and their war in Nicaragua. They are all authored by Elisabeth Reimann and all appeared in 1985-1987. The edition published in Argentina by Editorial Legasa is entitled *Confesiones de un contra*. Another edition, published in Mexico by Ediciones El Caballito, is entitled *La historia de Moisés: yo fuí un paladín de la libertad*.

Claire-lise Bernaud brought an edition published in Nicaragua by Vanguardia entitled *Yo fuí un contra* and another edition published in Peru by Editorial Horizonte entitled *Historia de Moisés*. Again, there is no mention of the other editions and the contents are exactly the same.

Possible reasons for its existence—I can offer a few possibilities to explain the abundance in our libraries of this type of difed. Alberto E.

Augsberger, in his article "Publishing in Latin America: An Overview," mentions that since 1973 two book laws have been adopted in Latin America to help control copyright issues. He states that

with the exception of these book laws, no state has adopted clearly defined book policies. There is a serious shortage of the reliable, up-to-date information needed to ascertain annual production—titles and print size, original works and translations, first editions and reprints or new editions, and so on. Although most countries have made it legally obligatory to deposit works to secure copyright protection, they do not maintain the copyright registers in a manner conducive to compiling statistics and classifying available information.[4]

With this in mind, it is possible that each publisher may have deposited its edition of this work to secure publishing rights without knowing the others had done so. It is plausible to assume that duplication was not caught because a system of checking may not be in place.

Another possibility for the occurrence of this type of difed is suggested by Philip G. Altbach and Eva-Maria Rathgeber who explain that "when a book . . . produced by an author or a small local publisher proves to have a modest level of success, it is reprinted or brought out in a second edition by a larger publisher."[5] They also explain that the primary motivation for writing a book for most scholarly authors may be from a genuine desire to share new ideas, the need for a book dealing with a certain issue, or just a desire to publish a book in order to fulfill promotion and rank advancement requirements.[6] Another explanation may be that the various publishers produce these books for their individual countries or areas of distribution, marketing them in whatever way will be most appealing to their potential buyers. Academic libraries, of course, would have the misfortune of collecting from all countries, thus creating the potential of duplication themselves.

These may all be legitimate explanations for the existence of this difed. In fact, they probably are exactly the reasons why it does occur. However, maybe because we do not really know how the difeds are produced, the suspicion remains that they are an intentional attempt to take advantage of a good thing. Whatever the reason, we now know that difeds exist and must now concern ourselves with what to do with them to make the information accessible to the people visiting our libraries.

Cataloging suggestion—Make a uniform title to allow the variant titles to index under one particular title. I chose to use the title from the place the item was first published. If more than one item appeared at the same time, I would select as my uniform title the one used on the item being published in the country where the subject content occurs. In the case of Klaus Barbie, I would use *Barbie en Bolivia.* In the case of the contras I would use the title *Historia de Moisés.* I would also make notes in the bibliographic records indicating the existence of the difeds with variant titles.

What are the future implications of Latin American difeds in our business of cataloging? As John P. Dyson said at the 1975 SALALM conference: "Existe la noción muy divulgada y, en mi experiencia, muy errónea, de que el mayor mercado para el libro en castellano en los Estados Unidos es la comunidad hispanoparlante." As a book vendor in the Midwest, it was his experience that "todo movimiento de materia editorial, sin excepción, se hace en virtud de una condicion única: la experiencia académica."[7] Based on Dyson's statement, and based on what appears to be a sizable sum spent annually for Latin American materials in U.S. institutions of higher learning, I think it is quite reasonable to state that the academic library community is an important market for Latin American materials.[8]

These occurrences happen as we purchase materials from Latin America. After periodically examining this problem for the past three years, and after reading several articles on the subject of Latin American printing and publishing, I cannot offer a foolproof method for catching these items and eliminating them at the vendor's point of receipt. The items can only be caught at the library, generally by catalogers who examine these materials, item by item.

So then, what can be done in the profiles we have set up with our individual vendors? Nothing. I think the profiles have been fine-tuned over a period of years to ensure that we are getting what we want. Can more training be done on the part of the library personnel to catch, or at least to notice, these difed types? Yes, I think the employees who perform pre-order searching and receipt ought to be trained to recognize these Latin American difed problems. Do our employees understand Spanish and Portuguese well enough to catch these difeds when the materials are in the acquisitions department? What about us as catalogers? Can we be more aware of what is going into our respective collections? Can we look at our cataloging as creating a catalog for a collection and not simply as a piecemeal operation of processing items in isolation? How can we as members of SALALM encourage the continued growth and revitalization of the Latin American publishing industry? Perhaps, the best way is simply to continue buying materials from Latin America.

One related problem is the misunderstanding of the word "edición." Does it mean edition, printing, reissue? I think that we as catalogers need to understand, from the Latin American point of view, just what it means. I recently read with interest a discussion on the Internet dealing with this very topic. A rather respected cataloger even suggested that as catalogers we are simply describing the item as it is, without passing any judgment or interpretation on the information found in the item. If the verso says 5a. edición, we should not question the legitimacy of the information. We should just record it in the 250 field according to the AACR2 rules. That indicates to me a very monolingual view of looking at the world. There are difficulties in applying Anglo-American rules to materials that come from Latin America. We use the rules as guidelines, but I think it is implicit in our roles as catalogers of Latin American materials to make those kinds of interpretations and judgments as to the meaning of the information found in the item in hand. That is why finding these dups will be a job that will fall almost entirely on the shoulders of the cataloger.

We do have a problem. We are acquiring unnecessary items in our collections. Just as Lynne Rienner did three years ago, we must ask ourselves: "Is the sky falling?" I hope that this presentation has not filled us with gloom. I have identified five types of difeds, discussed the possible reasons for the existence of each, and offered suggestions as to how we can deal with them in our individual cataloging assignments.

I would like to share with you one more memory which comes from a class that I took as an undergraduate. We were reading and discussing the essays of William James and evaluating the implications of that experience in our individual lives. I remember reading his classic essay "The Will to Believe" and being particularly struck by his discussion of knowing truth and avoiding error. He states: "We must know the truth; and we must avoid error—these are our first and great commandments as would-be knowers; but they are not two ways of stating an identical commandment, they are two separable laws."[9] I came to realize that the search to know truth did not equate with the avoidance of error. In fact, in my search for truth, I would undoubtedly encounter error. The true journey of the would-be knower includes the action taken as one seeks to know truth. The person who is afraid to search for fear of encountering error—for fear of being duped—loses the opportunity of finding truth as surely as the person who seeks not at all. James states: "For my own part, I have also a horror of being duped; but I can believe that worse things than being duped may happen to a man in this world."[10]

I, too, believe that there are worse things than being duped. And that goes for the library. There are worse things than receiving duplicates in the guise of difeds. The task of acquiring and making available items of truth makes our occasional run-ins with problems and with error all the more important because it shows that we are acting. And in this case, our action, which is our continuing to acquire, buy, and develop these collections of Latin American materials, may be the very thing that saves us all.[11]

NOTES

1. Lynne Rienner, "Is the Sky Falling? Scholarly Publishing in the 1990s," in Deborah L. Jakubs, ed., *Latin American Studies into the Twenty-First Century: New Focus, New Formats, New Challenges*, Papers of SALALM XXXVI (Albuquerque, NM: SALALM Secretariat, 1993), pp. 159-164.

2. Sally A. Taylor, "Argentina: Reaching Out," *Publisher's Weekly* 240 (May 17, 1993), S15.

3. Paco Ignacio Taibo, II and Rogelio Vizcaíno A., *Las dos muertes de Juan R. Escudero: la comuna de Acapulco, 1918-1923* (Mexico: Editorial Joaquín Mortiz, 1990), p. 8.

4. Alberto E. Augsberger, "Publishing in Latin America: An Overview," in Philip G. Altbach et al., *Publishing in The Third World: Knowledge and Development* (Portsmouth, NH: Heinemann, 1985), p. 160.

5. Philip G. Altbach and Eva-Maria Rathgeber, *Publishing in the Third World: Trend Report and Bibliography* (New York: Praeger, 1980), p. 29.

6. Ibid, pp. 33-34.

7. John P. Dyson, "La distribución del libro en castellano en los Estados Unidos: Otra perspectiva," in Pauline P. Collins, ed., *New Writers of Latin America: Final Report and Working Papers of the Twentieth Seminar on the Acquisition of Latin American Library Materials* (Austin, TX: SALALM, 1978), p. 180.

8. Dyson is not the only one who recognizes the important relationship between the United States and Latin American publications. In her interviews with various Latin American publishers, Sally Taylor learned that the U.S. buyers of Latin American materials are valued not because of the quantity of purchase but because they promptly pay for the materials. Many publishers value this and consider it a rarity in their normal business with other buyers. (Please see *Publisher's Weekly* 240 [May 17, 1993], S18.) BYU currently acquires an average of 363 items a month from seven Latin American vendors, spending approximately $6100.00. That averages $16.85 per item. In other words, if we had caught these difeds we could have purchased other books that would have helped our collection.

9. William James, "The Will to Believe," in Alburey Castell, ed., *Essays in Pragmatism* (New York: Hafner Press, 1948), pp. 88-109.

10. Ibid, p. 100.

11. Of course, I am speaking literally (or would pragmatically be a better word?) and not religiously. As buyers, we need the book publishers as much as they need us. We are both dependent on the other for our very existence. I'm not saying that selling in the U.S. market is a life or death situation for these publishers. What I am implying is that we as buyers need publishers to create the materials that we buy; publishers need buyers of their products so that they can have the necessary capital to continue producing. The fact that academic libraries continue to purchase Latin American materials allows the publishing industries to constantly grow. For a very interesting article on the increasingly difficult relationships among Publisher/Library/Reader, see Gordon Graham's "Publishers, Librarians and Readers," *Publishers Weekly* 238 (Jan. 18, 1991), S4.

43. Latin American Newspapers: Considerations in CD-ROM Publishing

Dan Havercamp

Research Publications International (RPI) is a publisher that traditionally has been known for its microform collections. In the past year, RPI has been making strong progress in efforts to expand into the area of CD-ROM and electronic publications. RPI has been in business since 1966, principally offering research collections and newspaper backfiles with current subscriptions available in microform or CD-ROM. In addition, it has been involved in many preservation projects under contract with individual libraries.

My comments revolve around the concerns of CD-ROM publication. My first professional position was at the Universidad Iberoamericana, in Mexico City, and since then I have remained involved, to one degree or another, around the edges of Latin American librarianship. Research Publications has asked me to take responsibility for our Latin American client base and to work closely with our Editorial Department on the development of new publications of Latin American materials, as well as materials from other regions that may be of interest to libraries in Latin America. I have had a number of conversations with SALALM members about your interest in preserving and publishing Latin American newspapers on film and/or CD-ROM. Research Publications is very much open to suggestions of titles that perhaps we should consider including in our project. It has the staff, the technical resources, and the experience to undertake a publication project of Latin American newspapers. This presentation is our progress report to you on our findings so far, as we consider this project.

1. The first consideration that we discussed was this: would Latin American newspapers fit our niche? We have a history of reproducing newspapers from outside the United States, in microform and, in recent years, in CD-ROM. We have contracts, for example, with *The Times* of London, *LeMonde*, Spain's *El País*, and twenty other newspapers from Europe, the Middle East, Asia, and Oceania. There is a lack of titles from Latin America and Africa, so we are interested in including those regions at some point. At the present time Latin America is the next region we would like to see represented in our title list.

We are aware of rumors of Latin American newspapers becoming available on compact disc. Yet when we begin to track down their availability, we usually discover that, in fact, these publications on CD-ROM are not yet available, or never get off the ground. To date we have confirmed the existence of only one Latin American newspaper actually currently available on CD-ROM. I would greatly appreciate hearing from other SALALM members if, in fact, there are more newspaper titles in the region currently being published in this format. Therefore, the newspapers of record of most Latin American countries are still available only as current subscriptions or as microform backfiles. Certainly, the opportunities to publish the region's newspapers on CD-ROM are there in abundance.

2. Before we even begin to concern ourselves about the production and sales aspects, we need to consider the acquisition of rights to publish newspapers in this format. Rights for reproduction can either be exclusive or nonexclusive. For most titles, Research Publications (as well as many other publishers) will seek exclusive rights of distribution for a given format. This makes sense from a business standpoint, especially when an investment will be in a title that will have limited appeal because of subject or geographic specialization. When publications are considered to be in the realm of public domain, the exclusivity issue goes out the window, and then it becomes more a question of who gets to market first with those titles.

Even when a newspaper grants a CD-ROM or microform publisher exclusive rights to reproduce its backfiles and current publication, we run into another rights or copyright issue. Generally only those portions of the newspaper that were written by the staff of that journal, or for which the newspaper has reproduction rights, can be reproduced. This issue must be examined newspaper by newspaper when considering news agency files or columnists under syndication. In some cases the newspaper will have the right to license or transfer the rights to a third party, but most times they will not.

3. Near and dear to any publisher's heart is the next consideration: the market size of the proposed publication. Assuming that one can obtain exclusive rights to publish the CD-ROM version, it is safe to assume that the market, for example, for Mexico's *Unomásuno* will be larger than for the major newspaper of a much smaller nation. Nonetheless, if one were to look even at a title such as *Unomásuno* or *O jornal do Brasil*, the total universe of potential subscribers to the CD-ROM version needs to be estimated without assuming upfront that it will be a commercial success. Is it cost effective for a commercial publisher to undertake the production of this CD? To answer that question, we now move on to another consideration: the costs of production and distribution.

4. First, scanning devices, that wonderful technology that saves us from having to key into a computer the text that we wish to reproduce, are at a stage of evolution in which the quality and regularity of scanning are still tricky enough that scanning from microfilm produces a more even, uniform output than does scanning from the original newspaper print version. Scanning microfilm offers an evenness of contrast that is not found when scanning newsprint. Today's scanners, at least those available at a reasonable price, are still not sophisticated enough to adjust automatically to variances in print, or to light contrast. But the scanners that we regularly use do a very creditable job scanning microfilm. This means that we may need to film the newspaper first, before creating the CD-ROM. If the title has already been filmed by another organization, we must first examine the quality of the film to ensure that it is of sufficiently high quality to be scanned. (This, of course, raises the question: if it is already available on film, will there be a market for the CD-ROM version?) Once the film has been scanned, the electronic file has been developed, and we have mounted the files on the search engine software, we can send the tapes to our CD-ROM manufacturer. In order to get to the point of mastering the compact disc, we need to expect to invest approximately $100,000. Obviously, a nonprofit institution, or an organization located in a place where labor costs are lower than they are in urban Connecticut, may be able to produce the CD-ROM for less. Much of the editorial cost, and some of the microfilming cost, in an academic institution may already be "hidden" in the institutional budget. However, for a product such as *LeMonde*, for example, for which RPI masters CD-ROMs four times per year, there is a significant capital expense involved. It is one of the reasons why not many newspaper publishers attempt to do this on their own.

For the sake of argument, assume that the additional marketing and sales costs of introducing a new CD-ROM title can be folded into the existing organizational structure. Adding a new title to the next catalog or producing one new brochure is not usually a major expense, compared with the preparation of the publication itself. This translates into the following calculation. In order just to break even on a capital expense of $100,000 for a new CD-ROM title, one must expect to sell at least fifty copies at $2,000 apiece, or a hundred copies at $1,000, and so forth.

5. This brings us to the tough decision regarding which newspapers to select for possible CD-ROM publication. The economic viability of a title or group of titles needs to be assessed before making the final decision to pursue the acquisition or rights. As RPI continues to look at a list of obvious Latin American newspaper titles, some SALALM members will be contacted for input. Would we be better off, both from publishing and library perspectives, with a focus on a few key newspaper titles for which

we would be building a historical archive on CD-ROM? Or, perhaps, should we consider specialized, finite products, such as publishing selected short runs from several newspapers from one country, to cover a particular historic event or time period? In this case we would be considering a one-time publication, involving a finite investment. A CD-ROM that covers certain events in Latin American history may be preferable from a library's budgetary viewpoint, as it would not involve the commitment to an expensive subscription.

6. When considering the potential market for subscriptions to a particular CD-ROM title, we try to look beyond our traditional market. Academic research libraries are just one part of the potential body of subscribers. We would look for ways to distribute new titles to larger public libraries, to national libraries, and to certain special libraries. If the SALALM pie is too small to support a particular new publication, we would look to expand the pie to include other segments of the market. Research Publications International seeks your input of suggestions for new CD-ROM titles.

II

The State of the Art in the
Publishing Industry

44. Nuevas temáticas y nuevos enfoques en la labor editorial latinoamericana

Adalberto Santana

El presente trabajo tiene por objeto mostrar las nuevas temáticas y enfoques que se realizan dentro de la labor editorial latinoamericana, en particular aquella que corresponde al trabajo editorial que se lleva a cabo en el Centro Coordinador y Difusor de Estudios Latinoamericanos (CCyDEL) y en la revista *Cuadernos Americanos*. Debido a que el CCyDEL es uno de los pocos centros de América Latina y el mundo dedicados a la difusión y coordinación de los estudios latinoamericanos, y en virtud de que una de sus actividades principales es la publicación de obras de este carácter, consideramos conveniente dar a conocer las temáticas y enfoques que se presentan en sus ediciones. Sobre todo al considerar que este panel está orientado a la adquisición de materiales bibliográficos latinoamericanos desde el punto de vista latinoamericano.

Para introducirnos en el tema específico del trabajo editorial de la revista *Cuadernos Americanos* y del Centro Coordinador y Difusor de Estudios Latinoamericanos, en primer lugar nos referiremos a buena parte de las funciones que realizan estas dos entidades académicas universitarias. Mencionaremos brevemente que ambas forman parte del quehacer de la Universidad Nacional Autónoma de México, particularmente en el ámbito de la investigación sobre América Latina y en la difusión de los estudios latinoamericanos. De igual forma esas dos entidades apoyan el trabajo de investigación y difusión de los estudios latinoamericanos en otras instituciones dedicadas al tema en la región, Norteamérica, Europa y el resto del mundo. Cabe señalar que el CCyDEL es un organismo asociado no gubernamental de la UNESCO, que a su vez coordina la Sociedad Latinoamericana de Estudios sobre América Latina y el Caribe (SOLAR) y la Federación Internacional de Estudios sobre América Latina y el Caribe (FIEALC),[1] entidades que reciben los materiales publicados y pueden a la vez presentar propuestas de edición.

Esto quiere decir que buena parte de las publicaciones que editan tanto el CCyDEL como *Cuadernos Americanos,* corresponde a una serie de autores provenientes de distintos países, con temas y enfoques diversos, los cuales tienen algo en común: compartir la publicación de un ensayo referido a una temática y a un enfoque latinoamericano.

Los artículos que se publican en el CCyDEL y *Cuadernos Americanos* tienen como requisitos esenciales para ser editadas: (*a*) contar con un rigor académico y que el trabajo resulte favorablemente dictaminado, y (*b*) que el trabajo tenga como reflexión central un tema latinoamericano.

Refiriéndonos a los antecedentes y condiciones actuales en que se desarrolla la revista *Cuadernos Americanos,* podemos abarcarlos con los siguientes aspectos. *Cuadernos Americanos* es la pionera de las publicaciones periódicas latinoamericanas y de aquellas que ostentan un profundo espíritu latinoamericanista. *Cuadernos Americanos* se fundó en la Ciudad de México en 1942, por un grupo de destacados intelectuales mexicanos y españoles —estos últimos refugiados en tierras mexicanas como consecuencia de la Guerra Civil Española. Fue su primer director el economista e historiador Jesús Silva Herzog. A la muerte de éste, en 1985, la revista siguió apareciendo en su segunda época. En el año de 1987, de acuerdo a la voluntad de su Director Fundador y por decisión de la Junta de Gobierno de *Cuadernos Americanos,* la revista dio comienzo a su Nueva Epoca. En este período quedó bajo la responsabilidad de la Universidad Nacional Autónoma de México, la que nombró como su nuevo director al eminente filósofo Leopoldo Zea.

Cuadernos Americanos en su Nueva Epoca continua como un lugar de encuentro y tribuna de la reflexión de destacados intelectuales y académicos de Latinoamérica y de diversas regiones del mundo. En la actualidad lleva editados 44 números desde enero-febrero de 1987 hasta marzo-abril de 1994, con una periodicidad bimestral y un tiraje de 2000 ejemplares. Sería bien recordar que por su volumen, la revista *Cuadernos Americanos* tiene propiamente el formato de un libro. Por su mismo formato, regularmente cuenta con un número estimado de más de 250 páginas.

La circulación y distribución internacional de *Cuadernos Americanos* se realiza en cuatro continentes, ya sea por medio del intercambio, canje y suscripciones en 19 países del continente americano, 18 de Europa, 3 de Asia y 1 de Oceanía y 1 de Africa, lo que suma un total de 649 ejemplares en su distribución internacional. Entre los países donde *Cuadernos Americanos* tiene una mayor distribución se destacan los Estados Unidos de Norteamérica, a los que se envía un estimado de 357 ejemplares, es decir, casi un 20% de su edición. A esto se suma la compra directa que realizan diversas agencias internacionales, con sede en Suiza, Francia y Canadá.

En lo que se refiere a la distribución nacional de *Cuadernos Americanos,* al intercambio y canje con otras publicaciones y el rubro de suscripciones, circulan en el territorio mexicano más de 300 ejemplares. Habría que apuntar que otro canal de distribución de la revista se realiza a través de los circuitos de las librerías universitarias y de algunas librerías particulares, especialmente en la zona metropolitana de la ciudad de México.

Existe otro canal de distribución, el cual se desarrolla en una forma más esporádica pero que tiene un sustantivo impacto para el crecimiento de su distribución. Nos referimos a la presentación de la revista en congresos académicos y en la participación en ferias de libros, ya sean universitarias, nacionales o internacionales.

Ligada a estos canales de distribución, la labor editorial de *Cuadernos Americanos* también se genera a través del intercambio de anuncios y publicidad, hecho que permite tomar contacto con una serie de publicaciones periódicas con propósitos e intereses semejantes. Tan sólo en el número 44 de la revista se publicaron 22 anuncios tanto nacionales como internacionales. De igual forma se logró que los anuncios de la revista se insertaran en 20 publicaciones de igual naturaleza.

El análisis de esta información nos muestra la demanda que tiene *Cuadernos Americanos,* el interés por los temas que publicamos y la creciente demanda de las instituciones o personas interesadas en la adquisición de la revista.

Un elemento más que ahonda la producción editorial de *Cuadernos Americanos* es la nueva colección de libros, Cuadernos de Cuadernos, que comenzó a editarse en 1991. Esta serie cuenta a la fecha con cinco títulos.[2]

En lo que se refiere a las publicaciones del Centro Coordinador y Difusor de Estudios Latinoamericanos, podemos mencionar en términos generales que cuenta con las siguientes colecciones:

Latinoamérica Anuario Estudios Latinoamericanos—La publicación periódica más antigua del CCyDEL. Desde su aparición en 1968 hasta nuestros días tiene publicados 25 números. En ellos se han aglutinado una gran cantidad de artículos, ensayos, notas, reseñas y documentos que son una muestra del proceso de investigación en los estudios latinoamericanos en este último cuarto de siglo.

Serie "Nuestra América"—Hasta el momento esta colección de monografías ha alcanzado un total de 42 títulos publicados, y tiene una gran variedad de temas y autores. Entre los más recientes trabajos publicados se destacan análisis multidisciplinarios sobre países latinoamericanos tales como Argentina, Bolivia, Perú y Belice.

Revista Nuestra América—Esta colección comprende un total de 25 números. Publicación periódica que muestra una gran variedad de temas monográficos así como una diversidad y conjunción de autores.

Colección 500 años después—Esta es una colección que surgió con motivo de la conmemoración del llamado V Centenario. Abarca hasta el momento 16 títulos. Como su mismo nombre lo señala, la serie está dedicada a mostrar una variedad de ensayos y reflexiones en torno a lo que ha acontecido en América Latina después de aquel axial año de 1492.

Panoramas de Nuestra América—Es la más reciente colección de publicaciones del CCyDEL. Nace al llegar a su conclusión la *Revista Nuestra América*. Lleva apenas editados ocho números monográficos.[3] Esta colección se encuentra dedicada a conjuntar una serie de avances de investigación que sobre un tema determinado han trabajado diversos autores. La mayoría de ellos son latinoamericanistas procedentes de distintos centros de estudios latinoamericanos, tanto de México como de América Latina y el resto del mundo.

La distribución de estas publicaciones, sobre todo las publicaciones periódicas como *Revista Nuestra América* y *Latinoamérica Anuario Estudios Latinoamericanos* se realiza a través del intercambio y canje con otras publicaciones de instituciones dedicadas a los mismos estudios latinoamericanos.

En el recuento y la distribución de las publicaciones periódicas del CCyDEL podemos mencionar que en este momento se distribuyen nacional e internacionalmente 390 ejemplares respectivamente de *Latinoamérica Anuario Estudios Latinoamericanos* y *Revista Nuestra América*. En esta distribución figura el envío internacional a 20 países del continente americano, 15 de Europa, 2 de Asia y 1 de Africa, destacando en el caso del *Anuario,* Argentina y Venezuela en el caso de la *Revista Nuestra América*.

Tanto la distribución de los libros como de las publicaciones periódicas se hace de manera directa a través de agencias de distribución internacional o bien por medio de la red universitaria de librerías que tiene la UNAM. En el primer caso, varios distribuidores internacionales de materiales bibliográficos latinoamericanos nos han comentado que existe "demanda por las publicaciones del CCyDEL en el mercado de los profesionales dedicados al estudio del área latinoamericana". De igual forma que para *Cuadernos Americanos,* otro canal de distribución de las publicaciones del CCyDEL es el que se realiza a través de la participación en ferias de libros, ya sean universitarias, nacionales e internacionales.

Sin embargo, hay que apuntar que la distribución de las publicaciones del CCyDEL se realiza básicamente a través del intercambio y el canje nacional e internacional. Esta es una política que a lo largo de varios años ha permitido enriquecer el acervo bibliográfico con el que cuenta el CCyDEL. Así, nuestra Biblioteca "Simón Bolívar", que comenzó a formarse en 1968, en su acervo especializado en materiales bibliográficos sobre América Latina, es una de las más destacadas de la región. Podemos mencionar que la Biblioteca "Simón Bolívar" recibe aproximadamente un 99% de las 630 publicaciones periódicas que ingresan al Centro a través del intercambio o canje.

De esta forma podemos señalar que la adquisición de materiales bibliográficos latinoamericanos para nuestra biblioteca —que actualmente cuenta con más de 12 mil ejemplares— se ha incrementado en buena medida por la magnitud del intercambio, la donación y el canje de libros y publicaciones periódicas.

Y en ese mismo sentido, podemos afirmar que de conformidad con esa política, las publicaciones del CCyDEL también se canalizan a la par de instituciones y centros especializados en estudios latinoamericanos, a bibliotecas nacionales e internacionales, a embajadas nacionales (tanto mexicanas como de países latinoamericanos) y a personas en lo individual. Esto ha resultado en el crecimiento de nuestro acervo bibliográfico, ya que la donación de libros que recibimos en 1993 llegó a cerca de 800 ejemplares sobre América Latina, editados en su mayoría fuera de México.

De igual forma el impacto de nuestras publicaciones se refleja tanto en los canales de distribución como en el hecho de ser fuentes obligadas de consulta e información de especialistas en estudios latinoamericanos. Un ejemplo reciente de esto último lo tenemos en el texto *500 años del ensayo hispanoamericano: Antología anotada,*[4] título publicado en Pretoria, Sudáfrica, donde se asienta que buena parte de sus referencias se remiten a ensayos aparecidos en *Cuadernos Americanos.* Con esto queremos reafirmar la importancia que tienen nuestras publicaciones y de allí nuestro interés por ampliar los canales de distribución.

Sin embargo, también habría que resaltar que las nuevas temáticas latinoamericanas y enfoques (sobre todo interdisciplinarios) que se manifiesta en las ediciones del CCyDEL y *Cuadernos Americanos,* no sólo son productos que van dirigidos a un reducido sector de especialistas. Por el contrario, en virtud de la misma temática el radio de su mercado es mucho más amplio. Podemos afirmar que ese mercado se encuentra determinado por una serie de sujetos o instituciones que tiene los más diversos orígenes y variantes. Con esto queremos decir que los productos derivados de los estudios latinoamericanos, y en especial el ensayo latinoamericanista, es consumido por una gama muy amplia y diversa de lectores.

De allí que se reconozca que el ensayo latinoamericano editado en publicaciones de corte *latinoamericanista* al ingresar al circuito de la distribución, se acomode "a una variedad de lectores unidos por un común interés en Hispanoamérica, para conocerla mejor o para revalorizarla".[5]

De esta forma el impacto de revistas como *Cuadernos Americanos* y las ediciones del CCyDEL nos sirve de ejemplo para percatarnos de su trascendencia. Tanto por la revitalización del ensayo latinoamericano como por una corriente del pensamiento difusor de lo que es América Latina, así como del trabajo de los que académicamente se autocalifican como latinoamericanistas. Pero también estamos conscientes de las exigencias de distribución que nos plantea ese mercado, sobre todo en un período signado por un dinámico proceso de globalización económica y de una novedosa revolución técnico-científica, dinámica en la que ese mismo desarrollo va acelerando la producción industrial y la extensión de los servicios. Ambos situaciones cobran un significado muy especial para la distribución de los productos editoriales latinoamericanos, y sobre todo de las ediciones procedentes de los círculos o instituciones académicas universitarias de las áreas de humanidades y las ciencias sociales.

Entre las publicaciones del Centro Coordinador y Difusor de Estudios Latinoamericanos están la Serie "Nuestra América", con 42 números hasta el momento; la Colección "Panoramas de Nuestra América" con 8 números; la Colección 600 años después con 16 números; revista *Nuestra América* con 25 números; y Latinoamérica, Anuario Estudios Latinoamericanos con 25 números. (Véase el cuadro, p. 415.)

NOTAS

1. La SOLAR es un organismo que reúne a diversas instituciones de Latinoamérica dedicadas a los Estudios Latinoamericanos, y la FIEALC hace lo propio con instituciones del mismo carácter en Europa, Norteamérica, Africa y Asia.

2. Fernando Ainsa et al., *La novela histórica;* José Luis Gómez Martínez, *Teoría del ensayo,* 1992; Varios autores, *Ibero-América 500 años después. Identidad e integración,* 1993; Leopoldo Zea, *Filosofar a la altura del hombre,* 1994 y David R. Maciel, *El bandolero, el pocho y la raza. Imagenes cinematográficas del chicano,* 1994.

3. Se anexa un listado de todos los números publicados en las colecciones del CCyDEL.

4. *500 años del ensayo hispanoamericanos: Antología anotada,* recopilación e introducción de Cathy Maree (Pretoria: University of South Africa, 1993).

5. Ibid., p. 3.

Publicaciones del Centro Coordinador y Difusor
de Estudios Latinoamericanos, UNAM

Número	Título	Autor
Serie "Nuestra América"		
1	Latinoamérica en la encrucificajada de su historia	Leopoldo Zea
2	Situaciones y ideologías en Latinoamérica	José Luis Romero
3	México en el horizonte liberal	Abelardo Villegas
4	Filosofía, filósofos y universidad en Latinoamérica	Arturo Roig
5	La Universidad necesaria	Darcy Ribeiro
6	Un eslabón perdido en la historia: piratería en el Caribe siglos XVI y XVII	Marta Jarmy de Chapa
7	El populismo en América Latina	Varios
8	Centroamérica: desafíos y perspectivas	Varios
9	En nacionalismo en América Latina	Varios
10	América Latina, sociedad, historia y geografía	Hanns Albert Steger
11	Humboldt, historiador y geógrafo de América, Vol. 1.	Charles Minguet
12	Humboldt, historiador y geógrafo de América, Vol. 2.	Charles Minguet
13	El problema de la identidad latinoamericana	Varios
14	Alejandro Korn: profesión y vocación	Juan Carlos Torchia
15	La latinidad y su sentido en América Latina	Varios
16	El perfil del Brasil contemporáneo	Varios
17	El perezjimenismo: génesis de las dictaduras desarrolladas	Felícitas Portillo Lopez
18	Filosofía y crisis: en torno a posibilidad de la filosofía latinoamericana	Caldera Alejandro Serrano
19	Cinco narradores argentinos: Mansilla, Dávalos, Alvarez, Arlt, Di Benetto	Carlos Orlando Nallim
20	El sacerdote en la novela hispanoamericana	María de las Nieves Pinillos Iglesias
21	La idea colombina del descubrimiento desde México, 1936-1986	Juan Antonio Ortega y Medina
22	Imperialismo y economía en América Latina	Varios
23	El militar argentino como proyecto literario	María Teresa Gutiérrez Haces
24	Las categorías de la cultura mexicana	Elsa Cecilia Frost
25	Sentido y trayectoria del pensamiento ecuatoriano	Carlos Paladines
26	Dos científicos de la Ilustración hispanoamericana: J.A. Alzate, F.J. de Caldas	García Alberto Saladino
27	Ecuador contemporáneo	Claudio Malo González (comp.)
28	Los usos de Sandino	Enrique Camacho Navarro
29	Cabrera Infante y otros escritores latinoamericanos	Ignacio Díaz Ruiz
30	Eugenio de Aviraneta y México: acercamiento a un personaje histórico literario	Salvador Méndez Reyes
31	Ezequiel Martínez Estrada y la interpretación del Martín Fierro	Liliana Weinberg de Magia
32	Belice: sus fronteras y destino	Francesca Gargallo y Adalberto Santana

Serie "Nuestra América"

Colección 500 años después

Revista "Nuestra América"

1 Bolívar. Ideología, utopía, historia
2 José Carlos Mariátegui. Ideología, política, literatura
3 El barroco latinoamericano
4 El Caribe. Sociedad y cultura / nación e imperialismo
5 Andrés Bello. Humanismo, americanismo
6 Relaciones Estados Unidos-América Latina
7 Economía de América Latina
8 Identidad y cultura latinoamericana
9 Marx y América Latina
10 Pedro Henríquez Ureña
11 Filosofía de la liberación
12 Migración de las ideas
13 Sendero luminoso
14 Nacionalismo y latinoamericanismo
15 De sayas y minifaldas: la mujer en América Latina
16 Relaciones México-Estados Unidos
17 México en el siglo XIX
18 Costa Rica contemporánea: un balance histórico
19 Novela histórica
20 La iglesia en América Latina
21 Afinidades iberoamericanas en el proceso republicano de consolidación
22 Rebeliones indígenas
23 Problema de fronteras
24 Movimiento obrero en Argentina
25 El inca. Garcilaso de la Vega

Anuario

11-1978 Latinoamérica Anuario Estudios Latinoamericanos
13-1980 Latinoamérica Anuario Estudios Latinoamericanos
17-1984 Latinoamérica Anuario Estudios Latinoamericanos
18-1985 Latinoamérica Anuario Estudios Latinoamericanos
20-1987 Latinoamérica Anuario Estudios Latinoamericanos
21-1988 Latinoamérica Anuario Estudios Latinoamericanos
22-1989 Latinoamérica Anuario Estudios Latinoamericanos
23-1990 Latinoamérica Anuario Estudios Latinoamericanos
24-1991 Latinoamérica Anuario Estudios Latinoamericanos
25-1992 Latinoamérica Anuario Estudios Latinoamericanos

About the Authors

GLORIA DE ALFARO, Bibliographer for Latin America, Spain, and Portugal and Lecturer in the Department of Spanish and Portuguese, University of Colorado, Boulder.

JEANNETTE ALFARO ULGADE, Director of the Centro de Información en Ciencia y Tecnología, Consejo Nacional de Investigaciones Científicas y Tecnológicas, San José, Costa Rica.

CECILIA AVILÉS VALDEZ, Director of the Centro de Enseñanza Técnica y Superior (CETYS), Mexicali, Baja California, Mexico.

ELSA BARBERENA BLÁSQUEZ, Professor at the Graduate School of Library Science and Library Coordinator of the Facultad de Filosofía y Letras, Universidad Nacional Autónoma de México, Mexico.

WALTER BREM, Assistant Curator for the Bancroft Collection, University of California, Berkeley.

ANGEL ESTEBAN DEL CAMPO, Professor at the Facultad de Filosofía y Letras, Universidad de Granada, Spain.

JOSEFINA CASTRO DE ROQUE, Coordinator of Technical Processes at the Library of the Universidad Centroamericana, San Salvador, El Salvador.

SARAH CORONA BERKIN, Professor at the Departamento de Educación y Comunicación, Universidad Autónoma Metropolitana, Mexico.

RUSS DAVIDSON, Curator of the Latin American and Iberian Collections at the University of New Mexico Library.

MARTA DOMÍNGUEZ DÍAZ, Owner/Director of Servicio Extensión Cultura (SEREC), Santiago, Chile.

GEORGE F. ELMENDORF, Executive Director of the Latin American Bibliographic Foundation, Tucson, Arizona.

MERLIN H. FORSTER, currently H. Darrel Taylor Professor of Latin American Literature at Brigham Young University, Utah, and formerly Professor at University of Illinois at Urbana-Champaign and University of Texas at Austin. Author of books and other publications, his research interests are Latin American poetry and drama and the history of experimental literature in Latin America during the twentieth century.

DAVID WILLIAM FOSTER, Regents' Professor of Spanish and Women's Studies at Arizona State University where he directs the Spanish Graduate Program. Author of numerous works with research emphasis on social ideology in contemporary Latin American narrative and theater. Past Fulbright Scholar in Argentina, Brazil, and Uruguay and Inter-American Development Bank Professor in Chile.

NELLY S. GONZÁLEZ, Head of Latin American Library Services Unit, University of Illinois Library at Urbana-Champaign, and SALALM President, 1993-1994.

FREDERICK W. GRAHAM, Latin American Area Support Team Specialist at the Family History Library, Salt Lake City, Utah.

LAURA GUTIÉRREZ-WITT, Director of the Nettie Lee Benson Latin American Collection, University of Texas at Austin, and SALALM President, 1980-1981.

DAN HAVERKAMP, Regional Sales Manager of Research Publications International for the mid-Atlantic/South region and Latin America.

ROBERT HOWES, Sub-Librarian in charge of collection management and information services, University of Sussex Library, Brighton, United Kingdom. Volunteer for London Friend lesbian and gay counseling organization.

HOWARD L. KARNO, Owner of Howard Karno Books, previously Libros Latinos, Valley Center, California.

HERMAN W. KONRAD, Professor at the Department of Anthropology and History, University of Calgary, Canada.

KAREN LINDVALL-LARSON, Librarian of Latin American Studies/Collection Management at the University of California Library at San Diego, California.

YOLANDA MALONEY, Business Librarian and Bibliographer for Latin American Studies at the University of Colorado, Boulder.

KAHLILE MEHR, Cataloging Supervisor for Central Europe, Asia, and the British Isles at the Family History Library, Salt Lake City, Utah.

CONNY MÉNDEZ ROJAS, Director of the Central Library, Universidad Centroamericana, Managua, Nicaragua, and a Mellon-Mortenson Associate at the University of Illinois at Urbana-Champaign.

NICOLE MICHAUD-OYSTRYK, Head of Elizabeth Dafoe Library and Subject Bibliographer for French, Spanish and Italian literature at the University of Manitoba, Canada.

MOLLY MOLLOY, Reference Librarian/Latin American Selector at the New Mexico State University, Las Cruces.

LUIZ MOTT, Professor in the Department of Anthropology at the Universidade Federal da Bahia in Bahia, Brazil, and President of the Grupo Gay da Bahia.

SHARON A. MOYNAHAN, Librarian and Assistant Professor at the University of New Mexico General Library, Albuquerque, New Mexico, and SALALM Executive Secretary.

CARMEN M. MURICY, Head of the Acquisition Section of the Library of Congress Office at Rio de Janeiro, Brazil. SALALM Member-at-large and Chair of Marginalized Peoples and Ideas Subcommittee.

GUILLERMO NÁÑEZ FALCÓN, Director of the Latin American Library, Tulane University, New Orleans, Louisiana.

VERA CRISTINA NEUMANN, Librarian in the Special Collections Department, Universidade Estadual de Campinas (UNICAMP), Brazil. A professional intern at the Oliveira Lima Library at Catholic University of America in 1994.

CLEMENTE PADÍN, Uruguayan poet and contributor to many international exhibits on Poesía Visual y Experimental.

TERRY CHARLES PEET, Coordinator of the Hispanic Acquisitions Program, Library of Congress, and Chair of SALALM Acquisitions Committee.

WANDA QUOIKA-STANKA, Legal Information Services Librarian at the Law Library, University of Alberta, Canada.

NORA D. S. ROBINS, History Librarian at the University of Calgary, Canada.

ADALBERTO SANTANA, Researcher of CCYDEL/UNAM and Academic Secretary of Programa Universitario de Difusión de Estudios Latinoamericanos (PUDEL/UNAM), Mexico.

SUSAN SCHNUER, Coordinator of the Mortenson Center for International Library Programs at the University of Illinois Library at Urbana-Champaign.

LAURA D. SHEDENHELM, Librarian, Cataloging Department of University of Georgia Libraries. ALA/USIA Library Fellow to the Colección Hondureña, Biblioteca Central, Universidad Nacional Autónoma de Honduras, Tegucigalpa (1994). Chair of SALALM Membership Committee.

SONIA T. D. G. SILVA, Director of Coleções Especiais, Biblioteca Central, Universidad Estadual de Campinas (UNICAMP), Brazil.

ILIANA SONNTAG-BLAY, Professor Emeritus, San Diego State University, California, and SALALM President, 1985-1986.

VÍCTOR TORRES ORTIZ, Head of the Biblioteca Regional del Caribe y de Estudios Latinoamericanos of the Universidad de Puerto Rico, Recinto de Rio Piedras, Puerto Rico.

SCOTT VAN JACOB, Librarian of the Boyd Lee Sphar Library, Dickinson College, Carlisle, Pennsylvania, and Chair of SALALM Serials Sub-Committee.

ESPERANZA B. DE VARONA, Assistant Head of the Archives and Special Collections Department and Curator of the Cuban Archives at the University of Miami Library, Florida.

LUIS M. VILLAR, Bibliographer/Reference Librarian for Spanish, Italian, and Portuguese at Dartmouth College, New Hampshire.

RAYMOND LESLIE WILLIAMS, Professor of Spanish, Director of Graduate Studies, and Director of the Novel of the Americas Project at the University of Colorado, Boulder. Author of books and articles on contemporary Latin American fiction. His most recent book is *The Colombian Novel, 1844-1987* (University of Texas Press, 1991).

JOHN B. WRIGHT, Authority Control Librarian at Harold B. Lee Library, Brigham Young University, Provo, Utah.

Conference Program

Monday, May 30

9:00 - 10:00 a.m.   Inaugural Session
                         Doubletree Hotel, Salt Lake City

Opening: *Nelly S. González*
                         SALALM President
                         University of Illinois at Urbana/Champaign

Welcome: *Ted E. Lyon*
                         Undergraduate Studies Director
                         David M. Kennedy Center for International
                         Studies
                         Brigham Young University

Welcome: *Gene R. Cook*
                         Family History Library
                         Salt Lake City, Utah

José Toribio Medina Award:

                         Robert McNeil
                         Presentation of Award

                         Laura Gutiérrez-Witt
                         Homage to Nettie Lee Benson

Welcome and Announcements:

                         Mark L. Grover
                         Local Arrangements
                         Brigham Young University

10:00 - 10:30 a.m.   Orientation for New Members and/or First-Time
                         Attendees

10:00 - 11:00 a.m.   Bookdealers' Book Exhibit Opening

11:00 a.m. - 12:15 p.m.   General Session
                          Merlin Forster, Brigham Young University
                          "Recent Trends in Latin American Poetry and
                          Drama, 1970-1994"
                          Introduction: Troy Cook

12:15 - 1:30 p.m.   Lunch

12:15 - 1:30 p.m.   José Toribio Medina Honoree Luncheon

1:30 p.m   Buses depart from hotel to Provo

1:30 - 2:45 p.m.   Travel to Brigham Young University (BYU)

3:00 - 4:30 p.m.   General Session
                          Raymond L. Williams, University of Colorado
                          "Recent Trends in the Spanish American Novel,
                          1970-1994"
                          Introduction: *Yolanda Maloney,* University of
                          Colorado

4:30 - 5:30 p.m.   Brigham Young University Reception

5:30 p.m.   Buses depart from BYU Museum of Art to Park
                          City

5:30 - 6:30 p.m.   Park City for no-host dinner

9:30 p.m.   Buses depart from Park City to hotel

Tuesday, May 31

8:00 - 9:15 a.m.   Workshop: Latin American Materials Micro-
                          filming Issues
                          Moderator: *Dan Hazen,* Harvard University
                          Rapporteur: Nancy Hallock, University of
                          Pittsburgh

                          Dan Haverkamp, Research Publications
                          "CD-ROM Publishing Considerations for Latin
                          American Library Materials"

Dan Hazen, Harvard University
"Procedural Ponderosity Perpetuates Preservation Progress: How Organization Has Brought Us Fame, Happiness, and Success: The Heartwarming (Albeit Tedious) Story of LAMP"

Peter Johnson, Princeton University
"Rectifying Bureaucratic Norms in the Struggle for Cuban Microfilm for the Year 2000: A History of Mass Mobilization of Bibliographic Workers for the Triumph of ICCG"

Mary Jo Zeter, University of Illinois at Urbana/Champaign
"The Humanities Preservation Project: Microfilming Monographic Literature at the University of Illinois"

8:00 - 9:15 a.m. Panel: Three Decades of Gay Literature in Mexico, Argentina, and Brazil
Moderator: *Carmen Muricy,* Library of Congress, Rio de Janeiro Office
Rapporteur: Tony Harvell, University of San Diego

David William Foster, Arizona State University
"Matters Related to Research on Sexual Dissidence in Latin American Cultural Production"

Robert Howes, University of Essex
"Contemporary Brazilian Gay Writers and Publications"

Víctor F. Torres, Universidad de Puerto Rico
"De los 41 a Luis Zapata: Del rechazo a la institucionalización del homosexual en la narrativa mexicana"

8:00 - 9:15 a.m. Panel: Themes in Mexican Literature
Moderator: *Ana María Cobos,* Saddleback College
Rapporteur: Gabriela Sonntag, California State University, San Marcos

Cecilia Avilés Valdez, CETYS, Mexicali
"Las escritoras mexicanas de los últimos tiempos"

Sarah Corona, Universidad Metropolitana, Ciudad
de México
"La literatura infantil mexicana: Su desarrollo de
1956 a 1993"

Liliana Irene Weinberg, UNAM
"Cuadernos Americanos: Los desafíos de una
empresa cultural"

9:15 - 9:30 a.m.   Coffee Break

9:30 - 11:00 a.m.   Panel: Access vs. Ownership: Learning to
                          Relate to the New Library Paradigm
                          (First of Two Parts)

                          Moderator: *Jared Loewenstein,* University of
                          Virginia
                          Rapporteur: Claire-Lise Bénaud, University of
                          New Mexico

                          Stella Bentley, University of California, Santa
                          Barbara
                          Terry Peet, Library of Congress
                          David Block, Cornell University
                          Molly Molloy, New Mexico State University

9:30 - 11:00 a.m.   Panel: Current Trends in Latin American
                          Publishing

                          Moderator: *Carl Deal,* University of Illinois at
                          Urbana/Champaign
                          Rapporteur: Carlos Delgado, University of
                          California, Berkeley

                          Carl Deal, University of Illinois at
                          Urbana/Champaign
                          "Academic Publishing in Chile, Ecuador, and
                          Mexico"

                          Marta Domínguez, SEREC
                          "Una nota bibliográfica sobre la nueva narrativa
                          chilena"

Juan Risso, Risso y Linardi
"Actuales tendencias en la narrativa uruguaya"

11:00 a.m. - 12:15 p.m. General Session
David William Foster, Arizona State University
"Latin American Literary Bibliography since the Boom"
Introduction: Rhonda Neugebauer, Arizona State University

12:15 - 1:30 p.m. Lunch

1:00 - 2:00 p.m. Family History Library Tours, Salt Lake City

2:00 - 3:30 p.m. Panel: Family History
Moderator: *James Bolt,* Collection Development Head, Family History Library
Rapporteur: Darlene Waller, University of Connecticut

Kahlile Mehr, Cataloging Supervisor, Family History Library
"Latin America and the Family History Library: A Historical Overview"

Fred Graham, Latin American Area Support Team, Family History Library
"The Latin American Collection of the Family History Library"

Rebecca Horn, Associate Professor of History, University of Utah
"Scholarly Uses of the Latin American Collection of the Family History Library"

4:00 - 5:30 p.m. General Session
Ted E. Lyon, Brigham Young University
"The Role of Journal Publications: Pop, Boom, Bang"
Introduction: Mark L. Grover, Brigham Young University

5:30 - 8:00 p.m.   Dinner

8:00 - 10:00 p.m.   Evening Presentations
                          Yolanda Maloney, University of Colorado at
                          Boulder
                          "Latin American Visions: Through the Eye of the
                          Camera"

                          Clemente Padin, Uruguayan "Concrete" Poet
                          Mr. Padin will present his works through readings
                          and video.

Wednesday, June 1

8:00 - 9:15 a.m.   Panel: Access vs. Ownership: Learning to
                          Relate to the New Library Paradigm
                          (Second of Two Parts)
                          Moderator: *Jared Loewenstein,* University of
                          Virginia
                          Rapporteur: Harold Colson, University of
                          California, San Diego

                          Peter Stern, Rutgers University
                          George Elmendorf, México Norte
                          Lynne Rienner, Lynne Rienner Publishers
                          Sharon Moynahan, SALALM Secretariat

8:00 - 9:15 a.m.   Panel: Experiences Abroad: The USIA/ALA
                          Library Program and the Mellon Foundation/
                          Mortenson Center Program at the University
                          of Illinois
                          Moderator: *Laura Shedenhelm,* University of
                          Georgia
                          Rapporteur: Rachel Barreto, Catholic University
                          of America

                          Laura Shedenhelm, University of Georgia
                          "A Library Fellow in Honduras: Automatización
                          de la colección hondureña"

Susan Schnuer, University of Illinois at Urbana/Champaign
"The Mellon Foundation-Mortenson Center Program for Central American Libraries"

Connie Méndez Rojas, Biblioteca Central, Universidad Centroamericana, Managua, Nicaragua
"The Biblioteca Central of the Universidad Centroamericana"

Jeannette Alfaro Ugalde, Centro de Información en Ciencia y Tecnología, San José, Costa Rica
"CONICIT y su biblioteca"

Josefina Castro de Roque, Universidad Centroamericana "J.S. Cañas," San Salvador, El Salvador

"La biblioteca universitaria"

9:15 - 9:30 a.m.	Coffee Break
9:30 - 11:00 a.m.	Town Hall Meeting Rapporteurs: Catherine Nelson and Maria Silva Kuhn, Tulane University
11:00 a.m. - 12:15 p.m.	General Session *Carlos Guillermo Wilson,* San Diego State University "The Emergence of Latin American Writers of African Ancestry" Introduction: William D. Ilgen, University of North Carolina
12:15 - 1:30 p.m.	Lunch
1:30 - 3:00 p.m.	Panel: La adquisición de materiales bibliográficos latinoamericanos desde el punto de vista latinoamericano Moderator: *Carlos Delgado,* University of California, Berkeley

Rapporteur: Marian Goslinga, Florida International University

Adalberto Santana, Centro Coordinador y Difusor de Estudios Latinoamericanos, UNAM
"Nuevas tendencias y nuevos enfoques en la labor editorial latinoamericana"

Micaela Chávez, El Colegio de México
"La adquisición de materiales bibliográficos latinoamericanos en las bibliotecas mexicanas"

1:30 - 3:00 p.m. **Workshop: Collection Analysis for Latin American Literatures: Three Reports from the Field**
Moderator: *Gayle Williams,* University of Georgia
Rapporteur: Olga Beshers, University of Miami

Walter Brem, University of California, Berkeley
"Mexico"

Russ Davidson, University of New Mexico
"Brazil"

Karen Lindvall-Larson, University of California, San Diego
"Chile"

3:00 - 4:30 p.m. **Panel: Themes in Latin American Literature**
Moderator: *Gloria de Alfaro,* University of Colorado
Rapporteur: Víctor Torres, Universidad de Puerto Rico

Eduardo Erazo, New Mexico State University
"Tragic Women Characters in the Novels of Elena Poniatowska"

Angel Esteban del Campo, Facultad de Letras, Universidad de Granada
"La muerte de los *Doce Cuentos Peregrinos* de Gabriel García Márquez"

Gloria de Alfaro and *Yolanda Maloney,*
University of Colorado
"Representations of the Prostitute in Latin
American Narrative"

3:00 - 4:30 p.m. Panel: The View from the North: Latin
American Studies and Collections in Canada

Moderator: *Sharon Neary,* University of Calgary
Rapporteur: Peter Bushnell, University of Florida

Nicole Michaud-Oystryk, University of Manitoba
"Librarian-Faculty Partnership: Challenges and
Opportunities"

Wanda Quoika-Stanka, University of Alberta
"Hispanic Collections at the University of Alberta
Library"

Nora Robins, University of Calgary Library
"Development During Adversity: The Latin
Americanist Collection at the University of
Calgary"

4:30 - 5:45 p.m. Panel: Library Services and Resources

Moderator: *Reynaldo Ayala,* San Diego State
University - IVC
Rapporteur: Rafael E. Tarrago, University of
Notre Dame

Reynaldo Ayala and *Marta Stiefel Ayala,* San
Diego State University - IVC
"Report Card on Public Libraries' Services to the
Latino Community: A REFORMA Project Funded
by the W. K. Kellogg Foundation"

Luis Villar, Dartmouth College
"Access to Sor Juana Inés de la Cruz's Poetry
through the Internet"

4:30 - 5:45 p.m.   Panel: Cataloging Latin American Literature
                          Moderator: *Claire-Lise Bénaud,* University of
                          New Mexico
                          Rapporteur: Rachel Barreto, Catholic University
                          of America

                          Vera Neumann, Catholic University of America
                          "Bibliotecas particulares de intelectuais
                          brasileiros: Tesouro desconhecido"

                          John Wright, Brigham Young University
                          "Latin American Different Editions: The Duping
                          of the Academic Library"

6:45 p.m.   Buses begin departing from hotel to reception at
                          Hidden Valley Country Club

7:00 - 10:00 p.m.   Bookdealers' Reception

9:30 p.m.   Buses begin departing from club to hotel

Thursday, June 2

8:00 - 9:15 a.m.   Panel: The Dixie-Latin American Connection:
                          Experience in Documenting Latin American
                          Culture at Three Southern Depositories
                          Moderator: *Lesbia Varona,* University of Miami
                          Rapporteur: *Barbara Stewart,* University of
                          Pittsburgh

                          Guillermo Náñez Falcón, Tulane University
                          "Central American Collections and a Treasury of
                          Mexican Documents in Tulane University"

                          Jane Garner, University of Texas at Austin
                          "Mexican and Mexican-American Manuscripts in
                          the Benson Latin American Collection"

                          Esperanza de Varona, University of Miami
                          "Cuban and Cuban-American Bilingual Archives
                          in the University of Miami Library"

8:00 - 9:15 a.m.   **Panel: Bibliographical Surveys of Latin American Literature**

Moderator: *Iliana L. Sonntag-Blay,* Professor Emeritus, San Diego State University
Rapporteur: Mina Jane Grothey, University of New Mexico

Nelly S. González, University of Illinois at Urbana/Champaign
"Facts Become Fiction: The Latin American Dictator through the Works of Valle-Inclán, Asturias, and García Márquez"

Iliana L. Sonntag-Blay, Professor Emeritus, San Diego State University
"An Index to Latin American Poetry in Anthologies"

Scott Van Jacob, Dickinson College
"A Bibliographic Survey of Views of Africa by Contemporary Afro-Hispanic American Writers"

9:15: - 9:30 a.m.   Coffee Break

9:30 - 11:00 a.m.   Workshop: Latin American Newspapers

Moderator: *Scott Van Jacob,* Dickinson College
Rapporteur: Christiane Erbolato-Ramsey, Brigham Young University

Carmen Muricy, Library of Congress, Rio de Janeiro Office
"Brazilian Newspapers"

David Block, Cornell University
"Results of Newspaper Holdings Survey"

11:00 a.m. - 12:00 p.m.   Closing Session and Business Meeting

12:00 - 1:30 p.m.   Lunch

1:30 - 3:30 p.m.   Executive Board Meeting